International Law and Pollution

This book includes the papers from the Tenth Sokol Colloquium on International Law at the University of Virginia.

International Law and Pollution

Edited by
Daniel Barstow Magraw

upp

UNIVERSITY OF PENNSYLVANIA PRESS   Philadelphia

Copyright © 1991 by the University of Pennsylvania Press
ALL RIGHTS RESERVED
Printed in the United States of America

Library of Congress Cataloging-in-Publication Data

International law and pollution / edited by Daniel Barstow Magraw.
    p.   cm.
Includes papers initially prepared for the 10th Sokol Colloquium
held at the University of Virginia School of Law on Apr. 15–16,
1988, and also some prepared for a panel on acid rain at the meeting
of the American Bar Association in Toronto on Aug. 7, 1988.
    Includes bibliographical references and index.
    ISBN 0-8122-3052-3
    1. Environmental law, International—Congresses.   2. Pollution—
Law and legislation—Congresses.   3. Acid rain—Law and
legislation—Congresses.   I. Magraw, Daniel Barstow.   II. Sokol
Colloquium (10th : 1988 University of Virginia School of Law)
III. American Bar Association. Meeting (1988 : Toronto, Canada)
K3584.6   1988
341.7′623—dc20   90-19454
                                                              CIP

This book is dedicated to
CAITLIN, KENDRA, KIM, SEAN,
and their descendants

Contents

Preface

The dramatic expansion of international law since World War II has affected all aspects of the international legal system. The international system broadened to encompass new substantive concerns, such as nuclear war, human rights, economic development, and environmental protection—including both of its branches, natural resource management and pollution control. At the same time, a myriad of new actors has emerged. New international organizations, such as the United Nations, the International Monetary Fund, and the International Bank for Reconstruction and Development, were formed and have assumed major global roles. Many new States were created as the world decolonized, bringing new values and concerns into the international lawmaking process. Nongovernmental organizations became more active internationally. Improvements in telecommunications and travel facilitated these changes and affected how they occurred.

These developments are interrelated, because movements and ideas do not evolve in a vacuum. Indeed, the entire world has become more interdependent—economically, politically, ecologically, ethically, and culturally—a fact that itself has influenced the content and scope of international law.

The result of these forces has been a massive codification and growth of international law. No one knows precisely how many international agreements are now in force. The United States is a party to approximately 7,500, and there are easily tens of thousands overall. Moreover, customary international law has continued to expand.

This book examines one of the areas of international law and policy that has gained increasing attention: international pollution. Attention to pollution is not entirely new, of course. Treaties have existed about international rivers, including environmental aspects of those watercourses, for hundreds of years. And human activities have long affected the environment, as evidenced by traditional slash-and-burn agriculture and vast irrigation projects such as those in the Nile Basin and Sri Lanka. But anthropogenic effects on the environment now threaten to be longer-lasting, more widespread, and more pernicious owing to changes in the magnitude and nature of human activities. The focus on international pollution thus is extremely important.

Unfortunately, in spite of the fact that some customary international law principles and hundreds of international agreements relate to the environment, today's international legal system is deficient both in preventing pollution and in providing compensation to victims of pollution. A partial recounting of recent international pollution problems demonstrates this proposition: the oil spill off the coast of Morocco; shipments of hazardous waste from developed to developing countries; the disaster at the nuclear-power plant in Chernobyl, U.S.S.R.; stratospheric ozone depletion from chlorofluorocarbons and other chemicals; acid rain in Canada caused by sulphur emissions in the United States; and possible climate change from the emission of greenhouse gases.

It is essential to improve the effectiveness of international law regarding pollution. It is the goal of this book to facilitate that process by discussing international law and pollution at both the general and the specific levels—the specific levels being pollution from nuclear accidents and acid deposition.

The contents of this book have three sources. Chapters 2 to 13 and 15 were initially prepared for the Tenth Sokol Colloquium on International Law at the University of Virginia School of Law, in Charlottesville, Virginia, on April 15–16, 1988. Chapters 14 and 16 were initially presented at a panel on acid rain at the annual meeting of the American Bar Association in Toronto, Canada, on August 7, 1988. Chapters 1 and 10 were written specifically for this book. For the most part, the chapters that were originally written in 1988 have been updated to take account of developments since then; the extent of update is indicated in the introductory note for each chapter.

Citations in this book follow *A Uniform System of Citation* (14th ed. 1986), which is the system commonly used by legal scholars and practitioners. For the convenience of readers not familiar with that system, a list of abbreviations used in the notes is provided following this Preface.

Finally, I would like to express my sincere appreciation to all contributing authors and to Edith Brown Weiss, Brian Flemming, John Lawrence Hargrove, and John Perry, who also participated as panel chairpersons or speakers in the Sokol Colloquium. I would also like to thank the following: the Sokol Foundation at the University of Virginia for funding the Sokol Colloquium; Richard Lillich, David Martin, and Richard Merrill for their assistance and support in planning the Sokol Colloquium; Maria White for administering the Colloquium; Deborah

Kennedy, Alan Kessel, Tom Marshall, and Andrew Sens for their help in preparing manuscripts; Debra Donahue, Izah Gallagher, Rosemary Kellogg, Rebecca Rains, Mary Scherschel, and Paul Schmidt for research assistance; Marge Brunner, Barbara Chavis, Anne Guthrie, Colleen Nunn, Joanna Rose, Jan Stewart, and Kay Wilkie for secretarial assistance; Jean Grismer Magraw and Steve McCaffrey for reviewing Chapter 1; Arthur Evans, Jo Mugnolo, and Ruth Veleta for seeing me through the preacceptance and production stages at the University of Pennsylvania Press; and the two anonymous reviewers for the University of Pennsylvania Press, whose unusually thorough and thoughtful critiques resulted in numerous improvements in the book. Lastly, I would like to express my deep gratitude to my wife, Lucinda Low, for her support during the preparation of this book, and to my children, who accepted my need to spend time on this book with good cheer and even some understanding that the book is intended to help preserve their heritage.

Abbreviations

A.	Atlantic Reporter
AM. J. CANCER	American Journal of Cancer
AM. J. INT'L L.	American Journal of International Law
AM. J. MED.	American Journal of Medicine
AM. SOC. INT'L L. PROC.	American Society of International Law Proceedings
ATMOS. ENV'T	Atmospheric Environment
ATOMIC ENERGY L.J.	Atomic Energy Law Journal
AUSTL. L.J.	Australian Law Journal
BEVINS	Treaties and Other International Agreements of the United States of America, 1776–1949 (Bevins)
BRITISH MED. J.	British Medical Journal
BRIT. Y.B. INT'L L.	British Yearbook of International Law
Cal.	California Reports
Cal. Rptr.	West's California Reporter
CAN. B. REV.	The Canadian Bar Review
CAN. Y.B. INT'L L.	Canadian Yearbook of International Law
COLO. J. INT'L ENVTL. L. & POL'Y	Colorado Journal of International Environmental Law and Policy
COLO. L. REV.	Colorado Law Review
COLUM. J. TRANSNAT'L L.	Columbia Journal of Transnational Law
CORNELL L. REV.	Cornell Law Review

D.C. Cir.	United States Court of Appeals for the District of Columbia Circuit
DEN. J. INT'L L. & POL'Y	Denver Journal of International Law and Policy
D. Kan.	United States District Court for Kansas
D. Utah	United States District Court for Utah
ECOLOGY L.Q.	Ecology Law Quarterly
ENVTL. POL'Y & L.	Environmental Policy and Law
F.	Federal Reporter
FAO	Food and Agriculture Organization
FOREIGN AFF.	Foreign Affairs
F. Supp.	Federal Supplement
G.A. Res.	General Assembly Resolution
GEO. L.J.	Georgetown Law Journal
Hague Acad. Int'l L.	Hague Academy of International Law
HARV. ENVTL. L. REV.	Harvard Environmental Law Review
HARV. INT'L L.J.	Harvard International Law Journal
HASTINGS L.J.	Hastings Law Journal
HOFSTRA L. REV.	Hofstra Law Review
I.A.E.A. BULL.	International Atomic Energy Agency Bulletin
I.C.J.	International Court of Justice Reports
I.C.R.P. Pub. No.	International Commission on Radiological Protection Publication Number
I.L.A.	International Law Association
I.L.C.	International Law Commission
I.L.M.	International Legal Materials
I.L.R.	International Law Reports
INT'L & COMP. L.Q.	International & Comparative Law Quarterly

Int'l Env't Rep. (BNA)	International Environment Reporter (Bureau of National Affairs)
INT'L ENVTL. AFF.	International Environmental Affairs
INT'L LAW.	International Lawyer
INT'L PRACTITIONER'S NOTEBOOK	International Practitioner's Notebook
J.L. & ECON.	Journal of Law and Economics
J. MAR. L. & COM.	Journal of Maritime Law and Commerce
J.O. COMM. EUR.	Journal Officiel des Communautés Européennes
J. SPACE L.	Journal of Space Law
LA. L. REV.	Louisiana Law Review
McGILL L.J.	McGill Law Journal
MICH. L. REV.	Michigan Law Review
Misc.	New York Miscellaneous Reports
NAT. RESOURCES J.	Natural Resources Journal
N.D. Ill.	United States District Court for the Northern District of Illinois
N.E.	North Eastern Reporter
NETH. Y.B. INT'L L.	Netherlands Yearbook of International Law
N.H. [in a case citation only]	New Hampshire Reports
NUCLEAR ENGINEERING INT'L	Nuclear Engineering International
N.Y. [in a case citation only]	New York Reports
N.Y.S.	West's New York Supplement
N.Y. Times	New York Times
O.E.C.D. Rec.	Organization for Economic Cooperation and Development Recommendation
O.J. EUR. COMM.	Official Journal of the European Community
Op. Att'y Gen.	Opinions of the Attorney General
P.	Pacific Reporter
P.C.I.J.	Permanent Court of International Justice

Pub. L. No.	Public Law Number
Rec. des Cours	Recueil des Cours
R. Int'l Arb.	United Nations Reports of International Arbitral Awards
Sci. Am.	Scientific American
S.D.N.Y.	United States District Court for the Southern District of New York
Stan. L. Rev.	Stanford Law Review
Stat.	Statutes at Large
Tex. Int'l L.J.	Texas International Law Journal
T.I.A.S.	Treaties and Other International Acts Series
Touro L. Rev.	Touro Law Review
T.S.	Treaty Series
U.C.C.	Uniform Commercial Code
U.L.A.	Uniform Laws Annotated
U.N. Doc.	United Nations Document
U.N.E.P.	United Nations Environment Programme
U.N. GAOR	United Nations General Assembly Official Record
U.N.T.S.	United Nations Treaty Series
U.S. [in a case citation only]	United States Reports
U.S. App. D.C.	United States Court of Appeals Reports
U.S.C.	United States Code
U.S. Dep't St. Bull.	United States Department of State Bulletin
U.S.T.	United States Treaties and Other International Agreements
Vand. L. Rev.	Vanderbilt Law Review
Wall St. J.	Wall Street Journal
Wash. L. Rev.	Washington Law Review
Water Resources Rev.	Water Resources Review
Weekly Comp. Pres. Docs.	Weekly Compilation of Presidential Documents

W.H.O.	World Health Organization
W.M.O.	World Meteorological Organization
YALE J. INT'L L.	Yale Journal of International Law
Y.B. INST. INT'L L.	Yearbook of the Institute of International Law
Y.B. INT'L L. COMM'N	Yearbook of the International Law Commission

Part I:
International Law and
Pollution: An Overview

Chapter 1
International Law and Pollution

Daniel Barstow Magraw

Overview: Distinctions and Definitions

International environmental issues can be divided into two great branches: (1) allocating and conserving natural and cultural resources and (2) preventing or otherwise dealing with pollution. These categories are related. For example, sulphur dioxide emitted in the United States damages natural and cultural resources in Canada.[1] Both categories ultimately must be taken into account to manage the world's resources adequately.[2] Nevertheless, natural resource management and pollution control are sufficiently distinct to allow them to be considered separately.

This book, as its title suggests, examines various aspects of the category of pollution control. For purposes of this book, pollution is defined as

the introduction by humankind, directly or indirectly, of substances or energy into the environment resulting in deleterious effects of such a nature as to endanger human health, harm living resources and eco-systems, impair amenities or interfere with other legitimate uses of the environment.[3]

Pollution is of concern to the international community, and thus may be subject to international legal norms, in three contexts.

The first context involves what I refer to as "intra-State pollution," that is, pollution that is caused solely by sources within one State and whose direct deleterious effects are experienced wholly within that State. The international community has an interest in intra-State pollution in several types of situations, for example, if intra-State pollution destroys an ecosystem and thus leads to a loss of genetic diversity.

The recognition that the international community has legitimate interests in intra-State pollution occurred relatively recently and has dramatic implications for international environmental law as well as for the international legal system as a whole.[4] Specifically, the international legal system is implicated if intra-State pollution occurs in a manner that abrogates an international agreement, such as a bilateral wildlife-preservation treaty[5] or the global World Heritage Convention.[6] Similarly, intra-State pollution can violate customary international law, such as international human rights norms. For example, the continued prevalence of dangerously polluted drinking water might violate established human rights relating to health[7] or an arguable human right to live in a decent environment.[8]

In the second context, pollution occurs across the borders of two or more States. Such "transboundary pollution" (also referred to as "transfrontier pollution") is defined as

any intentional or unintentional pollution whose physical origin is subject to, and situated wholly or in part within the area under, the national jurisdiction of one State and which has effects in the area under the national jurisdiction of another State.[9]

Transboundary pollution can violate the rights under international law of the State in which the effect occurs. The classic example of such a situation is Canada's liability to the United States for damage caused to property in Washington State by fumes from an iron ore smelter in Trail, British Columbia.[10] Transboundary nuclear pollution from the accident at the nuclear power reactor at Chernobyl, U.S.S.R. (discussed later, in Chapter 7), raises a similar set of issues. These issues are important, among other reasons, because they reflect a vision of the world as much more interdependent than had been the prevailing view in the past and because they involve the State's duty to regulate private activities within its jurisdiction or control.[11]

The third context in which pollution implicates international rights and duties is similar to that in which transboundary pollution occurs, except that the effects occur in a global commons—such as the high seas, outer space, the climate,[12] and, at least in one view, Antarctica—rather than in another State. I refer to this type of pollution as "commons pollution." Commons pollution differs from transboundary pollution because there typically does not exist any entity with the exclusive right to protest commons pollution or to claim or distribute compensation for commons pollution: no conventional regime now exists establishing an international organization with such authority vis-à-vis a global commons;[13] and no State has an exclusive right vis-à-vis other States regarding a global commons, because all States share an equal interest in the commons. Allowing individual States to protest instances of commons pollution could result in multiple and conflicting claims and difficult questions about possible acquiescence by non-protesting States and allocation of any reparations paid for damage to a commons. The result of not allowing individual States to protest commons pollution, however, would be even less tenable: pollution of the commons would be without remedy. Several approaches are potentially available regarding this situation, for example, the concept of wrongs *erga omnes* (against all States in the world) as discussed in the *Barcelona Traction* case[14] and recognized in the Restatement (Third) of Foreign Relations Law of the United States,[15] the concept of international crime recently put forward in the United Nations International Law Commission,[16] and the utilization of general-purpose international organizations as surrogates.[17] In any event, the legal issues associated with commons pollution are real and need to be addressed.

Intra-State pollution that implicates international law, transboundary pollution, and commons pollution are referred to together in this chapter as "international pollution."

International pollution encompasses an unfortunately vast array of effects and activities. International pollution harms or otherwise affects outer space, the atmosphere, the oceans, the weather and possibly the climate, freshwater bodies and groundwater aquifers, farmland, cultural heritage, and life forms (including humans, other animals, fish, birds, and plants). Specific pollution threats, which frequently are interrelated, include acid deposition due to the emission of sulphur dioxide and nitrogen oxides; nuclear contamination from accidents at nuclear power plants, disposal of nuclear wastes, and nuclear-weapons testing; debris in outer space; stratospheric ozone depletion from the release of chlorofluorocarbons and other gases; tropospheric ozone enhancement from volatile organic compounds; oil spills at sea; runoff into international rivers and marine areas of agricultural pesticides and fertilizers, sewage, and industrial effluents; introduction of toxic substances into the food chain; water and soil pollution following the export of hazardous wastes; damage from government and scientific activities, mineral exploitation, and tourism in Antarctica; destruction of ecosystems; altered rainfall patterns from deliberate weather modification such as cloud-seeding; dissemination of genetically altered organisms; climate change from the emission of carbon dioxide, methane, chlorofluorocarbons, and other "greenhouse" gases; nonnuclear military activities, such as those involving biological warfare or poison gas; and the ultimate ecological threat, nuclear war.[18] Some of these threats are primarily anthropogenic (i.e., generated by human activity), some are primarily nonanthropogenic, and some are an often indistinct mixture of the two.

The international-pollution threats just described are subject to one further distinction that should be made at the outset, that is, between pollution resulting from a *single event* (such as an accidental or, less frequently, an intentional discharge of a pollutant) and pollution resulting from a *chronic* condition (such as long-term, low-level emission of toxic fumes). These two types of pollution situations raise different policy and legal concerns. Generally speaking, with respect to single-event pollution, the community is concerned with (1) the probability that an event will occur and corresponding safety standards for the State in which the activity is occurring (the State of origin); (2) immediate response mechanisms, such as notification of States that potentially may be harmed (affected States) and assistance mechanisms to facilitate terminating the pollution, providing medical treatment, evacuating nearby populations, or other mitigation measures in all States concerned; (3) determination of accountability for injuries suffered, that is, ascertaining whether the State of origin met the appropriate standard of care; and (4) compensation of those who are actually injured. In contrast, in the case of chronic transboundary pollution, the community is concerned with (1) proving that the chronic problem has caused a recognizable injury in the affected State(s); (2) either eliminating or minimizing the chronic pollution without necessarily ending the activity causing the pollution, whose economic viability often depends on the chronic release; and (3) possibly compensating those injured by the chronic pollution, particularly if it is not eliminated completely.

Finally, it should be noted that it is sometimes convenient to describe international pollution, and efforts to control it, in terms of whether it concerns a geographic area (e.g., the high seas), a resource (e.g., salmon), or an activity (e.g., sulphur dioxide emission). Such descriptive schemes are only of limited utility, however. The contours of a particular pollution-control regime should be determined by all the pertinent characteristics of the pollution at issue—characteristics that typically are not defined solely in terms of geographic area, resource, or activity. Pollution-control regimes thus commonly cut across two or three of these parameters. For example, the 1987 Montreal Ozone Protocol deals with a geographic area (the stratosphere), a resource (the stratospheric ozone layer), and a set of activities (those producing and utilizing chlorofluorocarbons).[19]

Paradigmatic Responses Regarding International Pollution

General Approaches

Three general approaches might be adopted regarding international pollution.[20] These three approaches, which are briefly summarized below, have markedly different implications for the role of government and the content of relevant legal norms.

The first general approach is the "market" approach, which essentially would leave environmental-protection decisions to individual decision-makers in the marketplace. The market approach fails, in my view, for several reasons. One is that individual decision-makers cannot be expected to take account of externalities (i.e., effects of an activity that are experienced by a person other than the decision-maker), of which international pollution is a classic example.[21] In addition, some relevant interests (e.g., future generations) are not represented by individual decision-makers, and thus there is no reason to expect decisions by those individuals to reflect those interests adequately.[22] Furthermore, individual values and choices about pollution control may differ from collective values and choices about those same issues in ways that should be reflected in public policy but that will not if choices are made entirely by individual decision-makers.[23] This failure occurs regardless of whether the situation involves intra-State pollution, transboundary pollution, or commons pollution. The analysis is similar if States, rather than individuals, are viewed as the relevant decision-makers.[24]

The second general approach to international pollution is what may be referred to as the "remedial" approach. This approach focuses on remedying harm after it occurs, including compensating persons (or the State of which such persons are nationals) who suffer personal or property damage as a result of the pollution. The remedial approach can take either of two forms, depending on whether the costs of remedying the situation are borne directly by the polluter or are paid out of a general fund. These forms have different implications for deterrence. The remedial approach serves a valid and perhaps necessary function once a recognizable injury occurs (especially assuming an international norm is violated, and probably even if no norm is violated, as explained later in Chapter 4); but it often involves high transaction costs, and it is flawed because reparation typically is more costly than prevention and because much pollution damage is irremediable. For example, it is not possible to recover a historical monument damaged by acid rain or a life lost to nuclear contamination.[25]

The third general approach is what may be referred to as the "regulatory" approach. This approach focuses on preventing pollution before it occurs (and on attempting to manage the environment more generally) and thus does not suffer some of the disabilities of the remedial approach mentioned above. Because preventive regimes are unlikely to be completely effective (or even, in some circumstances, to *try* to eliminate completely all international pollution from a particular activity), however, the regulatory regime typically should be supplemented by remedial/compensatory mechanisms. Moreover, it would be imprudent to ignore the incentives for private behavior inherent in policy options or to assume blithely that government control decisions are inevitably more beneficial than private choices.

Whether or not the reader agrees with the foregoing evaluations of these approaches, it would seem obvious that these approaches must be considered in setting policy and specifying norms.

Degree of Internationalization and Role of International Organizations

Efforts to deal with international pollution problems can occur at the following levels: unilateral, bilateral, regional, multi-State (by which I mean an effort by several States that are not geographically grouped and whose number is significantly less than the number of all the States in the world, now approximately 165), and universal (i.e., open to participation by all the world's States). A problem can be approached at several levels simultaneously, especially if a relatively small number of States desire stricter standards or are willing to agree more quickly than the larger community.[26] Moreover, a variety of international organizations (governmental and non-governmental) might be involved in a particular effort.[27] The decisions as to which level is appropriate, which States or international organizations should participate, and what roles they should play depend not only on political parameters—for example, which States currently are cooperating on which types of issues—but also on the physical realities of cause and effect and the existence or nonexistence of norms implicating various States.

Solutions to problems of intra-State pollution can be unilateral in many situations, because all the relevant activities and direct harm occur in one State. Other States will have an interest in some circumstances, however, depending on the nature and contents of the norm involved. Moreover, involving an international organization such as the International Bank for Reconstruction and Development (the

World Bank) may be desirable to alleviate financial burdens, to provide expertise, or for other reasons.[28]

Pollution of an international river can involve just two countries, with no cause in any other State and no effects even reaching the ocean. For example, the proposed Cabin Creek coal mine in Canada would have polluted the spawning grounds of fish that migrate in the Flathead River flowing into the United States, with no noticeable effect in any other country; the two nations have pursued a bilateral strategy aimed at a bilateral solution.[29] A bilateral approach is necessary to dealing with that problem because a unilateral approach by the United States is impossible (the pollution source is in Canada), and a unilateral approach by Canada is unlikely to suffice (because the harm experienced by the United States is an externality). If the two countries were unsuccessful in protecting the river, however, it is possible that other States party to the World Heritage Convention[30] would have had an interest in the situation: the Flathead River is the western boundary of Glacier National Park, which has been nominated as a World Heritage Site pursuant to the Convention and which may qualify for protection under the Convention regardless of that designation.[31]

Pollution problems in other international rivers, such as the Rhine, involve causes and effects in more than two countries, so that a regional approach makes more sense.[32] A unilateral or bilateral approach would be incomplete, though possibly still better than nothing.

Ozone depletion by chlorofluorocarbons (CFCs) and other chemicals may allow, at least in the short term, a multi-State approach, because relatively few States currently control production and consumption of the ozone-depleting chemicals. In the long term, a universal approach is necessary in order to prevent production and consumption from increasing worldwide, especially in developing countries.[33] Marine pollution and other issues relating to the law of the sea were considered to require a universal effort. Initial post–World War II efforts were initiated in the United Nations International Law Commission and culminated in four treaties finalized at the First United Nations Conference on the Law of the Sea in 1958.[34] In response to perceived inadequacies, the United Nations again coordinated efforts, eventually resulting in the 1982 Convention on the Law of the Sea, part XII of which contains 46 articles on the "Protection and Preservation of the Marine Environment."[35] Climate change is another issue that ultimately requires a universal approach, although initial progress is now being attempted via a multi-State group (which in theory is open to participation by all States but which in practice currently involves considerably fewer), the Intergovernmental Panel on Climatic Change (IPCC), established under the auspices of two international organizations—the United Nations Environment Programme (UNEP)[36] and the World Meteorological Organization (WMO).[37]

The role of UNEP and WMO in organizing the IPCC raises the point that international organizations can potentially perform many important functions in the type of situation just described, or indeed in any environmental dispute-settlement or rule-making situation involving two or more States. One such role is to serve as an impartial intermediary, with a range of possible functions, such as providing a forum for discussion, as the United Nations organized regarding the law of the sea; facilitating communication between States not having diplomatic relations with one another;[38] providing a neutral fact-finding mechanism or making nonbinding recommendations (both of which were done by the standing Canada–United States International Joint Commission, apparently successfully, in the Cabin Creek controversy);[39] and making binding decisions on the merits, as was done by an *ad hoc* tribunal in the *Trail Smelter* arbitration.[40] Another intriguing role is that played by the World Bank in the Indus River controversy between India and Pakistan: by injecting outside funds, the World Bank transformed the dispute from a zero-sum game to a situation in which a gain by one country did not automatically cause an equivalent loss to the other country, thus facilitating a peaceful settlement to a bitter, theretofore intractable dispute.[41]

International organizations can also play an active functional role in implementing a regime. An example is the role of the International Atomic Energy Agency as the contact point for information about nuclear accidents.[42] It should also not be forgotten, of course, that international organizations and the activities they promote can be the source of pollution or other environmental degradation—a charge that has been leveled, for example, at the World Bank regarding its projects in the Amazon basin and elsewhere.[43] Finally, it should be pointed out that international organizations differ in their institutional competence with respect to different issues (because of their differing mandates, composition, and experience) and, particularly, that nongovernmental organizations (NGOs) can sometimes perform functions inaccessible to governmental organizations, because NGOs are subject to different constraints and are not necessarily tainted by identification with any political system.

The foregoing discussion does not exhaust the possible roles of international organizations in controlling pollution or the considerations relevant to determining their optimum involvement in a particular pollution-control effort. It does, however, establish the potential significance of international organizations in pollution-control efforts.

Specific Strategies: Initial Detailed, Comprehensive Treaty versus
Framework Convention and Subsequent Protocols

A final question relevant to establishing a conventional regime (i.e., a
regime established by an international agreement) concerning international pollution is whether to attempt to resolve all issues related to the
problem at one time in one comprehensive international agreement or
whether to specify general principles in a first international agreement
(typically referred to as a "framework convention") that is intended to
be supplemented in detail by one or more subsequent agreements
(typically referred to as "protocols" or "annexes"). The comprehensive
approach allows all issues to be resolved concurrently and may facilitate trade-offs between different activities leading to a specific type of
pollution (e.g., trade-offs between carbon dioxide and methane emissions in the climate-change situation).

The framework convention/protocol approach, on the other hand,
may facilitate progress because it focuses on general principles (such as
the obligation to cooperate in a specific area) without requiring detailed commitments. It also allows agreement on some details in one
protocol without being delayed by more intractable issues that are the
subject of future protocols. This approach also provides more flexibility in responding to changes in scientific knowledge, because the
details are contained in more limited protocols that are typically easier
to modify (although this can also lead to fragmented obligations when
some States balk at the new protocols and others do not).[44] The framework convention/protocol approach has been utilized concerning acid
deposition and ozone depletion and is contained in the U.N. International Law Commission's draft articles on the Law of the Non-Navigational Uses of International Watercourses.[45] It may be used in addressing bilateral transboundary air pollution between Canada and the
United States.

As one might imagine, it is possible to have more than two levels of
framework conventions in a single regulatory regime. For example, at
the February 1989 Meeting of Legal and Policy Experts on the Law of
the Atmosphere, convened in Ottawa, Canada,[46] one possibility considered was a multilayered system that would have at the most general
level an overarching framework convention on the law of the atmosphere, with more specific framework conventions on issues such as
nuclear pollution, acid deposition, ozone depletion, volatile organic
compounds, deforestation, and climate change, and even more detailed protocols pursuant to each of those. That strategic approach was
sharply disputed by some who argued that climate change is of such

high priority that international efforts should focus on preparing a comprehensive convention on that topic.[47] Regardless of one's views of the merits of that argument, the point is that the question of how to proceed is very important and highly debatable.

Assessment of the Current Situation and Prospects for the Future

International law and the international legal system can serve several important functions in dealing with international pollution. International law can specify relevant preventive norms, such as prescribing limits on the amount of a pollutant that may be emitted; and it can provide rules about accountability and reparations, for example, substantive rules that define when a State is accountable for international pollution and what remedies are appropriate and procedural rules establishing or governing arbitral or adjudicative mechanisms. With its long history, the international legal system also offers a rich menu of useful negotiation models for rule-making and dispute-settlement with respect to international pollution. Accordingly, it is not surprising that international law and institutions already have much to say about pollution and other international environmental issues.

Customary international law and general principles of law recognized by the world's major legal systems relate to some activities and problems, such as the dispute over the Trail smelter, mentioned above. It is now widely agreed that there is a general customary-law prohibition against causing (or allowing private activities within that State's jurisdiction or control to cause) significant pollution in another State or in a common area or to a common resource and that there is a general customary obligation to cooperate with other States to prevent international pollution.[48] These customary obligations are particularly important because they apply universally, even (generally speaking) to States that did not agree to them.[49]

There are over 200 international agreements (treaties, conventions, protocols, etc.) dealing expressly with international environmental questions.[50] There are hundreds of others prescribing regimes for international watercourses, which can be termed "environmental" because they deal with the condition or level of water.[51] The United States, for example, has environmental cooperation agreements with the three large countries with which it shares borders: Canada;[52] Mexico;[53] and the Soviet Union.[54] Many nonbinding environmental instruments with at least moral force also exist.[55]

Many international organizations—both governmental, such as the UNEP, and non-governmental, such as the International Union for

Conservation of Nature and Natural Resources (IUCN) and the International Law Association (ILA)[56]—currently work in the field. Moreover, major international efforts are under way with respect to many of the pollution issues identified above. One example is the Intergovernmental Panel on Climate Change (IPCC), mentioned above, which is examining the scientific, social, and policy aspects of climate change as a result of the emission of "greenhouse" gases.

Nevertheless, the reality is that, despite progress in some areas,[57] the international system does not perform adequately with respect to most pollution, whether the situation involves single-event pollution, such as transboundary environmental disasters, or a chronic-pollution situation.

As a general matter, the international legal system is characterized by three well-known systemic disabilities that hinder rapid and definitive regulatory regimes: there is no centralized lawmaking authority, international dispute-settlement mechanism with mandatory jurisdiction, or centralized enforcement authority.[58] As a result, international norms frequently do not exist with respect to a particular situation. Moreover, it is often difficult to know if there is an applicable rule, to identify its specific content (if a rule does exist), to determine how it applies to a particular dispute, and to enforce it. In these senses, therefore, the characteristics of the international legal and political systems operate as constraints on improving international-pollution control efforts.

This situation may be changing somewhat, as United Nations General Assembly resolutions approach lawmaking status[59] and if the current Soviet initiative to utilize the International Court of Justice for environmental disputes or other efforts to upgrade and strengthen international environmental management organizations succeed.[60] But the general situation will most likely remain largely unchanged, at least for the short term, interfering with the international legal system's ability to deal with the environmental issues.

More specifically, most international pollution situations are not covered by a conventional regime. Examples include the Chernobyl disaster, climate change, and pollution from volatile organic compounds.[61] The other two sources of international law—customary international law and general principles of law recognized by the major legal systems of the world[62]—typically are more vague than international agreements and are particularly uncertain and subject to contradictory interpretations regarding international environmental problems. For instance, disagreement exists about the degree to which the general prohibition against causing pollution in another State is subject to a standard of due diligence and about the precise contents of the

duty to cooperate in preventing pollution (e.g., the aspects of informing, consulting, and conducting environmental impact assessment). A
vivid example is the Chernobyl disaster. In attempting to apply customary norms to that situation, great confusion has apparently existed
about whether the Soviet Union is accountable to other States for
damage therein arising from the accident or from the Soviet Union's
failure to notify potentially affected States of it.[63] Similarly, imprecision
in the applicable customary law seems to have prolonged the acid-
deposition dispute between Canada and the United States.[64]

Many pollution situations are covered by conventional regimes, for
example, pollution caused by the transport of oil at sea[65] and by
activities in outer space;[66] and some improvement undoubtedly has
occurred. But often the conventional regimes that do exist are inadequate. Inadequacies can result if the norms in the international agreement are insufficient to deal with the problem (as apparently is the case
with the 1987 Montreal Ozone Protocol[67] and as several States and
NGOs argue is the case with the Antarctic Mineral Treaty),[68] if States
make reservations with respect to essential components of the agreement (as the United States and Soviet Union did with respect to the
mandatory dispute-settlement provision in the 1986 Notification Convention regarding nuclear accidents),[69] if essential States are not party
to the agreement (as is the case with the Paris and Vienna Conventions
on liability for nuclear damage),[70] or if the regime is not at the appropriate level (as is the case currently with respect to the international
transfer of hazardous waste, regarding which several subuniversal
treaties exist but no global agreement is yet in force).[71] It should also be
pointed out that noninternational regimes do not suffice to fill in the
gaps[72] and, as explained above,[73] cannot be expected to.

Moreover, the forces and activities leading to international pollution
will most certainly continue to grow. With the exception of increasing
energy efficiency, eliminating pollution typically is expensive;[74] and
there is no reason to expect dramatic technological breakthroughs to
alter that situation to any great degree.[75] Significant improvements in
energy efficiency are possible, which would presumably reduce harmful emissions.[76] Indeed, the United States (as well as Western Europe
and Japan) experienced such a situation earlier in its history: total
domestic energy consumption remained roughly level between 1973
and 1986, in spite of growth in population and Gross National Product.[77] But achieving greater energy efficiency will require changes in
private and institutional behavior that will not occur automatically and
might not occur at all. Moreover, the short-term pressures to indus-
trialize and to exploit natural resources, as well as the temptation to
ignore detrimental pollution effects experienced by other States or in

the commons, often prove irresistible to policymakers, who are influenced by political pressures.[78]

These pressures most likely will intensify. The world's population, which was 1.7 billion at the beginning of this century[79] and is 5 billion now,[80] is expected to grow to 8 to 9 billion by 2025.[81] Most of that increase is expected to occur in developing countries, and much of that increase in megalopolises that already have inadequate infrastructure.[82] Both the increase in the absolute number of people and the fact that those people (presumably especially in developing countries) will want improved standards of living imply that demands on the world's resources will intensify and that pollution will worsen. Increasing technological complexity will probably lead to a higher risk of breakdowns (again, especially in less technically sophisticated developing countries) and possibly also to a wider scope of effects if an accident occurs. Moreover, at least until recently, there was no widespread realization among policymakers and ordinary citizens that the costs of mitigating and adapting to international pollution can be extremely high[83] or, more generally, that long-term growth, prosperity, and health depend on environmental protection.

The last-mentioned factor has been ameliorated to some degree, for example by the publication and popularization of the Brundtland Commission Report, together with the concept of sustainable development: "Sustainable development is development that meets the needs of the present without compromising the ability of future generations to meet their own needs . . . ."[84] But that concept needs to be explicated and to be more widely understood, accepted, and implemented—no trivial tasks.

Another attitudinal shift that will affect the nature and effectiveness of efforts to control international pollution concerns the degree to which citizens and policymakers conceive of the earth as a single, interdependent, and fragile entity. Scientists have utilized the concept of the biosphere (i.e., the concentric layers of life-supporting land, water, and atmosphere) since the early to middle part of this century.[85] For scientists and nonscientists, there has been growing evidence of a variety of sorts that the world is increasingly interdependent—ecologically, economically, politically, ethically, and culturally—as demonstrated by the events in Eastern Europe in 1989, and that the biosphere is fragile and subject to severe and sometimes irreparable harm from anthropogenic activities.

Perhaps the most profound influence in prompting this attitudinal shift stems from human activities in outer space. As one astronaut said in a telephone conversation from outer space, "The world is beautiful."[86] She did not say, "San Francisco is beautiful" or "The Atlas

Mountains are beautiful": from outer space, the frame of reference instinctively is the entire Earth. The same effect is felt more popularly when people see a photograph of the Earth floating alone, cloud-covered, and vulnerable in space.[87] Intuitively and intellectually, the power of that image is undeniable. It has forever altered humankind's sense of ourselves and our environment.[88] That change enhances the potential for adequately controlling pollution and otherwise attaining ecological equilibrium on a global scale.

The shift in frame of reference and the growing recognition of the interdependence and fragility of the biosphere do not guarantee progress, however, just as articulating the concept of sustainable development does not guarantee environmentally responsible economic growth. Effective international action, involving more appropriate and more widely subscribed-to norms and more effective international institutions, thus is imperative to reduce and eliminate pollution and to ensure adequate response when pollution does occur—including compensation, where appropriate. Moreover, international action must be effectively coordinated with programs at the national and subnational levels.

Crosscutting Issues

Especially in dealing with environmental problems at the global level, three crosscutting issues tend to arise. The first is how to treat developing countries. Indeed, this is probably the most important substantive international environmental issue over the next several decades. These countries must be included in solutions because their activities increasingly add to pollution. For example, burning rain forests in Brazil increases carbon dioxide emissions, decreases the carbon sink, and thus affects the possibility of human-induced climate change. So also does coal burning in China. Moreover, most of the projected doubling of the world's population over the next century will occur in developing States, probably leading to higher-pollution activities.[89] Yet most of the current international pollution has been caused by developed States; so those States have built their comfortable standards of living relatively unconstrained by the limits those same States are now urging on developing States. It is thus understandable that developing States question whether such a pattern is equitable, especially when developed States still do not always follow their own advice (as evidenced, for example, by current exploitation of Hawaiian rain forests).[90] In addition, developed States have more resources with which to battle pollution and pursue remedies;[91] developing States have greater needs, for example to aid the "absolute poor" resident in them;[92] developing

States face a host of practical difficulties in implementing pollution-control measures;[93] and developing States contain most of the world's genetic library.[94] A particularly difficult issue, sometimes said to involve transboundary pollution, concerns the export of hazardous technology and substances (the export of "risk"): the risk is higher when the export is from a developed State to a developing State, with results such as the tragedy at the chemical plant in Bhopal, India.[95]

Powerful political, practical, and moral reasons thus exist to include developing States in efforts to protect the biosphere from pollution and to do so in a way that does not unduly interfere with those States' economic development.[96] Various approaches have been tried, such as in the 1982 United Nations Convention on the Law of the Sea[97] and the 1987 Montreal Ozone Protocol,[98] and new approaches will undoubtedly be undertaken. Some have spoken generally of a "global bargain" for survival between developing and developed States.[99] More specifically, one developing country (India) reportedly demanded that developed countries should pay it $2 billion in exchange for its becoming a party to the Montreal Ozone Protocol: $1.25 billion to revamp existing CFC plants and $.75 billion to operate those plants until suitable substitutes are developed.[100] Obviously, such trade-offs raise complicated and difficult issues. Another difficulty arises in that developing countries vary markedly in income level, resource base, and technical and regulatory capability; consider, for example, Bangladesh and Brazil. What is clear is that participation by developing States is critical *at all levels* of identifying environmental problems and designing, implementing, and refining solutions to those problems.[101]

The second crosscutting issue is that international environmental questions tend to be characterized by scientific uncertainty about causes, effects, and remedies (including their cost and effectiveness). From a policymaking perspective, the questions are what we know about the situation being considered and how much we need to know in order to make decisions. Climate change is perhaps the quintessential example of an international environmental problem raising these policy questions, requiring, among other expertise, intricate knowledge of solar rhythms and the behavior and interaction of the world's atmosphere, vegetation, and oceans, together with large- and small-scale modeling of temperature, precipitation, and wind patterns.[102] Many environmental problems susceptible to nonuniversal approaches are also beset by uncertainty, or at least entail detailed fact-finding efforts before the problem can be satisfactorily delineated. Moreover, liability and compensation regimes must often deal with uncertainty, for example, whether a particular injury (such as a cancer) was caused by the environmental insult at issue (such as exposure to radioactive fallout or a carcinogenic chemical).[103] To further complicate matters, States do not always agree on the extent to which further information and understanding are needed. As is described later in Chapter 10,[104] such has been the case in the Canada–United States acid rain dispute.

Paradoxically, however, the existence of scientific uncertainty (or even the assertion that such uncertainty exists) with respect to a particular international pollution issue can lead, over the long term, to progress in dealing with that pollution. Perceived uncertainty, for instance, often stimulates research to resolve it. Research on international pollution tends to be international in scope because its causes and effects, except for intra-State situations, are on an international scale. Moreover, even with respect to intra-State pollution, the international community's interest in the pollution problem tends to ensure either that the composition of the research team is multinational or that there are simultaneous, sometimes parallel, research efforts in more than one country. In either event, the scientific effort, unless unsuccessful or acrimonious (which typically is not the case), creates a commonly accepted data base, an international network of individuals familiar with each other and with the dimensions of the pollution at issue, and a momentum for addressing the problem. These factors make it difficult for policymakers to ignore an issue without confronting it. An example is the 1957–58 International Geophysical Year (IGY). Much of the IGY research occurred in Antarctica, which was (and still is) the subject of many territorial claims (some overlapping) by States and which at that time was not governed by any overarching regime, environmental or otherwise. The success of the IGY led to U.S. President Dwight Eisenhower's call for a conference to create a joint management regime in Antarctica and eventually to the Antarctica Treaty, which went into effect in 1961, and several subsequent treaties on the Antarctic environment.[105]

In addition, through international scientific research efforts, a large international group of scientists can come to share a belief that a serious pollution problem exists or even that a particular action is warranted, as in the Canada–United States acid rain controversy.[106] Such a group of individuals can exert a powerful influence on policymakers to take action concerning a pollution problem. Because of their involvement in the scientific method, individual scientists are less likely than politicians to be influenced by purely nationalistic sentiments— and thus are more likely to favor fact-based and equitable international solutions. Also, individual scientists may be more forthright in their public statements and in their advocacy efforts (or in their decision-making, if they are decision-makers) because of the knowledge that their position is shared by colleagues worldwide; in addition, their efforts may benefit from information or arguments collected with the assistance of those colleagues. The process of dealing with uncertainty thus may facilitate resolving the problem about which the uncertainty exists.

A third issue that cuts across international pollution-control efforts, as well as virtually all other environmental questions, is how to take into account the interests of future generations. Intuitively, it is clear to many people that subsequent generations have an interest in an unpolluted environment. It is far from obvious, however, how one should evaluate that interest (e.g., will future generations care more about unpolluted water than about unpolluted air) or balance it against the interests of present generations (e.g., should the interests of future generations outweigh the interests of the most destitute members of the present generation in improving their standard of living). Although important analyses have been conducted on intergenerational equity,[107] much theoretical and methodological work remains to be done.

In summary, major crosscutting issues affecting approaches to pollution are the treatment and involvement of developing countries, the role of scientific uncertainty, and intergenerational equity. Other variables affecting pollution-control efforts include whether the pollution is chronic or caused by a single event; the appropriateness of utilizing customary international law or international agreements; the appropriate governmental level of effort and management; the degree to which international organizations, including NGOs, should be involved; and the degrees to which international organizations already exist to help coordinate efforts. It is clear that these factors vary significantly among instances of international pollution.

Contents and Organization of This Book

This book discusses international law and pollution at both the general and the specific levels.

Part I of the book (Chapters 1 to 5) provides an overview of international law and pollution. In Chapter 1, I define certain fundamental concepts (pollution, intra-State pollution, transboundary pollution, commons pollution, and international pollution); describe the interface between pollution and the international legal system; identify various types of international pollution and analytic distinctions among them; and raise three major crosscutting issues, namely, treatment of developing States, the role of uncertainty, and intergenerational equity. In this chapter, I also discuss various paradigmatic approaches to international pollution and evaluate the effectiveness of the international legal system's current treatment of international pollution. In Chapter 2, I examine the interrelationship among pollution-control efforts and two other major international post–World War II efforts—to protect human rights and to achieve economic development—in order to place the book's remaining chapters in a more complete context of contemporary developments in international law.

Pierre-Marie Dupuy then presents an overview of existing and evolving customary international law principles relating to pollution, including the duties to prevent pollution and to cooperate and the components of each (Chapter 3). In his discussion, Dupuy distinguishes between so-called hard and soft law, that is, between directives that are normative and obligatory and those that are only hortatory or aspirational. In Chapter 4, Stephen C. McCaffrey describes recent developments regarding pollution in the U.N. International Law Commission, which is considering, among other issues, both pollution of international watercourses and the perplexing question of whether a State can be internationally accountable for transboundary pollution even if the pollution does not involve a wrongful act. The Commission's studies of these topics are significant not only as important examples of the progressive development of international law, but also because both of these topics are based on the potential conflict between the right of a sovereign State to be free to engage in activities in its own territory, on the one hand, and a State's duty not to interfere with another State's ability to be free to act as it wants in its own territory, on the other. That conflict must be resolved in a manner that reflects the pervasive ecological (and other) interdependence of today's world. In the final chapter in Part I, Ian Brownlie discusses how international law relating to pollution arises in the practice of public international law, drawing on his considerable experience in that regard (Chapter 5).

With this overview in mind, the book then shifts in Parts II and III to how international law has responded, and still needs to respond, to two specific types of pollution. As mentioned earlier, there are many sources and activities that give rise to transboundary pollution. Parts II and III focus on two areas of particularly acute concern—nuclear power and acid rain. These two problems are issues of current concern, but they also differ in several significant respects. Perhaps most important, they manifest the two distinct types of transboundary pollution risks: the concern with nuclear power is *single-event* accidental transboundary pollution, while the concern with acid rain involves a *chronic* condition. The relevant legal regimes thus must address different concerns, as is explained above.[108] In addition, acid deposition is primarily a regional or bilateral problem (because of the rate at which the acidic compounds fall to the earth), whereas nuclear pollution also has important global dimensions. This difference affects the number and the identity of States that must cooperate in designing and implementing a solution. The acid-deposition debate has also involved a more contentious use of the issue of uncertainty than have efforts to control nuclear pollution, although uncertainty is also an important component of nuclear-pollution debates. Furthermore, a framework convention/ protocol approach has been taken to acid deposition, at least in Europe, whereas that approach has not been taken with respect to nuclear pollution. Finally, an international governmental organization, the International Atomic Energy Agency (IAEA), exists whose function is precisely to coordinate efforts in the area of nuclear energy production (the activity most likely to lead to accidental nuclear pollution), whereas no corresponding institution exists with respect to acid deposition. Efforts to deal with transboundary acid deposition thus must occur within the framework of institutions with other or more general mandates, or wholly outside the framework of any existing international organization.

Part II (Chapters 6 to 9) examines international legal issues relating to pollution from nuclear accidents—a set of issues that is perhaps most appropriately approached at the universal level. Andronico O. Adede provides an overview of the legal regime relating to pollution from nuclear accidents (Chapter 6). Günther Handl discusses international accountability, including the puzzling question of the lack of diplomatic claims against the Soviet Union after the Chernobyl disaster (Chapter 7). Paul Szasz provides a framework for analyzing damages, including the element of uncertainty, in the case of nuclear accidents— a framework that is also instructive with respect to injuries from other types of pollution (Chapter 8). L.F.E. Goldie then examines the overarching theoretical framework in a discussion that synthesizes many of his insights about State accountability and applies them to the issues of nuclear pollution (Chapter 9).

Part III (Chapters 10 to 16) discusses acid deposition, focusing on the European and Canada–United States experiences. Chapter 10 provides an overview of the acid deposition problem, including a distillation of the differences and similarities in the Canadian and the U.S. positions in their dispute. James N. Galloway then describes the current state of scientific knowledge about acid deposition (Chapter 11). Johan G. Lammers examines the complicated, multilayered European approach to the problem, providing a wealth of detail in the process (Chapter 12). Lammers also raises several difficult and fundamental questions about how the European State practice relates to the general customary international law obligation to prevent transboundary pollution. Ross Glasgow (Chapter 13) and Edward G. Lee (Chapter 14) discuss the Canadian policy and legal perspectives about acid deposition, respectively. William A. Nitze and Scott A. Hajost present the U.S. counterpart positions in Chapters 15 and 16, respectively. These final four chapters thus provide valuable evidence of State practice in the international pollution area and demonstrate the dynamic of assertion/counterassertion in the formation of international law.

Acknowledgments

My views on several ideas expressed in this chapter evolved from conversations with many people, in particular with Edith Brown Weiss, Günther Handl, Robert Lutz, Stephen McCaffrey, and Paul Szasz. It has not proven possible, in retrospect, to extract from those discussions the exact source of an idea. I thus wish to identify my indebtedness to those individuals and to express my gratitude for the continual and typically unselfish dialogue that exists among the many persons involved in international environmental protection efforts and analyses. This does not mean, of course, that I speak for anyone else in this chapter; any mistakes are mine alone.

Notes

1. *See, e.g.*, Graedel & Crutzen, *The Changing Atmosphere*, Sci. Am. 58, 61 (Sept. 1989); *infra* Chapter 14.
   Questions relating to dispute settlement arguably constitute another category of international environmental issues. It is probably preferable to think about dispute settlement in the separate contexts of the categories mentioned in the text, because the techniques used appropriately vary according to the type of problem involved. In any event, dispute settlement does not constitute a major focus of this book.
2. *See, e.g.*, Clark, *Managing Planet Earth*, Sci. Am. 46 (Sept. 1989).
3. This definition is taken from the definitions adopted by the Organisation for Economic Co-operation and Development (OECD) Transfrontier Pollution Group. *See* OECD Res. C(77)28 (Final), *Annex*, Introduction, May 17, 1977, in OECD, OECD and the Environment 151 (1986).
4. Some of these implications are discussed in Chapter 2, *infra*.
5. *See, e.g.*, Convention for the Protection of Migratory Birds, Aug. 16, 1916, United States–Canada, 39 Stat. 1702, T.S. 628, 12 Bevins 375.
6. Convention Concerning the Protection of the World Cultural and Natural Heritage, Nov. 16, 1972, 27 U.S.T. 37, T.I.A.S. No. 8226 [hereinafter World Heritage Convention].
7. *See* U.N. Charter, arts. 1(3), 55, 56; Universal Declaration of Human Rights, G.A. Res. 217 (III), Dec. 10, 1948, U.N. GAOR (3d Sess.) at 71, art. 25, U.N. Doc. A/810 (1948).
8. *See, e.g.*, The Hague Declaration on the Environment (March 11, 1989), *reprinted in* 28 I.L.M. 1308 (1989); Steiger, Demel, Fey & Malanczuk, *The*

Fundamental Right to a Decent Environment, in Trends in Environmental Policy and Law 1 (W. Burhenne ed. IUCN 1980).

9. OECD Res. C (77) 28 (Final), Annex, Introduction, May 17, 1977, in OECD, OECD and the Environment 151 (1986).

10. *See* Trail Smelter (U.S. v. Can.), 3 R. Int'l Arb. Awards 1905 (1938 & 1941); *see also infra* Chapters 10, 14 & 16.

11. *See, e.g., infra* Chapter 4.

12. In December 1988, the U.N. General Assembly declared climate to be the "common concern of mankind." G.A. Res. 43/53 ("Protection of global climate for present and future generations of mankind"), Dec. 6, 1988, *reprinted in* 28 I.L.M. 1326 (1989). Malta, which introduced the resolution, had initially proposed the language "common heritage of mankind." For a discussion of this declaration, see Kirgis, *Standing to Challenge Human Endeavors that Could Change the Climate*, 84 Am. J. Int'l L. 525 (1990).

13. That situation will change with respect to the high seas and seabed if the U.N. Convention on the Law of the Sea, Oct. 21, 1982, U.N. Doc. A/CONF.62/121, *reprinted in* 21 I.L.M. 1261 (1982) [hereinafter Law of the Sea Convention], enters into force.

14. Barcelona Traction, Light and Power Company, Ltd. (Bel. v. Sp.), 1970 I.C.J. 3, 32.

15. American Law Institute, 2 Restatement (Third) of Foreign Relations Law of the United States §§ 602 Comment *a*, 902 Comment *a*, Intro. Note to pt. VI, at 101 (1987) [hereinafter Restatement (Third)]. For a discussion of this approach, see Kirgis, *supra* note 12.

16. *See* art. 19(3)(d) of Part I of the Draft Articles on State Responsibility, Report of the International Law Commission on the Work of its Twenty-eighth Session, 31 U.N. GAOR Supp. (No. 10) at 175 (1976), U.N. Doc. A/31/10. Draft article 19(3)(d), which has been provisionally adopted by the Commission, states that an international crime may result from "serious breach of an international obligation of essential importance for the safeguarding and preservation of the human environment, such as those prohibiting massive pollution of the atmosphere or the seas." *Id.* As currently proposed to the Commission by the Special Rapporteur (but not yet endorsed by the Commission), every State apparently would have standing to protest an international crime. *See* art. 14 of Part II of the Draft Articles on State Responsibility, Report of the International Law Commission on the Work of its Thirty-fifth Session, 40 U.N. GAOR Supp. (No. 10) at 42 (1985), U.N. Doc. A/40/10.

17. The United Nations, for example, might receive reparations paid for commons pollution and be authorized to decide what to do with the reparations.

18. For discussions of several of these issues, see *Managing Planet Earth*, 261 Sci. Am. No. 3 (Special Issue) (Sept. 1989).

For discussions of these issues (in various combinations, see J. Brunnée, Acid Rain and Ozone Layer Depletion: International Law and Regulation (1988); Lammers, Pollution of International Watercourses (1984); International Environmental Law (L. Teclaff & A. Utton eds. 1974); Transboundary Resources Law (A. Utton & L. Teclaff eds. 1987); World Climate Change: The Role of International Law and Institutions (V. Nanda ed. 1983).

19. Montreal Protocol on Substances that Deplete the Ozone Layer, Sept. 16, 1987, *reprinted in* 26 I.L.M. 1550 (1987) [hereinafter Montreal Ozone Protocol].

20. For discussions of the processes by which international environmental agreements come into existence, see Jacobson & Kay, *A Framework for Analysis*, in ENVIRONMENTAL PROTECTION: THE INTERNATIONAL DIMENSION 1 (D. Kay & H. Jacobson eds. 1983); Hahn & Richards, *The Internationalization of Environmental Regulation*, 30 HARV. INT'L L.J. 421 (1989).

21. *See, e.g.*, Hardin, *The Tragedy of the Commons*, 162 SCIENCE 1243 (1968). For an example of an analysis of acid rain that ignores externalities, see *No Pap from NAPAP*, Wall St. J., Jan. 26, 1990, at A14, col. 1 (Western ed.).

22. *See, e.g.*, E. BROWN WEISS, IN FAIRNESS TO FUTURE GENERATIONS: INTERNATIONAL LAW, COMMON PATRIMONY, AND INTERGENERATIONAL EQUITY (1989).

23. *See, e.g.*, Sax, *The Legitimacy of Collective Values: The Case of the Public Lands*, 56 COLO. L. REV. 537 (1985).

24. Various models exist to explain decision-making by States. *See, e.g.*, G. ALLISON, ESSENCE OF DECISION (1971). The points made in the text remain valid when applied to States regardless of the model used and the type of pollution involved, with only one major exception. That exception is that the difficulties mentioned in the text do not necessarily occur if the issue involves only intra-State pollution that does not implicate the interests of the international community.

25. For an elaboration of this idea in the context of State accountability more generally, see Magraw, *International Legal Remedies*, in TRANSFERRING HAZARDOUS TECHNOLOGIES AND SUBSTANCES: THE INTERNATIONAL LEGAL CHALLENGE (G. Handl & R. Lutz eds. 1989).

26. An example of a multilayered approach is the international transfer of hazardous waste: the United States has a relatively strict set of domestic laws restricting the export of hazardous wastes, *see* Comment, *U.S. Controls on International Disposal of Hazardous Waste*, 22 INT'L LAW. 775 (1988), and bilateral treaties with Canada and Mexico, and it participated in the negotiations leading to the universal 1989 Basel Convention, *see infra* note 69.

27. *See generally* L. CALDWELL, INTERNATIONAL ENVIRONMENTAL POLICY—EMERGENCE AND DIMENSIONS 91–100 (1984).

28. *See infra* text accompanying note 43.

29. *See* International Joint Commission (Canada–United States), *Recommendations Regarding the Proposed Cabin Creek Coal Mine* (Dec. 1988); Keiter & Sax, *Glacier National Park and Its Neighbors: A Study of Federal Inter-Agency Cooperation* in OUR COMMON LANDS: DEFENDING THE NATIONAL PARKS 175 (D. Simon ed. 1988).

30. World Heritage Convention, *supra* note 6.

31. *See* Magraw, *International Law and Park Protection: A Global Responsibility*, in OUR COMMON LANDS: DEFENDING THE NATIONAL PARKS 147–49, 162–63 (D. Simon ed. 1988).

32. *See, e.g.*, International Commission for Protection of Rhine Against Pollution, Apr. 29, 1963, 994 U.N.T.S.

33. *See, e.g.*, [12 Current Report] Int'l Env't Rep. (BNA) 105–7 (Mar. 8, 1989); *id.* at 389 (Aug. 9, 1989).

34. *See, e.g.*, Convention on the High Seas, art. 25(1), Apr. 29, 1958, 13 U.S.T. 2312, T.I.A.S. No. 5200, 450 U.N.T.S. 82. There is also an extensive regional seas program. *See infra* Chapter 3, nn. 98–103.

35. Law of the Sea Convention, *supra* note 13, at Part XII.

36. UNEP is the primary environmental agency in the United Nations.

37. WMO is a U.N. scientific agency that conducts operational programs (including World Weather Watch) and provides a networking function among States for monitoring and forecasting weather.

38. An analogous situation occurred in ending the hostage crisis between the United States and Iran. Each country entered into binding agreements with Algeria that resulted, among other things, in releasing the hostages and establishing the Iran–United States Claims Tribunal in the Hague.

39. *See supra* text accompanying note 29.

40. Trail Smelter (U.S. v. Can.), 3 R. Int'l Arb. Awards 1905 (1938 & 1941).

41. Non-governmental organizations can also serve a similar function, as is indicated by their role in debt-for-nature swaps. *See* CONSERVATION INTERNATIONAL, THE DEBT-FOR-NATURE EXCHANGE: A TOOL FOR INTERNATIONAL CONSERVATION (Sept. 1989).

42. *See infra* Chapter 6.

43. *See, e.g.,* Wirth, *The World Bank and the Environment,* ENVIRONMENT 33 (Dec. 1986).

44. Consider, for example, the snarled stalemate that exists regarding international law relating to carriage of goods by sea. The original "Hague Rules" were adopted in the Brussels Convention of 1924 and were given effect in approximately 85 States. The Hague Rules were amended by the "Hague-Visby Rules" contained in the Brussels Protocol of 1968, to which 13 States are parties; those States thus have abandoned the Hague Rules in favor of the Hague-Visby Rules. A third set of rules—the "Hamburg Rules"—was adopted in the 1978 United Nations Convention on the Carriage of Goods by Sea. Three sets of regulations thus exist regarding maritime transport. *See* N. HORN & C. SCHMITTHOFF, THE TRANSNATIONAL LAW OF INTERNATIONAL COMMERCIAL TRANSACTIONS 25 (1982).

45. The 1979 Convention on Long-Range Transboundary Air Pollution, Nov. 13, 1979, T.I.A.S. No. 10541, *reprinted in* 18 I.L.M. 1442 (1979), is a framework convention. Three subsequent protocols to that Convention have been finalized, regarding financing the cooperation program (Geneva, 1984), sulphur dioxide (Helsinki, 1985), and nitrogen oxides (Sofia, 1988), as described in Chapter 12. The Vienna Convention for the Protection of the Ozone Layer, Sept. 16, 1987, *reprinted in* 26 I.L.M. 1516 (1987), is a framework convention, to which the Montreal Ozone Protocol, *supra* note 19, is a protocol. Regarding the International Law Commission's study of international watercourses, see *infra* Chapter 4.

46. For the final report of that meeting, see *Statement of the Meeting of Experts on the Law of the Atmosphere, Ottawa, Canada* (Feb. 1989).

47. *See also* EEC Council Resolution on the Greenhouse Effect and the Community, June 21, 1989, para. 2, *reprinted in* 28 I.L.M. 1306 (1989); UNEP Governing Council Decision on Global Climate Change, May 25, 1989, paras. 9–10, *reprinted in* 28 I.L.M. 1330 (1989); The Cairo, Egypt, Compact of Dec. 21, 1989, on Responding to Climate Change, *reprinted in* [13 Current Report] Int'l Env't Rep. (BNA) 33 (Jan. 10, 1990) [hereinafter Cairo Compact] (urging the completion of a framework convention on climate change).

48. These principles are discussed in Chapter 3. They appear, for example, in principles 21 and 24 of the Stockholm Declaration on the Human Environment, June 16, 1972, U.N. Doc. A/CONF.48/14 & Corr.1, *reprinted in* 11 I.L.M. 1416 (1972), in principle 21 of the World Charter for Nature, G.A. Res. 7 (XXXVII), 36 U.N. GAOR Supp. (No. 51) at 17, U.N. Doc. A/51 (1982),

reprinted in 12 ECOLOGY L.Q. 992 (1985), in articles 8 and 9 of the U.N. International Law Commission's study of International Watercourses, *see infra* Chapter 4, in article 197 of the Law of the Sea Convention, *supra* note 13, and in article 30 of the Charter of Economic Rights and Duties of States, G.A. Res. 3281 (XXIX), 29 U.N. GAOR Supp. (No. 31) at 51, U.N. Doc. A/9946 (1974). These principles are also related to the general principle of law sic utere tuo ut alienum non laedas (the duty to exercise one's rights in a way that does not harm the rights of others).

49. 1 RESTATEMENT (THIRD), *supra* note 15, § 102 & Comments *a, d.* The latter comment refers to the fact that States that persistently object to a general customary norm during its formation are not bound by it; such situations are rare.

50. For international agreements relating to the environment, see REGISTER OF INTERNATIONAL TREATIES AND OTHER AGREEMENTS IN THE FIELD OF THE ENVIRONMENT (UNEP 1989), U.N. Doc. UNEP/GC.15/Inf.2. *See also* OECD, OECD AND THE ENVIRONMENT (1986); INTERNATIONAL PROTECTION OF THE ENVIRONMENT—TREATIES AND RELATED DOCUMENTS (B. Ruster, B. Simma & M. Bock eds. 1975–1982); *id.,* SECOND SERIES (1990).

51. For conventions dealing with international watercourses, see *Report of the Secretary-General on the Legal Problems relating to the Utilization and Use of International Rivers and documents of the twenty-sixth session of the Commission prepared by the Secretariat,* especially U.N. Doc. A/5409 and U.N. Doc. A/CN.4/274, *reprinted in* 2 Y.B. INT'L L. COMM'N, pt. 2, at 1, 33, 265 (1976); LEGISLATIVE TEXTS AND TREATY PROVISIONS CONCERNING THE UTILIZATION OF INTERNATIONAL RIVERS FOR OTHER PURPOSES THAN NAVIGATION, U.N. Doc. ST/LEG/SER.B/12 (U.N. Legislative Series, undated but probably published in 1963).

52. *See, e.g.,* Agreement on Great Lakes Water Quality, Nov. 22, 1978, United States–Canada, 30 U.S.T. 1383, T.I.A.S. No. 9257.

53. *See, e.g.,* Agreement of Cooperation Regarding Transboundary Air Pollution Caused by Copper Smelters Along Their Common Border, Jan. 29, 1987, United States–Mexico, *reprinted in* 26 I.L.M. 33 (1987).

54. Agreement on Cooperation in the Field of Environmental Protection, May 23, 1972, United States–U.S.S.R., 23 U.S.T. 845, T.I.A.S. No. 7345.

55. *See, e.g.,* World Charter for Nature, G.A. Res. 37/7, Oct. 28, 1982.

56. Sixty-two governments, 130 State agencies, and more than 400 NGOs active in 120 countries are members of the IUCN. Holdgate, *Planning for Our Common Future—Options for Action,* ENVIRONMENT 14, 41 (Oct. 1989). The ILA is a private membership organization formed in Brussels in 1873 whose purposes include the study and advancement of international law. It has approximately 4,000 members worldwide, divided into approximately 40 national branches.

57. An example of an area in which there has been significant progress is the transport and dumping of oil and other materials at sea, but recent spills in Alaska and off the coast of Morocco indicate that not enough has been done.

58. The U.N. Security Council has enforcement authority under some circumstances, *see* U.N. Charter, arts. 39–44, but that authority has been effectively enervated by the veto power of the five permanent members of the Security Council.

59. *Cf.* Military and Paramilitary Activities in and Against Nicaragua (Nicar. v. U.S.), Merits, 1986 I.C.J. 14, 99 ¶ 188.

60. *See, e.g.,* The Hague Declaration, *supra* note 8.

61. In fact, only two universal conventional regimes exist defining liability to private persons for specific pollution activities: transport of oil at sea, *see infra* note 65, and nuclear accidents, *see infra* note 70 & Chapter 6. The former is quite elaborate but does not always function satisfactorily, as indicated by the slow process of the case of the Amoco Cadiz oil spill. The latter schemes do not have participation of many important States. *See infra* note 70. Other regimes exist regarding liability to *affected States. See*, *e.g.*, Convention on International Liability for Damage Caused by Space Objects, Oct. 9, 1973, 24 U.S.T. 2381, T.I.A.S. No. 7762.

62. *See*, *e.g.*, 1 RESTATEMENT (THIRD), *supra* note 15, at § 102.

63. *See infra* Chapter 7.

64. *See infra* Chapter 10.

65. *See*, *e.g.*, International Convention on Civil Liability for Oil Pollution Damage, Nov. 29, 1969, 973 U.N.T.S. 3; International Convention on the Establishment of an International Fund for Oil Pollution Damage, Dec. 18, 1971, *reprinted in* 11 I.L.M. 284 (1972).

66. *See*, *e.g.*, Treaty on Principles Governing the Activities of States in the Exploration and Use of Outer Space, Including the Moon and Other Celestial Bodies, Jan. 27, 1967, 18 U.S.T. 2410, T.I.A.S. No. 6347, 610 U.N.T.S. 205.

67. Montreal Ozone Protocol, *supra* note 19; *see* London Adjustments and Amendments to the Montreal Protocol, June 29, 1990.

68. Convention on the Regulation of Antarctic Mineral Resource Activities, June 2, 1988, *reprinted in* 27 I.L.M. 868 (1988) [hereinafter Antarctic Minerals Convention]; *see Antarctic Mineral Development Convention Encounters Major Obstacles at Paris Meeting*, [12 Current Report] Int'l Env't Rep. (BNA) 529 (Nov. 8, 1989).

69. Convention on Early Notification of a Nuclear Accident, I.A.E.A. Doc. INFIRC/335/GC(SPL.I)/RES(1986), *opened for signature* Sept. 26, 1986, *reprinted in* 25 I.L.M. 1370 (1986) (entered into force Oct. 27, 1986).

70. Paris Convention on Third-Party Liability in the Field of Nuclear Energy, July 29, 1960, *reprinted in* 55 AM. J. INT'L L. 1082 (1961) (14 States are parties); Vienna Convention on Civil Liability for Nuclear Damage, May 21, 1963, *reprinted in* 2 I.L.M. 727 (1963) (11 States are parties).

71. The United States, for example, has bilateral hazardous-waste treaties with Mexico and Canada. *See* Agreement on the Transboundary Shipments of Hazardous Waste and Hazardous Substances, Nov. 12, 1986, United States–Mexico, *reprinted in* 26 I.L.M. 25 (1987); Agreement Concerning the Transboundary Movement of Hazardous Waste, Oct. 28, 1986, United States–Canada. A universal treaty has been finalized but is not yet in force. *See* Basel Convention on the Control of Transboundary Movements of Hazardous Wastes and their Disposal, Mar. 22, 1989, *reprinted in* 28 I.L.M. 657 (1989).

72. *See*, *e.g.*, McCaffrey, *Expediting the Provision of Compensation to Accident Victims*, in TRANSFERRING HAZARDOUS TECHNOLOGIES AND SUBSTANCES: THE INTERNATIONAL LEGAL CHALLENGE (G. Handl & R. Lutz eds. 1989).

73. *See supra* text accompanying notes 21–24 and 29.

74. *For Consumers, Ecology Comes Second*, Wall St. J., Aug. 23, 1989, at B1, col. 3 (Western ed.).

75. There are some wild cards that could radically alter the situation, such as the commercial development of cold fusion or major increases in efficiency of photovoltaic cells.

76. *See*, *e.g.*, J. GOLDEMBERG, T.B. JOHANSSON, A.K.N. REDDY & R.H. WIL-

LIAMS, ENERGY FOR A SUSTAINABLE WORLD (World Resources Institute 1987); N.Y. Times, Sept. 3, 1989, at E5, col. 1 (nat'l ed.). Japan has reduced its carbon dioxide emissions during its period of explosive growth.

77. *E.g.*, COUNCIL ON ENVIRONMENTAL QUALITY, ENVIRONMENTAL QUALITY—1987–88 ANNUAL REPORT 300 (1989).

78. *See, e.g., Starting Over: Romanians Address an Economy that Left Their Lives Threadbare*, Wall St. J., Jan. 2, 1990, at 1, col. 1 (Western ed.) (quoted *infra* Chapter 10, at n. 10). Political pressures, of course, tend to be local (as the old saying goes, "All politics are local.").

79. Lambert, *Global Spin*, HOWARD MAGAZINE, Jan.–Feb. 1990, at 17, 27.

80. Keyfitz, *The Growing Human Population*, 119 SCI. AM. (Sept. 1989).

81. *E.g., id.* For a comparison of major population studies, see Ygdrassil, Gold, Anderson & Hizsnyik, *A Critical Review of Population Projections for the Study of Long-Term, Large-Scale Interactions between Development and Environment*, in SCENARIOS OF SOCIOECONOMIC DEVELOPMENT FOR STUDIES OF GLOBAL ENVIRONMENTAL CHANGE: A CRITICAL REVIEW at 13 (F. Toth, E. Hizsnyik & W. Clark eds. IIASA 1989).

82. Lambert, *supra* note 79, at 27.

83. *See, e.g.*, J. Dronkers, R. Boeije & R. Misdorp, *Socioeconomic, Legal, Institutional, Cultural and Environmental Aspects of Measures for the Adaptation of Coastal Zones at Risk to Sea Level Rise* (Draft Nov. 11, 1989).

84. WORLD COMMISSION ON ENVIRONMENT AND DEVELOPMENT, OUR COMMON FUTURE 43 (1987) [hereinafter BRUNDTLAND COMMISSION REPORT]. For additional language, see *infra* Chapter 2 at text accompanying note 29.

85. The focus on the biosphere was prompted by, among others, the Austrian geologist Edward Suess (1831–1914) and the Soviet mineralogist V. I. Vernadsky (1863–1945).

86. Telephone conversation between Marsha S. Ivins and U.S. President George Bush, rebroadcast on National Public Radio on Jan. 17, 1990.

87. For such a photograph, see TIME, Jan. 2, 1989, at 73. The cover of that issue contains a less lovely vision.

88. *Accord* BRUNDTLAND COMMISSION REPORT, *supra* note 84, at 1.

89. *See* McNamara, *Time Bomb or Myth: The Population Problem*, 62 FOREIGN AFF. 1107 (1985).

90. *See, e.g., Hawaii Debates Peril to Rain Forest as an Energy Project Taps a Volcano*, N.Y. Times, Jan. 26, 1990, at A13, col. 1 (nat'l ed.). For a comparison of developed- and developing-country sulphur dioxide emissions, see *Monitoring the Global Environment: An Assessment of Urban Air Quality*, ENVIRONMENT 6 (Oct. 1989).

91. The fund, recently announced by the U.N. Secretary-General to assist States in settling disputes via the International Court of Justice, might prove helpful with respect to pursuing remedies for international pollution. *See* Secretary-General's Trust Fund to Assist States in the Settlement of Disputes through the International Court of Justice, announced Nov. 1, 1989, *reprinted in* 28 I.L.M. 1589 (1989).

92. Robert McNamara, formerly President of the World Bank, defined "absolute poverty" as a form of existence so characterized by exposure to the elements, malnutrition, illiteracy, and disease as to be below any reasonable standard of human decency. *See* McNamara, *supra* note 89, at 1118–19.

93. *See* Magraw, *The International Law Commission's Study of International Liability as It Relates to Developing States*, 61 WASH. L. REV. 1041, 1050–52 (1986).

94. *See, e.g.*, Linden, *The Death of Birth*, TIME, Jan. 2, 1989, at 32.

95. The international transfer of hazardous technology, products, and waste is not considered in this book, except in part in Chapter 4. For analyses of various aspects of this set of issues, see TRANSFERRING HAZARDOUS TECHNOLOGIES AND SUBSTANCES: THE INTERNATIONAL LEGAL CHALLENGE (G. Handl & R. Lutz eds. 1989).

96. *See, e.g.*, principle 23 of the Stockholm Declaration on the Human Environment, *supra* note 48. For a discussion of the treatment of developing States under current international environmental law, see Magraw, *Legal Treatment of Developing Countries: Differential, Contextual, and Absolute Norms*, 1 COLO. J. INT'L ENVTL. L. & POL'Y (1990).

97. Oct. 21, 1982, U.N. Doc. A/CONF.62/121, *reprinted in* 21 I.L.M. 1261 (1982).

98. *Reprinted in* 26 I.L.M. 1550 (1987).

99. *See, e.g.*, TIME, Jan. 2, 1989, at 54.

100. [12 Current Report] Int'l Env't Rep. (BNA) 389 (Aug. 9, 1989).

101. *See, e.g.*, Cairo Compact, *supra* note 47; *Statement of the Meeting of Experts on the Law of the Atmosphere, Ottawa, Canada* (Feb. 1989).

102. For contrasting views about the likelihood that global warming will occur, see Brookes, *The Global Warming Panic*, FORBES, Dec. 25, 1989, at 96; Schneider, *The Changing Climate*, SCI. AM. 58 (Sept. 1989); Ramirez, *A Warming World*, FORTUNE, July 4, 1988, at 102.

103. *See infra* Chapter 8.

104. *See also infra* Chapters 11, 13–16.

105. Antarctic Treaty, Dec. 1, 1959, 12 U.S.T. 794, 402 U.N.T.S. 71; Convention on the Conservation of Antarctic Seals, June 1, 1972, 29 U.S.T. 441, T.I.A.S. No. 8826; Convention on the Conservation of Antarctic Marine Living Resources, May 20, 1980, T.I.A.S. No. 10240; *cf.* Antarctic Mineral Convention, *supra* note 68 (not yet in force).

106. *See, e.g., infra* Chapter 11.

107. *See, e.g.*, E. BROWN WEISS, IN FAIRNESS TO FUTURE GENERATIONS: INTERNATIONAL LAW, COMMON PATRIMONY, AND INTERGENERATIONAL EQUITY (1989); d'Arge, *Ethical and Economic Systems for Managing the Global Commons* 327, in CHANGING THE GLOBAL ENVIRONMENT (1989).

108. *See supra* text following note 18.

Chapter 2
International Pollution, Economic Development, and Human Rights

Daniel Barstow Magraw

Introduction

This chapter examines the relationship among three sets of international efforts that have played major roles in defining the international legal system since World War II. These three are the attempts to understand and control or otherwise cope with international pollution of various types;[1] to achieve economic development (defined differently by different persons) for developing countries;[2] and to define and protect political and social rights of individuals.[3] The goals of this chapter are, by illuminating the relationships among these three areas, to identify linkages within the current international legal system and to place the international pollution-specific discussions appearing elsewhere in this book in the broader perspective of that system.

Conceptual Framework

An attempt to parse the relationship of these three areas involves dealing with several complicating factors. A conceptual question exists in that it is not possible to isolate three elements from the intellectual history of a period. Other currents—including decolonization, expansion of the roles and scopes of international law and organizations, developments in trade law, population growth, the amassing of nuclear arsenals, and improvements in telecommunications—have influenced the post–World War II decades strongly. Most of these other currents are somewhat different from the international pollution, human rights, and economic development efforts because these three efforts concern growth in areas of substantive law. In any event, this chapter does not deny the relevance of such factors, but rather attempts to examine the interaction of the international pollution, economic development, and human rights areas within the overall post–World War II experience, which necessarily includes those other factors.

Another conceptual complexity arises from the facts that attention on these three areas increased roughly simultaneously and that there rarely are any "smoking guns" regarding causal relationships; determining cause and effect is thus very difficult. In many instances, it is possible only to identify trends or shared characteristics.

The set of relationships among these three areas is also complicated. At least in theory, the three areas relate not only all together in a tripartite fashion (international pollution–economic development–human rights), but also in pairs: international pollution–economic development; international pollution–human rights; and economic development–human rights. It is conceptually easier to analyze a relationship between two variables than a relationship among three. But practically speaking, that approach encounters the difficulty that these pairs interact in the context of other activities and developments, including the remaining area considered in this chapter. After identifying an instance in which one area has affected another area, I attempt to discern whether the remaining area has been, or is likely to be, affected.

Additionally, those relationships are complex because they exist on several levels and may be analyzed accordingly. I identify and discuss five such levels in this chapter.

The first level concerns the content of norms or goals, including the identity and nature of the relevant actors and intended beneficiaries. The question is whether the content of international norms or goals regarding one area has affected the content of international norms or goals in the other areas. An example is whether the unprecedented emphasis of human rights norms on the rights of individuals, rather than States, has influenced norms and goals in the areas of international pollution and economic development.[4]

The second level concerns practical implementation. Is complying with norms or accomplishing goals with respect to one area affected by the existence of international norms relating to, and attempts to achieve norms or goals with respect to, the other areas, or, phrased differently, do the norms or goals in one area impose constraints or create opportunities with respect to the other areas? For instance, does achieving economic growth affect efforts to protect the environment?[5]

The third level relates to law creation. Has the method of creating international norms in one area affected the method of creating international norms in the other areas? One might thus ask whether the rapid movement from aspirational to obligatory norms in the human rights area has eased the way for a similar transformation regarding international pollution.[6]

The fourth level concerns structure. Has the structure of international norms in one area affected the structure of international norms in the other areas? For example, has the existence of the obligation to pay compensation to an alien for nationalized property—which exists even if no international delict has yet occurred, but which results in a delict if no compensation is paid—affected the willingness to find an obligation to pay compensation for international pollution that does not entail an international wrong?[7]

The fifth and final level involves methodologies of monitoring, enforcement, and dispute settlement.[8] Have the monitoring of compliance with norms, the enforcement of norms, and the settlement of international disputes arising in one area affected monitoring, enforcement, and dispute settlement in the other areas? For example, has the role of non-governmental organizations (NGOs), such as Amnesty International, in monitoring human rights violations led to similar roles in monitoring compliance with international pollution norms?[9]

The interaction of international pollution, economic development, and human rights efforts thus does not occur on one plane in a "triangle," to use the term that appeared in the title of a panel that considered the interrelationships of these areas at the 1988 Annual Meeting of the American Society of International Law.[10] Rather, these three areas interact in a type of three-dimensional matrix containing at least the five levels identified above—levels that may, themselves, interact.[11]

A final complication arises from the fact that the legal regimes with respect to these areas are still relatively embryonic. Dialogues in each area thus consider both norms and aspirations. The distinction between the two is often neither sharp nor agreed-upon, as demonstrated by the debate about the normative content of the New International Economic Order[12] and the apparent confusion about whether the Soviet Union is internationally accountable for harm in other States from the disaster at the nuclear power plant at Chernobyl.[13] In addition, norms and aspirations are subject to relatively rapid change, as evidenced by the dynamic evolution of human rights law. Moreover, these areas are at different stages of being governed by norms, as distinguished from aspirations, and at different degrees of conformance to whatever norms do exist. In the first two analytic levels, the possibilities of goals affecting norms, or vice versa, are raised. And the third level deals in part with the process of transforming aspirations to legal norms. The fact that the international pollution, economic development, and human rights areas are at different evolutionary stages thus should be borne in mind.

The full range of the relationships just described deserves examination. This chapter focuses on presenting an analytic framework for examining those relationships and on identifying examples of the most significant interactions that have occurred or are likely to occur. Often, it has been possible only to describe an effect or relationship without investigating it in detail, because of time constraints. An interesting question not considered here, for example, is under what circumstances an effect of one area on another has led to an effect on a third. Additional analysis is desirable to explore the linkages within the international legal system.

Definitions

Before examining the levels of interaction, it is necessary to define the terms "pollution," "international pollution," "human rights," and "economic development." By pollution, I mean

the introduction by humankind, directly or indirectly, of substances or energy into the environment resulting in deleterious effects of such a nature as to endanger human health, harm living resources and ecosystems, impair amenities or interfere with other legitimate uses of the environment.[14]

By international pollution, I mean pollution that is generated within the territory or control of one State and results in harm in another State or an international commons (e.g., the transboundary flux of sulphur dioxide from the United States to Canada or oil spills that pollute the high seas). I also mean to include pollution that is generated within a State and has its direct effects entirely within that State ("intra-State pollution"), if that pollution engages an interest of the international community (e.g., extinction of a species).[15]

By human rights, I mean those rights recognized in the United Nations Charter,[16] the Universal Declaration of Human Rights,[17] the International Covenant on Civil and Political Rights[18] and its Optional Protocol,[19] and the International Covenant on Economic, Social and Cultural Rights.[20] As these documents comprise the core of the International Bill of Human Rights, I will concentrate on them without much reference to the many other international human rights conventions.

Economic development here means growth in per capita Gross National Product (GNP). I exclude from the concept of economic development questions of distributive justice. I also do not address the question whether economic development, as defined herein, should be pursued primarily through the agricultural, industrial, or service sectors, or through some combination of them. I choose that exclusively growth-oriented definition because the questions that are the focus of this chapter would be trivialized or blurred by defining economic development to include the achievement of attributes that are central to the usual concept of pollution or freedom from it—such as clean air or water—or of economic or political rights—such as equality of income and wealth distribution or participation in the political process.

From a policy perspective, defining "development" is critically important. That concept typically now includes just such environmental and political attributes; and recently or currently favored approaches to development, such as sustainable development,[21] growth-with-equity,[22] and basic human needs,[23] were designed specifically to recognize and attain those attributes. Indeed, as is discussed below, the reasons such approaches gained ascendancy may be due, in large part, to ecological and human rights concerns. I use the term societal development to refer to development in the broader sense. From the perspective of examining the relationships between the three areas that are the subject of this chapter, however, such a comprehensive definition of development would be counterproductive without a narrower term limited solely to the growth-oriented aspect of development, because that would not allow the areas to be separated for analytical purposes. Both terms—economic development and societal development—thus are necessary for this chapter.

Content and Scope

Focus on Health, Safety, and Individual Well-being

Societal development (in the broad sense defined above), human rights, and environmental protection efforts all share concerns about health, safety, and individual well-being. The movements to protect human rights and to control pollution recognized these concerns at their inception.[24] Not so the early efforts to achieve economic development; these focused on industrialization and removing capital constraints on development, rather than on what was actually happening to individuals.[25] That focus, which was partly based on the belief—subsequently discredited—that benefits from laissez faire economic growth would automatically "trickle down" to the masses, shifted in the 1970s toward considering distributive issues, achieving growth-with-equity, and meeting basic human needs of the poor, especially those persons living in absolute poverty (i.e., that condition of existence so characterized by exposure to the elements, malnutrition, illiteracy, and disease as to be beneath any reasonable standard of human decency).[26] The basic-human-needs approach became predominant in the early 1980s, and it remains a central concern—if not the central concern— even in today's context of policy disarray.[27]

Historically, it seems clear that human rights and environmental concerns contributed to the redefinition of "economic development" away from considering purely growth-oriented concerns to including other aspects—and those concerns may have been influential in re-orienting the approach to achieving development, even purely eco-nomic growth, toward local participation—by emphasizing, publiciz-ing, and popularizing ideas relating to issues such as the health of the population. Human rights debates and activities probably provided the most impetus to increased attention being paid to income- and wealth-distribution, local participation, and worker safety and health, and to the adoption of the growth-with-equity and basic-human-needs ap-proaches to development. Similarly, environmental concerns most probably have increased the attention paid by economic-development efforts to the long-term perspective, to quality of life, to the importance of cultural continuity, and to health and safety issues generally. For example, the underpinnings of the New International Economic Or-der, as expressed in the 1974 Charter of Economic Rights and Duties of States, include the "protection, preservation and enhancement of the environment" and "promot[ing] . . . economic, social and cultural development."[28]

The report of the World Commission on Environment and Develop-ment (the "Brundtland Report") reflects the influence of both the human rights and the environmental protection emphases in these regards. Those influences are evident, for example, in the Brundtland Report's definition of the critical concept of "sustainable develop-ment":

Sustainable development is development that meets the needs of the present without compromising the ability of future generations to meet their own needs. It contains within it two key concepts:
—the concept of 'needs,' in particular the essential needs of the world's poor, to which overriding priority should be given; and
—the idea of limitations imposed by the state of technology and social organization on the environment's ability to meet present and future needs.

Thus the goals of economic and social development must be defined in terms of sustainability in all countries—developed or developing, market-oriented or centrally planned.[29]

Environmental efforts presumably also increase awareness of the health and safety aspects of human rights norms and goals (hereafter, references to "norms" include both norms and goals, unless the context indicates otherwise).

Individuals as Subjects of International Law

International human rights norms define the rights of individuals and, on occasion, even provide individuals the right to make claims directly against States.[30] Some human rights norms also provide that individuals have duties.[31] It has been argued that there exists an international human right to a healthy and decent environment.[32] The 1989 Hague Declaration on the Environment expressly ties international pollution to traditional human rights:

> The right to live is the right from which all other rights stem. Guaranteeing this right is the paramount duty of those in charge of all States throughout the world.
> Today, the very conditions of life on our planet are threatened by the severe attacks to which the earth's atmosphere is subjected.[33]

It has also been argued that there is a right to economic development.[34] The concept of human rights thus has been important in terms of expressing and furthering the goals of environmental protection and economic development.

Moreover, to the extent norms in these areas focus on individuals as having rights or duties under international law or as being the beneficiaries of international-law duties of States, they represent an expansion of international law beyond its previous almost-exclusive preoccupation with the rights and duties of States. It was recognized, at least after the Permanent Court of International Justice's Advisory Opinion in the case concerning the Jurisdiction of the Courts of Danzig,[35] that international agreements can create rights and obligations for individuals. An example of such obligations is that individual soldiers could be held responsible for killing or torturing in violation of the law of war (activities that now, interestingly, are proscribed by human rights norms). That possibility was given effect after World War II in the war-crimes trials (and subsequent punishment) of German and Japanese government officials.[36]

The incidence of individual rights and obligations has grown significantly since then. This important post–World War II development owes much of its impetus to the three areas discussed in this chapter, and especially to human rights norms, which are the most advanced in this respect. I expect this trend to continue, especially in respect of international pollution.

The focus on the rights and duties of individuals will probably be tempered, however, by another recent development in international law. That development, which also departs from the international legal system's historical preoccupation with States as legal actors, is the recognition that *humankind as a whole* has an interest in managing and deriving benefits from specific natural resources or conditions. In 1967, for example, the Outer Space Treaty stated that "The exploration and use of outer space, including the moon . . . , shall be carried out for the benefit and in the interests of all countries . . . and shall be the province of all mankind."[37] The 1982 U.N. Convention on the Law of the Sea uses the same concept of "mankind" but expands the interest mankind has, declaring that the sea-bed beyond the limits of national jurisdiction is the "common heritage of mankind."[38] The 1988 U.N. General Assembly Resolution on Protection of Global Climate for Present and Future Generations of Mankind declares that "climate change is a common concern of mankind."[39] Express recognition of the interests of humankind (a term preferable to "mankind" because the latter can be viewed as sexist) thus has occurred in contexts involving economic (or societal) development or international pollution, or both.

Focusing on humankind as the possessor of rights has different legal implications from defining rights in terms of individuals or of States. Such a focus is attractive for several reasons. It reflects the growing interdependence of human life on Earth and parallels the recognition that the biosphere is an integrated whole (although the focus on humankind does not include nonhuman life). Emphasizing the concept of humankind also may provide a helpful way of approaching the difficult question of how to take into account the interests of subsequent generations. For example, the concept of humankind implies temporal (as well as spatial) continuity. It also eliminates the need to be able to identify specific individuals—which is impossible but which would be necessary, at least theoretically, if intergenerational equity is conceptualized in terms of the rights of individuals living in the future. But focusing on humankind also raises difficult questions. Some of those questions involve the presumed need to predict the overall characteristics, needs, and preferences of future populations. Others are similar to those involved in protecting against pollution of global commons: for example, who has the right to, or the duty to, manage resources, bring claims, and allocate benefits or compensation?[40] These questions, though difficult, are not intractable. I do not expect they will prevent the increased utilization of the concept of humankind in economic development and international pollution control efforts.

Relevance of International Law to a State's Treatment of Its Own Nationals

A related point is that international law traditionally had little, if anything, to do with a State's treatment of its own nationals. The classic example is the set of norms regarding State responsibility for injuries to aliens: the rules applied only to a State's treatment of aliens, and no comparable rules governed a State's treatment of its own nationals or how a State might dispose of any amount it received from another State as compensation for the latter State's having injured a national of the former State.[41] The Nuremberg trials following World War II broke this precedent, in particular by prosecuting individuals for crimes against humanity, which included "murder, extermination, enslavement, deportation, and other inhumane acts committed against *any civilian population*."[42] International human rights norms carried this further, explicitly dealing with how a State treats its nationals in a wider set of activities, thus expanding the reach of international law. Attention to how States affect the environment of their own residents, including their own nationals, probably has increased as a result, including to the extent that intra-State pollution is of interest to international law as a result of violating human rights norms.[43] The same is probably true with respect to how the fruits of economic development are distributed within a State, including to its nationals. The reference to "sustainable *and equitable* development" in the International Labour Organisation's Convention Concerning Indigenous and Tribal Peoples in Independent Countries may be a step in that direction.[44] I expect this trend to continue, especially regarding international pollution norms.

Articulation of Norms and the Relevance of Resource Availability and Technical and Regulatory Capacity

The concern about economic development has affected the content and articulation of international pollution norms and, to a lesser degree, human rights norms in a fashion different from those described above. The story can best be told chronologically.

Article 2, paragraph 1, of the 1966 International Covenant on Economic, Social and Cultural Rights provides that all Parties undertake steps to achieve progressively the full rights recognized in the Covenant.[45] Paragraph 3 of that article, however, contains an exception applicable only to developing countries: "Developing countries . . . may determine to what extent they would guarantee the economic rights recognized in the present Covenant to non-nationals."[46]

Article 2(3) is an example of what I refer to as "differential norms," that is, norms that on their face provide different, presumably more advantageous, standards for one set of States than for another set.[47] Theoretically, the sets of States can be distinguished on any grounds (other than simply that one State or set of States is acting and another State or set of States is being affected).[48] Article 2(3) is the first differential norm of which I am aware that differentiates on the basis of whether a State is "developing" or not. The term "developing countries," by the way, is not defined in the Covenant, although it presumably encompasses countries with a vast range of characteristics (e.g., both Burundi and Brazil are commonly referred to as developing countries). Article 2(3) does not appear to have been widely cited or discussed.

The next development, which was much more significant from an international pollution-control perspective, occurred in 1972. Principle 23 of the 1972 Stockholm Declaration on the Human Environment declared that the economic-development situation of a State is relevant to determining appropriate environmental standards:

Without prejudice to such criteria as may be agreed upon by the international community, or to standards which will have to be determined nationally, it will be essential in all cases to consider the systems of values prevailing in each country, and *the extent of the applicability of standards which are valid for the most advanced countries but which may be inappropriate and of unwarranted social cost for the developing countries.*[49]

Principle 23 reflects the facts not only that different countries have different values and that the need to improve standards of living properly affects developing countries' priorities but also that developing countries face several disadvantages affecting environmental protection. For example, developing countries are less likely to have sufficient information to predict transboundary harm as a result of activities in their territories, especially where the activities are foreign-controlled; and they are less likely to have sufficient technical expertise to evaluate potential harm and monitor ongoing activities or sufficient legal, regulatory, and administrative skills to draft and effectuate pollution-control laws.

These ideas were taken up in a broader context in 1974, when the U.N. General Assembly passed three resolutions that, taken together, called for a New International Economic Order (NIEO). NIEO is based on the propositions that developing States must develop economically, that the economic differential between developed and developing States must narrow, and that resources must be transferred to developing States to achieve those ends.[50] These three resolutions were the Declaration on the Establishment of a New International Economic Order; the Programme of Action on the Establishment of a New International Economic Order; and the Charter of Economic Rights and Duties of States (CERDS), article 30 of which provides that "The environmental policies of all States should enhance and not adversely affect the present and future development potential of developing countries."[51]

Although not legally binding, principle 23 of the Stockholm Declaration and article 30 of CERDS have been very influential and constitute the foundation for applying differential norms to environmental issues. In each of them (as was the case with article 2(3) of the Economic, Social and Cultural Covenant),[52] the differential norms provide different standards for developing and developed States.

Since 1974, several international agreements and declarations regarding the environment have included such differential norms or goals. Examples include the 1982 U.N. Convention on the Law of the Sea (e.g., article 207, concerning pollution from land-based sources, provides that parties shall "tak[e] into account . . . the *economic capacity of developing States and their need for economic development*");[53] the 1985 Vienna Convention for the Protection of the Ozone Layer (article 4 provides that States shall cooperate in promoting the development and transfer of technology "taking into account in particular the *needs of developing countries*");[54] the 1987 Montreal Protocol on Substances that Deplete the Ozone Layer (articles 2 and 5 provide different reduction standards for developing and developed countries, defined in terms of annual per capita consumption of controlled ozone-depleting substances);[55] and the 1989 Basel Convention on Hazardous Waste (e.g., article 10(3) requires States to "employ appropriate means to cooperate in order to assist *developing countries*" in implementing specified provisions in the Convention).[56] Since 1972, therefore, differential norms have been used to give simultaneous effect to the concerns for economic development and environmental protection.

Another method for taking concurrent account of multiple values already existed (i.e., by 1972), however, and had been used in a variety of areas. Many international agreements and declarations—concerning the environment and otherwise—contain what I refer to as "contextual norms," that is, norms that on their face provide identical treatment to all States affected by the norm, including developing and developed States, but the application of which requires (or at least permits) consideration of factors that might vary from State to State. The use of contextual norms antedates World War II, but that use has escalated dramatically since that time—most probably for reasons that go well beyond the focus and interaction of the three areas discussed in this chapter.[57]

Some contextual norms are general in nature; that is, by their terms they do not limit the factors that may be considered. An example is the 1972 Convention on International Liability for Damage Caused by Space Objects.[58] The Convention, which provides absolute liability on the part of the launching State, allows an injured State to make a claim until one year after that State "could *reasonably* be expected to have learned of the facts,"[59] and it provides that compensation should be determined by reference to "principles of *justice and equity*."[60] Other contextual norms are limited in that some boundaries are indicated regarding what facts and circumstances may be taken into account. For example, article 194 of the Law of the Sea Convention contains the general obligation to take steps necessary to prevent, reduce, and control marine pollution "using for this purpose the *best practicable means at their disposal and in accordance with their capabilities*":[61] a contextual qualification thus applies, but it is limited to considering elements such as resource availability and technological capacity.

For purposes of this analysis, the most interesting contextual norms are those environmental norms taking account of factors that correspond typically, but not necessarily unvaryingly, to the economic-development level of a State. Some international environmental agreements containing such contextual norms antedated 1972, for example, the 1949 Convention for the Regulation of Whaling (whales taken under permits for scientific research shall be processed and dealt with "*as far as possible*" according to the permit);[62] the 1958 Convention on the Continental Shelf (the exploitation of the continental shelf and its resources "must not result in any *unjustifiable* interference with . . . conservation of the living resources");[63] and the 1969 Convention on Civil Liability for Oil Pollution Damage (ship owner is exempt from liability if he proves damage is due to "the *negligence* . . . of any . . . authority responsible for the maintenance of lights" and owners of all ships discharging oil are jointly and severally liable for "damage which is not *reasonably* separable").[64] Others were finalized between the 1972 Stockholm Convention and the 1974 NIEO trio, for example, the 1972 Convention Concerning the Protection of the World Cultural and Natural Heritage (each party "will do *all it can* to [protect cultural and natural resources], to the *utmost of its own resources*")[65] and the 1973 Convention on International Trade in Endangered Species of Fauna and Flora (parties "shall take *appropriate* measures" to enforce the Convention and prohibit trade in violation thereof).[66] Still others came after 1974, such as the 1979 LRTAP Convention (e.g., States "shall endeavour . . . *as far as possible*, [to] gradually reduce and prevent air pollution"),[67] the 1982 Law of the Sea Convention (e.g., States are generally obligated to take steps "necessary" to prevent, reduce, and control marine pollution "using for this purpose the *best practicable means at their disposal* and *in accordance with their capabilities*"),[68] the 1985 Vienna Ozone Convention (States shall, "in accordance with the *means at their disposal* and *their capabilities*," cooperate and adopt certain measures),[69] and the Basel Convention on Hazardous Waste ("Each Party shall take *appropriate* measures to: (a) Ensure that the generation of hazardous wastes and other wastes within it is reduced to a minimum, *taking into account social, technological and economic aspects*").[70]

Thus, after the 1972 Stockholm Declaration on the Human Environment and the formal call for NIEO in 1974, some international environmental norms have been articulated in a way that expressly reflects the drive for economic development, that is, via differential norms that depend upon distinguishing between developing and developed countries. Also, an alternative, less explicit way of taking into account differences in economic resources and technical and regulatory capabilities—i.e., contextual norms—had already been in use and has continued to be used in articulating environmental norms and goals. Indeed, contextual environmental norms appear to occur more frequently than differential environmental norms. An effect of the concern for economic development—or at a minimum the recognition that resource availability and technical and regulatory capability affect the degree to which States can protect the environment, together with the belief that norms should not demand the impossible[71]—is even evident in the use of contextual norms, however: since 1972, contextual environmental norms are more likely to refer specifically to resource availability and capability.

The concern about economic development also appears to have influenced the content and articulation of human rights norms, though the effect is visible at an earlier date and does not appear to be as prevalent. As indicated above,[72] article 2 of the 1966 International Covenant on Economic, Cultural and Social Rights provides both differential treatment and contextual treatment. I am not aware of other examples of economic-development-based differential norms in the human rights area; and the contextual norms that appear in human rights laws are less likely to refer to, or otherwise have particularly to do with, resource availability or technical or regulatory capability. For example, the contextual norms in the Convention on the Elimination of All Forms of Discrimination Against Women are phrased in terms of "appropriate"[73] and "equitable";[74] even the provision establishing a globally representative Committee on the Elimination of Discrimination Against Women lists equitable geographical distribution, different forms of civilization, and different legal systems, but not different levels of economic development.[75] The same situation exists with respect to the Convention Against Torture and Other Cruel, Inhuman or Degrading Treatment or Punishment.[76]

Some human rights conventions, however, contain override clauses that allow a State to restrict the exercise of some rights if required by the national interest, which is described in various ways. Applying these contextual norms could involve considering the economic importance of a particular asset or activity. For example, although the African Charter on Human and People's Rights does not contain any differential norms, the right to property is subject to encroachment "in the interest of public need or in the general interest of the community."[77] The Universal Declaration of Human Rights is subject to a comprehensive override of "the just requirements of morality, public order and the general welfare in a democratic society."[78]

Human rights efforts, in turn, may, by focusing on distributive questions, reinforce NIEO's claims for international pollution norms capable of considering characteristics associated with development status. In this respect, it would not seem to matter whether the norms were differential or contextual.

Use of Norms Calling for Progressive Realization

Another interaction of human rights, economic development, and international pollution activities involves the use of goals calling for States to attempt to achieve an end or to make progress toward achieving that end, rather than requiring that a State achieve something or (as was probably more common before World War II) prohibiting a State from an activity. Article 56 of the U.N. Charter, for example, obligates States to "take joint and separate action in cooperation with the [United Nations] *to achieve*" the human rights and other goals set forth in article 55 of the Charter.[79] Similarly, article 2 of the International Covenant on Economic, Social and Cultural Rights obligates a State to "take steps . . . to the maximum of its available resources, *with a view to achieving progressively* the . . . rights recognized in the present Convention."[80] This type of obligation, which is referred to as "progressive realization," was subsequently utilized in international pollution norms (e.g., article 2 of the 1979 LRTAP Convention obligates States to "*endeavour to limit* and, as far as possible, *gradually* reduce and prevent air pollution")[81] and in economic development declarations (e.g., article 15 of CERDS provides that "All States have the duty to *promote* the *achievement* of . . . disarmament . . . and to utilize the resources released . . . for development").[82]

A striking aspect of progressive-realization norms is that it is almost impossible to determine whether a State is violating them, especially given that there typically does not exist any dispute-settlement mechanism with mandatory jurisdiction to decide the question. The contours and edges of the obligation are so undefined that it is arguable that no real obligation exists at all. In this regard, progressive-realization norms are similar to contextual norms (of which progressive-realization norms may, in fact, be a subset). Contextual norms also typically leave wide latitude for arguments about whether a State has or has not complied. Consider, for example, the principle that shared natural resources should be utilized in an equitable and reasonable manner[83] or the U.S. position about acid rain, discussed here in Chapters 10 and 13 to 16.[84]

The willingness to utilize such norms in these three (and other) areas reflects the facts that, although States agree there is an issue appropriately dealt with internationally and that restrictions on State behavior are required, reaching agreement on specific obligations may not be possible, at least initially. In this respect, the use of progressive-realization norms is related to the use of contextual norms and of framework conventions, discussed earlier in Chapter 1.[85]

Many issues in the human rights, international pollution, and economic development areas fit that description: States have decided that it is better to have some guiding norm, even if it is generally unenforceable because it is so ambiguous, than to have no governing rule at all. States might reach that conclusion for quite different reasons. For example, a State might genuinely desire progress on the issue and decide that something is better than nothing, it might prefer an ambiguous norm because of such a norm's ability to incorporate (without amendment) changes in scientific knowledge or other likely developments, or it might want to create the impression that progress is occurring while still maintaining the ability to claim that its own behavior is lawful.

In any event, the frequent use of contextual norms and progressive-realization norms indicates a willingness on the part of States to utilize, at least in the short term, norms that are relatively unenforceable. That willingness may reflect, among other things, pessimism about the world community's ability to agree on more effective rules or optimism about the increasing sophistication of the international legal system (e.g., that the existence of unenforceable norms will not weaken the strength of more enforceable norms), or both.

Standing of States to Make Claims

Ordinarily, only a State to which an international obligation is owed has standing to claim that the obligation has been violated.[86] This doctrine presents difficulties with respect to human rights norms—including human rights norms that relate to the environment—because the right belongs to individuals, not to States. Although an individual whose human right was violated might in some instances have standing to bring a claim (as discussed above), because an individual cannot take self-help measures that are available to a State and is not likely to have resources on par with the allegedly violating State, the contest will be unequal. Moreover, it is not feasible to assign the right to make human rights claims generally to the State of which the individual victim is a national (as is the case with State responsibility for injuries to aliens) because the allegedly violating State is often that very State. Norms and goals about economic development raise similar concerns. A somewhat different difficulty is presented regarding international norms that concern pollution of the commons: as explained in greater detail in Chapter 1,[87] no State (or any other entity) has an exclusive right to protest against pollution of global commons or to claim or distribute compensation for commons pollution. Similar questions exist with respect to environmental rights of humankind and the interests of subsequent generations.

The need to resolve these difficulties has contributed to the expansion of a heretofore somewhat obscure concept (wrongs *erga omnes*, that is, wrongs against all States in the world) and to the development of a controversial proposal (international crimes). Wrongs *erga omnes* were discussed approvingly by the International Court of Justice (ICJ) in the 1970 *Barcelona Traction* case (rejecting the conclusions of the same court in a case decided four years earlier)[88] with particular reference to norms outlawing "acts of aggression [and] genocide, as also . . . the principles and rules concerning the basic rights of the human person."[89] Nevertheless, the idea that some obligations are owed to all States in the world and that all States thus have standing to protest violations of those obligations was not given much practical effect until recently. The Restatement (Third) of Foreign Relations Law of the United States now recognizes that any State may protest "a significant injury to the general environment [or] a denial of human rights in violation of customary international law."[90] In a somewhat similar vein, the U.N. International Law Commission has provisionally approved the concept of international crimes as including certain serious breaches of human rights and international pollution norms;[91] and the special rapporteur has proposed (although the Commission has not yet endorsed) that all States would have standing to protest (and, indeed, would have an obligation to resist the situation created by) international crimes.[92]

The attention on human rights and international pollution thus has served to expand international law about standing, at least with respect to wrongs *erga omnes* and possibly with respect to international crimes (if that proposal eventually becomes law).

Practical Implementation

One of the issues at this level can be phrased as the question, Does the existence of international pollution (and directly related norms) significantly affect the efforts to develop economically and to achieve greater human rights, and, if so, what are the effects? Other questions can be framed simply by exchanging terms: Does the effort to develop economically (and directly related norms) significantly affect the efforts to combat international pollution and to achieve human rights? Does the effort to achieve human rights (and directly related norms) significantly affect the efforts to combat international pollution and to develop economically?

In addressing these questions, it is not sufficient to refer only to the manifold interdependencies—cultural, ecological, ethical, economic, and political—of today's world, or to the interconnectedness of those interdependencies.[93] That is the case even though the fact of that interdependence has international legal consequences.[94] The analysis must be more refined.

A comprehensive analysis of the relationship between the environment and development was undertaken in *Our Common Future*, the report of the U.N. World Commission on Environment and Development (the Brundtland Report).[95] The Commission concluded that there is a two-way causal connection between environmental protection (including pollution control and natural resource management) and economic development (as defined in this chapter). The Commission also concluded that there is a relationship among those two phenomena and achieving some aspects of human rights, that is, at least the economic, health, and safety aspects (which are referred to as "economic, social, and cultural" rights, as distinguished from "civil and political" rights). These conclusions are typified by the following quotation:

[E]nvironmental stresses and patterns of economic development are linked one to another. Thus agricultural policies may lie at the root of land, water, and forest degradation. Energy policies are associated with the global greenhouse effect, with acidification, and with deforestation for fuel wood in many developing nations. These stresses all threaten economic development. Thus economics and ecology must be completely integrated in decision-making and lawmaking processes not just to protect the environment, but also to protect and promote development. Economy is not just about the production of wealth, and ecology is not just about the protection of nature; they are both equally relevant for improving the lot of humankind.[96]

From other portions of the Brundtland Report, it is evident that the Commission's concerns about "improving the lot of humankind" include (in addition to increasing generally the economic condition of people in the Third World) improvements in health, education, nutrition, housing and protection from adverse weather, adequate treatment of women and children, and empowerment of indigenous or tribal peoples.[97] Each of these individual concerns is also expressed in international human rights law.[98]

Although the Commission did not expressly cast its analysis or conclusions in terms of human rights, the primary focus of the Commission was on sustainable development, defined above.[99] As evident from that definition and from the attention to the individual concerns just mentioned,[100] the Commission conducted its analysis with respect to a concept of development that goes beyond *economic* development to encompass ideas of economic well-being, nutrition, health, safety, distributive justice, and intergenerational equities—ideas that are directly related to human rights.

Similarly, the influential report of the Independent Commission on International Development Issues, *North-South: A Program for Survival* (the "Brandt Report"), is founded on a concept of development that expressly includes many of the individual issues that concerned the Brundtland Commission (e.g., health, education, nutrition, protection from the elements, treatment of women and children), as well as distributive justice, intergenerational equity, and human rights more generally.[101] The Brandt Commission was created in order to consider development strategies generally rather than the relationship between the environment and development. It concluded—as did the Brundtland Commission seven years later—that there is a fundamental and critical connection between environmental protection, economic development (as defined in this chapter), and human rights:

[T]here has been an awakening to the need to protect the environment from over-exploitation, pollution and contamination. The United Nations Conference on the Human Environment in 1972 was an important milestone, and much progress in awareness has been made in the years since then. It can no longer be argued that the protection of the environment is an obstacle to development. On the contrary, the care of the natural environment is an essential aspect of development.[102]

Both the Brandt and the Brundtland Commissions concluded that the environment–development–human rights linkage is international in scope. The Brundtland Commission explained:

Ecology and economy are becoming ever more interwoven—locally, regionally, nationally, and globally—into a seamless net of causes and effects.

Impoverishing the local resource base can impoverish wider areas: Deforestation by highland farmers causes flooding on lowland farms; factory pollution robs local fishermen of their catch. Such grim local cycles now operate nationally and regionally. Dryland degradation sends environmental refugees in their millions across national borders. Deforestation in Latin America is causing more floods, and more destructive floods, in downhill, downstream nations. Acid precipitation and nuclear fallout have spread across the borders of Europe. Similar phenomena are emerging on a global scale, such as global warming and loss of ozone. Internationally traded hazardous chemicals entering foods are themselves internationally traded [sic]. In the next century, the environmental pressure causing population movements may increase sharply, or barriers to that movement may be even firmer than they are now.[103]

The Brandt Commission described the international linkage between environmental protection and economic development from a somewhat different perspective:

There is . . . a temptation for a country to set lower standards than another in order to attract industry and create jobs. There is an obvious need to harmonize standards, to prevent a competitive debasement of them. Developing countries . . . have an interest in establishing and enforcing standards for environmental protection. The same norms will not be appropriate for all countries, and they must make their own judgement of the trade-offs involved. But to seek to attract industry at the expense of environment might cause damage that is more costly to undo than to prevent, and it would also be likely to contribute to protectionist pressures in industrial countries.

Environmental impact assessment should be undertaken wherever investments or other development activities may have adverse environmental consequences whether within the national territory concerned, for the environment of neighbouring countries or for the global commons. There should be guidelines for such assessments, and when the impact falls on other countries there should be an obligation to consult with them. Development banks should be mindful of such factors in the development of their own projects, and be ready to assist environmental impact studies to ensure that an ecological perspective is incorporated in development planning.[104]

Without undertaking to detail the data or reasoning in the Brandt and Brundtland Reports, it suffices to say that the Commissions' conclusions are fundamentally sound. A strong and ineluctable linkage exists between the effort to combat pollution (and to protect the environment more generally) and the effort to achieve economic development; and success in those two efforts is necessary before the realization of human rights can be improved in the Third World—at least economic, social, and cultural rights, and perhaps civil and political rights. Moreover, those linkages are international in scope and must be approached at that level (as well as at the domestic level).

Perhaps policymakers' most sobering realization of the past several decades, however, has been that achieving economic growth—and, by extension, improving pollution control—does not automatically lead to improvements in the living and working conditions of most people (especially most poor people), specifically, in the realization of economic, social, and cultural human rights. Although in some countries rapid economic growth led to rising standards of living for the majority of the population, the more common experience was much more dismal: unemployment and underemployment worsened; the number of people in absolute poverty[105] increased; and inequalities of income and wealth within society grew.[106] This realization has been partly responsible for the shift in policy emphasis (away from trickle down, growth-dominated policies toward, for example, basic human needs) and for the redefinition of "development" (away from economic development toward social development, as those terms are defined herein), described above.[107]

The past few decades' experience also does not support the conclusion that economic growth necessarily leads to enhancing civil and political rights. Indeed, the recent rush to democracy in Eastern Europe might plausibly lead one to argue the inverse, that is, that failure to develop economically leads to achieving civil and political rights.

Law-Creation

One of the most striking developments in substantive international law since World War II has been the rapid transformation of aspirational goals to binding customary obligations in the international human rights area (i.e., as some describe it, from "soft" law to "hard" law). It is now widely acknowledged, for example, that many human rights norms are part of customary international law and that some of those have even risen to the status of *jus cogens*, that is, peremptory norms that cannot be abrogated by agreement.[108] It has been strongly argued that the entire 1948 Universal Declaration of Human Rights, which unquestionably was aspirational when originally adopted, has become part of customary international law.[109]

Many reasons account for this transformation. Several human-rights or analogous norms, for example, prohibition of slavery[110] and State responsibility for injuries to aliens (although the latter, in particular, retains a separate policy basis and jurisprudence),[111] existed before

World War II. The fundamental concept of human rights is widely accepted, at least in word (such as in national constitutions), if not in deed.[112] Human rights have a powerful moral appeal. Moreover, perhaps because of the previously mentioned factors, States are extremely reluctant to speak out against human rights (even if failing to do so is blatantly hypocritical, such as was the case when the General Assembly unanimously approved the Convention Against Torture).[113] Nevertheless, the transformation of human rights aspirations to customary norms, in particular, is remarkable for several reasons: the time frame was relatively short, a substantial amount of contrary State practice occurred during the period,[114] most of the consistent State practice was comprised of refraining from acting,[115] and much of that refraining was already required by international agreements.[116]

The efforts to control international pollution and, to a lesser extent, to achieve economic development share many of the characteristics just described. The momentum created by the human rights transformation certainly has given hope to international pollution-control and economic development-rights activists. It quite easily could have a substantive-law impact as well, for example, by increasing the willingness of diplomats, judges, and commentators to find that the transformation to customary law has occurred.

Another manner in which law-creation in one area may affect law-creation in another is through the role of international governmental agencies and international non-governmental organizations (NGOs) in propagating norms and goals. Agencies and NGOs played an important role in formulating international human rights documents and transforming those documents from aspirational to normative status. For example, the International Labour Office (now the International Labour Organisation [ILO]) helped conclude a convention on forced labor in 1930 and, most recently, NGOs were very influential in preparing the 1989 Draft Convention on the Rights of the Child.[117] An in-depth analysis, written by David Trubek, examines how the international community seeks to protect economic, social, and cultural rights and describes the roles of the ILO and the World Health Organization in that effort.[118]

That pattern is recurring in the international pollution area and, to a lesser extent, in the economic development area. NGOs played an active role in the deliberations at the 1972 Stockholm Conference on the Human Environment and in many environmental-convention drafting conferences since then (e.g., in the 1989 conference in Basel on the Convention on Hazardous Waste).[119] Currently NGOs are involved in observing and influencing the Inter-governmental Panel on Climate Change (IPCC),[120] drafting climate change conventions for consideration by the IPCC (e.g., a workshop sponsored by the Climate Institute prepared such a draft convention), and planning the 1992 Conference on Environment and Development in Brazil (commemorating the twentieth anniversary of the Stockholm Conference).

International governmental organizations and agencies have also played major roles in law-creation in the area of environmental protection. The 1989 Convention Concerning Indigenous and Tribal Peoples in Independent Countries, for example, was prepared under the auspices of the International Labour Organisation.[121] The United Nations Environment Programme (UNEP) has been active in promoting environmental protection measures (such as the Montreal conference that concluded the 1987 Ozone Protocol),[122] and UNEP and the World Meteorological Organization were primarily responsible for establishing the IPCC process.

NGOs and, to a lesser extent, intergovernmental agencies have served similar functions in propagating economic-development goals and attempting to transform them to norms (although that transformation has progressed to a more limited degree).[123]

Structure of Norms

The fundamental rule regarding State responsibility for injury to aliens, which can be viewed as a precursor to modern international human rights norms, even though their policy bases and jurisprudence have remained distinct,[124] is that, provided that appropriate compensation is paid, a State may expropriate an alien's property without any international wrong occurring.[125] What is particularly interesting and unusual about that norm and its structure is that the expropriating State has an obligation to pay compensation even though it has done nothing that is wrongful under international law. Only if the expropriating State fails to pay appropriate compensation does it commit an international wrong, in which case it is required to make reparation under the usual rules of State responsibility (as contrasted with the similar term, also discussed in this paragraph, "State responsibility for injuries to aliens").[126]

In the international pollution area, the U.N. International Law Commission is now studying the perplexing problem of whether and, if so, under what circumstances, a State (the State of origin) should be internationally accountable for pollution arising in its territory or control that crosses a boundary and results in damage in another State (the affected State), even when the activity giving rise to the pollution is not wrongful (e.g., even if that activity does not violate a treaty and is undertaken with due care). The Commission's study of this topic (referred to as the "Liability" topic) is highly controversial, as described in detail in Chapter 4. The point to make here is that the Commission currently appears disposed to adopt an approach that would allow the State of origin to engage in or allow on its territory activities resulting in transboundary pollution and subsequent harm *without violating international law as long as appropriate compensation is paid to the affected State*. If such compensation is not paid, however, an international wrong is committed, and reparation would be due according to the usual rules of State responsibility.[127]

The structure of the rule on Liability now under consideration by the International Law Commission thus is identical to that of State responsibility for injuries to aliens. Moreover, the latter may have formed a conceptual template for the Liability rule, not only because the injuries-to-aliens rule is well-known, but also because it represents a balance between a State's need and right to exercise authority in its own territory, on the one hand, and the need to protect other States' rights (i.e., other States' interest in their nationals), on the other—a balance that is also necessary to achieve in the area of international pollution.[128] In addition, the Commission came to study the Liability topic as an offshoot of its study of State responsibility, which itself was initially defined in terms of State responsibility for injuries to aliens.[129] It may thus have been natural to relate the areas of Liability and injuries to aliens.

In any event, the fact that the structure of the injuries-to-aliens rule has functioned smoothly since well before World War II—the controversy about the rule has concerned the standard of compensation, not whether compensation is due—indicates that there is nothing unworkable in the structure of the Liability rule being considered by the International Law Commission.

Monitoring, Enforcement, and Dispute Settlement

Non-governmental international organizations (NGOs) have been active in monitoring compliance with human rights norms. The best-known example is Amnesty International, which prepares periodic reports regarding human rights compliance on a country-by-country basis, observes trials of dissidents or other persons whose human rights are or appear to be endangered, publicizes the plight of such persons, and organizes letter-writing campaigns to responsible governments (and government officials) about such persons. Other groups also engage in such activities. For example, the Section on Individual Rights and Responsibilities of the American Bar Association has an active trial-observation program.

These activities are based in part on the belief that governments can be embarrassed into modifying their ways, or at least that governments will wish to avoid adverse publicity. In this sense, these NGOs are involved in *enforcing* human rights norms, not simply monitoring them.

Another example of the same approach involves the monitoring groups established in many participating States of the Conference on Security and Cooperation in Europe (CSCE)[130] to monitor compliance with the 1975 Helsinki Final Act, in particular the human rights provisions of the Helsinki Final Act.[131] The Helsinki Final Act specifically states that "governments, institutions, organizations and persons have a positive role to play" in accomplishing the Helsinki Final Act's aims (which, presumably, include the environmental goals in the second chapter, as well as the human rights provisions in the first chapter).[132] The CSCE's 1989 Vienna Final Act goes further, providing in addition that the participating States

will respect the right of persons to observe and promote the implementation of CSCE provisions. . . . They will facilitate direct contacts and communications among these persons, organizations and institutions within and among participating States. . . . They will also take effective measures to facilitate access to information on the implementation of CSCE provisions and the free expression of views on these matters.[133]

Similarly, international governmental agencies and NGOs have been active in seeking such goals. They have sought, for example, to increase compliance with environmental norms and aspirations. Worldwatch Institute publishes the annual report *State of the World*. The World Resource Institute gathers data and publishes reports. Greenpeace International stages activities regarding marine-mammal protection and nuclear-testing prevention. The National Audubon Society monitors acid rain,[134] the Environmental Defense Fund participated in shaping President George Bush's acid rain policy, and the Natural Resource Defense Council has been active in monitoring nuclear-testing norms.[135]

International governmental agencies and NGOs have also devoted their efforts to achieving economic development, such as the activities of the United Nations Development Programme and the Overseas Development Council; to arranging debt-for-nature swaps in the Third World, such as the deals organized by Conservation International, the Nature Conservancy, and World Wildlife Fund; and to convincing foreign-aid donors such as the World Bank to consider environmental implications when designing and evaluating projects. Moreover, agencies and NGOs in the international pollution area have adopted many of the same techniques as those used in working for human rights. Ninna Rösiö, a Swedish participant at the Government of Canada's 1989 Meeting of Experts on the Law of the Atmosphere, for example, spoke of the need to "mobilize shame" on the part of polluting countries in order to help convince them to stop polluting.

The important role of NGOs was presaged in article 71 of the U.N. Charter, which expressly allows the Economic and Social Council to consult with NGOs.[136] That role will almost certainly continue, given their official access to many relevant international meetings, the dedication of their members, the resources at their disposal, and their ability to participate and offer suggestions free from the constraint of being identified with, or bound by, the policies of a particular country.[137] Moreover, NGOs are essential to mobilize public involvement and to serve as a check on governments, which are polluters themselves (e.g., because of military and energy-production activities) and which are subject to shortsightedness, ignorance, incompetence, and corruption.

To the extent that treaties dealing with any one area have led to satisfactory experiences with formal international dispute-settlement procedures—for example, the Canada–United States and Mexico–United States boundary waters treaties and their mechanisms for solving disputes—settlement via similar mechanisms of disputes in the other two areas may be more likely. Conversely, unsatisfactory experiences in such a situation may decrease the likelihood of using such mechanisms to settle disputes in the other two areas. More speculatively, situations in which no dispute-settlement mechanisms are available might lead to a greater realization of the need for such mechanisms generally.

It is also possible that the application of municipal law and access to municipal courts have been affected. For example, the utilization of international human rights law in U.S. cases such as *Filartiga*[138] may affect the likelihood that U.S. courts would apply international environmental law. This possibility would not seem to have any relationship to economic development, however, until that area comes to include or be governed by well-recognized norms.

Notes

1. For a discussion of post–World War II international environmental protection efforts generally, see L.K. CALDWELL, INTERNATIONAL ENVIRONMENTAL POLICY—EMERGENCE AND DIMENSIONS 19–100 (1984).

2. For an analysis of post–World War II economic-development efforts, see

DEVELOPMENT STRATEGIES RECONSIDERED (J.P. Lewis & V. Kallab eds. 1986); G. MYRDAL, ASIAN DRAMA (1968).

3. For a table of international human rights conventions demonstrating the increased rate of activity in this area since World War II, see 2 RESTATEMENT (THIRD) OF FOREIGN RELATIONS LAW OF THE UNITED STATES 148–49 (1987) [hereinafter RESTATEMENT (THIRD)]. For a description of post–World War II efforts to protect international human rights, see R. LILLICH & F. NEWMAN, INTERNATIONAL HUMAN RIGHTS 1–12 (1979).

4. *See infra* text accompanying notes 30–36.

5. *See infra* text accompanying notes 95–107.

6. *See infra* text accompanying notes 108–16.

7. *See infra* text accompanying notes 124–29.

8. These could be considered three distinct levels, but I treat them together for purposes of this chapter for reasons of convenience.

The second and fifth levels differ because the second level concerns the actual progress, stasis, or regression that is occurring, whereas the fifth level concerns the methods, techniques, and procedures used in attempting to achieve progress.

9. *See infra* text accompanying notes 129–35.

10. 1988 AM. SOC. INT'L L. PROC. (forthcoming).

11. For example, the expanded role of NGOs in monitoring human rights violations (level five) may affect the practical implementation of international pollution controls (level two).

12. *See, e.g.*, M. BULAJIC, PRINCIPLES OF INTERNATIONAL DEVELOPMENT LAW (1986).

13. *See infra* Chapter 6.

14. This definition is taken from definitions adopted by the Organization of Economic Cooperation and Development (OECD) Transfrontier Pollution Group. *See* OECD Res. C(77)28 (Final), *Annex*, Introduction, May 17, 1977, in OECD, OECD AND THE ENVIRONMENT 151 (1986).

15. For a more expansive discussion of the term "international pollution," see *supra* Chapter 1, at text accompanying notes 4–17.

16. *See, e.g.*, U.N. Charter art. 55.

17. Universal Declaration of Human Rights, G.A. Res. 217 (III), U.N. Doc. A/810 (1948).

18. International Covenant on Civil and Political Rights, 999 U.N.T.S. 171, *reprinted in* 6 I.L.M. 368 (1967).

19. Optional Protocol to the International Covenant on Civil and Political Rights, 999 U.N.T.S. 171, *reprinted in* 6 I.L.M. 383 (1967).

20. International Covenant on Economic, Social and Cultural Rights, G.A. Res. 2200A (XXI), 993 U.N.T.S. 3, *reprinted in* 6 I.L.M. 360 (1967).

21. *See* WORLD COMMISSION ON ENVIRONMENT AND DEVELOPMENT, OUR COMMON FUTURE (1987) [hereinafter BRUNDTLAND REPORT].

22. *E.g.*, Wilber & Jameson, *Paradigms of Economic Development and Beyond*, in DIRECTIONS IN ECONOMIC DEVELOPMENT 1, 12 (K. Jameson & C. Wilber eds. 1979) [hereinafter Wilber & Jameson].

23. *E.g.*, R. AYRES, BANKING ON THE POOR 83 (1985).

24. *E.g.*, Slavery Convention, Sept. 25, 1926.

25. *E.g.*, DEVELOPMENT STRATEGIES RECONSIDERED, *supra* note 2, at 5–7; Wilber & Jameson, *supra* note 22.

26. *See* McNamara, *Time Bomb or Myth: The Population Problem*, 62 FOREIGN AFF. 1107, 1118–19 (1985).

27. DEVELOPMENT STRATEGIES RECONSIDERED, *supra* note 2, at 9.

28. Art. 30, G.A. Res. 3281 (XXIX), 29 U.N. GAOR (No. 31) at 51, U.N. Doc. A/9946 (1974) [hereinafter CERDS].

29. BRUNDTLAND REPORT, *supra* note 21, at 43.

30. *See infra* text accompanying note 34; Filartiga v. Peña-Irala, 630 F.2d 876 (2d Cir. 1980).

31. *See* Optional Protocol to the International Covenant on Civil and Political Rights, *supra* note 19. Traditional international law was not totally devoid of rights and duties for individuals. *See, e.g., infra* text accompanying notes 34–35.

32. W.P. GORMLEY, HUMAN RIGHTS AND ENVIRONMENT: THE NEED FOR INTERNATIONAL CO-OPERATION 1 (1976); The Hague Declaration on the Environment, Mar. 11, 1989, *reprinted in* 28 I.L.M. 1308 (1989).

33. The Hague Declaration on the Environment, *supra* note 32.

34. *See, e.g.*, M. BULAJIC, PRINCIPLES OF INTERNATIONAL DEVELOPMENT LAW (1986).

35. Jurisdiction of the Courts of Danzig (Danzig v. Pol.), 1928 P.C.I.J. (ser. B) No. 15 (Mar. 3).

36. *See, e.g.*, International Military Tribunal (Nuremberg) Judgment and Sentences, *reprinted in* 41 AM. J. INT'L L. 172 (1946).

37. Treaty on Principles Governing the Activities of States in the Exploration and Use of Outer Space, Including the Moon and Other Celestial Bodies, Jan. 27, 1967, art. 1, 18 U.S.T. 2410, T.I.A.S. No. 6347, 610 U.N.T.S. 205.

38. Oct. 21, 1982, preamble, U.N. Doc. A/CONF.62/121, *reprinted in* 21 I.L.M. 1261 (1982) [hereinafter UNCLOS].

39. U.N.G.A. Res. 43/53, U.N. Doc. A/RES/43/53 (Dec. 6, 1988), *reprinted in* 28 I.L.M. 1326 (1989). When originally proposed by Malta, Resolution 43/53 referred to climate as the "common heritage of mankind," but that formulation was not accepted.

40. *See supra* Chapter 1, at text accompanying notes 12–17.

41. *See* 2 RESTATEMENT (THIRD), *supra* note 3, § 902 Comment *a*.

42. Charter of the International Military Tribunal, Aug. 8, 1945, 59 Stat. 1546, 1547, 83 U.N.T.S. 279 (emphasis added).

43. *See supra* Chapter 1, at text preceding notes 7–8; *see also* D'Amato & Engel, *State Responsibility for the Exportation of Nuclear Power Technology*, 74 VA. L. REV. 1011 (1988).

44. June 27, 1989, art. 23, *reprinted in* 28 I.L.M. 1382 (1989).

45. International Covenant on Economic, Social and Cultural Rights, *supra* note 20, art. 2(1).

46. *Id.* art. 2(3).

47. For a further exploration of these ideas, see Magraw, *Legal Treatment of Developing Countries: Differential, Contextual, and Absolute Norms*, 1 COLO. J. INT'L ENVTL. L. & POL'Y 69 (1990). In that article, I identify two other types of norms appearing in international law: "contextual" norms (defined *infra* at text following note 51) and "absolute" norms (i.e., norms that are neither differential nor contextual). No bright line exists between contextual norms and absolute norms.

48. Thus, international norms regarding diplomatic immunity are not differential, even though they distinguish between sending and receiving States.

49. Sept. 16, 1972, U.N. Doc. A/CONF.48–14 & Corr. 1, prin. 23, *reprinted in* 11 I.L.M. 1416 (1972) (emphasis added).

50. *See, e.g.*, CERDS, *supra* note 28, Preamble, arts. 15, 18, 19, 21, 22, 23. *See generally* MEAGHER, AN INTERNATIONAL REDISTRIBUTION OF WEALTH AND POWER (1979).

51. G.A. Res. 3201 (S–VI), 6 (Special) U.N. GAOR Supp. (No. 1) at 3, U.N. Doc. A/9556 (1974); G.A. Res. 3202 (S–VI), 6 (Special) U.N. GAOR Supp. (No. 1) at 5, U.N. Doc. A/9956 (1974); CERDS, *supra* note 28, art. 30.

Article 25 of CERDS further differentiates among developing countries, directing the world community to pay "special attention to the particular needs and problems of the least developed among the developing countries, of landlocked developing countries and also island developing countries."

52. *Supra* text accompanying note 46.

53. UNCLOS, *supra* note 38, art. 207. Articles 202 and 203 also provide differential treatment.

54. Mar. 22, 1985, *reprinted in* 26 I.L.M. 1516 (1987).

55. Sept. 16, 1987, *reprinted in* 26 I.L.M. 1550 (1987); *see also* art. 10 & Preamble.

56. Convention on the Control of Transboundary Movements of Hazardous Wastes and Their Disposal, Mar. 22, 1989, art. 10(3), *reprinted in* [1 Ref. File] Int'l Env't Rep. (BNA) 21:3701 (1989) [hereinafter Basel Convention on Hazardous Wastes]. *See also id.* arts. 10(4), 4(2)(e).

57. *See* Magraw, *supra* note 47.

58. Mar. 29, 1972, art. 2, 24 U.S.T. 2389, T.I.A.S. No. 7762, 961 U.N.T.S. 187.

59. *Id.* art. 10 (emphasis added).

60. *Id.* art. 12 (emphasis added). Regarding the meaning of "equity," Judge Jiménez de Aréchaga stated in an individual opinion in the Tunisia-Libya case: "To resort to equity means, in effect, to appreciate and balance the relevant circumstances of the case, so as to render justice, not through the rigid application of general rules and principles and of formal legal concepts, but through an adaptation and adjustment of such principles, rules and concepts to the facts, realities and circumstances of each case. . . . In other words, the judicial application of equitable principles means that a court should render justice in the concrete case, by means of a decision shaped by and adjusted to the relevant 'factual matrix' of that case. Equity is here nothing other than the taking into account of a complex of historical and geographical circumstances the consideration of which does not diminish justice but, on the contrary, enriches it. . . . All the relevant circumstances are to be considered and balanced; they are to be thrown together into the crucible and their interaction will yield the correct equitable solution of each individual case." Case Concerning the Continental Shelf (Tunisia & Libyan Arab Jamahiriya), 1982 I.C.J. 18, 106, 109, *reprinted in* 21 I.L.M. 225 (1982). The concept of "equity" thus mandates that the individual characteristics of developing countries be taken into account if they are relevant to a case.

61. UNCLOS, *supra* note 38, art. 194 (emphasis added). Article 2(1) of the International Covenant on Economic, Social and Cultural Rights, *supra* note 20, contains a similar contextual norm ("to the maximum of its available resources").

62. Dec. 2, 1946, art. 8(2), T.I.A.S. No. 1849, 4 Bevins 248, 161 U.N.T.S. 72 (emphasis added).

63. Apr. 29, 1958, art. 5(1), 15 U.S.T. 471, T.I.A.S. No. 5578, 499 U.N.T.S. 311 (emphasis added).

64. Nov. 29, 1969, arts. 3(2)(c) & 5, *reprinted in* 9 I.L.M. 45 (1970) (emphasis

added). *See also id*. art. 1(7) ("'Preventive measures' means any reasonable measures taken by any person after an incident has occurred to prevent or minimize pollution damage.").

65. Nov. 16, 1972, art. 4, 27 U.S.T. 37, T.I.A.S. No. 8226 (emphasis added). *See also id*. arts. 5 & 11.

66. Mar. 3, 1973, art. 8(1), 27 U.S.T. 1087, T.I.A.S. No. 8249 (emphasis added). *See also id*. arts. 8(3) ("[a]s far as possible"), 13(2) ("as soon as possible").

67. Nov. 13, 1979, art. 2, T.I.A.S. No. 10541, *reprinted in* 18 I.L.M. 1442 (1979) (emphasis added) [hereinafter 1979 LRTAP Convention]. *See also id*. arts. 4 ("as far as possible"), 6 ("compatible with balanced development, in particular by using the best available technology which is economically feasible"), 7 ("as appropriate to [the party's] needs").

68. UNCLOS, *supra* note 53, art. 194 (emphasis added).

69. Vienna Convention for the Protection of the Ozone Layer, Mar. 22, 1985, art. 2, *reprinted in* 26 I.L.M. 1516 (1987) (emphasis added).

70. Basel Convention on Hazardous Wastes, *supra* note 56, art. 4(2).

71. This combination, which seems unobjectionable, has played a role in the U.N. International Law Commission's study of International Liability, described *infra* at text accompanying notes 122–24 and Chapter 4.

72. G.A. Res. 2200A (XXI), art. 2, 21 U.N. GAOR Supp. (No. 16), U.N. Doc. A/6316 (1966).

73. Dec. 18, 1979, arts. 2, 3, 5, 6, 7, 8, 10, 11, 12, 14, 16, G.A. Res. 180 (XXXIV), *reprinted in* 19 I.L.M. 33 (1980).

74. *Id*. art. 17.

75. *Id*.

76. Dec. 10, 1984, Annex G.A. Res. 46 (XXXIX), *reprinted in* 23 I.L.M. 1027 (1984) and, as modified, 24 I.L.M. 535 (1985).

77. June 27, 1981, art. 14, *reprinted in* 21 I.L.M. 58 (1982) (not yet in force).

78. Art. 29, G.A. Res. 217 (III), U.N. Doc. A/810 (1948).

79. U.N. Charter art. 56.

80. International Covenant on Economic, Social and Cultural Rights, *supra* note 20, art. 2.

81. 1979 LRTAP Convention, *supra* note 67, art. 2.

82. CERDS, *supra* note 28, art. 15.

83. *E.g.*, Lammers, *The Present State of Research Carried Out by the English-Speaking Section of the Centre for Studies and Research*, in TRANSFRONTIER POLLUTION AND INTERNATIONAL LAW 89, 91 (Hague Academy of International Law).

84. *See, e.g., infra* Chapter 10, at text accompanying notes 46–52.

85. *Supra* Chapter 1, at text accompanying notes 44–47.

86. 2 RESTATEMENT (THIRD), *supra* note 3, § 902 Comment *a*.

87. *Supra* Chapter 1, at text accompanying notes 12–17.

88. South West Africa (Second Phase) (Ethiopia & Liberia v. South Africa), 1966 I.C.J. 6, 47.

89. Barcelona Traction, Light and Power Co., Ltd. (Bel. v. Sp.), 1970 I.C.J. 3, 32.

90. 2 RESTATEMENT (THIRD), *supra* note 3, § 902 Comment *a*, § 602 Comment *a*, § 703(2).

91. *See supra* Chapter 1, at note 16.

92. *Id*.

93. For example, countries that are closely tied economically are likely to have increased political interdependence and cultural cross-fertilization.

94. *See, e.g.*, River of Oder (Czech., Dk., Fr., Ger., Gr. Br., Swed. & Pol.), 1929 P.C.I.J. (ser. A) No. 23, at 26–27 (Sept. 10).

95. BRUNDTLAND REPORT, *supra* note 21.

96. *Id.* at 37. Note that the Brundtland Commission may use a different definition of "economic development" from that used in this chapter.

97. *See, e.g., id.* at 54, 103, 109, 111, 118, 189, 250, 257, 114.

98. *See, e.g.*, the documents cited *supra* notes 16, 17, 18, 19, 20, 73.

99. *Supra* text accompanying note 29.

100. *See supra* text accompanying note 97.

101. INDEPENDENT COMMISSION ON INTERNATIONAL DEVELOPMENT ISSUES, *North-South: A Program for Survival* 54, 57, 90, 56, 59, 16, 24, 25, 223 (1980) [hereinafter BRANDT REPORT]. The Brandt Commission was also expressly concerned about treatment of refugees, *id.* at 112, a subject that is also part of international human rights law. *See* Convention Relating to the Status of Refugees, July 28, 1951, 189 U.N.T.S. 137; Protocol Relating to the Status of Refugees, Jan. 31, 1967, 606 U.N.T.S. 267, *reprinted in* 6 I.L.M. 78 (1967).

102. BRANDT REPORT, *supra* note 101, at 114. Note that the Brandt Commission's concept of development includes human rights aspects, as discussed *supra* at text accompanying note 101.

103. BRUNDTLAND REPORT, *supra* note 21, at 5.

104. BRANDT REPORT, *supra* note 101, at 114–15.

105. *See supra* text accompanying note 26.

106. *See, e.g.*, BRANDT REPORT, *supra* note 101, at 127; Wilber & Jameson, *supra* note 22, at 13. The Brandt Report attributed this pattern partly to international factors and partly to the fact that, in the Commission's diplomatic language, "those who benefit most from the present distribution of wealth and economic power, whether in the North or the South, commonly fail to give the highest priority to their shared responsibility for improving the lot of the poorest in the world. . . . [B]enefits accrue mainly to minorities who have been able to invest or work in the modern sectors of industry and agriculture or occupy the higher rungs of the public services and the professions." BRANDT REPORT, *supra* note 101, at 127.

107. *See supra* text accompanying notes 24–29.

108. *See, e.g.*, 2 RESTATEMENT (THIRD), *supra* note 3, § 702 & Reporters' Note 11.

109. *See, e.g.*, M. MCDOUGAL, H. LASSWELL & CHEN, HUMAN RIGHTS AND WORLD PUBLIC ORDER 273–74, 325–27 (1980).

110. 1926 Slavery Convention, *supra* note 24.

111. *See, e.g.*, 2 RESTATEMENT (THIRD), *supra* note 3, at 145–46.

112. *See, e.g., id.* § 702 Reporters' Note 1.

113. *Supra* note 76.

114. *See, e.g.*, the annual reports on human rights violations published by Amnesty International.

115. *See generally* S.S. Lotus (Fr. v. Turk.), 1927 P.C.I.J. (ser. A) No. 10 (Sept. 7).

116. *Compare* Military and Paramilitary Activities in and Against Nicaragua (Nicar. v. U.S.), Merits, 1986 I.C.J. 14, 99 (the ICJ found that there exists a customary law prohibition on the aggressive use of force in the situation where almost all States in the world were already bound by the U.N. Charter's provisions to the same effect).

117. 2 RESTATEMENT (THIRD), *supra* note 3, § 702 Reporters' Note 4; Cohen,

The Role of Nongovernmental Organizations in the Drafting of the Convention on the Rights of the Child, 12 HUM. RTS. Q. 137 (1990).

118. Trubek, *Economic, Social and Cultural Rights in the Third World: Human Rights Law and Human Needs Programs* 205, in INTERNATIONAL PROTECTION OF HUMAN RIGHTS (T. Meron ed. 1984).

119. *See* Stockholm Declaration on the Human Environment, *supra* note 49; Basel Convention on Hazardous Wastes, *supra* note 51. Greenpeace International played a particularly active role leading up to and in this conference.

120. For a description of the IPCC, see *supra* Chapter 1, at text accompanying note 36.

121. *See supra* note 44.

122. *Supra* note 55.

123. *See, e.g.*, Chinkin, *The Challenge of Soft Law: Development and Change in International Law*, 38 INT'L & COMP. L.Q. 850 (1989).

124. 2 RESTATEMENT (THIRD), *supra* note 3, at 145–46.

125. Borchard, *Theoretical Aspects of the International Responsibility of States*, in 1 ZEITSCHRIFT FÜR AUSLÄNDISCHES ÖFFENTLICHES RECHT UND VÖLKERRECHT 223, 233–39 (1929).

126. *See, e.g.*, 2 RESTATEMENT (THIRD), *supra* note 3, § 712. *See generally* INTERNATIONAL LAW OF STATE RESPONSIBILITY FOR INJURIES TO ALIENS (R. Lillich ed. 1983).

127. For a discussion of the Commission's study of liability, see Magraw, *Transboundary Harm: The International Law Commission's Study of "International Liability*,*"* 80 AM. J. INT'L L. 305 (1986).

128. *Id.* at 308–9; *supra* Chapter 1, "Contents and Organization of this Book."

129. For the evolution of these studies, see Magraw, *supra* note 127, at 306–7.

130. The CSCE, formed in 1973, is composed of all European States (except Albania), Canada, and the United States. For a description of CSCE activities, see Bloed, *Institutional Aspects of the Helsinki Process After the Follow-up Meeting of Vienna*, 36 NETH. INT'L L. REV. 342 (1989).

131. Conference on Security and Cooperation in Europe: Final Act (Aug. 1, 1975), ch. 1, prin. VII, *reprinted in* 14 I.L.M. 1292 (1975).

132. *Id.* ch. 1, prin. IX.

133. Concluding Document of the third follow-up meeting of the Conference on Security and Cooperation in Europe, Jan. 19, 1989, ch. 1, art. 26, *quoted in* Bloed, *supra* note 125, at 345 n. 8.

134. *See Skeptical Audubon Society Will Track Acid Rain*, N.Y. Times, Sept. 30, 1987, at A19, col. 1 (nat'l ed.).

135. *See* Schrag, *Policy, Procedures, and People: Governmental Response to a Privately Initiated Nuclear Test Monitoring Project as a Case Study in National Security Decision-Making*, 21 N.Y.U. J. INT'L L. & POL. 1 (1988).

136. U.N. CHARTER, art. 71. For a description of the three categories of NGO consultation, see E. OSMANCZYK, ENCYCLOPEDIA OF THE UNITED NATIONS AND INTERNATIONAL AGREEMENTS 565 (1985).

137. For a discussion of NGOs and the international environmental protection movement, see Sands, *The Environment, Community and International Law*, 30 HARV. INT'L L.J. 393 (1989).

138. Filartiga v. Peña-Irala, 630 F.2d 876 (2d Cir. 1980).

Chapter 3
Overview of the Existing Customary Legal Regime Regarding International Pollution

Pierre-Marie Dupuy

Introduction

The existing customary international legal regime regarding international pollution consists of principles and rules of which a large number have been defined in the last two decades by the progressive gathering of recurrent treaty provisions, recommendations made by international organizations, resolutions adopted at the end of international conferences, and other texts that can be said to have influenced State practice. From a strict point of view, this legal regime should consist only of those principles that receive a concrete application in the usual conduct and behavior of States, so that they materialize the general *opinio juris* and can then be considered as part of customary international law.

Nevertheless, everybody knows that it has become more difficult than in the past to define very precisely the contents of present customary rules, given the rapid evolution of modern general international law. In the field of international environmental law in particular, international institutions, both intergovernmental and, at a lower stage, non-governmental (e.g., the Institut de Droit Internationale, the International Law Association, and the International Union for Conservation of Nature) have played an important role.

A number of *guidelines* emitted by these bodies have penetrated gradually into contemporary State practice. In certain cases, these guidelines bring an important contribution to the definition of international standards on the basis of which the due diligence to be expected from "well-governed" modern States can be established. "Soft law"—

by which I mean international directives or undertakings that are not, strictly speaking, binding in themselves—thus is a phenomenon of real importance in this branch of international law. Soft law must be taken into account in the tentative analysis and interpretation of what is certainly already "hard law," that is, international directives or undertakings that are binding of their own accord under international law. Examples of this process will be encountered later in this chapter.

The terms "pollution" and "international pollution" or, more often used, "transfrontier pollution" have been defined as follows by international bodies, in particular the United Nations Environment Programme (UNEP)[1] and the Organization for Economic Cooperation and Development (OECD) Transfrontier Pollution Group:[2]

> The term pollution means the introduction by man, directly or indirectly, of substances or energy into the environment resulting in deleterious effects of such a nature as to endanger human health, harm living resources and eco-systems, impair amenities or interfere with other legitimate uses of the environment;
> Transfrontier pollution means any intentional or unintentional pollution whose physical origin is subject to, and situated wholly or in part within the area under, the national jurisdiction of one State and which has effects in the area under the national jurisdiction of another State.[3]

These two definitions are adopted herein in consideration of their intrinsic quality and acceptance by the community of States.

This chapter is founded on the work which has been undertaken by the French-speaking Section of the Hague Academy of International Law in 1985 on "Transfrontier Pollution and International Law," taking into account the international legal evolution since that date.[4] Like the original report published in French by the Hague Academy, the present one provides an enunciation of and commentary on the major principles and rules that seem to characterize the actual state of positive general international law in this field. It is then presented like a kind of codification report. Three main topics, which must be clearly distinguished, are discussed in this chapter: prevention of transfrontier pollution (the second section), which implies international cooperation between States and international organizations (covered in the third section), and reparation of damages caused by existing transfrontier pollution (fourth section).

The scope covered by this chapter is limited in two respects. First, it deals with legal principles of which the customary character is actually emerging or already well established. Some valuable guidelines are not commented on, or are touched on only briefly, because they constitute until now merely interesting proposals and not even "soft law." Second, from a substantive point of view, this chapter does not examine all rules relating to the international protection of the environment, including the principles referring to the protection of nature (flora and fauna), but only those that concern international action against transfrontier pollution, constituting but one part of the actual international environmental law.

Obligation to Prevent Transfrontier Pollution

The basic principle governing transfrontier environmental pollution is that States shall prevent or abate any such damaging interference that causes or entails a significant risk of causing substantial harm. On the basis of a broad comparison of treaty law, international resolutions, and regional practice, it seems possible to define this well-established rule as follows:

> In the exercise of their sovereign rights to exploit and use, pursuant to their development policies, their natural resources, States shall take into account the impact of actual or anticipated activities in areas placed under their jurisdiction on the environment situated beyond their national frontiers. They shall take, in good faith and with all due diligence, appropriate measures to prevent transfrontier pollution by elaborating, in particular, rules and procedures adapted to the requirements of the protection of the environment, and see to it that these are effectively applied.

Let us examine the origin and legal basis of the principle and its implications as well as some of the best ways of implementing it.

Origin and Legal Basis of the Principle

Support for the obligation not to cause substantial harm by transfrontier pollution is to be found in the classic statement in the international arbitral award of the *Trail Smelter* case (United States v. Canada) which reads:

> Under the principles of international law, as well as the law of the United States, no State has the right to use or permit the use of its territory in such a manner as to cause injury to the properties or persons therein, when the case is of serious consequences and the injury is established by clear and convincing evidence.[5]

Confirmation of this ruling may be found in the attitude taken by the International Court of Justice in the *Corfu Channel* case (United Kingdom v. Albania) regarding which it proclaimed "the obligation of every State not to allow its territory to be used for acts contrary to the rights of other States."[6] These cases emphasize the interdependence of States and the requirement to take other States' interests into account.

It would be a mistake to think that this principle could be applied only to the relations established between neighboring States and not in a wider geographical context. This question is of definite importance in view of the behavior of certain kinds of transfrontier pollution. For example, air pollution caused by some gaseous substances often reaches places very far from the place where the toxic emissions originated.[7] One can normally impose the above obligation in such situations of long-distance pollution because the rule regarding the *harmless use of territory* can quite well dispense with arguments based on actual contiguity; the rule is a natural corollary of a sovereign State's exclusive jurisdiction over its territory, as pointed out, for example, in the *Island of Palmas* arbitration (United States v. Netherlands) delivered by Max Huber in 1928.[8]

This fundamental principle seems to have been accepted by the actual world community of States. It is one case in which international declarations and institutional resolutions support the expression of a universal *opinio juris*. The duty not to cause substantial harm through transfrontier pollution in the area under the jurisdiction of another State may be deemed to have been explicitly accepted in many collective statements of States, among which Principle 21 of the Declaration on the Human Environment, adopted nearly twenty years ago during the 1972 United Nations Conference, is no doubt one of the most important. It provides as follows:

States have, in accordance with the Charter of the United Nations and the principles of international law, the sovereign right to exploit their own resources pursuant to their own environmental policies, and the responsibility to ensure that activities within their jurisdiction or control do not cause damage to the environment of other States or of areas beyond the limits of national jurisdiction.[9]

This formulation is of paramount importance, in particular for developing countries,[10] because it is made of two balancing elements: on the one hand, the right of a State to develop its economy and, on the other hand, the duty not to cause transfrontier environmental damage.

The substance of Principle 21 has been reaffirmed by several international bodies and in particular the U.N. General Assembly, in Resolution 3129 of December 1973 on Co-operation in the Field of Environment Concerning Natural Resources Shared by Two or More States,[11] and Resolution 3281 of December 1974 proclaiming the Charter of Economic Rights and Duties.[12] One can also refer to Principles 3 and 6 of the 1973 European Economic Community (EC) Programme of Action on the Environment;[13] the 1974 OECD Council Recommendation C(74)224 concerning Transfrontier Pollution (Annex, Title B);[14] the 1974 OECD Council Recommendation C(74)220 and 221, respectively, on the Control of Eutrophication of Waters and on Strategies for Specific Pollutants Control;[15] the 1975 Final Act of the Conference on Security and Cooperation in Europe;[16] and Principle 3 of the 1978 UNEP Draft Principles of Conduct on Shared Natural Resources.[17]

Numerous treaty provisions formulate the same general obligation, generally in a more precise and also more relative way, by referring to any "substantial" or "significant" harm to be prevented. Illustrations of this can be found, for example, in article 58(2)(e) of the 1960 Frontier Treaty concluded between the Federal Republic of Germany and the Netherlands, which provides:

The contracting Parties shall . . . take or support . . . all measures required: . . . (e) to prevent such excessive pollution of the boundary waters as may substantially impair the customary use of the waters by the neighbouring State.[18]

Other examples of such an approach are to be found, for instance, in the 1964 Agreement concerning Frontier Watercourses concluded between Finland and the U.S.S.R.,[19] the Agreement between Mexico and the United States concerning the Permanent and Definitive Solution to the International Problem of the Salinity of the Colorado River,[20] followed by another treaty between the same States in 1983 inspired by an identical orientation, on Cooperation for the Protection and Improvement of the Environment in the Border Area.[21]

One should note the somewhat stricter formulation in the 1982 U.N. Convention on the Law of the Sea, article 192(2) of which reads as follows:

States shall take all measures necessary to ensure that activities under their jurisdiction or control are so conducted as not to cause damage by pollution to other States and their environment, and that pollution arising from incidents or activities under their jurisdiction or control does not spread beyond the areas where they exercise sovereign rights in accordance with this Convention.[22]

As easily observed, this multilateral codification treaty provision is a faithful retaking of the declaratory Principle 21 of Stockholm quoted above,[23] although it does not balance the obligation not to cause transfrontier pollution with a right to develop economically.

A confirmation of the customary value of the obligation to prevent transfrontier pollution is to be found, without being paradoxical, in the argumentation developed by States in concrete cases, when they seem partly to ignore this general rule of law. In fact, they take due care to refer expressly to the legal value of this principle, explaining that their precise behavior in the case does not violate it. The attitude both of Brazil in relation with Argentina in the Itaipu barrage affair and, even more, of India in the context of its difficulties with Bangladesh relating to the diversion of a part of the Ganges waters is interesting in this regard.[24]

This general obligation cannot be considered as an absolute one, however. States cannot be deemed to have violated international law every time they have not been able to prevent the occurrence of transfrontier pollution. This obligation of prevention exists only to the extent that the risk of causing international environmental damage is reasonably foreseeable. It can be strengthened in regard to special areas that require particular ecological protection, such as areas the 1980 World Conservation Strategy[25] refers to as "life-support systems," such as ecosystems of plants, animals, and microorganisms together with the nonliving components of their environment and related ecological processes essential for the functioning of the biosphere in all its diversity. For one of the more recent conventional requirements in this field, see articles 10 and 11 of the 1985 Association of South East Asian Nations (ASEAN) Agreement on the Conservation of Nature and Natural Resources.[26]

Implications and Means of Implementing the Principle

The first implication of the principle delineated above seems clearly to be the death of the *Harmon Doctrine*—if, indeed, it was still extant.[27] According to that doctrine regarding international watercourses, which Chief Justice Harmon of the U.S. Supreme Court expressed more than one hundred years ago, every State is free, within the frontiers delimiting its area of jurisdiction, to undertake or let develop any action that it considers beneficial for the national interest, without taking into account the material consequences of such decision outside the national territory.[28] The demise of the Harmon Doctrine has occurred even though, case by case, there can always be temptations for States engaged in concrete development projects to forget part of their actual duties in this area.[29]

This general obligation of prevention implies that the State must consider what can or could be the eventual interferences of present and anticipated activities on the environment situated in the territory of other States. This idea has inspired procedures generally designated as "environmental impact assessments"[30] in several countries, for example, the United

States, Canada, France, the Federal Republic of Germany, and Ireland. The recourse to such procedures has been recommended several times in international texts, in particular in Principle 4 of the 1973 EC Programme of Action on the Environment, and in different recommendations of the OECD.[31] It has also been recommended by the conclusions contained in chapter C of the 1981 UNEP Conclusions of the Study on the Legal Aspects concerning the Environment related to Off-shore Mining and Drilling within the Limits of National Jurisdiction, which were reached by the UNEP Working Group of Experts on Environmental Law and were subsequently endorsed by the U.N. General Assembly in Resolution 37/217 of March 24, 1983, on International Co-operation in the Field of the Environment.[32]

Nevertheless, this special procedure, as such, cannot be implemented on a customary basis. To get any compulsory value, it must be established in an international agreement. This situation is realized in several recent treaties, like the Apia Convention on Protection of Nature in the South Pacific[33] or the most recent UNEP conventions on protection of regional seas, such as the Kuwait Convention or the Jeddah Treaty touching respectively on the interests of the Persian Gulf and the Red Sea.[34]

In any event, international customary law has not developed sufficiently to define precisely what kind of procedures should be enforced by States to apply their general obligation to prevent transfrontier pollution. One can certainly take into consideration the level of development of the concerned States in assessing what kind of procedure they should enforce. International impact statements probably already constitute part of the implementation of "due diligence," as far as industrialized countries are concerned. Is it absolutely possible, however, to reach the same conclusion as far as developing countries are concerned?

The same question should be asked with regard to the rules of *nondiscrimination* and *equality of access*, which have been increasingly proposed by recommendations and some conventions in the past few years. The 1985 Draft Articles set up by the Hague Academy Centre of Research contain a provision that reads as follows:

1. In keeping with their rights and obligations in the matter of protection of the environment, States shall respect the principle of non-discrimination between their own environment and that of other States as regards the elaboration and application of laws and regulations in the domains of prevention, reparation and repression of pollution.
2. States shall allow persons concerned with a transfrontier pollution, acting jointly or severally, access to the administrative and judicial proceedings available to persons concerned with inland pollution.[35]

Such a regime should enable environmental protection in States to be reinforced precisely because it aims to ensure that the protection against transfrontier pollution is not inferior to that existing in relation to pollution occurring within the State of origin of that transfrontier pollution, but without requiring that State to expend more effort in relation to transfrontier pollution than it would in similar conditions within its own territory. The regime can contribute in particular to giving victims of transfrontier pollution possibilities of protecting their environment no less effective than those available to victims of comparable pollution within the State of origin.[36]

In practice, the implementation of such a regime can lead to a large proportion of transfrontier pollution problems being avoided, among them problems of a local or regional nature that may arise between countries with fairly similar policies in environmental matters. Indeed, by facilitating the use of domestic proceedings and ensuring the nondiscriminatory treatment of applications by the victims of transfrontier pollution, such a regime may enable many transfrontier problems to be resolved in a direct manner. It also may bring about a significant reduction in the number of situations likely to lead to invoking the international liability of the State of origin, a turn of events that, as is well known, would pose very difficult legal and political questions.

Until now, these rules have been implemented only between Western industrialized countries, as described later. The explanation for this is that the application of such a regime requires, to be efficient, a similar level of economic development and ecostandards for quality and safety between the interested States. Even in this context, this regime contributes to the establishment of a *minimum standard of behavior* and in no way prejudices stricter obligations resulting from international law applicable between the States concerned, in particular as regards transfrontier pollution damage.

Nondiscrimination and equal treatment were first introduced into inter-State practice by the 1974 Nordic Environmental Protection Convention between Finland, Sweden, Denmark, and Norway, which have an ancient tradition in common.[37] It was then quite systematically introduced in the OECD Council Recommendations regarding transfrontier pollution, and, in particular, it was developed in the 1977 Recommendation C(77)28 for the Implementation of a Regime of Equal Right of Access and Non-Discrimination in Relation to Transfrontier Pollution.[38] The principle has also been retaken by UNEP, however, in its 1978 Draft Principles of Conduct in the Field of the Environment for the Guidance of States in the Conservation and Harmonious Utilization of Natural Resources Shared by Two or More States.[39] Even more interesting, one can observe that, despite its special conditions of implementation, the principle has been also laid down in a convention aimed at establishing a new legal regime on a universal scale, namely articles 194(4) and 227 of the 1982 U.N. Law of the Sea Convention.[40]

One can hardly believe, however, that this principle forms part of general international law in this matter. It is much more to be considered as a *lex ferenda* on its way to progressive customary crystallization. Nevertheless, the actual trends of treaty law and soft law guidelines defined by international institutions can be taken into consideration to define more concretely the material contents of "due diligence," which is referred to in the proposed formulation of this principle.[41]

One might argue, both with respect to the obligations to prevent transfrontier pollution and to exercise due diligence, as well as to the obligation to cooperate discussed later, that these principles are currently so imprecise as to lack normative character. The fact that a particular rule may encompass a wide range of acceptable behavior, and thus be imprecise in some sense, does not negate its normative quality, however. The use of "good faith" in U.S. contract law is illustrative. The Uniform Commercial Code contains the obligation of good faith and defines that concept somewhat imprecisely.[42] Nevertheless, one cannot plausibly argue that there is no such obligation or that all behavior, however outrageous, satisfies the standard.[43]

Obligation to Cooperate

One can formulate the principle of the obligation to cooperate as follows:

1. States have the obligation to cooperate, in a spirit of solidarity, with one another as well as with competent international organizations with a view to preventing, diminishing, and eliminating transfrontier pollution.

2. To discharge this obligation, States shall inform and consult one another, in all good faith, on their activities or measures, undertaken or projected, that are likely to cause transfrontier pollution.

3. Without prejudice to paragraph 2 above, States shall inform one another on their respective pollution prevention policies, consult with one another about all questions likely to arise between them in connection with the management of their environments and take concerted action aimed at harmonizing their environmental policies.

This very large principle raises different kinds of problems: what are its legal basis, its material contents, and its methods of implementation?

Legal Basis of the Obligation of Cooperation

From a general point of view, it is possible to say that contemporary international law is no longer a law of coexistence of sovereign States as it was during the entire nineteenth century and as is still reflected in the Permanent Court of International Justice award in the *Lotus* case in 1927.[44] It has also become a law of cooperation, if not yet, in a few fields, a law of the International Community. The general obligation of cooperation in the field of prevention of transfrontier pollution is deeply implanted in the law of the United Nations as defined in particular in article 1(3) of the U.N. Charter.[45] Moreover, as pointed out by the International Court of Justice in its 1986 award in the Case Concerning Military and Paramilitary Activities in and Against Nicaragua, the main principles established by this Charter today have acquired a customary value, independently of it and without possible discussion.[46] This customary value is particularly the case for those general rules that have been stated again in the U.N. General Assembly Resolution 2625 on Friendly Relations and Cooperation Between States.[47]

There are also concordant and numerous elements, however, that found a specific ground for the obligation of cooperation in preventing transfrontier pollution. On the one hand, cooperation is the general means by which States will implement the substantive rights and duties regarding the use of transboundary natural resources. On the other hand, various rules of conduct that are becoming parts of contemporary international custom, such as the principle of information and consultation to be commented on later,[48] are in fact implied by the more general principle of cooperation, from which they cannot be isolated.

Already *before* the development of modern international environmental law, which begins quite late, that is, contemporary to the 1972 U.N. Conference on the Human Environment,[49] the Arbitral Tribunal in the *Lac Lanoux* case recognized in 1957 the duty of the States to cooperate in the use of the waters of an international watercourse in the following terms:

In fact, States are today perfectly conscious of the importance of the conflicting interests brought into play by the industrial use of international rivers, and of the necessity to reconcile them by mutual concessions. The only way to arrive at such compromises of interests is to conclude agreements on an increasingly comprehensive basis. International practice reflects the conviction that States ought to strive to conclude such agreements; there would thus appear to be an obligation to accept in good faith all communications and contacts which could, by a broad confrontation of interests and by reciprocal good will, provide States with the best conditions for concluding agreements.[50]

The repetitive reference in this statement of the tribunal to good faith as a condition and an inspiring rule for the behavior of States in this matter is particularly relevant. One can note here the evident link between the principle of cooperation and the substantive rule of prevention of transfrontier pollution.

Support for the duty of States to cooperate in maintaining or restoring a reasonable and equitable use of transboundary natural resources or, more generally speaking, in preventing transfrontier pollution is also to be found in the numerous nonbinding recommendations and declarations adopted by member States of the international organizations that have considered the matter. Some examples are Principle 24 of the Stockholm Declaration on the Environment,[51] reiterated by the U.N. General Assembly in several resolutions, in particular Resolutions 2995,[52] 3129,[53] and 34/186[54]—the last-mentioned being devoted to cooperation in the field of protecting the environment of shared natural resources, inspired by the 1978 UNEP Principles of Conduct on Shared Natural Resources.[55] OECD Council Recommendations C(74)224,[56] C(77)115 (Final),[57] C(77)28 (Final),[58] and C(78)77 (Final),[59] which all deal with general or particular aspects of transfrontier pollution, refer also to the general obligation of cooperation and define some of its means of realization.

In addition, the great number of treaties referring to the necessity of cooperation shows the conviction of States regarding the implementation of a general customary obligation in this field. The classical argument that says that if an obligation is put in a treaty, this inclusion brings the proof that the same obligation does not exist in general international law, can be viewed here as irrelevant, in particular for the reasons already put forward.[60] These conventions must be considered as legal instruments making this general duty more precise and adapting it to specific areas and matters. By way of illustration, consider the following: the 1963 Berne Convention on the International Commission for the Protection of the Rhine against Pollution (amended in 1976);[61] the 1964 Agreement concerning the Use of Water Resources in Frontier Waters concluded between Poland and the USSR;[62] the 1968 African Convention on the Conservation of Nature and Natural Resources (art. 16);[63] the 1971 Act of Santiago concerning Hydrologic Basins concluded between Argentina and Chile (arts. 3–8);[64] the 1974 Paris Convention for the Prevention of Pollution from Land-based Sources;[65] the 1974 Helsinki Convention for the Protection of the Marine Environment of the Baltic Sea Area;[66] the 1976 Barcelona Convention for Protection of the Mediterranean Sea,[67] followed by many other conventions established on the same model for the protection of other regional seas; the 1978 Great Lakes Water Quality Agreement between Canada and the United States (arts. 7–10);[68] the 1979 ECE Convention on Long-Range Transboundary Air Pollution;[69] the 1982 U.N. Law of the Sea Convention (arts. 63, 66–67, 197, and following arts.);[70] and last but not least, the 1985 ASEAN Agreement on the Conservation of Nature and Natural Resources (arts. 19 and 20).[71]

Material Contents of the Obligation of Cooperation

The content of the obligation to cooperate is difficult to describe in abstract terms. It depends very much on the great variety of concrete situations; what is required of a State in any particular situation can be determined only by examining the relevant facts and circumstances of that situation.[72] Nevertheless, observation of the practice of States, of treaty provisions, and of guidelines set up by international recommendations gives a clear idea of the main orientations of general international law in this field. Certainly, two of the main implications of the general principle, closely interconnected, are the rules of information and consultation, which concern different levels of threats and State behavior.

A first kind of delivery of information seems to have already acquired the stature of a compulsory general norm, as the first expression of a spirit of cooperation and good faith. It is what one could name the *ad hoc* information and consultation that one State has to give to another before realizing activities capable of provoking damaging interferences in the environment within the other country's jurisdiction. This rule can be considered as the logical prolongation of the obligation of prevention of transfrontier pollution, which implies taking into account in an appropriate manner these eventual transboundary interferences.[73] The application of this rule extends also to damages that have not yet occurred but represent a danger for the neighboring country. This kind of information has been pointed out by many recommendatory texts. Of these, Title E of the 1974 OECD Recommendation on Principles Concerning Transfrontier Pollution,[74] often taken later as reference by other international bodies, including UNEP, is of prime importance. Title E reads as follows:

> Prior to the initiation in a country of works or undertakings which might create a significant risk of transfrontier pollution, this country should provide early information to other countries which are or may be affected. It should provide these countries with relevant information and data, the transmission of which is not prohibited by legislative provisions or prescriptions or applicable international conventions, and should invite their comments.
> Countries should enter into consultation on an existing or foreseeable trans-

frontier pollution problem at the request of a country which is or may be directly affected and should diligently pursue such consultations on this particular problem over a reasonable period of time.

Countries should refrain from carrying out projects or activities which might create a significant risk of transfrontier pollution without first informing the countries which are or may be affected and, except in cases of extreme urgency, providing a reasonable amount of time in the light of circumstances for diligent consultation. Such consultations held in the best spirit of co-operation and good neighbourliness should not enable a country to unreasonably delay or to impede the activities or projects on which consultations are taking place.[75]

A second category of exchanges purports to meet the need of States for a more general exchange of information on a regular basis concerning not only the prevention of transfrontier pollution but also the use and management of shared natural resources, such as the watercourses of an international river basin. Such information exchange often takes place in the framework of a permanent regional institution. The model for such an institution is the International Joint Commission, formed at the beginning of this century by the United States and Canada.[76]

This second category of exchange of information, even more than the first one, cannot be separated from ordinary consultation. It seems to be the most appropriate way of establishing a reasonable and equitable use of shared natural resources, as is required by international law. Indeed, the equitable apportionment of such resources can best be defined by way of negotiation, in order to harmonize the different economic, political, and social interests existing in each concerned State as to how the resource will be utilized. The experience provided by the management of international watercourses abundantly illustrates such situations.[77]

To reflect the treaty practice relating to a duty of information and consultation, one can consider the most important part of the agreements already cited[78] that contain provisions incorporating such an obligation. Many other conventions could be referred to, however, particularly in the field of development, protection, and use of international watercourses, such as article 6 of the 1960 Indus Waters Treaty between India and Pakistan,[79] article 9 of the 1974 Agreement concerning Co-operation in Water Economy Questions in Frontier Rivers concluded by the German Democratic Republic and Czechoslovakia,[80] and article 9 of the 1978 Agreement on Great Lakes Water Quality concluded between Canada and the United States.[81] Several articles of the 1979 ECE Convention on Long-Range Transboundary Air Pollution also refer expressly to the obligations of both information and consultation.[82] Article 206 of the 1982 U.N. Convention on the Law of the Sea reconciles pertinently a reference to the international impact assessment procedures and the application of the information principle.[83]

A faithful echo of the same rules can be found in the major OECD and UNEP Recommendations and Draft articles cited above,[84] as well as in the U.N. Resolutions referring to the protection of the international environment, especially General Assembly Resolution 3129[85] and article 3 of the 1974 Charter of Economic Rights and Duties of States.[86] The latter stresses the interrelationship between the obligation of prevention and the obligation of cooperation, of which the rules of information and consultation form a fundamental part. Support for the duty to give prior notice is also to be found in the 1982 EC Council Directive on Major Accident Hazards of Certain Industrial Activities,[87] and the 1985 EC Council Directive on the Assessment of the Effects of Certain Public and Private Projects on the Environment.[88]

Finally, it is impressive that practically all the international bodies that have tried, in the last ten years, to codify the principles constituting the actual substance of customary law in this field have insisted on the importance of information and consultation as major means to implement the general duty to cooperate to protect the environment against transfrontier pollution. This is the case for the Institut de Droit Internationale (IDI) Resolutions of 1979 on Pollution of Rivers and Lakes in International Law,[89] adopted in September 1979 at the Athens Session, as well as of another IDI Resolution of September 1987, adopted at its Cairo Session, on Air Transfrontier Pollution.[90] It is also the position adopted in the 1982 ILA Resolution adopted in Montreal.[91] The same conclusion has been reached by Stephen Schwebel and Jens Evensen in their respective reports to the U.N. International Law Commission about the law relating to utilizations of international watercourses other than navigation, as well as by the current special rapporteur, Stephen McCaffrey.[92]

Nevertheless, even if there is no doubt about the customary character of the rules of information and consultation, one should not underestimate the difficulties that applying these rules is able to provoke in practice. The two well-known examples of Brazil/Argentina and India/Bangladesh difficulties remain in everyone's memory.[93]

A particular place should be reserved for a third kind of information, usually referred to as "notification" of accidents that have occurred in one country and are able to provoke transfrontier pollution. The obligation to provide this type of information is clearly established by the different international legal instruments (both soft and hard, i.e., conventional) already cited above in connection with the information and consultation procedures, as a classical rule of conduct. The accident at Chernobyl,[94] however, has proved that at least the U.S.S.R. did not consider it as an existing part of customary international law, as a result of which two special treaties (discussed below)[95] have been negotiated in the framework of the International Atomic Energy Agency (IAEA) in 1986.

Subject-matter and Means of Implementing the General Obligation of Cooperation for the Prevention of Transfrontier Pollution

The participants in the 1985 session of the Hague Academy Centre for Studies and Research conducted a large and systematic analysis of State practice related to cooperation on environmental matters.[96] That analysis led to the same conclusion that has been reached by the other international bodies which tried in the past to summarize the actual state of international law on this question: the most significant and efficient means of cooperation is the negotiation of special agreements between the States that have interests in the protection of the same transboundary resource, whether it be an international river basin or the air and atmosphere in a defined area.

This conclusion does not mean that there is actually in general customary international law an *obligatio de negociandi*, or obligation to negotiate. Fundamentally, the assertion laid down by the 1957 *Lac Lanoux* arbitration—that the duty to inform and consult does not mean that an initiative capable of causing damage to the environment out of national boundaries depends on the reaching of an agreement with the interested country (or countries)—remains true.[97] One must clearly distinguish among the compulsory rule of information, the compulsory rule of consultation, and a *method* of cooperation, which is the negotiation of a special agreement. With this observation in mind, it has seemed possible to synthesize both the reference to that contractual method and the main subject-matters of it in the following terms:

Agreements on Cooperation

In order to ensure the implementation of the principles and rules stated in the preceding articles, and to adapt their application to the special circumstances of each case, States draw their inspiration from the following guidelines and endeavor to conclude bilateral and multilateral agreements providing, in particular, for

(a) protection of natural resources situated in the territories of more than one State against all threats emanating from activities conducted in the territory or under the control of one or more from among them, and elaboration and conservation plans endowed with adequate means of execution and based upon an equitable and reasonable use of the said resources;

(b) elaboration of emergency plans for cases of accidental pollution;
(c) solution of town and country planning problems, in frontier regions and of common interest;
(d) establishment and, in due course, joint or concerted management of specially protected zones;
(e) cooperation in the domain of scientific studies and research;
(f) creation or habilitation of bodies entrusted, among other matters with the duty of compiling lists of substances the disposal of which will be either forbidden or controlled and establishing qualitative environmental norms as well as quantified criteria and thresholds, or revising them periodically or enforcing them;
(g) setting up of appropriate institutional structures aimed at ensuring the continuity and permanence of the cooperation; and
(h) the settlement of disputes which could be created by transfrontier pollution problems.

The simple reading of the previous provisions is sufficient to ascertain the fact that they contain many propositions that cannot be yet regarded as compulsory under general international law. As already stated, they are the result of both a synthesis and a systematization of the observation of recurrent treaty articles and also, in some aspects—paragraphs (d) to (h)—a description *de lege ferenda* of what should be the inspiration of future practice. A valuable indication of actual trends in that matter is given in particular by the several UNEP Conventions for protection of the Regional Seas: the 1976 Barcelona Convention for the Protection of the Mediterranean;[98] the 1978 Kuwait Convention for the Persian Gulf;[99] the 1981 Abidjan Convention for the West and Central African Region;[100] the 1982 Jeddah Convention for the Red Sea;[101] the 1983 Cartagena de Indias Convention for the Wider Caribbean Region;[102] and the 1985 Convention on the Protection of East African Coastal Zones.[103]

Let us examine several points of the provisions enumerated above. Paragraph (a) refers explicitly to what is often called the "principle of equitable use of internationally shared resources." In fact, it appears more like a general inspiring concept, which, as already mentioned, can hardly be improved without the help of a concrete negotiation between the concerned parties, on the basis of all the ecological, economic, social, and political factors interesting them. As has been rightly pointed out by Johan Lammers,

the essence of the principle of equitable utilization is that instead of laying down a norm with more or less specific contents, it rather prescribes a certain *technique* aimed at reaching an equitable result in each case. The extremely flexible character of the principle, however, has also a disadvantage in that the principle does not provide a directive for the States concerned.[104]

In fact, there is more than an analogy between this reference to equity and the one that has been developed in an apparently very different field, which is the law of delimitation of sea areas and continental shelves between States as it has been defined by arbitral tribunals and, mainly, by the International Court of Justice.[105] In that respect, as is well known, *equity is not taken in itself but as part of a legal principle*, which implies that delimitation will be established upon the due taking into consideration of equitable principles. That consideration leads to the evaluation of the pertinent circumstances that should not be ignored in each actual case.

The situation is about the same in defining the concrete conditions of an equitable apportionment of an ecological resource. Lists of typical factors to be considered in this respect have been drawn up by several international bodies in relation to equitable utilization, for example, in particular, articles 4 to 8 of the 1966 ILA Helsinki Rules on the Uses of the Waters of International Rivers,[106] article 6 of the ILA Belgrade Articles on the Regulation of the Flow of Waters of International Watercourses,[107] title B of OECD Council Recommendation C(74)224 on Principles Concerning Transfrontier Pollution,[108] and the very detailed article 8 of Evensen's 1983 project presented to the International Law Commission,[109] the substance of which has been even more enriched in draft articles 6 and 7 proposed by McCaffrey.

Paragraph (c) of the article presented above makes express reference to standing international commissions and other international institutional frameworks that have been actively developed in the last half of a century, but more intensively during the last twenty years, especially in frontier regions. Without recalling again the very rich experience of the United States–Canada International Joint Commission, one can notice the many creations that West European countries have known more recently. Consider, for instance, the 1975 French-German-Swiss Rhine Commission, or the 1978 Aachen Commission between the Federal Republic of Germany and the Netherlands.[110] This kind of international commission has generally a larger mandate than the classical international river commissions that had been created earlier. They consider not only protection of the environment but also all other aspects of regional cooperation that have an influence on the management of the concerned region. They are often closely linked with so-called low-level transfrontier cooperation between regional governments, *Länder*, districts, or even municipalities. A long-term cooperation can hardly be conceived without the existence and action of such transfrontier structures. The activities of such regional cooperation commissions enable us to look to new normative developments that could help in implementing international liability, as will be discussed later, by defining on a concrete basis, adapted to the specificities of each region, the precise criteria of lawful utilization of the interested resource.

Paragraph (f) refers to the drawing up of lists of substances, the disposal of which would be either forbidden or controlled. It mentions as well the establishment by these commissions of qualitative environmental norms as well as quantified criteria and thresholds, and the possibility of revising them periodically. Examples of such practices can be found in the action of several international commissions, such as the United States–Canada International Joint Commission, or in Europe, the Meuse, Moselle, or Lake Leman Commissions, the powers of which have been progressively enlarged in order to harmonize as much as possible the ecostandards recognized in each interested country.[111]

The system of lists is today very well known. It has been introduced by different protection-of-the-sea conventions in the early seventies, for instance by the 1972 Oslo and London conventions on prohibition of immersion of dangerous wastes,[112] and has become an ordinary technique for international management of the international environment. Article 210(4) of the 1982 Law of the Sea Convention foresees the establishment of norms by States, both on universal and regional levels, in the framework of international institutions, to be periodically revised.[113]

Responsibility and Reparation

The question of responsibility and liability for transfrontier pollution has been one of the most discussed in the last fifteen years. Two major opinions have been presented, not only by authors but also by national delegations presenting the viewpoint of their government in the framework of international organs, in particular the Sixth Commission of the U.N. General Assembly and the Third U.N. Conference on the Law of the Sea. It has been also studied, under the leadership of Robert Quentin Quentin-Baxter and Ambassador Julio Barboza in the International Law Commission (ILC).[114]

Some writers, such as Wilfred Jenks and L.F.E. Goldie,[115] taking into account the evolution which has affected municipal legislation regarding liability for ultrahazardous activities and the actual development of such activities on an international scale, have proposed a regime of strict if not always absolute liability for transfrontier pollution. This point of view received strong support in the 1970s from some governments, such as those of Canada, Australia, and some developing countries. This position has inspired the early beginning of the ILC work on International Liability for Injurious Consequences Arising Out of Acts Not Prohibited by International Law.

Other writers, such as Günther Handl and this author,[116] have defended another opinion, according to which State responsibility in this field stays under the classical regime defined by International Law, specifically, responsibility for acts or omissions that are illegal under international law. This opinion is shared not only by the majority of industrialized countries, but also, it seems, by an enlarging number of developing countries that, in the meantime, have evaluated the practical and economic consequences of implementing strict liability of States.

The practice of States during the same period, culminating with the *de facto* irresponsibility of the U.S.S.R. for the internationally proved damages provoked by the radioactive cloud that has passed over several Western European countries, has shown where the reality is.[117] From a more formal point of view, the same evidence has been brought by the evolution of negotiations inside the Third U.N. Conference on the Law of the Sea. In spite of prior propositions tending to impose a regime of strict liability for international pollution of the marine environment, the final wording of article 235 clearly attests that agreement could be reached only upon formulating a classical regime of responsibility for violation of an international obligation.[118]

It is clear that many practical arguments of the defenders of strict liability are quite valuable. Nevertheless, what is true today more than ever is that customary international law does not entail a general obligation to make reparation for every damage caused by transfrontier pollution. There is no strict liability in customary international law for transfrontier pollution or even for damages caused by ultrahazardous activities. A report published in October 1984 by the Environment Committee of the OECD Council, under the title "Responsibility and Liability in Relation to Transfrontier Pollution," is interesting in this regard. The report is not the result of the work of individual experts, but proceeds from the thorough discussions and negotiations of member States' delegations during several years inside the Transfrontier Pollution Group. The report states:

International liability for transfrontier pollution derives from general legal principles. It is engaged by a failure to comply with a customary or treaty obligation. In the opinion of most Member countries, this liability remains based on a State's failure to comply with an international obligation embodied in the above-mentioned rule concerning due diligence, the origin of which may be found not only in treaty law (violation of the terms of a bilateral or multilateral treaty) but also in customary law.[119]

Nevertheless, it is still true that the implementation of regimes of strict liability or of regimes inspired by it, established on the basis of *leges specialia*, or special agreements, should ensure a much better protection of victims of certain kinds of transfrontier pollution damage. That is the reason why the Draft Articles of The Hague Academy Research Centre, after having noted that State responsibility for transfrontier pollution remains under the classical regime, propose a solution that seems to facilitate a reparation of such damages, by making the release of liability of the offending State much easier. The Draft Articles read as follows:

Responsibility: In accordance with international law, the breach of those of the preceding provisions that have an obligatory character as well as of the obligations assumed in virtue of agreements of co-operation shall engage the international responsibility of the State.

Reparation: Unless otherwise provided, when quantified environmental norms prescribing specific values have been established, the fact of the thresholds fixed by the said norms being exceeded shall entail the liability of the responsible State to pay compensation, except duly proved cases of force majeure or act of God.[120]

As far as the legal basis of State responsibility for transfrontier pollution is concerned, one can revisit what has been said earlier about the legal ground of the obligation to prevent such pollution: there is a "primary obligation" (in the sense laid down by Roberto Ago in his reports to the ILC on State Responsibility)[121] which is the obligation of harmless use of territory. Its content, as mentioned above,[122] has been quite precise in the past twenty years, as determined both by the practice of States (including treaty practice) and by the soft law resolutions which,- in the medium term, can be considered as expressing progressively what is or, in certain cases, will be soon, the common *opinio juris* inside the world community.

These resolutions also make it easier to define what should be the average behavior of a "well-governed State" in regard to transfrontier pollution problems. Accordingly, the standards of international "due diligence" can be expected to become more and more definite with the progress of international cooperation. Due diligence appears here as the measure of international responsibility. It is both the counterpart to the exclusive exercise of territorial jurisdiction and the limiting factor on international responsibility flowing from failure to act in accordance with international norms.

But one must see that there is also a place for special regimes defining *rationae materiae* (i.e., for some kinds of damages by pollution, for instance chemical ones) or *rationae loci*. Here we meet again the actual and potential importance of *regional* cooperation inside or even outside international standing bodies. We are confronted again with the efficiency of agreements of cooperation as they have been defined earlier in this chapter. And the definition of special ecological quality standards by such treaties will make it easy to strengthen the regime of liability by giving to it the advantages for the victims that usually are found in regimes of strict liability. All, in this matter, is a question of burden of proof and standard of proof.

International ecostandards are essentially divided in two categories. The first is composed of what one could call qualitative ecostandards. They are basically parameters to be taken into account because respecting them has an influence on the quality of the environment and the ecological equilibrium of a given natural resource (for instance, the elements referred to earlier in regard to the definition of what should be, in a concrete case, the equitable apportionment of a shared natural resource).[123] They are useful, but nevertheless still open to discussion.[124]

The second category, that of quantitative ecostandards, is adopted on the basis of an agreement between technicians and experts in the matter concerned. This kind of ecostandard is frequently encountered in technical annexes or, more seldom, in the text of conventions for the protection of the environment. One can give many illustrations of this technique: the 1972 United States–Canada Agreement on the Water Quality of the Great Lakes;[125] the 1973 Agreement concerning the Permanent and Definitive Solution to the International Problem of the Salinity of the Colorado River concluded between Mexico and the United States;[126] the 1974 treaty between Sweden and Denmark about the protection of the Oresund against pollution; the 1984 Agreement between the Federal Republic of Germany and the Netherlands referring to the management of the Ems Dollart Territory; or the two 1976 conventions for protecting the waters of the Rhine, together with their technical annexes.[127]

From the point of view of international responsibility, what is interesting about these quantitative ecostandards, adopted by way of treaty law, is that they can be precisely controlled by technical measures and accomplished by technicians, even if one must not overevaluate the objectivity of technical criteria and evaluations. They are not susceptible to determination by lawyers, arbitrators, or judges on the ground of personal convictions. *A concrete and official statement that the standard has been exceeded will then suffice to establish prima facie that the State from which the water flows, for instance, is liable to repair the damages caused by such a violation of the internationally agreed norm.* Let us take, as an illustration, this extract from the 1973 United States-Mexico Agreement:

1. Referring to the annual volume of Colorado River waters guaranteed to Mexico under the Treaty of 1944, of 1,500,000 acre-feet (1,850,234,000 cubic meters):
a) The United States shall adopt measures to assure that not earlier than January 1, 1974, and not later than July 1, 1974, the approximately 1,360,000 acre-feet (1,677,545,000 cubic meters) delivered to Mexico up-stream of Morelos Dam, have an annual average salinity of no more than 115 p.p.m. ± 30 p.p.m. U.S. count (121 p.p.m. ± 30 p.p.m. Mexican count) over the annual average salinity of Colorado River waters which arrive at Imperial Dam.[128]

Here we are confronted with a definition of legality which leaves almost no room for approximative evaluation and later discussions. Even if not possible in all cases, the recourse to such a form of international ecostandards could, for the reasons mentioned above, greatly help in the efficiency of international responsibility, which stays otherwise, as it is daily shown, practically unemployed.

Technically, the system of responsibility described here is not a regime of strict liability. The responsible State will be liable not only because it has caused damage but also because this damage is the emanation of the breach of an international obligation. From a practical point of view, that means first of all that, for the interest of the victim, the situation is as comfortable as one under a strict liability regime. The victim will not personally have to bring any proof of the illicit act caused by the defaulting State (even if the problem of the causal link between the activity under the jurisdiction of the State of origin and the damage provoked may still exist). For the State parties, the advantage is that they know exactly what the content of their responsibility is and how to be in accordance with their international obligations.

Without offering a solution for every case, the system here proposed can probably help "to develop further the international law regarding liability and compensation for the victims of pollution and other environmental damage caused by activities within the jurisdiction or control of such States to areas beyond their jurisdiction," which is, after all, the exact wish formulated by the Principle 22 of the Stockholm Declaration of 1972.[129]

Acknowledgments

A valuable complement to this chapter is the Final Report adopted by the Expert Group on Environmental Law established in 1985 by the

World Commission on Environment and Development. *See Final Report: Legal Principles for Environmental Protection and Sustainable Development*, WCED/86/23/Add.1 (June 1986). The *Final Report* covers a larger scope than the present chapter, embracing aspects of environmental protection in addition to transfrontier pollution.

Notes

1. UNEP is the principal United Nations agency involved in international environmental protection efforts. The activities of several other United Nations agencies also directly concern the environment, however, including the Food and Agriculture Organization (FAO), the United Nations Educational, Scientific and Cultural Organization (UNESCO), and the World Meteorological Organization (WMO).

2. The OECD is an economic policymaking organization composed primarily of industrialized countries. Its 24 members are Australia, Austria, Belgium, Canada, Denmark, the Federal Republic of Germany, Finland, France, Greece, Iceland, Ireland, Italy, Japan, Luxembourg, the Netherlands, New Zealand, Norway, Portugal, Spain, Sweden, Switzerland, Turkey, the United Kingdom, and the United States. This author has been the legal adviser to the OECD Transfrontier Pollution Group throughout its existence.

3. *See, e.g.*, OECD Res. C(77)28 (Final), *Annex*, Introduction (May 17, 1977), in OECD, OECD AND THE ENVIRONMENT 151 (1986).

4. *See Corpus of Principles and Rules Relative to the Protection of the Environment against Transfrontier Pollution Established by the French-speaking Section*, in Centre for Studies and Research in International Law and International Relations, Hague Academy of International Law, LA POLLUTION TRANSFRONTIÈRE ET LE DROIT INTERNATIONAL—TRANSFRONTIER POLLUTION AND INTERNATIONAL LAW 27 (1985) [hereinafter LA POLLUTION TRANSFRONTIÈRE]; P.M. Dupuy, *Bilan de Recherches*, in LA POLLUTION TRANSFRONTIÈRE, *supra* this note, at 33; *see also* Lammers, *The Present State of Research Carried Out by the English-speaking Section of the Centre for Studies and Research*, in LA POLLUTION TRANSFRONTIÈRE, *supra* this note, at 89.

5. Trail Smelter (U.S. v. Can.), 3 R. Int'l Arb. Awards 1905, 1965 (1938 & 1941).

6. Corfu Channel (U.K. v. Alb.), 1949 I.C.J. 4, 22 (Judgment of Apr. 9).

7. *See, e.g.*, the discussion in Chapter 11, *infra*.

8. Island of Palmas (U.S. v. Neth.), 2 R. Int'l Arb. Awards 829 (1928). For a discussion of this case, see *infra* Chapter 9.

9. Report of the United Nations Conference on the Human Environment, Stockholm, June 5–16, 1972, pt. 1, ch. 1, *reprinted in* 11 I.L.M. 1416 (1972).

10. *See* INSTITUTO DE INVESTIGACIONES JURIDICAS, UNIVERSIDAD NACIONAL AUTONOMA DE MEXICO, LEGAL PROTECTION OF THE ENVIRONMENT IN DEVELOPING COUNTRIES (1976).

11. G.A. Res. 3129 (XXVIII), U.N. GAOR Supp. (No. 30A), U.N. Doc. A/9030/Add.1 (1973).

12. Charter of Economic Rights and Duties of States, Dec. 12, 1974, G.A. Res. 3281, 29 U.N. GAOR Supp. (No. 31) at 50, U.N. Doc. A/9631 (1975), *reprinted in* 14 I.L.M. 251 (1975).

13. EC Programme of Action on the Environment, 16 O.J. EUR. COMM. (No.

C 12/6) (1973); 20 O.J. Eur. Comm. (No. C 139) (1977); 26 O.J. Eur. Comm. (No. C 46) (1983). For a description of the EC, see *infra* Chapter 12, at note 4.

14. *Supra* note 3.

15. *Reprinted in* OECD, OECD and the Environment 44, 45 (1986).

16. Conference on Security and Cooperation in Europe: Final Act (Aug. 1, 1975), *reprinted in* 14 I.L.M. 1292 (1975).

17. UNEP Draft Principles of Conduct on Shared Natural Resources, prin. 3 (1978) (unpublished).

18. Frontier Treaty, Apr. 8, 1960, Netherlands-F.R.G., art. 58(2)(c), 508 U.N.T.S. 14.

19. Agreement Concerning Frontier Watercourses, Apr. 24, 1964, Finland-U.S.S.R., 537 U.N.T.S. 231.

20. Agreement Concerning a Solution to the International Problem of the Salinity of the Colorado River, Aug. 30, 1973, United States–Mexico, 24 U.S.T. 1968, T.I.A.S. No. 7708, *reprinted in* 12 I.L.M. 1105 (1973).

21. Agreement for Cooperation on Environmental Programs and Transboundary Problems, Aug. 14, 1983, United States–Mexico, art. 2.1, T.I.A.S. No. 10827, *reprinted in* 22 I.L.M. 1025 (1983).

22. Third United Nations Conference on the Law of the Sea, Dec. 10, 1982, art. 192(2), U.N. Doc. A/Conf.62/121, *reprinted in* 21 I.L.M. 1261 (1982).

23. *See supra* text accompanying note 9.

24. *See* C. Caubet, *Le Barrage d'Itaipu et le droit international fluvial*, thèse doctorat d'Etat, Université de Toulouse I (Dec. 6, 1983); P.M. Dupuy, *La Gestion concertée des ressources naturelles: à propos du différend entre le Brésil et l'Argentine relatif au barrage d'Itaipu*, [1978] 24 Annuaire Français de Droit International 866. In these two cases, the State of origin of transfrontier pollution was prevailing itself with its rights of sovereignty, in a way which recalled in a certain way the Harmon Doctrine, described *infra* at text accompanying note 28.

25. *See* V.C. de Klemm, *Conservation of Species, the Need for a New Approach*, 9 Envtl. Pol'y & L. 117 (1982).

26. ASEAN Agreement on the Conservation of Nature and Natural Resources, *opened for signature* July 9, 1985, arts. 10 & 11, *reprinted in* 15 Envtl. Pol'y & L. 64 (1985).

27. *See* McCaffrey, *Transboundary Environmental Relations Between Mexico and the United States*, in Transatlantic Colloquy on Cross-Border Relations: European and North American Perspectives (S. Ercmann ed. Zurich 1987).

28. *See* U.S. Attorney General J. Harmon, *Treaty of Guadalupe Hildalgo—International Law*, 21 Op. Att'y Gen. 274 (1895); Austin, *Canadian-United States Practice and Theory Respecting the Law of International Rivers: A Study of the History and Influence of the Harmon Doctrine*, 37 Can. B. Rev. 391, 408 (1959).

29. *See* Handl, *Territorial Sovereignty and the Problem of Transfrontier Pollution*, 69 Am. J. Int'l L. 50 (1975); P.M. Dupuy, La responsabilité des Etats pour les dommages d'origine technologique et industrielle 26 (Paris, Pédone, 1976); Le Droit de l'environnement et la souveraineté des Etats—Bilan et perspectives, in Hague Acad. Int'l L., The Future of the International Law of the Environment 29 (1985).

30. *See* UNEP Report, U.N. Doc. ENV/GE.1/R.11/Rev.1 (Nov. 22, 1984).

31. *See* OECD Rec. C(79)114 (May 8, 1978), in OECD, OECD and the Environment 162 (1986). *See also* OECD Rec. C(89)2 (Final) (Mar. 3, 1989), concerning an Environmental Checklist for Possible Use by High-Level Deci-

sion Makers in Bilateral and Multilateral Development Assistance Institutions, *reprinted in* 28 I.L.M. 1314 (1989).

32. UNEP Doc. 1.G.12/2 (1978) (Concl. no. 8); International Co-operation in the Field of the Environment, G.A. Res. 37/217, U.N. GAOR Supp. (No. 51) at 145, U.N. Doc. A/37/51 (1983).

33. *Reprinted in* UNEP REFERENCE SERIES 3, SELECTED MULTILATERAL TREATIES IN THE FIELD OF ENVIRONMENT 47, 463 (A.C. Kiss ed. 1983).

34. Kuwait Regional Convention for Cooperation on Protection of the Marine Environment from Pollution, Apr. 24, 1978, art. 2, *reprinted in* 17 I.L.M. 511 (1978); Jeddah Regional Convention for the Conservation of the Red Sea and Gulf of Aden Environment, *opened for signature* Feb. 14, 1982, art. 11, *reprinted in* 9 ENVTL. POL'Y & L. 56 (1982). One could also refer to the Nairobi Convention of June 21, 1985 for the protection of the coastal regions of East Africa, *infra* note 103.

35. LA POLLUTION TRANSFRONTIÈRE, *supra* note 4, at 29–31.

36. *See Report on the Implementation of a Regime of Equal Right of Access and Non-Discrimination in Relation to Transfrontier Pollution*, in OECD, LEGAL ASPECTS OF TRANSFRONTIER POLLUTION 37 (1977); OECD Rec. C(77)28, *supra* note 3, at 150. *See also* S. McCaffrey, Sixth Report on Non-navigational Uses of International Watercourses, Feb. 23, 1990, U.N. Doc. A/CN.4/427, §§ 38–39.

37. Convention on the Protection of the Environment, Feb. 19, 1974, *reprinted in* 13 I.L.M. 591 (1974).

38. *See supra* note 36.

39. UNEP Doc. 1.G.12/2 (1978).

40. *Supra* note 22, arts. 194(4), 227.

41. *See* P. Zannas, *La Responsabilité des Etats pour les actes de négligence*, Montreux, Ganguin & Laubscher; P.M. Dupuy, *Due Diligence in the International Law of Liability*, in OECD, LEGAL ASPECTS OF TRANSFRONTIER POLLUTION 369 (1977).

42. U.C.C. §§ 1–203 (obligation of good faith), 2–103(b) ("'Good faith' in the case of a merchant means honesty in fact and observance of reasonable commercial standards of fair dealing in the trade."), 1 U.L.A. 109, 185 (1989).

43. *See also* American Law Institute, RESTATEMENT (SECOND) OF THE LAW OF CONTRACTS § 205 (Duty of Good Faith and Fair Dealing) (1981).

44. S.S. Lotus (Fr. v. Turk.), 1927 P.C.I.J. (ser. A) No. 10 (Sept. 7).

45. U.N. CHARTER art. 1(3).

46. Military and Paramilitary Activities in and against Nicaragua (Nicar. v. U.S.), Merits, 1986 I.C.J. 14 (Judgment of June 27).

47. G.A. Res. 2625(XXV), U.N. GAOR Supp. (No. 28) at 121, U.N. Doc. A/8028 (1970).

48. *See infra* text accompanying notes 72–95.

49. *See supra* note 9.

50. Lac Lanoux (Fr. v. Spain), 24 I.L.R. 101, 129–30 (1957) (English); 12 Rep. Int'l Arb. Awards 281 (1957) (French), *reprinted in* 53 AM. J. INT'L L. 156 (1959).

51. *Supra* note 9, at prin. 24.

52. Cooperation Between States in the Field of the Environment, G.A. Res. 2995 (XXVII), U.N. GAOR Supp. (No. 30), U.N. Doc. A/8730 (1972).

53. Cooperation in the Field of the Environment Concerning Natural Resources Shared by Two or More States, *supra* note 11.

54. Cooperation in the Field of the Environment Concerning Natural Re-

sources Shared by Two or More States, G.A. Res. 34/186, U.N. GAOR Supp. (No. 46) at 128, U.N. Doc. A/34/46.

55. *See supra* note 39.

56. *Supra* note 3.

57. OECD Res. C(77)115 (Final) (July 22, 1977), in OECD, OECD AND THE ENVIRONMENT 181 (1986). *See also* the Declaration of Brasilia emanating from the Sixth Ministerial Meeting on the Environment in Latin America and the Caribbean held in Brasilia on March 30–31, 1989, especially § 2: "The Ministers endorse the principle that each State has the sovereign right to administer freely its natural resources. This does not, however, exclude the need for international cooperation at the subregional, regional and world levels; rather, it reinforces it." *Reprinted in* 28 I.L.M. 1311 (1989).

58. OECD Res. C(77)28 (Final) (May 17, 1977), in OECD, OECD AND THE ENVIRONMENT 150 (1986).

59. OECD Res. C(78)77 (Final) (Sept. 21, 1978), in OECD, OECD AND THE ENVIRONMENT 154 (1986).

60. *See supra* text preceding note 36.

61. *Reprinted in* TRACTATENBLAD VAN HET KONINKRIJK DER NEDERLANDEN, No. 104 (1963).

62. Agreement Concerning the Use of Water Resources in Frontier Waters, July 17, 1964, Poland-U.S.S.R., 552 U.N.T.S. 175.

63. Sept. 15, 1968, 1001 U.N.T.S. 3.

64. Vol. 1 at 180, U.N. Doc. A/CN.4/274.

65. Feb. 21, 1974, *reprinted in* 13 I.L.M. 352 (1974).

66. Mar. 22, 1974, *reprinted in* 13 I.L.M. 546 (1974).

67. Convention for the Protection of the Mediterranean Sea Against Pollution, *opened for signature* Feb. 16, 1976, *reprinted in* 15 I.L.M. 290 (1976).

68. Agreement on Great Lakes Water Quality, Nov. 22, 1978, United States-Canada, 30 U.S.T. 1383, T.I.A.S. No. 9257.

69. Convention on Long-Range Transboundary Air Pollution, Nov. 13, 1979, T.I.A.S. No. 10541, *reprinted in* 18 I.L.M. 1442 (1979). For a description of the ECE, see *infra* Chapter 12 note 3.

70. *Supra* note 22.

71. *Supra* note 26.

72. *Cf.* Lammers, *"Balancing the Equities" in International Environmental Law*, in L'AVENIR DU DROIT INTERNATIONAL DE L'ENVIRONNEMENT—THE FUTURE OF THE INTERNATIONAL LAW OF THE ENVIRONMENT 153 (R.J. Dupuy ed. 1985).

73. *See supra* text accompanying notes 31–35. *See also* S. McCaffrey, Fifth Report to the International Law Commission on the Law of the Non-navigational Uses of International Watercourses, U.N. Doc. A/CN.4/412 (1988), draft articles 12 to 16.

74. OECD Rec. C(74)224 (Nov. 14, 1974), in OECD, OECD AND THE ENVIRONMENT 142 (1986).

75. *Id.* at Title E.

76. For a description of the International Joint Commission, see R.B. BILDER, WHEN NEIGHBORS QUARREL: CANADA-U.S. DISPUTE-SETTLEMENT EXPERIENCE 54–60 (Inst. for Legal Studies, Univ. of Wis.-Madison Law School, May 1987) (The Claude T. Bissell Lectures, University of Toronto 1986–87. Dispute Processing Research Program, Working Papers Series 8).

77. *See, e.g.*, Niamey Act Regarding Navigation and Economic Cooperation Between the States of the Niger Basin, Oct. 26, 1963, 587 U.N.T.S. 9.

78. *See supra* text accompanying notes 61–71.

79. Indus Waters Treaty, Sept. 19, 1960, India-Pakistan, 419 U.N.T.S. 125.

80. *Reprinted in* Sozialistische Landeskultur Umweltschutz, Textansgabe ausgewählter Rechtsvorschriften, Staatsverslag der Deutsch Dem. Rep. 375 (Berlin 1978).

81. *Supra* note 68.

82. *Supra* note 69.

83. *Supra* note 22. *See* 1987 Revue Générale de Droit International Public 769, 781.

84. *See supra* text accompanying notes 56–59.

85. *Supra* note 53.

86. *Supra* note 12.

87. EEC Directive 82/501/CEE, art. 8, J.O. Comm. Eur. (No. L 230) (1982).

88. EEC Directive 85/337/CEE, art. 7, J.O. Comm. Eur. (No. L 175) (1985). *See also* OECD Council Decision-Recommendation C(88)85 (Final) concerning the communication of information to the public and the participation of the public in the decision-making process relating to measures of prevention and intervention applicable to accidents caused by dangerous substances, *reprinted in* 1988 Revue Générale de Droit International Public 808.

89. 58 Y.B. Inst. Int'l L., pt. II, 199 (Kaiser 1980), 1979 Athens Session, art. 6.

90. 62 Y.B. Inst. Int'l L., pt. II, 300 (Pédone 1988), 1987 Cairo Session, art. 8.

91. 60 ILA Reports 175, art. 8 (Harpell's Press 1983).

92. Schwebel, Third Report on the Law of the Non-navigational Uses of International Watercourses, art. 9, U.N. Doc. A/CN.4/348 (1981), *reprinted in* [1982] 2 Y.B. Int'l L. Comm'n, pt. 1, at 65; Evensen, First Report on the Law of the Non-navigational Uses of International Watercourses, art. 9, U.N. Doc. A/CN.4/367, *reprinted in* [1983] 2 Y.B. Int'l L. Comm'n, pt. 1, at 155, U.N. Doc. A/CN.4/SER.A/1983/Add.1; S. McCaffrey, *supra* note 73, draft arts. 10, 17, 18.

93. *See supra* text accompanying note 24.

94. The details of the Chernobyl accident are described in Chapter 7 *infra*. *See also* Handl, *Après Tchernobyl: Quelques reflexions sur le programme legislatif multilateral à l'ordre du jour*, in 1988 Revue Générale de Droit International Public at 62.

95. *See infra* Chapter 6.

96. *See* La Pollution Transfrontière, *supra* note 4.

97. *Supra* note 50.

98. *Reprinted in* 15 I.L.M. 290 (1976).

99. Kuwait Regional Convention for Cooperation on the Protection of the Marine Environment from Pollution, Apr. 24, 1978, *reprinted in* 17 I.L.M. 511 (1978).

100. Abidjan Convention for Co-operation in the Protection and Development of the Marine Environment of the West and Central African Region, March 23, 1981, *reprinted in* 20 I.L.M. 746 (1981).

101. *Supra* note 34.

102. Cartegena de Indias Convention for the Protection and Development of the Marine Environment of the Wider Caribbean Region, *reprinted in* 22 I.L.M. 227 (1983).

103. Convention for the Protection, Management and Development of the Marine and Coastal Environment of the Eastern African Region, June 21,

1986, *summarized in* II ANNUAL REVIEW OF OCEAN AFFAIRS: LAW AND POLICY, MAIN DOCUMENTS 1985–1987, at 686 (UNIFO Publishers 1989).

104. *Supra* note 4, at 91–92.

105. *See* P. WEIL, PERSPECTIVES DU DROIT DE LA DELIMITATION MARITIME (Paris, Pédone, 1988). For the application of equity to the environment, see L.F.E. Goldie, *Reconciling Values of Distributive Equity and Management Efficiency in the International Commons*, in THE SETTLEMENT OF DISPUTES ON THE NEW NATURAL RESOURCES 335 (1983); Handl, *Equitable Use and Transfrontier Pollution*, in OECD, TRANSFRONTIER POLLUTION AND THE ROLE OF STATES 95 (Paris 1981).

106. ILA, REPORT OF THE 52ND CONFERENCE 484 (1967) (factors of equitable use of international basin waters include geography, hydrology, past utilization, economic and social needs of each State, population dependence on basin waters, avoidance of unnecessary waste in utilization, and degree to which needs of each State may be satisfied without substantial injury to other States).

107. ILA, REPORT OF THE FIFTY-NINTH CONFERENCE, BELGRADE, 1980 (1982).

108. *Supra* note 74, Title B.

109. *Supra* note 92, art. 8 (article 8 lists relevant questions of equitable use of waters to include comparison of needs, uses and contribution to waters, availability of alternative water resources, cooperation in projects to attain optimum utilization, and pollution by system States); to be compared with articles 6 and 7 proposed by McCaffrey, in his Second Report, U.N. Doc. A/CN.4/399/Add.1 & 2 (1986).

110. *See* OECD, PROTECTION OF THE ENVIRONMENT IN TRANSFRONTIER REGIONS (1979).

111. *See* Contini & Sand, *Methods to Expedite Environmental Protection*, 66 AM. J. INT'L L. 37 (1972); Sand, *The Creation of Transnational Rules for Environmental Protection*, in IUCN, TRENDS IN ENVIRONMENTAL POLICY AND LAW 311 (1980).

112. Convention for the Prevention of Marine Pollution by Dumping from Ships and Aircraft, Feb. 15, 1972, *reprinted in* 11 I.L.M. 262 (1972); Convention on the Dumping of Wastes at Sea, Nov. 13, 1972, *reprinted in* 11 I.L.M. 1291 (1972).

113. *Supra* note 22, art. 210(4).

114. Quentin-Baxter submitted five reports before his death in 1984. Ambassador Barboza has been the special rapporteur since then. This topic is discussed in Chapter 4 *infra*.

115. Jenks, *Liability for Ultra-Hazardous Activities in International Law*, 117 REC. DES COURS 99 (1966); Goldie, *Liability for Damage and the Progressive Development of International Law*, 14 INT'L & COMP. L.Q. 1189 (1965); Goldie, *International Principles of Responsibility for Pollution*, 2 COLUM. J. TRANSNAT'L L. 283 (1970); Kelson, *State Responsibility and the Abnormally Dangerous Activity*, 13 HARV. INT'L L.J. 197, 243 (1972).

116. *See supra* note 29; Handl, *State Liability for Accidental Transfrontier Environmental Damage by Private Persons*, 74 AM. J. INT'L L. 525 (1980); *The Environment: International Rights and Responsibilities*, 1980 AM. SOC. INT'L L. PROC. 223; P.M. Dupuy, *Le fait générateur de la responsabilité internationale des Etats*, 188 REC. DES COURS 9 (1984); *La réparation des dommages causés aux nouvelles ressources*, in THE SETTLEMENT OF DISPUTES ON THE NEW NATURAL RESOURCES, *supra* note 105, at 427–46; *see also* the most interesting Report by

the OECD Environment Committee, RESPONSIBILITY AND LIABILITY OF STATES IN RELATION TO TRANSFRONTIER POLLUTION (OECD 1984).

117. The response by States to Chernobyl is discussed in Chapter 7 *infra*.

118. *Supra* note 22, art. 235.

119. RESPONSIBILITY AND LIABILITY IN RELATION TO TRANSFRONTIER POLLUTION 7 (OECD 1984).

120. *Id.*

121. *See, e.g.*, Report of the International Law Commission to the General Assembly, 31 U.N. GAOR Supp. (No. 10) at 165, U.N. Doc. A/31/10 (1976), *reprinted in* [1976] 2 Y.B. Int'l L. Comm'n, pt. 2, at 1, 71 U.N. Doc. A/CN.4/SER.A/1976/Add.1.

122. *See supra* Part II.

123. *See supra* text following note 50.

124. *See* P.M. Dupuy, *Limites matérielles des pollutions tolérées*, in RECHTSFRAGEN GRENZÜBERSCHREITENDER UMWELTBELASTUNGEN/LES PROBLÈMES JURIDIQUES POSÉS PAR LES POLLUTIONS TRANSFRONTIÈRES, WORKSHOP SARREBRUKEN, 1982, at 27–42 (Erich Schmidt Verlag 1984).

125. Agreement on Great Lakes Water Quality, Apr. 15, 1972, United States–Canada, 23 U.S.T. 301, T.I.A.S. No. 7312 (amended as per note 68, *supra*).

126. *Supra* note 20.

127. Convention on the Protection of the Rhine against Chemical Pollution, Dec. 3, 1976, *reprinted in* 16 I.L.M. 242 (1977); Bonn Convention on the Protection of the Rhine against Pollution by Chlorides, Dec. 3, 1976, *reprinted in* 16 I.L.M. 265 (1977).

128. *Supra* note 20.

129. *Supra* note 9, prin. 22.

Chapter 4
International Liability and International Watercourses: The Work of the International Law Commission Relating to International Pollution

Stephen C. McCaffrey

Introduction

In its 1987 Report to the United Nations General Assembly, the World Commission on Environment and Development[1] reminded us that there are "environmental trends that threaten to radically alter the planet, that threaten the lives of many species upon it, including the human species."[2] The Commission identifies these trends as including desertification, deforestation, acid deposition, global warming (the "greenhouse effect") caused by the burning of fossil fuels, depletion of the ozone layer by other industrial gases, and the introduction of toxic substances into the human food chain and underground water tables.[3] Indeed, no one would dispute that humankind has ample reason to be aware of the environmental problems confronting spaceship Earth.[4] It is also beyond peradventure that the technology exists to control the environmentally deleterious byproducts of human civilization— and, indeed, of human life itself—that we refer to as pollution. Pollution control can be costly, however, not only in terms of the necessary technology but also, ultimately, in terms of profits, jobs, and development.

Moreover, there are two sides to the coin of technological advancement: one helps us to deal with the wastes of human and economic activity, but the other creates new risks, in the form of hazardous substances, products, and processes.[5] Recent events—Chernobyl, Bhopal, the Rhine chemical spill—have reminded us only too forcefully of the dark side of technological advancement.

The United Nations International Law Commission[6] is currently engaged in efforts to codify and develop progressively norms of international law concerning two topics that bear on international pollution. The titles of these topics are International Liability for Injurious Consequences Arising Out of Acts Not Prohibited by International Law ("International Liability") and The Law of the Non-Navigational Uses of International Watercourses ("International Watercourses"). This chapter will discuss selected aspects of the Commission's work on these topics, both of which concern international pollution generally rather than pollution from a specific source such as acid rain or nuclear accidents. The chapter will focus upon International Liability because that topic, unlike International Watercourses, deals almost exclusively with problems of international pollution.

International Liability

For more than thirty years, the International Law Commission has been struggling with the monumental task of codification of the law of State responsibility,[7] a subject dealing with internationally wrongful acts of States. The Commission has recognized, however, that a State can engage in activities that are not prohibited by international law—such as those involving space objects and nuclear reactors—but that may, through no fault of that State, give rise to injurious consequences in other States. Accordingly the Commission decided in 1970 to treat separately the question of liability for the harmful transfrontier consequences of such activities.[8] This topic came to be entitled "International Liability for Injurious Consequences Arising out of Acts Not Prohibited by International Law." The need for separate treatment of International Liability was explained in the following terms:

The Commission fully recognizes the importance, not only of questions of responsibility for internationally wrongful acts, but also of questions concerning the obligations to make good any harmful consequences arising out of certain lawful activities, especially those which, because of their nature, present certain risks. . . . [T]he latter category of questions cannot be treated jointly with the former.[9]

The category of issues to be dealt with in the context of International Liability had earlier been described by the special rapporteur for State responsibility as "questions relating to responsibility arising out of the performance of certain lawful activities—such as spatial and nuclear activities . . . [o]wing to the entirely different basis of the so-called responsibility for risk."[10]

International Liability was included in the Commission's current program of work in 1978, and the first special rapporteur for the topic, R. Q. Quentin-Baxter, was appointed in that year. Quentin-Baxter submitted five reports to the Commission before his death in 1984. By that time, the Commission had reached a general understanding that the scope of the topic would be confined to "physical activities, giving rise to physical transboundary harm."[11] In his third report, Quentin-Baxter presented a "Schematic Outline" that sets forth the basic principles governing the rights and duties of States in cases falling within the topic's scope. The current special rapporteur, Ambassador Julio Barboza, has indicated his intention to follow the general approach indicated in the outline; it thus continues to serve as the basis of the Commission's work on International Liability. The principles contained in the outline include the following: the duty to inform other States of activities that are giving or may give rise to injury in those other States (Section 2(1)); the right of an actually or potentially affected State to require the source State (also referred to as the State of origin) to provide information concerning actually or potentially injurious activities (Section 2(2)); the establishment of joint fact-finding machinery (Section 2(4)–(7)); reparation for loss or injury, to be ascertained in accordance with the "shared expectations" of the States concerned, as therein defined (Section 4(2)–(4)); and provision of adequate measures of prevention (Section 5(2)).

In his report submitted in 1982, Quentin-Baxter made the following remarks concerning the nature of the topic and the operation of the procedures and rules set forth in the schematic outline:

> The distinctive feature of the present topic is that no deviation from the rules it prescribes will engage the responsibility of the State for wrongfulness except ultimate failure, in case of loss or injury, to make the reparation that may then be required. In a sense, therefore, the whole of this topic, up to that final breakdown which at length engages the responsibility of the State for wrongfulness, deals with a conciliation procedure, conducted by the parties themselves or by any person or institution to whom they agree to turn for help.
> A reference to the schematic outline . . . will show how this works out in practice. There is a preliminary phase of consultation and fact-finding, without substantive commitment by the States concerned. There is a second phase of negotiation among those States to establish a regime reconciling their conflicting interests; but the only sanctions for refusal to negotiate or failure to reach agreement are a continuation of the conflict of interest, and the possibility that a State which has failed to cooperate may be at some disadvantage if a loss or injury entailing questions of reparation subsequently occurs . . . .
> . . . In relation to the establishment of regimes of prevention and reparation,

all loss or injury is prospective; in relation to the establishment of an obligation to provide reparation, all loss or injury is actual.[12]

It is only "[a]t the very end of the day," according to Quentin-Baxter, "when all the opportunities of regime-building have been set aside— or, alternatively, when a loss or injury has occurred that nobody fore- saw—[that] there is a commitment, in the nature of strict liability, to make good the loss."[13]

These remarks reveal that Quentin-Baxter's ideas about the topic had reached a fairly advanced stage by 1982. It may thus come as something of a surprise that, at the time this chapter was written, in November 1989, the Commission had yet to adopt a single article on International Liability, even though it referred ten articles to the Draft- ing Committee in 1988 and then referred nine replacement articles to the Drafting Committee in 1989.[14]

The fact that the Commission has not made more progress in the twelve years that the topic has been on its active agenda is partly the result of the cautious attitude States have taken toward it, but also testifies to the complexity and delicacy of the issues it raises.[15] A perusal of the summary of the Commission's discussion of Interna- tional Liability at its 1987[16] and 1988[17] sessions reveals that members of the ILC still do not agree upon the basic question of whether general international law recognizes a principle of strict liability for the inju- rious consequences of the kinds of activities in question. Furthermore, and perhaps even more fundamentally, there seems to be no clear understanding of exactly what kinds of activities are involved. Some members would confine the study of International Liability to what might be termed "ultrahazardous" activities, such as spatial and nu- clear activities, while others would include within its ambit any activity having adverse transfrontier environmental consequences. It is also unclear to what extent injury to an international commons should be included, or whether, instead, only injury in or to another State's territory should be covered.[18]

While Ambassador Barboza has approached the development of the liability topic along the same general lines as his predecessor, he has been somewhat bolder in emphasizing the duty of prevention and in indicating that the "main basis" of the obligation of reparation (in cases of the kind here at issue) is strict liability.[19] In 1987, he submitted for the Commission's preliminary consideration a set of six introductory articles.[20] His 1988 report revised those and included additional arti- cles, bringing the total to ten.[21] He revised those ten articles in 1989, at a point too late in the publication process of this chapter to discuss them in detail.[22] For present purposes, articles 1, 2, and 4 from his

1987 report and articles 1, 2, and 3 from his 1988 report, reproduced below, are most pertinent. Articles 1, 2, and 4 from his 1987 report read as follows:

Article 1

Scope of the present articles

The present articles shall apply with respect to activities or situations which occur within the territory or control of a State and which do or may give rise to a physical consequence adversely affecting persons or objects and the use or enjoyment of areas within the territory or control of another State.

Article 2

Use of terms

In the present articles:

(1) 'Situation' means a situation arising as a consequence of a human activity which does or may give rise to transboundary injury;

(2) The expression 'within the territory or control':

(a) In relation to a coastal State, extends to maritime areas whose legal regime vests jurisdiction in that State in respect of any matter;

(b) In relation to a flag State, State of registry or State of registration of any ship, aircraft or space object, respectively, extends to the ships, aircraft and space objects of that State even when they exercise rights of passage or over-flight through a maritime area or airspace constituting the territory of or within the control of any other State;

(c) Applies beyond national jurisdictions, with the same effects as above, thus extending to any matter in respect of which a right is exercised or an interest is asserted;

(3) 'State of origin' means a State within the territory or control of which an activity or situation such as those specified in article 1 occurs;

(4) 'Affected State' means a State within the territory or control of which persons or objects or the use or enjoyment of areas are or may be affected;

(5) 'Transboundary effects' means effects which arise as a physical consequence of an activity or situation within the territory or control of a State of origin and which affect persons or objects or the use or enjoyment of an area within the territory or control of an affected State;

(6) 'Transboundary injury' means the effects defined above which constitute such injury.

Article 4

Liability

The State of origin shall have the obligations imposed on it by the present articles, provided that it knew or had means of knowing that the activity in question is carried out within its territory or in areas within its control and that it creates an appreciable risk of causing transboundary injury.[23]

The revisions to the preceding articles that Ambassador Barboza submitted in 1988 are as follows:

Article 1

Scope of the present articles

The present articles shall apply with respect to activities carried out under the jurisdiction of a State as vested in it by international law, or, in the absence of such jurisdiction, under the effective control of the State, when such activities create an appreciable risk of causing transboundary injury.

Article 2

Use of terms

For the purposes of the present articles:

(a) "Risk" means the risk occasioned by the use of substances whose physical properties, considered either intrinsically or in relation to the place, environment or way in which they are used, make them highly likely to cause transboundary injury throughout the process.

"Appreciable risk" means the risk which may be identified through a simple examination of the activity and the substances involved;

(b) "Activities involving risk" means the activities referred to in article 1;

(c) "Transboundary injury" means the effect which arises as a physical consequence of the activities referred to in article 1 and which, in spheres where another State exercises jurisdiction under international law, is appreciably detrimental to persons or objects, or to the use or enjoyment of areas, whether or not the States concerned have a common border;

(d) "Source State"[24] means the State which exercises the jurisdiction or the control referred to in article 1;

(e) "Affected State" means the State under whose jurisdiction persons or objects, or the use or enjoyment of areas, are or may be affected.

Article 3

Attribution

The source State shall have the obligations imposed on it by the present articles, provided that it knew or had means of knowing that an activity involving risk was being, or was about to be, carried out in areas under its jurisdiction or control.[25]

These articles, as well as the others proposed by Ambassador Barboza, raise a host of interesting and complex issues. This chapter will deal with only two of them: the requirement that the source State have "control" over the activity in question, and the question of whether a State from which hazardous technology is exported should be liable under the draft for injurious consequences of its use that are confined to the importing State.

The Requirement of Control

Article 1 as proposed by the special rapporteur in 1987 defines the scope of the draft *ratione materiae* as being confined to "activities or situations which occur within the territory *or* control of a State." Article 4, according to the special rapporteur,

. . . set[s] out two important conditions, both of which ha[ve] to be fulfilled to engage the liability which the articles impose[] on States: first, the State of origin ha[s] to have knowledge or the means of knowing that the activity in question was taking place or was about to take place in its territory, and, second, the activity create[s] an appreciable risk of transboundary injury.[26]

The special rapporteur found support for these conditions in the *Corfu Channel* case and the award in the *Trail Smelter* arbitration, "notwithstanding the opinion that these two decisions applied to cases of State responsibility for wrongful acts."[27] He explained further that, in his view,

The question of liability for prevention or reparation of harm would be subject to special review in cases of those developing countries with large territories or vast spaces such as the Exclusive Economic Zone, where the means for effective monitoring might be lacking.[28]

Finally, the special rapporteur emphasized the importance of the requirement that the activity be one which creates an "appreciable risk." He explained that this expression means "that the risk involved must be of some magnitude and must be clearly visible or easy to deduce from the properties of the things or materials used."[29] The fact that there was no such restriction in article 1, the general "scope" article, made the criterion a necessary element of article 4, in his view.

The revisions submitted by Ambassador Barboza in 1988 retain the approach just described, although the means vary somewhat. Revised article 1 defines the scope of the draft as being activities[30] occurring within the jurisdiction of a State or, in the absence of such jurisdiction, under the effective control of the State, when such activities create an appreciable risk of causing transboundary injury. The requirement of jurisdiction or control is thus maintained in article 1; the requirement of "appreciable risk" is moved to article 1[31] and thus does not appear in revised article 3 (which corresponds to article 4 of the 1987 draft);[32] and the definition of "appreciable risk" (as contained in revised article 2(a)) does not appear to have changed substantially.[33] Revised article 3 retains the requirement that obligations will be imposed under the draft only if the source State knew or had means of knowing of the activity in question.[34]

The effect of revised article 3 is still uncertain, because it only goes as far as providing that, even if the two conditions are satisfied, the source State "shall have the obligations imposed on it by the present articles." What those obligations will be remains to be seen. But assuming, as is likely, that they will include an obligation to make good losses suffered in the other State(s), the article would appear, to that extent, to provide for strict liability.[35] At least in terms of the way in which the Commission has organized its work, this construction would seem appropriate: the State responsibility topic covers internationally wrongful acts, while the question of liability without fault for injurious transfrontier consequences of activities that are lawful but may be considered "abnormally dangerous" or "ultrahazardous" is to be dealt with in the context of the International Liability topic.[36]

The issue of strict liability will be revisited later in this chapter. Even assuming that strict liability is the applicable standard of liability, however, the question arises whether the injurious activity must not only be located in the territory of the source State but must also be shown to be under the effective control of that State in order to engage its liability. For the purpose of this inquiry, "effective control" means not legal authority (since it is assumed that the State would have such authority with regard to activities within its territory) but the capability of the source State to regulate the activity in question effectively, that is, to manage the risk that the activity entails.

The wording of article 1 of the 1988 draft—which introduces the term "effective control" into Ambassador Barboza's draft articles[37]— suggests that effective control is not necessary if the activity occurs under the jurisdiction of the source State, because the term "effective control" appears only after the phrase "or, in the absence of . . . jurisdiction." Although that language does not expressly exclude the possibility that jurisdiction will be insufficient without effective control, Ambassador Barboza's commentary appears relatively specific on that point:

> When the activity is carried out in a State's own jurisdiction, there are no differences regarding the basis of attribution of liability between an activity carried out by the State and one carried out by private persons. In both cases, liability is attributed by virtue of the mere fact that the activities are carried out in areas under the State's jurisdiction.[38]

Even that comment may not be conclusive, however, because a State will presumably always have effective control over activities that it carries out itself.[39]

With respect to the 1987 draft, article 2 leaves little doubt that by the phrase "areas within its control" the special rapporteur had in mind, in particular, "maritime areas whose legal regime vests *jurisdiction* in [a coastal] State in respect of any matter."[40] Article 1 employs the expression "territory or control"; article 2 does offer a nonexhaustive definition of the expression "within the territory or control," but unfortunately provides no assistance in determining whether the term "control" includes the notion of *effective* regulation or control of an activity by the State of origin.[41] The corresponding provision of the schematic outline is somewhat more general, but brings us little closer to an answer.[42]

Indeed, it is fairly clear that the original special rapporteur used the term "control" in the sense of "jurisdiction" or "legal authority to regulate," rather than "ability to regulate." The word "control" was the result of Quentin-Baxter's search for a term that would encompass acts and injuries that occur outside of the territory of a State, but that nonetheless are committed in, or affect, a thing or area over which the State has some authority or in which it has an interest. Of course, the typical case to which the Liability topic is addressed involves an activity in one State that produces adverse consequences in another. But as Quentin-Baxter has pointed out,

> The distinction is [often] only quasi-territorial: for example, the activities of one State's ships on the high seas may give rise to incidental or accidental losses or injuries either to coastal States—in which case there is a literal transboundary element—or to other States which are users of the high seas—in which case the dividing line is between national jurisdictions.[43]

Quentin-Baxter then went on to note that the Commission had arrived at a consensus during its 1981 session "that the term which best describes the quasi-territorial dividing line is 'control' "; he explained that "this meaning is fixed by the use of the term in the composite phrase 'territory or control' " and then, in a statement of direct relevance to this chapter, declared: "The ambit of this phrase does not extend to matters in which the territorial jurisdiction of a receiving [affected] State is paramount."[44] Thus, the term "control" would not apply when the activity in question was situated within the territory of the source State. While subsequent paragraphs of his Third Report demonstrate that Quentin-Baxter was sensitive to the concerns of developing countries to which hazardous technology is exported,[45] it seems clear that the term "control," as used in the schematic outline, has little or nothing to do with the allocation of responsibility, as between an exporting and an importing country, for accidents caused by exported technology.

This review of the background of the articles presented to the Commission suggests that neither article 4 (1987) nor article 3 (its 1988 counterpart) may require that the harmful activity be under the effective control (as distinguished from the legal authority) of the source State in order for that State's liability to be engaged by the draft articles. This possibility was noticed in 1987 by at least one member of the

Commission, Chief Justice Razafindralambo of Madagascar, who made the following observations at that year's session:

[T]he concept of control had to be defined more clearly as far as private activities were concerned. . . . That question had arisen in the case of the activities of multinational corporations, in which it was often difficult to identify the authority that was actually in control. He had in mind, for example, the disaster which had occurred at a Union Carbide factory in Bhopal. The mere fact that a multinational corporation which exported investments and technology was located in the territory of a State was not enough automatically to entail the responsibility of that State, which actually had to be in control of the local subsidiary. He was therefore of the opinion that provision had to be made for the two-fold requirement of territory and control.[46]

This passage, while somewhat ambiguous, could be taken to mean that a State in the position of India would be liable for transfrontier consequences of a Bhopal-like disaster only if it had effective control of the local subsidiary whose plant emitted the noxious gas. Indeed, generally accepted norms of State responsibility would, in effect, hold a State responsible for the injurious consequences of private conduct only if the activity involved was or should have been under the effective control of that State.[47]

Such a requirement would seem no less appropriate in the context of the Liability topic. If effective control were not required, a State's mere knowledge of an activity within its territory or jurisdiction (e.g., the dumping of hazardous wastes) could engage its liability for injurious transfrontier consequences—even if the State were unable to prevent or otherwise control the activity. The effect of the special rapporteur's statement that "special review" would have to be given to cases involving "developing countries with large territories or vast spaces such as the Exclusive Economic Zone, where the means for effective monitoring might be lacking,"[48] is not entirely clear. If all that is meant is that the source State must have had the capability of "monitoring" the activity, this would seem to import no more than the "knowledge" requirement. If something more akin to an "effective control" requirement is intended for activities within a State's jurisdiction, this is not clear either from the text of the article or from the special rapporteur's explanation of it.

Should the Commission decide that effective control is a precondition to liability, the meaning of that requirement in a case such as Bhopal, as well as the effect of lack of compliance with it, will have to be examined. It seems clear that control presupposes, among other things, knowledge of the risks posed by the activity and the means to regulate or manage those risks effectively. The definition of "appreciable risk" contained in article 2 (1988) indicates that the special rapporteur intended article 3 to embody a "knowledge-of-risk" or "reason-to-know-of-risk" requirement.[49] But neither the articles thus far proposed by the current special rapporteur nor the schematic outline[50] contains a requirement that the source State have the means to regulate the risk involved. It would probably not be realistic to presume that a developing country would have this knowledge and capability in every case involving imported high technology,[51] although it is well established that a State must possess a legal and administrative structure that is sufficient to permit it to fulfill its obligations of "due diligence."[52] The position of developing countries was emphasized by several members of the Commission, whose concerns are succinctly summarized in the Commission's 1987 Report as follows:

> Other members stated that multinational corporations were at the forefront of the development and utilization of science and complex technology. These corporations often operated, beyond State control, as the result of financial power and the sole custody of knowledge on advanced science and technology. The developing countries were in a particularly disadvantageous position. They needed the multinational corporations to operate within their territory in order to generate some economic development; at the same time, they lacked the expertise to appreciate the magnitude of risk that the work of these corporations could cause and the power to compel the companies to disclose such risks. In this context, these developing countries were also victims. Their legitimate interest should therefore be taken into account.[53]

These considerations in turn raise the issue of "prior informed consent" and its variants (such as prior notification and impact assessment), which are beyond the scope of this chapter.[54]

If it is established, however, that the State of origin knew or should have known of the risk involved in the operation of the activity in question, and had the capability (in terms of expertise and infrastructure)[55] of regulating it but failed to do so adequately, that State could be found to have breached an obligation to other States to exercise due diligence in regulating or controlling the activity.[56] If found in breach of this obligation, the source State would have committed an internationally wrongful act and would be under a duty to make good the losses occasioned thereby.[57] Theoretically, however, such a situation would fall not within the study of International Liability, but within that of State responsibility which, as already noted, deals precisely with internationally *wrongful* acts.

These principles may be applied to a Bhopal-type fact situation as follows: If the Bhopal disaster had entailed injurious transfrontier consequences, and if the accident could be shown to be the result of India's breach of its obligation to exercise due diligence in regulating or controlling the plant to assure its safe operation, India could be found to be liable for the injurious transfrontier consequences under rules of State responsibility. The more difficult question is whether India would be liable for those consequences even if it had not breached an obligation of due diligence, that is, even if it had done all it could reasonably be expected to do to assure that the plant was operated safely and that the risk of transfrontier injury was properly minimized. This question lies at the heart of the Liability topic. It essentially asks whether States will be strictly liable for the injurious transfrontier consequences of certain kinds of activities—such as nuclear power plants and certain chemical plants—which, even when stringently regulated, pose a risk, albeit a very slight one, of causing disastrous consequences.

This question, which has aroused much controversy both in the Sixth Committee and in the Commission, has not yet been resolved.[58] Both special rapporteurs have clearly indicated that strict liability must form a part of the regime to be developed, at least as a last resort.[59] It seems clear that this position is correct, but it is equally clear that States would not accept unconditional liability without fault to an unlimited monetary extent. Some means of reasonably confining liability, in terms of both the conditions under which it will attach and its monetary extent, must therefore be devised. The procedures set forth in the schematic outline, which are designed to produce a negotiated regime for compensation, offer a sound basis for this effort. It remains to be seen whether the Commission will be able to reach agreement on such a system, or whether it will retreat to the field of internationally wrongful acts.

The "Transfrontier" Element

A second issue that should be touched upon is whether the rules developed by the Commission on International Liability will apply to a case in which technology exported from one State to another causes harmful consequences wholly within the territory of the latter State. The suggestion was made by one member of the Commission at its 1987 session that the Liability draft should provide that a State, such as the United States, would be liable for disasters such as that which occurred at Bhopal. The proposition advanced is thus, in essence, that a State in which a multinational corporation (MNC) is incorporated or headquartered or from which hazardous technology is exported (the "home" or "exporting" State) should be liable for injurious consequences in another State (the "host" or "importing" State) caused either by the operation there of a plant by a subsidiary of the MNC or by the imported technology. In this scenario the "transfrontier" element would consist not of pollution crossing a border, but of the export of hazardous substances or technology. This argument was based in part upon the premise that developing countries lack the "means of knowing" whether activities exported from developed countries by MNCs entail "an appreciable risk of causing transboundary harm," as required by the draft articles. The argument is that "the State of nationality of the corporation [the home state], which did have the means of knowing the risk[,] should be held liable for the damage caused."[60]

As indicated earlier, several members of the Commission were indeed concerned about the ability of developing countries to exercise effective control over imported hazardous substances and technology.[61] The question is whether this concept means that, in a Bhopal-like situation, the Commission's rules on International Liability should provide that the home or exporting State would be liable for the disaster's wholly domestic injurious consequences. To put the question another way, should the United States or India be considered the "source State" under draft article 3 in a case such as Bhopal?

If the question were whether the United States could be found liable under contemporary international law for the injuries occasioned by the Bhopal disaster, the short answer, in my view, would be "no." Although an internationally sanctioned regime may be necessary to regulate the transfer of hazardous technology,[62] it seems far-fetched and even undesirable to suggest that general international law obligates an MNC's home state to decide what kinds of technology may be exported to developing countries such as India, and the conditions under which it will allow such export.[63] The paternalistic overtones of such an approach would doubtless be unwelcomed by developing countries.[64]

Of course, whether the rules being elaborated by the Commission in its work on the international liability topic *should* provide for the liability of technology-exporting countries under these circumstances is a separate question. It is clear enough that the Commission did not have this question in mind when it originally framed the liability topic.[65] Instead, the topic was conceived as "regulating liability for the dangers inherent in certain major fields of activity made possible by modern technology."[66] Thus, the liability draft was originally intended to cover such situations as the Chernobyl disaster (assuming the Soviet Union in that case did not commit an internationally wrongful act, e.g., by failing to regulate the nuclear plant adequately). It is doubtful that significant world order values would be served by extending the topic to cover situations such as Bhopal. Several points seem worthy of consideration in this connection.

First, a factor that cannot be ignored is that a regime that would make the home State of the exporter liable in cases such as Bhopal would most likely be unacceptable to any technology-exporting country—and this includes developing countries, such as India, that export technology. The fashioning of rules that would not be acceptable to the very States they would principally affect would do little to advance the rule of law in this field. Second, under what circumstances could the exporting State be said to have "control" over technology that has been exported? In the absence of agreement with the importing State, it would not have the right to exercise effective control over the technology since this would amount to an interference with the sovereignty of the importing State. Not even expansive theories of extraterritorial jurisdiction could justify such a right to control.

Finally, what would be the economic and social consequences of such an extension of the topic? Among other things, imposing liability upon the State from which hazardous technology is exported would tend to discourage that State from allowing such exports, or at least would lead to an imposition of much stricter controls upon the kinds of technology that could be exported, and upon the operation of the MNC in the developing country to which the technology is exported. This situation would make it more expensive for multinationals to operate in the Third World and would thus result in shifting jobs (and other wealth-producing activities) from the developing South back to the industrialized North, which would hardly seem to represent a net gain efficiency of resource allocation or in the world-order values of development and self-determination.

The question the Commission must confront (and with which it is best equipped to deal) is the following: where an activity in one State, which is lawful and properly regulated, nevertheless goes awry, producing injurious transfrontier consequences of a physical nature in another State, should the second State, which is entirely "innocent" or blameless, be left to bear its loss alone?[67] The various solutions to this problem range from imposing strict liability solely upon the source State to some form of cost-sharing, perhaps in pursuance of a prearranged regime. It seems doubtful that the Commission would be well advised (or even that the General Assembly intended for the ILC) to venture beyond the original conception of the topic, which was mapped by the Commission at the outset of its work, into the stormy and uncharted seas that swirl about the question of liability of technology-exporting States.

International Watercourses

The discussion of International Watercourses will be brief, as the Commission has as yet devoted little attention to the aspect of the topic dealing with pollution. By way of background, the Commission began work on the topic in 1974, but progress has been slowed by the fact that there have been four different special rapporteurs between that year and 1989. In 1980, the Commission provisionally adopted six introductory articles on watercourses under the rapporteurship of Stephen Schwebel, but these were reopened by his successor as special rapporteur, Jens Evensen. Minister (now Judge) Evensen presented a complete draft convention on the topic to the Commission in 1983, but resigned from the Commission (on his election to the International Court of Justice) before the ILC was able to adopt even one of his articles. In 1987 (under the rapporteurship of the present author), the Commission again provisionally adopted the first six articles of the draft, four of which are of an introductory nature and two of which are substantive. The latter (articles 6 and 7) concern equitable and reasonable utilization and participation, and factors relevant to equitable and reasonable utilization. In 1988, the Commission provisionally adopted 14 additional articles.[68]

A landmark in the Commission's work on International Watercourses is the Third Report of Judge Schwebel.[69] The special rapporteur began work on this report prior to his election to the World Court, but submitted it thereafter, for the consideration of a successor rapporteur and of the Commission. The report provides the foundation for the work that has followed and contains a wealth of material spanning the entire topic. This report contained a draft article on "Environmental Pollution and Protection," which will be set forth here in pertinent part because it has influenced the drafts prepared by subsequent rapporteurs:

Article 10

Environmental protection and pollution

1. For the purposes of this article, 'pollution' means any introduction by man, directly or indirectly, of substances, species or energy into the waters of an international watercourse system which results in effects detrimental to human health or safety, to the use of the waters for any beneficial purpose, or to the conservation or protection of the environment.

. . .

3. Consistent with article 6 on 'Equitable participation,' article 7 on 'Equitable use determinations' and article 8 on 'Responsibility for appreciable harm' of these articles, a system State is under a duty to maintain pollution of shared water resources at levels sufficiently low that no appreciable harm is caused in the territory of any other system State, provided that a system State is under no

duty to abate pollution emanating from another system State in order to avoid causing appreciable harm to a third system State as a result of such pollution, except in concert on an equitable basis with other system States.

. . .

5. At the request of any system State, the system States concerned shall consult with a view to preparing and approving lists of dangerous substances or species, the introduction of which into the waters of the international watercourse system shall be prohibited, limited, investigated or monitored, as appropriate.[70]

Provision is also made for "pollution or environmental emergenc[ies]." In the event of such an emergency, both the State in whose territory it originates and any State having knowledge of it are to notify all potentially affected States as rapidly as possible and take immediate mitigating action.[71]

The report submitted to the Commission at its 1988 session by the current special rapporteur contained three proposed articles relating to pollution of international watercourses.[72] But several articles bearing generally on the subject were provisionally adopted by the Commission in 1988, including most significantly article 8, which is one of the two most fundamental provisions of the draft (the other being article 6, on equitable and reasonable utilization). Article 8 contains a general, well-established rule of which subsequent provisions on harm from transboundary pollution will be specific applications.[73] Article 8 provides as follows:

Article 8

Obligation not to cause appreciable harm

Watercourse States shall utilize an international watercourse [system] in such a way as not to cause appreciable harm to other watercourse States.[74]

A problem that lies at the heart of article 8 is the relationship between the obligation not to cause appreciable harm through pollution of an international watercourse and the principle of equitable utilization (article 6).[75] That is, because of the limited carrying capacity of an international watercourse, it could conceivably be within State A's right to equitable utilization to cause State B pollution-related harm that is "appreciable" in character (as that term is used in the Watercourses draft). The relationship between the principles of "no appreciable harm" and "equitable utilization" has been discussed at length elsewhere[76] and will not be dwelt upon here. Suffice it to say that such discussions of the issue as occurred in the Commission prior to 1988 (which were very brief and preliminary) reveal that, as might be expected, opinions of members were divided.

Of the few members that addressed the issue, some believed that the "no harm" principle should prevail over that of equitable utilization. Under this view, a polluting State could not successfully defend a claim based on the no harm principle—that is, a claim that it had caused appreciable harm to another State through water pollution—by establishing that the pollution was within its rights of equitable utilization of the watercourse. Other members subscribed to precisely the opposite position. It is evident, on one hand, that the former position is the more "environmentally sound," in that it would make it unlawful for a State to pollute an international watercourse in a manner or to an extent that exceeds the "appreciable harm" threshold.[77] If, on the other hand, the equitable utilization principle were controlling, a greater amount or extent of pollution, in absolute terms, could theoretically be permissible.

When the Commission adopted article 8 in 1988, it decided that articles 6 and 8 should be complementary but that, at least *prima facie*, a use causing appreciable harm is not equitable. The Commission also recognized, however, that an equitable use may result in appreciable harm to a downstream State. In that event, the necessary accommodations would be reached by a specific agreement between the affected States.[78]

Other articles provisionally adopted by the Commission in 1988 that have implications for pollution are articles 9, 10, and 12 to 20. Articles 12 to 20 contain procedural rules applicable when a State plans measures that may have adverse effects (including pollution effects) on other watercourse States; those provisions will not be set forth here.[79] Article 9 lays down the duty to cooperate, including specifically the obligation to cooperate in protecting the watercourse:

Article 9
General obligation to co-operate

Watercourse States shall co-operate on the basis of sovereign equality, territorial integrity and mutual benefit in order to attain optimum utilization and adequate protection of an international watercourse [system].[80]

Article 10 deals with the regular exchange of information:

Article 10
Regular exchange of data and information

1. Pursuant to article 9, watercourse States shall on a regular basis exchange reasonably available data and information on the condition of the watercourse [system], in particular that of a hydrological, meteorological, hydrogeological and ecological nature, as well as related forecasts.

2. If a watercourse State is requested by another watercourse State to provide

data or information that is not reasonably available, it shall employ its best efforts to comply with the request but may condition its compliance upon payment by the requesting State of the reasonable costs of collecting and, where appropriate, processing such data or information.

3. Watercourse States shall employ their best efforts to collect and, where appropriate, to process data and information in a manner which facilitates its utilization by the other watercourse States to which it is communicated.[81]

Three articles dealing specifically with environmental protection, pollution, and related matters were submitted by the special rapporteur and discussed at the Commission's 1988 session. Two were referred to the Drafting Committee.[82] The third ("pollution or environmental emergencies")[83] will be revised by the special rapporteur and resubmitted as part of a general article on water-related incidents and emergencies.[84]

At its 1989 session, the Commission was unable to act on the two articles sent to the Drafting Committee in 1989, because of the priority given other topics. It seems almost certain that the Commission will eventually adopt an article on pollution of international watercourses; the only question is how strict the obligation embodied in that article will be.

It is safe to predict, however, that the Commission's draft will not make pollution of an international watercourse wrongful per se. Indeed, it is probable that mere pollution of an international watercourse is not prohibited by international law.[85] The question is one of degree. As with the topic of International Liability, it is likely that the Commission will endeavor to arrive at a formulation that allows States some flexibility. Making equitable utilization the controlling principle would accomplish this objective, but it does not appear likely that the Commission will adopt that approach, for two reasons. First, the Commission has interpreted the no-harm rule of article 8, adopted in 1988, as overriding the rule of equitable utilization (article 6) in the case of conflict. Second, many members have recognized that allowing a State to cause water pollution harm to another State in the name of equitable utilization would create the potential for abuse and would not promote values of pollution prevention and environmental protection. In any event, it is to be hoped that the balance that is ultimately struck will be one that recognizes the relationship between environmental protection and sustainable development.[86]

Conclusion

The current work of the International Law Commission on the topics of International Liability and International Watercourses raises a number of interesting questions relating to transfrontier pollution. Some of these issues, for example, that of "control" of an activity and that of the liability of an exporting State, pit the industrialized North against the developing South. Others, for example, that of strict liability and that of the standard to be applied to water pollution, would arise irrespective of the stage of development of the States involved. As we are reminded by the report of the World Commission on Environment and Development,[87] sustainable development—and, indeed, our survival as a species—is dependent upon major adjustments in the way humans view the world and societies function. It is hoped that the work of the International Law Commission will contribute, at least in a small way, to this process of adjustment.

Acknowledgments

This chapter was initially completed in March 1988. It has been updated to take into account developments at the 1988 and, to a lesser extent, the 1989 sessions of the International Law Commission.

Notes

1. The World Commission on Environment and Development was established by authority of U.N. General Assembly Resolution 38/161 of 1983.

2. WORLD COMMISSION ON ENVIRONMENT AND DEVELOPMENT, OUR COMMON FUTURE 2 (1987) [hereinafter OUR COMMON FUTURE], also published as U.N. Doc. A/42/427, Annex (1987).

3. *Id.* at 2–3. *See also* Environmental Perspective to the Year 2000 and Beyond, U.N. Doc. UNEP/GC.14/24, Annex II (1987), adopted by the Governing Council of UNEP, Decision 14/13, June 19, 1987, and by the U.N. General Assembly in Resolution 42/186 of Dec. 11, 1987, especially paras. 16, 20, and 21.

4. The 1972 United Nations Conference on the Human Environment was, of course, the watershed event which dramatized the world community's realization that it could no longer ignore environmental considerations and, in particular, the close relationship between environmental protection and sustainable development. *See* Report of the United Nations Conference on the Human Environment, June 16, 1972, U.N. Doc. A/CONF.48/14/Rev.1, *reprinted in* 11 I.L.M. 1416 (1972); and General Assembly Resolutions 2995 (XXVII), U.N. GAOR Supp. (No. 30), U.N. Doc. A/8730 (1972), and 2996 (XXVII), U.N. GAOR Supp. (No. 30), U.N. Doc. A/8730 (1972). *See also* Resolution on the World Charter for Nature, G.A. Res. 7, 36 U.N. GAOR Supp. (No. 51) at 17, U.N. Doc. A/51 (1982). The following preambular paragraphs are particularly pertinent: "The General Assembly, . . . Aware that: (a) Mankind is a part of nature and life depends on the uninterrupted functioning of natural systems which ensure the supply of energy and nutrients, [and that] (b) Civilization is rooted in nature, which has shaped human culture

and influenced all artistic and scientific achievement, and living in harmony with nature gives man the best opportunities for the development of his creativity, and for rest and recreation." *Id. See also* OUR COMMON FUTURE, *supra* note 2, especially at 2–9; Environmental Perspective to the Year 2000 and Beyond, *supra* note 3.

5. The World Commission on Environment and Development has emphasized the benefits and risks of high technology in the following terms: "A mainspring of economic growth is new technology, and while this technology offers the potential for slowing the dangerously rapid consumption of finite resources, it also entails high risks, including new forms of pollution and the introduction to the planet of new variations of life forms that could change evolutionary pathways." OUR COMMON FUTURE, *supra* note 2, at 4–5.

6. The International Law Commission of the United Nations (the Commission or ILC) is a group of 34 experts who serve in their individual capacities and who are charged with the codification and progressive development of international law. The Commission was established in 1947 by the General Assembly to carry out article 13, paragraph 1, of the U.N. Charter, which provides that the Assembly "shall initiate studies and make recommendations for the purpose of . . . encouraging the progressive development of international law and its codification." U.N. CHARTER, art. 13, para. 1. For a discussion of the extent to which a distinction can be drawn between codification and progressive development, see McCaffrey, *Codification and Progressive Development: Law and the World Environment*, 7 HARV. INT'L REV. 8 (1984).

7. The Commission selected State responsibility as one of the topics it considered suitable for codification at its first session in 1949. F.V. Garcia Amador was appointed the first special rapporteur for the topic at the Commission's 1955 session. He submitted six reports on the topic from 1956 to 1961. In 1963, the Commission reconsidered its approach to the topic and decided to embark upon a different course. Under this new approach, the Commission would not attempt to define the "primary" rules imposing obligations upon States, but would undertake to identify the "secondary" rules that determine the legal consequences of failure to fulfill obligations established by the "primary" rules. Roberto Ago was appointed special rapporteur in 1963, Garcia Amador no longer being a member of the Commission; Ago submitted his first report in 1969. On the basis of eight reports submitted by Ago, who is now a judge on the International Court of Justice, the Commission in 1980 completed the "first reading," or provisional adoption, of Part 1 of the draft, which is entitled "The Origin of International Responsibility." Since 1980, the Commission has been working on Part 2 of the draft, entitled "The Content, Forms and Degrees of International Responsibility." For a summary of the background of the Commission's work on State responsibility, and its status as of 1980, see UNITED NATIONS, THE WORK OF THE INTERNATIONAL LAW COMMISSION 80–88 (1980). Accounts of subsequent work may be found in the Commission's annual reports to the General Assembly. *See, e.g.,* Report of the International Law Commission on the Work of its Thirty-eighth Session, 41 U.N. GAOR Supp. (No. 10), U.N. Doc. A/41/10, [1986] 2 Y.B. INT'L L. COMM'N, pt. 2, at 35–39 (1987).

One aspect of the Commission's study of State responsibility deals expressly with pollution. Article 19(3)(d) of Part 1, in defining the controversial distinction between international crimes and international delicts, states that an international crime may result from "serious breach of an international obligation of essential importance for the safeguarding and preservation of the human environment, such as those prohibiting massive pollution of the atmosphere or the seas." Report of the International Law Commission on the Work of its Twenty-eighth Session, 31 U.N. GAOR Supp. (No. 10) at 175, U.N. Doc. A/31/10 (1976). Article 19(3)(d) was provisionally adopted by the Commission. Article 14 of Part 2, as proposed by the special rapporteur, would define some of the consequences of determining that an activity is an international crime. Report of the International Law Commission on the Work of its Thirty-fifth Session, 40 U.N. GAOR Supp. (No. 10) at 42, U.N. Doc. A/40/10 (1985).

For discussions of the Commission's studies of International Liability and State responsibility, see *Symposium on State Responsibility and Liability for Injurious Consequences Arising Out of Acts Not Prohibited by International Law*, 16 NETH. Y.B. INT'L L. XI–XVI, 1–300 (1985); Magraw, *Transboundary Harm: The International Law Commission's Study of "International Liability"*, 80 AM. J. INT'L L. 305 (1986).

8. *See* [1970] 2 Y.B. INT'L L. COMM'N 178.

9. [1977] 2 Y.B. INT'L L. COMM'N, pt. 2, at 6, U.N. Doc. A/CN.4/Ser.A/1977/Add.1.

10. Ago, Second Report on State Responsibility, [1970] 2 Y.B. INT'L L. COMM'N 178, U.N. Doc. A/CN.4/SER.A/1970/Add.1.

11. R. Q. Quentin-Baxter, Fourth Report on International Liability for Injurious Consequences Arising Out of Act Not Prohibited by International Law, U.N. Doc. A/CN.4/373, at 48 (1983), *reprinted in* [1983] 2 Y.B. INT'L L. COMM'N, pt. 1, at 201, 220 (1985) [hereinafter R. Q. Quentin-Baxter, Fourth Report]. Some members of the Commission, as well as some delegations in the Sixth (Legal) Committee of the General Assembly, had argued that the scope of the topic should extend, among other matters, to economic activities resulting in transboundary harm. Although scattered statements to this effect continue to be made in both fora, the current special rapporteur appears determined to keep the topic's scope confined to physical activities causing physical transfrontier harm. *See, e.g.*, Report of the International Law Commission on the Work of its Thirty-ninth Session, 42 U.N. GAOR Supp. (No. 10) at 102, paras. 154 & 155, U.N. Doc. A/42/10 (1987) [hereinafter 1987 ILC Report]; Topical Summary of the Discussion [of the ILC Report] Held in the Sixth Committee of the General Assembly During its Forty-second Session, Prepared by the Secretariat, U.N. Doc. A/CN.4/420, at 63, para. 214 (1988).

12. R. Q. Quentin-Baxter, Third Report on International Liability for Injurious Consequences Arising Out of Acts Not Prohibited by International Law, U.N. Doc. A/CN.4/360 and Corr. (1982), *reprinted in* [1982] 2 Y.B. INT'L L. COMM'N, pt. 1, at 51, 58, 59 [hereinafter R. Q. Quentin-Baxter, Third Report].

13. *Id.* at 60. Quentin-Baxter explained that he found it "hard to see how it could be otherwise, taking into account the realities of transboundary dangers and relations between States, and the existing elements of a developing chapter of international law." *Id.* But he pointed out that, "even at this final stage, the resort to strict liability is by no means automatic. The States concerned are compelled by nothing except the logic of their situations, the persuasiveness of the [guiding] principles in section 5 [of the outline], and the need to pay for damage done if no better arrangement can be worked out." *Id.*

14. *See* Report of the International Law Commission on the Work of its Fortieth Session, 43 U.N. GAOR Supp. (No. 10), U.N. Doc. A/43/10 (1988) [hereinafter 1988 ILC Report].

At the ILC's 1989 session, the special rapporteur submitted a revised set of nine introductory articles that were intended to replace the ten referred to the Drafting Committee in 1988. *See* J. Barboza, Fifth Report on International Liability for Injurious Consequences Arising Out of Acts Not Prohibited by International law, U.N. Doc. A/CN.4/423 and Corr. 1 & 2 (1989) [hereinafter J. Barboza, Fifth Report]. These nine articles were themselves referred to the Drafting Committee at the Commission's 1989 session. *See* Report of the International Law Commission on the Work of its Forty-first Session, 44 U.N. GAOR Supp. (No. 10) at 221, U.N. Doc. A/44/10 (1989) [hereinafter 1989 ILC Report]. The nine articles are reprinted *infra* in note 22.

15. For a description of the current status of the Commission's work on the topic, see 1989 ILC Report, *supra* note 14.

16. *See* 1987 ILC Report, *supra* note 11, at 89 et seq.

17. *See* 1988 ILC Report, *supra* note 14, at 10–44; 1989 ILC Report, *supra* note 14, at 221–57.

18. This question was raised by the special rapporteur in his 1989 report and discussed in the Commission. The discussion was inconclusive, but the special rapporteur indicated that he would study the matter further and report to the ILC in 1990. 1989 ILC Report, *supra* note 14, at 242.

19. *See, e.g.*, 1987 ILC Report, *supra* note 11, at 111, para. 183. *See also* J. Barboza, Second Report on International Liability for Injurious Consequences Arising Out of Acts Not Prohibited by International Law, U.N. Doc. A/CN.4/402, paras. 51–54 (1986). This is not to suggest that Quentin-Baxter did not call attention to the importance of prevention. *See, e.g.*, R. Q. Quentin-Baxter, Third Report, *supra* note 12, at 53.

20. J. Barboza, Third Report on International Liability for Injurious Consequences Arising Out of Acts Not Prohibited by International Law, U.N. Doc. A/CN.4/405 and Corr. 1 & 2 (1987) [hereinafter J. Barboza, Third Report].

21. J. Barboza, Fourth Report on International Liability for Injurious Consequences Arising Out of Acts Not Prohibited by International Law, U.N. Doc. A/CN.4/413, at 6 (1988) [hereinafter J. Barboza, Fourth Report].

22. As submitted by special rapporteur Barboza in 1989 and referred to the Drafting Committee that same year, articles 1–9 read as follows:

"Chapter I, General Provisions, *Article 1, Scope of the present articles*: The present articles shall apply with respect to activities carried out in the territory of a State or in other places under its jurisdiction as recognized by international law or, in the absence of such jurisdiction, under its control, when the physical consequences of such activities cause, or create an appreciable risk of causing, transboundary harm throughout the process.

"*Article 2, Use of terms*: For the purposes of the present articles:

"(a) 'Risk' means the risk occasioned by the use of things whose physical properties, considered either intrinsically or in relation to the place, environment or way in which they are used, make them likely to cause transboundary harm throughout the process, notwithstanding any precautions which might be taken in their regard.

"'Appreciable risk' means the risk which may be identified through a simple examination of the activity and the substance involved, in relation to the place, environment or way in which they are used, and includes both the low probability of very considerable (disastrous) transboundary harm and the high probability of minor appreciable harm.

"(b) 'Activities involving risk' means the activities referred to in the preceding paragraph, in which harm is contingent, and 'activities with harmful effects' means those causing appreciable transboundary harm throughout the process.

"(c) 'Transboundary harm' means the effect which arises as a physical consequence of the activities referred to in article 1 and which, in the territory or in places under the jurisdiction or control of another State, is appreciably detrimental to persons or objects, to the use or enjoyment of areas or to the environment, whether or not the States concerned have a common border. Under the regime of these articles, 'transboundary harm' always refers to 'appreciable harm.'

"(d) 'State of origin' means the State in whose territory or in places under whose jurisdiction or control the activities referred to in article 1 take place.

"(e) 'Affected State' means the State in whose territory or under whose jurisdiction persons or objects, the use or enjoyment of areas, or the environment, are or may be appreciably affected.

"*Article 3, Assignment of obligations*: The State of origin shall have the obligations established by the present articles, provided that it knew or had means of knowing that an activity referred to in article 1 was being, or was about to be, carried out in its territory or in other places under its jurisdiction or control.

"Unless there is evidence to the contrary, it shall be presumed that the State of origin has the knowledge or the means of knowing referred to in the preceding paragraph.

"*Article 4, Relationship between the present articles and other international agreements*: Where States Parties to the present articles are also parties to another international agreement concerning activities referred to in article 1, in relations between such States the present articles shall apply, subject to that other international agreement.

"*Article 5* [The special rapporteur proposed two alternatives for article 5. *Ed.*], *Absence of effect upon other rules of international law*: [The fact that the present articles do not specify circumstances in which the occurrence of transboundary harm arises from a wrongful act or omission of the State of origin shall be without prejudice to the operation of any other rule of international law.]

"[The present articles are without prejudice to the operation of any other rule of international law establishing liability for transboundary harm resulting from a wrongful act.]

"Chapter II, Principles, *Article 6, Freedom of action and the limits thereto*: The sovereign freedom of States to carry out or permit human activities in their territory or in other places under their jurisdiction or control must be compatible with the protection of the rights emanating from the sovereignty of other States.

"*Article 7, Co-operation*: States shall co-operate in good faith among themselves, and request the assistance of any international organizations that might be able to help them, in trying to prevent any activities referred to in article 1 carried out in their territory or in other places under their jurisdiction or control from causing transboundary harm. If such harm occurs, the State of origin shall co-operate with the affected State in minimizing its effects. In the event of harm caused by an accident, the affected State shall, if possible, also co-operate with the State of origin with regard to any harmful effects which may have arisen in the territory of the State of origin or in other places under its jurisdiction or control.

"*Article 8, Prevention*: States of origin shall take appropriate measures to prevent or, where necessary, minimize the risk of transboundary harm. To that end they shall, in so far as they are able, use the best practicable, available means with regard to activities referred to in article 1.

"*Article 9, Reparation*: To the extent compatible with the present articles, the State of origin shall make reparation for appreciable harm caused by an activity referred to in article 1. Such reparation shall be decided by negotiation between the State of origin and the affected State or States and shall be guided, in principle, by the criteria set forth in these articles, bearing in mind in particular that reparation should seek to restore the balance of interests affected by the harm." 1989 ILC Report, *supra* note 14, at 222–25 (note replaced with editor's note to article 5).

The text of these revised articles is included for the reader's information. The submission of the newly revised articles and the ILC's discussion of them occurred at a point in the publication process that was too late to permit their detailed consideration in this chapter. It will perhaps suffice to note that under the 1989 version of article 1, the scope of the topic is no longer limited to activities involving risk; it also includes those that cause transboundary harm even if they did not create a risk (as that term is defined in article 2(a) [1989]) of causing such harm. Both harm and risk are limited to those that are "appreciable." *See id.* at 225–26.

23. J. Barboza, Third Report, *supra* note 20, at 4–5; 1987 ILC Report, *supra* note 11, at 90–91.

24. A footnote appears at this point in Ambassador Barboza's text contrasting the use of the terms "source State" and "State of origin." J. Barboza, Fourth Report, *supra* note 21, at 7. No substantive difference is evident.

25. *Id.* at 6–7; 1988 ILC Report, *supra* note 14, at 10–13. Articles 1, 2, and 3 appear in Chapter 1, General Provisions.

26. 1987 ILC Report, *supra* note 11, at 94.

27. *Id.* The special rapporteur stated his view of the effect of those decisions in the following terms: "In the *Trail Smelter* case, the State of origin could be declared liable even though all the precautions imposed by the regime established by the Court had been taken if by accident the level of pollution passed over a certain limit; in the *Corfu Channel* case there was no reason why the presumption that a State had knowledge of everything that was happening in its territory should be limited to responsibility for wrongful acts." *Id.* The *Corfu Channel* case is also discussed in the special rapporteur's Fourth Report, *supra* note 21, at 24–26.

28. 1987 ILC Report, *supra* note 11, at 94. The quoted statement was elaborated upon somewhat in Ambassador Barboza's Fourth Report, *supra* note 21, at 25.

29. 1987 ILC Report, *supra* note 11, at 95.

30. The reference to "situations" was removed, but that does not affect the analysis in the text.

31. That requirement is also retained in article 1 of the 1989 version. *See supra* note 22.

32. The concept of "appreciable risk" also appears in article 1 of the 1989 version. *See supra* note 22.

33. *Compare* the definition of "appreciable risk" (which presumably incorporates the immediately preceding definitions of "risk") in revised article 2(a) in J.

Barboza, Fourth Report, *supra* note 21, *with* Ambassador Barboza's 1987 explanation of "appreciable risk," *supra* text accompanying note 29. *See also* J. Barboza, Fourth Report, *supra* note 21, at 11–14, 29.

34. The version of article 3 submitted in 1989 contains a new second paragraph which creates a presumption, unless there is contrary evidence, that the State of origin has the knowledge or the means of knowing about activities in its territory or under its jurisdiction or control. 1989 ILC Report, *supra* note 14, at 224. Article 3 (1989) is reprinted in note 22, *supra*.

35. Article 10 (1988) concerns reparation generally, but does not contain details about the nature or extent of the reparation that will ultimately be required. *See* 1988 ILC Report, *supra* note 14, at 12–13. The same is the case with article 9 (1989). *See supra* note 22.

36. The discussion of the Liability topic in 1988 seemed to indicate a trend within the Commission not to restrict the scope of the topic to international liability for nonprohibited activities, but to broaden the scope to include all liability for transboundary harm.

37. The draft articles do not define "effective control." Ambassador Barboza states in the commentary: "article 1, when it states 'activities . . . under the effective control,' aims to cover not only activities carried out in territories over which a State has *de facto* jurisdiction, but also activities carried out by the State itself in any jurisdiction, its own or another jurisdiction." J. Barboza, Fourth Report, *supra* note 21, at 22. For discussions of the term "control," see *id*. at 10 & 21.

The term "effective" does not appear in the 1989 version of article 1. *See supra* note 22. The special rapporteur explained that the word "was deleted . . . because it was felt that unless control was effective it was not control." J. Barboza, Fifth Report, *supra* note 14, at 13.

38. J. Barboza, Fourth Report, *supra* note 21, at 22–23.

39. Regardless of whether the requisite jurisdiction or effective control exists, there is an unresolved question of how to treat force majeure. *See id*. at 12.

40. 1987 ILC Report, *supra* note 11, at 91 (emphasis added). The special rapporteur also mentioned activities "in territories under hostile occupation, or in Mandated, Trust or Non-Self-Governing Territories." He noted that "the concept of 'territory' does not cover such situations." J. Barboza, Fourth Report, *supra* note 21, at 10.

41. As used in the proposed 1987 articles, the term "control" is evidently intended to cover situations in which the activity in question is not situated within the territory of the source State but is within its control by virtue of its being within the jurisdiction of that State. Examples are activities in maritime areas under the jurisdiction of the State, and ships flying the flag of, or space objects registered in, the State. 1987 ILC Report, *supra* note 11, at 91, art. 2(2)(a)–(b). In article 1 as proposed in 1988, quoted *supra* at text accompanying note 24, the special rapporteur uses the term "effective control." Regarding the 1989 version of article 1, see *supra* note 36.

42. Section 1, part 2(d) of the schematic outline provides in part as follows: "(d) 'Territory or control' includes, *in relation to places not within the territory of the acting State*, (i) any activity which takes place within the substantial control of that State. . . ." R. Q. Quentin-Baxter, Third Report, *supra* note 12, at 62 (emphasis added).

43. *Id*. at 60 (footnote omitted).

44. *Id.* (footnote omitted).

45. *See*, in particular, *id.* at 60–61, para. 45. Quentin-Baxter here recognizes that "developing countries may lack the experience and high technology skills to regulate such an activity effectively." He continues: "Quite conceivably, there are situations of this kind in which the 'exporting' State should be prepared to share with the receiving State authority and responsibility for the establishment and monitoring of appropriate technical standards; the arrangements made might have a bearing upon the definition and application of the term 'control.'" *Id.* at 61. Even here, however, Quentin-Baxter stops short of applying the term "control" to such situations.

46. Provisional Summary Record of the 2019th Meeting of the International Law Commission, June 23, 1987, U.N. Doc. A/CN.4/SR.2019, at 21 (July 6, 1987).

47. *See, e.g.*, P.-M. Dupuy, *International Liability of States for Damage Caused by Transfrontier Pollution*, in OECD, LEGAL ASPECTS OF TRANSFRONTIER POLLUTION 345, 354 (1977). Dupuy observes that "it has to be established whether the private person's action completely eluded the controls which the State authorities might be expected to maintain, or whether on the contrary, it meant that those authorities maintained insufficient control of polluting activity (or whether the country's legislation was unsuitable)." *Id.* A country's legislation could be found to be "unsuitable," according to Dupuy, if it "proved to be at variance with the criteria normally adopted by the other States or ignored the standards defined jointly by countries co-operating in international organisations." *Id.* at note 2.

It is important to note that we are not concerned here with "attribution" of private conduct to the State, strictly speaking. According to article 8(a) of the Draft Articles on State Responsibility provisionally adopted by the International Law Commission, the acts of private persons will be attributed to a State only "if it is established that those persons were in fact acting on behalf of the State." [1980] 2 Y.B. INT'L L. COMM'N, pt. 2, at 30–34, U.N. Doc. A/CN.4/SER.A/1980/Add.1.

See also Handl, *State Liability for Accidental Transnational Environmental Damage by Private Persons*, 74 AM. J. INT'L L. 525, 527, 558 (1980); *cf.* Principle 21 of the Stockholm Declaration on the Human Environment, Report of the Stockholm Conference, U.N. Doc. A/CONF.48/14, at 7, *reprinted in* 11 I.L.M. 1416, 1420 (1972).

48. *See supra* text accompanying note 28.

49. *See supra* text accompanying notes 29–33.

50. At least as interpreted by Quentin-Baxter: see the treatment of the expression "territory or control" in his Third Report, *supra* note 12, at 60–61, discussed *supra* in text accompanying notes 43–44.

51. *Cf.* the statement of Quentin-Baxter quoted *supra* note 45.

52. *See* Dupuy, *Due Diligence in the International Law of Liability*, OECD Doc. ENV/TFP/76.11, *reprinted in* OECD, LEGAL ASPECTS OF TRANSFRONTIER POLLUTION 369 (1977); S. McCaffrey, Fourth Report on the Law of the Non-Navigational Uses of International Watercourses, U.N. Doc. A/CN.4/412/Add.2, nn. 278–301 and accompanying text (1988) [hereinafter S. McCaffrey, Fourth Report]. The applicability of the principle of due diligence is discussed *infra* at text accompanying notes 55–58.

53. 1987 ILC Report, *supra* note 11, at 101, para. 151.

54. *See, e.g.*, Walls, *Chemical Exports and the Age of Consent: The High Cost of*

International Export Control Proposals, 20 N.Y.U. J. Int'l L. & Pol'y 753 (1988). The environment ministers of the European Community recently rejected prior informed consent as the basis for regulations concerning the import and export of dangerous chemicals. The ministers decided instead on a regime of prior notification. [10 Current Report] Int'l Env't Rep. (BNA) 639 (Dec. 9, 1987). *See also* "London Guidelines for the Exchange of Information on Chemicals in International Trade," developed by the Ad Hoc Working Group of Experts for the Exchange of Information on Potentially Harmful Chemicals (in particular pesticides) of the United Nations Environment Programme (UNEP), U.N. Doc. UNEP/GC/14/17, annex IV; UNEP Governing Council decision 14/27, "Environmentally safe management of chemicals, in particular those that are banned and severely restricted in international trade," in UNEP, Report of the Governing Council on the work of its fourteenth session, June 8–19, 1987, U.N. GAOR Supp. (No. 25), U.N. Doc. A/42/25 (1987) (requesting the Executive Director of UNEP to "convene an *Ad Hoc* Working Group of Experts with a view to: (a) Developing modalities of prior informed consent and other approaches which could usefully supplement the modalities of the London Guidelines"); Principles and Guidelines for the Safe Transfer of Technology, Apr. 15, 1987, prepared by the European Council of Chemical Industry Federations, Ave. Louise 250, Bte. 71, 1050 Bruxelles, Belgium.

55. Creation by a State of a risk of substantial transboundary harm, where the State lacks adequate infrastructure to control the risk, may itself constitute a breach of an international obligation. *See supra* note 44 and accompanying text.

56. On the requirement of due diligence, see Dupuy, *supra* note 52, and Handl, *supra* note 47, at 540 (citing the resolution of the Institute of International Law on The Pollution of Rivers and Lakes and International Law, arts. II and III(1), adopted at the Athens session of the Institute, Sept. 4–13, 1979). *See also supra* note 47.

57. If the Bhopal accident had caused transfrontier injuries, the determination of whether India had breached this obligation could properly take into account India's ability to foresee risks and to regulate them. This would seem to be implicit in the notion of "due" diligence, which may be taken to refer not only to the amount of care required under the circumstances, but also to the characteristics and capabilities of the State involved. If India had no means of knowing of the risk, or if it had done all that it could reasonably have been expected to do under the circumstances, it would presumably not be found in breach of this duty.

58. *See* 1987 ILC Report, *supra* note 11, at 111–13.

59. *See* R. Q. Quentin-Baxter, Third Report, *supra* note 12, at 60. *But cf.* R. Q. Quentin-Baxter, Fourth Report, *supra* note 11, at 218 (sounding cautionary notes, exemplified by the following passage: "However, it should also be borne in mind that, in making the leap to the strict liability of the State, legal doctrine falters and models in State practice are few"). Ambassador Barboza's views are summarized in 1987 ILC Report, *supra* note 11, at 113.

60. Provisional Summary Record of the 2016th Meeting of the International Law Commission, 17 June 1987, U.N. Doc. A/CN.4/SR.2016, at 9, 14 (1987) (statement of Professor B. Graefrath of the German Democratic Republic).

61. *See supra* text accompanying note 52.

62. *See generally* The Transfer of Hazardous Substances and Technology: The International Legal Challenge (G. Handl & R. Lutz eds. 1989);

McGarity, *Bhopal and the Export of Hazardous Technologies*, 20 Tex. Int'l L.J. 333 (1985).

63. This is not intended to suggest that States have no responsibilities whatsoever concerning the export of hazardous materials, products, or processes. The *Trail Smelter* award (U.S. v. Can.), 3 R. Int'l Arb. Awards 1905, 1965 (1938 & 1941), and Principle 21 of the Stockholm Declaration on the Human Environment, Report of the United Nations Conference on the Human Environment, June 16, 1972, U.N. Doc. A/CONF.48/14, at 7, *reprinted in* 11 I.L.M. 1416, 1420 (1972), suggest that a State may, under some circumstances at least, be obligated to inform the importing country of known risks associated with the exported items. The exact contours of this duty, and the relative burdens on the exporting and importing states, are less clear. This area is presently undergoing rapid development, especially with regard to hazardous wastes. *See also supra* note 53.

64. This is the main problem with the "high road" approach to the problem of exportation of hazardous technology described by Thomas McGarity. McGarity, *supra* note 62, at 335. Under this approach, all operations of multinational corporations would be subjected to the standards applicable in the source State (in the Bhopal case, the United States). McGarity observes that "[p]roponents of the 'high road' . . . are subject to the charge of 'economic imperialism,'" because this approach would have the effect, among other things, of discouraging the export of jobs. *Id.*

65. *See supra* text accompanying notes 9 and 10; more particularly, Report of the Working Group on International Liability for Injurious Consequences Arising Out of Acts Not Prohibited by International Law, U.N. Doc. A/CN.4/L.284 and Corr. 1, *reprinted in* [1978] 2 Y.B. Int'l L. Comm'n 150, pt. 2, U.N. Doc. A/CN.4/SER.A/1978/Add.1.

66. *Id.*, [1978] 2 Y.B. Int'l L. Comm'n at 151.

67. *See* 1987 ILC Report, *supra* note 11, at 100–101.

68. For discussions of these articles, see McCaffrey, *The Fortieth Session of the International Law Commission*, 83 Am. J. Int'l L. 153, 160 (1989); 1988 ILC Report, *supra* note 14, at 75–139.

69. S. Schwebel, Third Report on the Law of the Non-Navigational Uses of International Watercourses, [1982] 2 Y.B. Int'l L. Comm'n (Part One) 65 (1984).

70. *Id.* at 144–45. The article contains 14 paragraphs.

71. *Id.* at 145, art. 10, para. 9.

72. *See* S. McCaffrey, Fourth Report, *supra* note 52.

73. *See* 1988 ILC Report, *supra* note 14, at 92.

74. *Id.* at 78.

75. Article 6 provides: "*Equitable and reasonable utilization and participation*: 1. Watercourse States shall in their respective territories utilize an international watercourse [system] in an equitable and reasonable manner. In particular, an international watercourse [system] shall be used and developed by watercourse States with a view to attaining optimum utilization thereof and benefits therefrom consistent with adequate protection of the international watercourse [system].

"2. Watercourse States shall participate in the use, development and protection of an international watercourse [system] in an equitable and reasonable manner. Such participation includes both the right to utilize the international watercourse [system] as provided in paragraph 1 of this article and the duty to co-operate in the protection and development thereof, as provided in article. . . ." *Id.* at 77.

76. *See, e.g.,* S. McCaffrey, Second Report on the Law of the Non-Navigational Uses of International Watercourses, U.N. Doc. A/CN.4/399 and Add. 1 & 2, at Add. 2, 1–3; Handl, *National Uses of Transboundary Air Resources: The International Entitlement Issue Reconsidered,* 26 NAT. RES. J. 405, 409–27 (1986); McCaffrey, *The Law of International Watercourses: Some Recent Developments and Unanswered Questions,* 17 DEN. J. INT'L L. & POL'Y 505, 508–10 (1989).

77. This is the view subscribed to by Handl in the article cited *supra* note 76.

78. 1988 ILC Report, *supra* note 14, at 84. For discussions of the standard of liability and the requirement of "appreciable" harm, see McCaffrey, *supra* note 68, at 164–65.

79. For the text of articles 11–21 and some commentary, see McCaffrey, *supra* note 68, at 161–66; 1988 ILC Report, *supra* note 14, at 79–82, 114–39.

80. 1988 ILC Report, *supra* note 14, at 78.

81. *Id.* at 78–79.

82. These two draft articles, as proposed, read as follows: "*Pollution of international watercourse[s] [systems]*: 1. As used in these draft articles, 'pollution' means any physical, chemical or biological alteration in the composition or quality of the waters of an international watercourse [system] which results directly or indirectly from human conduct and which produces effects detrimental to human health or safety, to the use of the waters for any beneficial purpose or to the conservation or protection of the environment.

"2. Watercourse States shall not cause or permit the pollution of an international watercourse [system] in such a manner or to such an extent as to cause appreciable harm to other watercourse States or to the ecology of the international watercourse [system].

"3. At the request of any watercourse State, the watercourse States concerned shall consult with a view to preparing and approving lists of substances or species, the introduction of which into the waters of the international watercourse [system] is to be prohibited, limited, investigated or monitored, as appropriate.

"*Protection of the environment of international watercourse[s] [systems]*: 1. Watercourse States shall, individually and in co-operation, take all reasonable measures to protect the environment of an international watercourse [system], including the ecology of the watercourse and of surrounding areas, from impairment, degradation or destruction, or serious danger thereof, due to activities within their territories.

"2. Watercourse States shall, individually or jointly and on an equitable basis, take all measures necessary, including preventive, corrective and control measures, to protect the marine environment, including estuarine areas and marine life, from any impairment, degradation or destruction, or serious danger thereof, occasioned through an international watercourse [system]." S. McCaffrey, Fourth Report, *supra* note 52, at Add. 2, 21–22.

83. This draft article, as proposed, reads as follows: "*Pollution or environmental emergencies*: 1. As used in this article, 'pollution or environmental emergency' means any situation affecting an international watercourse [system] which poses a serious and immediate threat to health, life, property or water resources.

"2. If a condition or incident affecting an international watercourse [system] results in a pollution or environmental emergency, the watercourse State within whose territory the condition or incident has occurred shall forthwith notify all potentially affected watercourse States, as well as any competent international organization, of the emergency and provide them with all available data and information relevant to the emergency.

"3. The watercourse State within whose territory the condition or incident has occurred shall take immediate action to prevent, neutralize or mitigate the danger or damage to other watercourse States resulting therefrom." *Id.* at 23.

84. This draft article, submitted in the special rapporteur's 1989 report, reads as follows: *"Article 23, Water-related dangers and emergency situations*: 1. A watercourse State shall, without delay and by the most expeditious means available, notify other, potentially affected States and relevant intergovernmental organizations of any water-related danger or emergency situation originating in its territory, or of which it has knowledge. The expression "water-related danger or emergency situation" includes those that are primarily natural, such as floods, and those that result from human activities, such as toxic chemical spills and other dangerous pollution incidents.

"2. A watercourse State within whose territory a water-related danger or emergency situation originates shall immediately take all practical measures to prevent, neutralize or mitigate the danger or damage to other watercourse States resulting from the danger or emergency.

"3. States in the area affected by a water-related danger or emergency situation, and the competent international organizations, shall co-operate in eliminating the causes and effects of the danger or situation and in preventing or minimizing harm therefrom, to the extent practicable under the circumstances.

"4. In order to fulfil effectively their obligations under paragraph 3 of this article, watercourse States, together with other potentially affected States, shall jointly develop, promote and implement contingency plans for responding to water-related dangers or emergency situations." S. McCaffrey, Fifth Report on the Law of the Non-Navigational Uses of International Watercourses, U.N. Doc. A/CN.4/421 and Add. 1 & 2 (1989); 1989 ILC Report, *supra* note 14, 342–43.

85. To this effect, see Sette-Camara, *Pollution of International Rivers*, 186 REC. DES COURS 117, 160, 163.

86. *See, e.g.*, OUR COMMON FUTURE, *supra* note 2, at 9, 13–17; *supra* Chapter 2.

87. OUR COMMON FUTURE, *supra* note 2.

Chapter 5
State Responsibility and International Pollution: A Practical Perspective

Ian Brownlie

In this chapter, I discuss the problems of pollution from a slightly different perspective, from the perspective of someone who deals with problems of State responsibility on quite a broad stage, and who tends to see things more like an old-fashioned lawyer in terms of actual disputes and claims. There is, of course, a general question as to the actual role of the lawyer: what role can a lawyer play in relation to the problems of pollution? Quite often, in this field, the lawyer without the scientist is not really of much value.

The lawyer's particular role is that of examining the ex post facto consequences of disaster. The lawyer looks at the pathology of a situation: things have gone wrong, what do we do to deal with them next? That process leads to the rather specialized problem of liability, or what in international law parlance tends to be referred to as "responsibility."

It could, of course, be argued that liability (or responsibility) is the least important of the various aspects of the pollution problem. The key issues, almost certainly, are the problems of prevention. Prevention is a matter of feeding in principles, standards, mechanisms for monitoring, and so forth at the planning stage. And even municipal law—which has many more links with the process of a central government—is not really very far advanced in introducing pollution controls at the planning stage of projects.

The other key aspect is loss distribution. In municipal law, generations of tort lawyers have considered that the action for damages is only a part, and perhaps a rather crude part, of the general problem of loss distribution, which is at least a more qualitative aspect of the issue of liability as such. Loss distribution immediately takes us into some delicate questions of the proper role of the State, the condition of the insurance market, and whether an insurance market can deal with the level of risk that is raised by nuclear facilities and other major sources of pollution.

In spite of the relative unimportance of the problem of responsibility, however, there probably is some interaction between the issue of responsibility and these other issues—prevention and loss distribution—because I think it is still true to say that in a general way, both the layperson and the lawyer pay more attention to policy issues if somewhere ahead there is the defined possibility of liability or responsibility. Moreover, there is a curious, though not necessarily very clear, interaction between the concept of liability—putting a hard edge on rights—and these more sophisticated problems of prevention and loss distribution. Also, the policy problems behind pollution are infinite. There is, as so often is the case with modern programs and modern ethics, a major conflict, a tension, between one program and another. The Western industrialized States' approach to pollution thus may be in some tension with the right to develop, the development ethic, which is another program fraught with United Nations politics. But those tensions are beyond the scope of this chapter.

Returning to State responsibility, I would like first to refer to the sources of the law. I do not intend to discuss the doctrine of the formation of rules of customary law. I want to talk about the sources in the simplest sense—what documents, what materials should we be looking at? I have no quarrel with the sort of materials which have been mentioned most helpfully in Chapter 2 prepared by Pierre-Marie Dupuy; but I think it would be better if people in universities made more use of some excellent raw material which lies to hand, even in law libraries. For example, there is a curious disinclination to use the pleadings in cases. Some of the finest material, with extensive resources lying behind its preparation, is to be found in the written and oral pleadings in disputes before international tribunals. The pleadings prepared for the *Gulf of Maine* case by the U.S. government and the Canadian government contain a great deal of material.[1] It astonishes me how people in universities constantly rifle the legal periodicals but seem to manage to ignore the contents of pleadings. In the case of pollution, there are valuable documents produced in contested cases, such as the interesting memorials prepared by good teams of lawyers on behalf of Australia and New Zealand in connection with the *Nuclear Tests* cases.[2] I do not think such materials should be left out of account.

In the sphere of State practice, there are plenty of examples which tend to be ignored in the literature, for example, the Japanese claims against the United States for the consequences of nuclear tests in the

Pacific.[3] Some of that material can be found in texts such as White-man's Digest:[4] fourteen volumes and a volume of index, and if you study it carefully (the index is not álways very helpful), there is some very useful material there. There is also a splendid set of volumes produced by the Micronesian Claims Commission, the U.S. agency that decided the Micronesian claims.[5] Some of those claims involved what might be called "fallout," and the reports contain some quite useful material on how to quantify the losses to real people and how to approach the problems caused by polluting activities carried out by States. Also available for consultation is the Canadian statement of claim prepared in the wake of the disaster caused by the burnout of the Soviet Cosmos 954 satellite in 1978, where the distribution of radioactive material created substantial cleanup expense for the Canadian government.[6] There are other examples; the point is that these are the type of materials international lawyers should use.

Moreover, I think that there is a methodological problem. The law is not helped by overspecialization. I am not convinced that it is a good thing for lawyers to put on blinkers with labels on the sides saying, "international environmental law," which means that they are so expert that if they come across other materials not directly related to pollution, these are ignored because they are not related to the environment, as such. An example would be the tort lawyer who is interested in problems of pollution and will only deal with those types of nuisance which involve certain agents of pollution. That is a very curious form of legal reasoning, to say it is only physically similar activities such as smelly drains which are relevant to a legal problem. In international law, as Professor Dupuy has pointed out,[7] it would not occur to anyone to say that the *Corfu Channel* case[8] was irrelevant to a pollution problem because it did not concern pollution as such. Similarly, there is substantial literature on the responsibility of States for the harboring of armed bands who cause harm to neighboring States. The State practice on harboring armed bands goes back well into the nineteenth century; it is an old problem and there are many examples of State practice. In terms of legal reasoning, those principles, like the issues in the *Corfu Channel* case, are directly relevant to pollution problems.

I find it appalling that in international law writers arrange material in curious boxes which are inimical to the normal principles of legal relevance. There is a thing called "environmental law": only articles which have titles which refer to the environment are cited, and other matters are not referred to, however relevant a lawyer would say they were. State responsibility is not and should not be divided up into separate boxes with labels on them.

One of the most relevant problems to the present subject matter is the issue of State control of private activities. This is the subject of article 9 of the draft articles provisionally adopted by the International Law Commission, on the basis of the excellent reports prepared by Judge Roberto Ago.[9] That issue is very relevant: the Chernobyl nuclear power plant at which the disaster occurred apparently was organized by a State entity with a considerable degree of legal autonomy. Without getting into the complexities of Soviet municipal law, the reality is that a lot of pollution is caused under the auspices of private law entities, and the responsibility of the State must depend on an assumed duty on the part of States to control the activities on their territory of such entities.

State responsibility must, of course, evolve, just as the duty of care in the law of tort has had to evolve in the context of changes in society and changes in risk-creating activity. The Chernobyl disaster raises the issue, which is already foreshadowed by one or two writers, of a liability for failure to give notice of the creation of intolerable dangers. The law, as in the context of the municipal law of tort, depends on the changing standards of use and tolerability. Turning to Chernobyl again—and relying only on anecdotal evidence that I have not had the time to research—the questions arise: How did other States, at the level of claim, react to the appallingly harmful consequences of Chernobyl? Did they make claims? Did they at least reserve the right to claim?

The impression I have is that there are a number of States, including, for example, West Germany, that did not claim, or did not even privately reserve the right to make a claim.[10] And I am hypothesizing, simply in order to make a point. The problem is that a number of States are in exactly the same position as the Soviet Union. They already have their potential Chernobyls *in situ*, and they are, as it were, not very willing to throw stones at other glass houses. If that is the case, and I am not saying it is, but if this is an example of the changing levels of tolerability, then in some areas the level of tolerability may rise. States in the same position as the Soviet Union, with the same kind of facilities on their territory, are not willing to create normative boomerangs by producing claims against the Soviet Union. We thus cannot take the complacent view that all the standards are gradually rising as people are progressively horrified by the risks of which we have knowledge. It may in fact work sometimes the other way.

The final point in this chapter concerns very much a lawyer's approach to things, a lawyer's technique: the relevance of causes of action. If we are looking at things as lawyers, we should pay attention to the way in which particular forms of pollution damage can be fitted into the rules of international law according to the actual heads of claim. In international law, as in the law of tort, the forms of action, the heads of claim, are significant.[11] In the *Nuclear Tests* cases, the Australian memorial—and also the Australian oral pleadings—made skillful use of different heads of claim. The Australian written pleadings referred to the violation of the sovereignty of a State caused by what they called "the deposit of radio-active fallout" on the territory of Australia and its dispersal in Australian airspace without the country's consent in terms of violating Australia's sovereignty over its territory.[12] The oral pleadings invoked[13] the concept of the violation of the "decisional sovereignty of a State" as a result of the dissemination of radioactivity following the nuclear tests in the atmosphere of the Pacific.[14] The Australian pleadings also invoked the cause of action denominated "infringement of the freedom of the high seas."[15] And in the *Nicaragua* case, on the question of liability in that case, the Nicaraguans got the benefit of the distinction between causes of action based on multilateral treaties and causes of action based on customary international law.[16]

In summary, along with so-called soft law, for example, the duty of cooperation, international lawyers thus might occasionally look in their books, examine what is being done in actual pleadings and adjudications, and pay more attention to the causes of action.

Notes

1. Delimitation of the Maritime Boundary in the Gulf of Maine Area (Can. v. U.S.), 1984 I.C.J. 246. The volumes in the I.C.J. Pleadings series are published after each case is finished. The series normally contains all the documents in the case—including pleadings and evidence—and the oral statements of counsel in their original language. The materials for the *Gulf of Maine* case have not yet been published.

2. Memorial of Australia (Austl. v. Fr.) [1978] I I.C.J. Pleadings (Nuclear Tests) 249 (Nov. 23, 1973) [hereinafter Memorial of Australia]; Memorial of New Zealand (N.Z. v. Fr.), [1978] II I.C.J. Pleadings (Nuclear Tests) 145 (Oct. 29, 1973).

3. *See, e.g.*, 4 M. WHITEMAN, DIGEST OF INTERNATIONAL LAW 565, 585–86 (1965).

4. M. WHITEMAN, DIGEST OF INTERNATIONAL LAW (volumes and index published from 1963–73).

5. Unpublished decisions of the U.S. Micronesian Claims Commission, 1972–76 (pursuant to the Micronesian Claims Act of 1971, Pub. L. No. 92–39, 85 Stat. 92, 94 (1971)), on file with the U.S. Department of Interior and with the U.S. Foreign Claims Settlement Commission, Washington, D.C.

6. Dep't. of External Aff. (Can.), *Claim Against the Union of Soviet Socialist Republics for Damage Caused by Soviet Cosmos 954*, Jan. 23, 1979, No. FLA–268, *reprinted in* 18 I.L.M. 899 (1979).

7. *See supra* Chapter 3.

8. Corfu Channel (U.K. v. Alb.), 1949 I.C.J. 4 (Judgment of Apr. 9).

9. Report of the International Law Commission to the General Assembly, 35

U.N. GAOR Supp. (No. 10) at 31, U.N. Doc. A/35/10 (1980), *reprinted in* [1980] 2 Y.B. INT'L L. COMM'N, pt. 2, at 1, 31, U.N. Doc. A/CN.4/SER.A/1980/Add.1.

10. For a more complete discussion of this situation, see *infra* Chapter 7.

11. *See generally* I. BROWNLIE, SYSTEM OF THE LAW OF NATIONS: STATE RESPONSIBILITY (PART 1), 53–88 (1983) (Ch. V: Causes of Action in the Law of Nations).

12. *E.g.*, Memorial of Australia, *supra* note 2, at 331. *See also* Application of Australia (Austl. v. Fr.) [1978] I.I.C.J. Pleadings (Nuclear Tests) 3, 14 (May 9, 1973) [hereinafter Application of Australia].

13. I believe this was the idea of Professor Dan O'Connell, formerly Chichele Professor of Public International Law, Oxford University.

14. *See also* Nuclear Tests (Austl. v. Fr.), Joint Dissenting Opinion of Judges Oneyama, Dillard, Jiménez de Aréchaga, and Sir Humphrey Waldock, 1974 I.C.J. 312, 360–62 (¶ 101), 369 (¶ 116).

15. *E.g.*, Memorial of Australia, *supra* note 2, at 337; *see also* Application of Australia, *supra* note 12, at 14.

16. Military and Paramilitary Activities in and against Nicaragua (Nicar. v. U.S.), Merits, 1986 I.C.J. 14 (Judgment of June 27).

Part II:
Pollution from Nuclear
Accidents

Chapter 6
Overview of Legal and Technical Aspects of Nuclear Accident Pollution
Andronico O. Adede

Introduction

The concern with the adequacy of international legal regimes for dealing with pollution problems arising from nuclear accidents and the need to strengthen international technical standards for enhancing nuclear safety received a notable impetus following the 1986 Chernobyl nuclear accident in the U.S.S.R. Governments seemed more ready to consider specific international measures in response to the Chernobyl nuclear accident with its transboundary effects than they were following the 1979 Three Mile Island nuclear accident (TMI) in the U.S.A.

TMI, let it be observed briefly, encouraged the preparation by the International Atomic Energy Agency (IAEA)[1] of two sets of nonlegally binding instruments, namely, the Guidelines on Emergency Assistance Arrangements in Connection with a Nuclear Accident or Radiological Emergency,[2] and the Guidelines on Reportable Events, Integrated Planning and Information Exchange in a Transboundary Release of Radioactive Materials.[3] As is well known, TMI also resulted in a large number of measures and programs to improve nuclear safety through improved engineering devices and more competent operation of nuclear plants. It prompted federal supervision and redesign of nuclear plants leading to more diligent evaluation of safety aspects of nuclear installations both by the U.S. government, through the National Regulatory Commission (NRC), and by the industry itself, through the Atlanta-based Institute of Nuclear Power Operations (INPO).

The Chernobyl accident, in contrast, resulted in the immediate elaboration of two legally binding international instruments by the IAEA, namely, the Convention on Early Notification of a Nuclear Accident (IAEA Notification Convention)[4] and the Convention on Assistance in the Case of a Nuclear Accident or Radiological Emergency (IAEA Assistance Convention).[5] Both of these have been acknowledged as landmarks in the history of the treaty-making process.[6] It also resulted directly in the expanded program on nuclear safety and improvements by the IAEA and additional activities for the IAEA support missions in the field of nuclear safety and radiological protection. Such support missions, which are usually undertaken only upon request by a member State of the IAEA, include the Operational Safety Review Team (OSART),[7] the Assessment of Significant Safety Event Team (ASSET),[8] the Operational Safety Indicator Program (OSIP),[9] the program of Integrated Safety Assessment of Research Reactor (INSARR),[10] and the Radiation Protection Advisory Team (RAPAT).[11] Apart from an increased demand for these support missions, at the request of member States, there was also an increased awareness of the role played by the IAEA Incident Reporting System (IAEA-IRIS)[12] and the International Nuclear Information System (INIS).[13] There also emerged a concern with finding ways to make legally binding the IAEA Nuclear Safety Standards (NUSS)[14] and the evolution of the equally important question of nuclear waste disposal through the IAEA Waste Management Advisory Program (WAMAP).[15]

In order to present an overview of the legal and technical aspects of nuclear accident pollution, which is the scope of this chapter, the following central points should be mentioned at the outset. It is possible only to outline, on the one hand, the efforts toward establishing legal principles dealing with the injurious consequences of nuclear activities (e.g., appropriate remedies for victims of nuclear accident pollution) and, on the other hand, the search for effective technical standards for enhancing nuclear safety to prevent or minimize the possibilities of nuclear accidents (preventive measures). With that in mind, it is important to note at once that, while the efforts to find appropriate remedies for the victims of nuclear-accident pollution have resulted in international measures through the elaboration of international legal instruments, international technical standards for enhancing nuclear safety have not been amenable to formulation into internationally binding legal instruments. As will be noted further, nuclear safety remains a primary responsibility of individual States enforcing their national regulations and is still the subject of the non-legally binding guidelines such as those developed by the IAEA under its NUSS program.

Treaty Law on Nuclear Accidents Before and After TMI and Chernobyl

Before TMI and Chernobyl, several multilateral treaties were concluded to deal specifically with the question of civil liability for nuclear accidents in land-based nuclear installations, thus providing remedies for the victims of nuclear-accident pollution. Other treaties were aimed at ensuring physical protection of nuclear material especially from theft or acts of sabotage, which could lead to exposure of the public to ionizing radiation, and treaties establishing liability for accidents arising from transportation of nuclear material and operation of nuclear ships. A checklist of these treaties, focusing on the instruments dealing specifically with the problems of pollution damage from nuclear accidents, includes:[16]

1. the Paris Convention on Third-Party Liability in the Field of Nuclear Energy, July 29, 1960, as amended in 1964 and 1982 (adopted within the framework of Organization for Economic Cooperation and Development [OECD] and therefore regional in character);[17]

2. the Vienna Convention on Civil Liability for Nuclear Damage, May 21, 1963 (adopted within the framework of the IAEA and therefore global in character);[18]

3. the Brussels Convention on the Liability of Operations of Nuclear Ships, May 25, 1962;[19]

4. the Nordic Mutual Emergency Assistance Agreement in Connection with Radiological Accidents, 1963;[20]

5. the Brussels Convention Relating to Civil Liability in the Field of Maritime Carriage of Nuclear Material, December 17, 1971 (adopted within the framework of the International Maritime Organization [IMO]);[21]

6. the Vienna Convention on the Physical Protection of Nuclear Material, March 3, 1980;[22]

7. the IAEA Convention on Early Notification of a Nuclear Accident, 1986;[23] and

8. the IAEA Convention on Assistance in the Case of a Nuclear Accident or Radiological Emergency, 1986.[24]

There have also been a number of bilateral agreements dealing specifically with cooperation in nuclear safety matters such as exchange of information and consultation. The usefulness of these bilateral agreements was endorsed in the IAEA Assistance Convention, which regards bilateral arrangements as additional means of giving effect to the broad framework of the multilateral convention. The checklist of bilateral agreements includes the following:[25]

1. Federal Republic of Germany (F.R.G.)–United Kingdom—arrangements for a continuing exchange of information on significant matters pertaining to the safety of nuclear installations and on collaboration in the development of regulatory safety criteria (April 1979);

2. Denmark–F.R.G.—agreement regulating the exchange of information on the construction of nuclear installations along the border (July 4, 1977);

3. Netherlands–F.R.G.—memorandum on the exchange of information and consultation on nuclear installations near borders (September 27, 1977);

4. Portugal–Spain—cooperative agreement in nuclear safety (March 31, 1980);

5. Guidelines for Nordic Cooperation Concerning Nuclear Installations in the Border Areas (November 15, 1976);

6. F.R.G.–Switzerland—agreement on radiation protection in case of emergency (May 31, 1978);

7. F.R.G.–Luxembourg—agreement on the exchange of information in case of accident which could have radiological consequences (October 18, 1979);

8. F.R.G.–Luxembourg—agreement on mutual assistance in case of disasters or major accidents (March 2, 1978);

9. France–Switzerland—agreement on the exchange of information in case of accident which could have radiological consequences (October 18, 1979);

10. Belgium–France—agreement on radiological protection concerning the installations of the nuclear power plant at Ardennes (March 7, 1967);

11. France–F.R.G.–Switzerland—exchange of notes concerning the establishment of an intergovernmental commission on neighborhood problems in border areas (October 27, 1975); and

12. Belgium–U.S.A.—arrangement for exchange of technical information in regulatory matters and in cooperation in safety research and in standards development (June 6, 1978).

The existence of this network of bilateral agreements on specific aspects of nuclear events, especially within Europe, helped governments in identifying quickly what aspect of the problem needed to be tackled through multilateral arrangements which the Chernobyl accident made necessary. Thus, the IAEA Notification and Assistance Conventions were based on solid precedents.

Toward the Harmonization of the Paris and Vienna Conventions on
Civil Liability for Nuclear Damage

Efforts toward the harmonization and possible simultaneous application of the Paris Convention on Third-Party Liability in the Field of
Nuclear Energy and the Vienna Convention on Civil Liability for
Nuclear Damage (the first two in the checklist of multilateral instruments) in case of a nuclear accident started as far back as 1970, both by
the IAEA and by the Nuclear Energy Agency of the Organization for
Economic Cooperation and Development (NEA/OECD). Both conventions apply to damage caused by nuclear incidents occurring in
land-based nuclear installations and during transport of nuclear materials. They are based on the following identical principles: (1) absolute
and exclusive liability of the operator of the nuclear installation concerned; (2) limitation of the operator's liability in amount and in time;
(3) obligation for the operator to cover its liability by insurance or other
financial security; (4) unity of jurisdiction and enforcement of judgments; and (5) nondiscrimination as regards the victims of a nuclear
accident.

Although the Paris and Vienna Conventions have the same basic
approach to the question of civil liability, there exists no relationship
between them. Attempts to encourage the parties to the regional Paris
Convention also to become parties to the global Vienna Convention
did not materialize, although such attempts led to the 1964 amendment of the Paris Convention. In any case, it would have led to conflicting obligations for parties to the two conventions as they were. That is
why, in fact, no State has become party to both conventions. The
situation is that neither convention would apply to nuclear damage
suffered in the territory of a contracting party to the other Convention.
For example, if a nuclear incident were to occur in a nuclear installation situated in the territory of a contracting party to the Paris Convention and cause damage to persons or property in a State party to the
Vienna Convention, the Paris Convention would be inapplicable to
such damage, and vice versa. Moreover, if a nuclear incident should
occur during transport of nuclear materials between nuclear installations situated in two States, one of which is party to one of the conventions and the second of which is party to the other convention, the rules
concerning noncontracting States would apply as well: the operators of
those installations are liable only for nuclear incidents occurring and
nuclear damage suffered in the territories of the respective contracting
parties, and the sending and receiving operators do not benefit from

the provisions of either convention relating to the transfer of liability as these are applicable only in case of transport between contracting parties.

The IAEA and NEA/OECD have endeavored since the 1970s to work out a solution aimed at establishing a relationship between the Vienna and Paris Conventions. The efforts toward elaborating a joint protocol for that purpose dealt with the following two objectives: (1) elimination of conflicts of law that might arise from simultaneous application of the two conventions in the event of a nuclear accident involving parties to both conventions; and (2) mutual extension of the civil liability regime established under each convention for the wider protection of victims of a nuclear accident.

The work toward producing a protocol for the above purposes was diligently pursued by both the IAEA and the NEA/OECD from 1974. Chernobyl gave the additional incentive to complete the project. Thus by the end of 1987, the two organizations concluded a Joint Protocol Relating to the Application of the Vienna and Paris Conventions on Civil Liability for Nuclear Damage, adopted at a joint IAEA-NEA/OECD Working Group meeting in Vienna, October 27–30, 1987.[26]

As explained by both the IAEA and NEA/OECD Secretariats, the first principle underlying the Joint Protocol is to create a link or a bridge between the two conventions by abolishing the distinction between contracting parties and noncontracting parties as regards the operative provisions of either convention. The second principle consists in making either the Vienna or the Paris Convention exclusively applicable to a nuclear accident by means of appropriate conflict of law rules. There remains the standing appeal by the IAEA member States for wider acceptance of relevant conventions.

Addressing the Question of State Responsibility for Nuclear Damage

The efforts that resulted in the above Joint Protocol relating to the Paris and Vienna Conventions on civil liability for nuclear damage were being undertaken simultaneously within the IAEA with the work on the question of State responsibility for nuclear damage (international liability) that the Chernobyl accident brought to focus. It was observed that both the Paris and Vienna Conventions, even if harmonized by a Joint Protocol as discussed above, deal with the questions of liability for nuclear damage primarily under civil law, limiting themselves to liability of nuclear plant operators for damage resulting in loss of life or for damage to the property of individuals. Thus, there was a need to consider the matter in a broader context by taking up the question of State responsibility for injurious consequences of nuclear activities leading to the possibility of elaboration of a new multilateral instrument based on the law of State responsibility. The new instrument, if elaborated, would include international claims against States and also deal unambiguously with the question of nuclear damage to the environment in general rather than damage to individual property or loss of life, as is clearly the focus of both the Paris and Vienna Conventions.

With appreciation of the current work of the United Nations International Law Commission (ILC) on this question generally,[27] the IAEA started to explore the question of international liability for nuclear damage. The IAEA efforts on this question are proceeding with a great deal of caution, given the unwillingness of some member States to let the organization deal with issues touching upon the law of State responsibility until that law is settled by the ILC. Others, however, feel that the IAEA is eminently suited to deal with the aspects of that law in the specific context of nuclear activities by establishing recognition and acceptance of State responsibility for damage arising from nuclear activities, as opposed to dealing with the question of international liability, in general, for injurious consequences of all acts causing pollution damage, which is the ILC's approach. Thus, success in dealing with the question of State responsibility for nuclear damage and modalities for handling claims for compensation is indeed one of the challenges now facing the IAEA, and the results are eagerly awaited. At its meeting in February 1988, the Board of Governors further authorized the IAEA to continue its study on this matter, especially on the basis of the views of the member States on the whole question already requested by the Secretariat.

On the issue of modalities for handling compensation claims, it is important to bear in mind that a mechanism that relies solely upon the legal process based on the concept of equal access to local tribunals by victims of nuclear pollution (foreigners and nationals of the local State) will not provide the needed comprehensive solution.[28] Account should be taken of the position of a number of socialist States of Eastern Europe, which would prefer the procedure of establishing a government machinery for receiving, evaluating, and deciding on the compensation to be awarded to the claims of nations (collected nationally) and claims by foreign nationals (also collected and presented by their respective foreign States) without going through court proceedings. Thus, a combination of these two mechanisms (equal access to the local courts and presentation of claims to a national claims commission) would provide victims of nuclear damage options for pursuing their claims by established local procedures. In the event of lack of satisfaction through such local means, the individual claimants may turn to an international claims settlement mechanism, which may also be established under the new instrument for that purpose. But first, the State which is the origin of the nuclear accident causing the nuclear pollution should be given the opportunity to settle the claims by its local means.

In this context, it is useful to look closely again at Articles III–XIV of the 1971 Convention on International Liability for Damage caused by Space Objects as a model for a multilateral instrument relating to claims brought by States against each other, including claims arising from injuries to individuals or damage to their property.[29]

Recognizing the Focus of the IAEA Notification and Assistance Conventions

As noted briefly earlier, the IAEA already succeeded in producing two conventions in direct response to Chernobyl, focusing on the matter clearly signaled in the title of each convention: the Convention on *Early Notification* of a Nuclear Accident;[30] and the Convention on *Assistance* in the Case of a Nuclear Accident or Radiological Emergency.[31]

These two conventions were tailored to address the specific issues among those exposed by the Chernobyl accident and with respect to which the IAEA member States believed international legal instruments were achievable as a matter of urgency. The member States singled out the need to establish a treaty obligation to notify a nuclear accident with potential transboundary effects: whom to notify, how to notify, and the information to be notified. The emphasis was on the early warning following a nuclear accident that might have transboundary consequences, alerting States likely to be affected and thus enabling them to take some precautionary measures addressing, in that connection, the special needs of the developing countries. Whether or not the notification would include nuclear accidents arising from military activities of a State became a make-or-break conference issue and was indeed settled in a subtle way, as explained in the drafting history of the relevant articles of the Convention.[32]

The IAEA also singled out the need to establish a multilateral legal framework for providing emergency assistance promptly: how to request the assistance; how to render it, the modalities for undertaking an assistance mission itself, having regard to the applicable bilateral arrangements;[33] the question of equipment and personnel; and also the financial aspects of assistance. The financial aspects of assistance, it may be noted, also became another make-or-break conference issue, which defied solution until the last hours of negotiations of the conventions, as indicated in the drafting history of the relevant article.[34]

The two conventions are already in force. Through the continued collaborative efforts between the IAEA, the World Meteorological Organization (WMO), and the Global Telecommunication System (GTS), the machinery established for early warning of a nuclear accident under the Notification Convention has now been successfully tested to evaluate its efficacy. It may also be observed that assistance in an actual radiological emergency has been rendered through the IAEA to a member State (Brazil) in the framework of the Assistance Convention in connection with the radiological emergency caused by a disused cesium-137 source in that member State.

The work on these two conventions clearly demonstrated the vital role played by the IAEA as an organization respected by its member States as a forum in which they could consult and cooperate in solving a specific international problem. It is expected that such cooperation will continue to be maintained with other relevant international organizations, such as the World Health Organization (WHO), the International Labor Organization (ILO), and other United Nations bodies, including United Nations Environment Programme (UNEP) and the United Nations Scientific Committee on the Effects of Atomic Radiation (UNSCEAR).

The basic approach of the IAEA with respect to the Notification and Assistance Conventions was to stay close to what was evidently achievable and to avoid the temptation of trying to solve at once, all conceivable problems which might flow from a transboundary nuclear accident and radiological emergency. Thus, certain issues were deliberately left out of consideration of the two conventions in order to focus upon the obligation to notify a transboundary nuclear accident and on the framework for providing prompt assistance in the event of a nuclear accident or radiological emergency.

Commentators unfamiliar with the drafting history of the two conventions will always wonder why (and some of those who took part in the negotiations will continue to lament the fact that) the two IAEA conventions did not

1. define the term "radiological safety significance";

2. contain provisions on intervention level which may be a trigger factor for notification of accidents; and

3. address the question of State responsibility and compensation for nuclear damage.

Apart from the last point, on which the IAEA has commenced a study toward an appropriate solution, as briefly outlined above, the issues were, in fact, considered during the drafting process of the two conventions. One of them—intervention level—has been singled out for subsequent scientific study under the auspices of the IAEA. Recognizing the focus chosen for the two conventions, it was necessary to limit the scope of the two instruments, in the course of their elaboration, to the specific concern articulated by the member States while leaving open the consideration of other related questions to treatment elsewhere. The two conventions clearly achieved the purpose for which they were intended and thus should be acknowledged as such.

Toward Strengthening International Standards for Nuclear Safety: The Soft Law Before and After TMI and Chernobyl

The question of liability for nuclear damage was the subject of a series of treaties, and work toward additional legal regimes on the same question continues, as noted above. The efforts toward producing legally binding international standards for nuclear safety, however, have remained in the domain of "soft law," that is, recommendations to member States as opposed to obligatory requirements enshrined in a treaty.

This status should not be too surprising since it is consistent with a basic position accepted by the IAEA. Thus, echoing the conclusions reached at the IAEA Special Session of the General Conference (September 1986) in response to Chernobyl, the Director General of the IAEA, Hans Blix, made the following statement in an article: "It is clear that the ultimate responsibility for nuclear safety rests with our member States. Only national authorities have the capacity to establish detailed safety and radiation protection rules and to supervise and enforce their implementation."[35] Nevertheless, as Blix further observed in the same article, the Chernobyl accident demonstrated that the need for closer cooperation among States on this question, using the IAEA as a forum, was clearly felt. It became evident that efforts toward establishing an international safety regime are worth exploring. Treating the question of nuclear safety in an international plane had in fact been recognized by the seven major industrialized nations meeting in Tokyo, May 1980. In their final statement, commenting on the implications of Chernobyl nuclear accident they observed that, for each country, the maintenance of nuclear safety and security was an *international responsibility*.[36] Certainly, as the Director General of the IAEA also noted in the course of his above-mentioned article, "a number of what could be called an international safety regime were already in place." He was referring to a series of the "soft law" that the IAEA and other relevant international organizations have developed in the field of nuclear safety and radiological protection and also the work of the IAEA's International Nuclear Safety Advisory Group (INSAG). Here again, an illustrative checklist will help tell the story in a nutshell. The soft law list thus includes the following:

1. the recommendations on international cooperation in developing safety regulations for handling, storing, and transporting radioactive material, prepared by the United Nations Scientific Committee on the Effects of Atomic Radiation (UNSCEAR) established by the General Assembly in 1955 by resolution 913(X);[37]

2. the recommendations on international radiation protection standards proposed by the non-governmental International Commission on Radiological Protection (ICRP),[38] including the principle of dose limitation on cost-benefit analysis;

3. the IAEA Regulations for Safe Transport of Radioactive Material contained in the *Safety Series No. 6* (the 1985 edition was supplemented in 1986)—the recommendations in this series have been adopted by a number of States;[39]

4. the IAEA Basic Safety Standards (BSS) for Radiation Protection, contained in the *Safety Series No. 9*; first issued in 1962, revised in 1967 and lastly in 1982—the 1982 edition was cosponsored by NEA/OECD and by the International Labor organization, incorporating the latest recommendations of the ICRP;[40] and

5. the IAEA Nuclear Safety Standards (NUSS), comprising presently sixty volumes in the form of five codes of practice accompanied by safety guides.[41]

In Search of Ways for Achieving Wider Use of the NUSS Codes as International Safety Standards

One of the issues that the 1986 Special Session of the IAEA General Conference, convened in response to the Chernobyl accident, referred to the IAEA Board of Governors for action was the question of mandatory international safety standards. The Board of Governors subsequently had before it at its meeting of February 1987 a paper prepared by the IAEA Secretariat concerning possibilities for establishing mandatory international Safety Standards and commenting basically on the IAEA-NUSS codes. The five codes of practice deal with (1) *governmental organization* for regulation of nuclear power plants; (2) safety in nuclear power plant *siting*; (3) *design* for safety of nuclear power plants; (4) safety in nuclear power plant *operation*, including commissioning and decommissioning; and (5) *quality assurance* for safety in nuclear power plants.

Admittedly, the above five codes of practice contain only an extremely general guideline. Thus, to make them more acceptable to those who insist on stringent safety standard, the idea of updating the NUSS codes was brought up. The upshot of the debate in the IAEA Board of Governors was that member States remained skeptical of the need to produce the so-called minimum international safety standard, albeit through updating and "internationalizing" the codes and making them mandatory.

But the fears that efforts toward producing international safety standards would tend to diminish rather than enhance such standards are somewhat exaggerated. In fact, aspects of the NUSS codes have been used as models by a number of countries in the preparation of their domestic legislation on nuclear safety. Such was the case in Argentina, Brazil, China, Egypt, Mexico, Morocco, and the Philippines. But Turkey and Yugoslavia went even further by incorporating major sections of NUSS into their national regulations.

It may turn out that, even with respect to certain industrialized countries, some of the NUSS codes are already incorporated in their domestic regulations. Therefore, the real reason for their resistance to the introduction of mandatory international safety standards may be no more than natural bureaucratic inertia. The introduction of mandatory, self-contained international safety standards would certainly compel States to abandon the comprehensive national regulations that they have labored to develop—a prospect about which they are understandably unenthusiastic. Given the force of bureaucratic inertia and the skepticism about the possibility of producing strong international safety standards, perhaps what the IAEA has planned to do is the most reasonably achievable:[42] ascertaining the opinion of each member State as to how exactly it regards the codes and what use, if any, it makes of them and thereafter finding ways by which member States could be encouraged to make more use of the NUSS codes, as may be updated from time to time.[43]

It should also be recalled that the question of making the NUSS codes mandatory became bound up with the problem of establishing an international safety inspectorate to supervise the implementation of the international standards. The experience of the European Economic Community (which is composed of countries with almost homogeneous safety standards) with such a safety inspectorate has not been encouraging. The IAEA Director General, following a visit to the headquarters of the United States Institute of Nuclear Power Operations (INPO) in Atlanta and getting firsthand information on INPO's inspection activities, remained cautious about the viability of an analogous international inspectorate for nuclear safety by the IAEA along the lines of IAEA inspectorate for its safeguards system. He later stated: "obligatory international safety inspections of nuclear installation—a parallel of safeguards—are not likely to be introduced."[44]

Certainly, within a given country, for example, the United States, the General Accounting Office (the congressional watchdog) may have to cajole the Nuclear Regulatory Commission (NRC) and the nuclear industries themselves (with the help of INPO) to enforce specific national safety measures.[45] If that is how the international safety standards may also have to be implemented, it is imperative that the establishment of an appropriate institutional arrangement should be considered thoroughly.

Developments Concerning International Standards for Radiation Protection

On the question of radiation protection, efforts toward the formulation of international standards have long been possible on account of the invaluable tasks performed by the International Commission on Radiological Protection (ICRP). Thus, ICRP's recommendations, which set out fundamental principles for radiation protection, have served as the common basis for international standards and national regulations in this field.

As mentioned in point 4 of the preceding soft law checklist, the IAEA Basic Safety Standards for Radiation Protection—first issued in 1962 and revised in 1967—were last revised and issued in 1982. The 1982 Basic Safety Standards fully incorporate the latest ICRP recommendations and further expand and interpret them in practical terms, giving detailed guidance for their application. The ICRP system of dose limitation sets individual dose limits which are not to be exceeded, and this is a requirement common to norms for health protection. But the new system also introduces source-related requirements, a device rarely used in other protective systems. These requirements imply that, regardless of how low an individual dose may be, two conditions must be fulfilled: (1) every activity involving exposure to radiation must be justified by the advantages associated with the activity; and (2) further efforts to reduce radiation exposure must be undertaken whenever the benefit—in terms of dose reduction—warrants the efforts to achieve it. The second condition is known as "optimization of radiation protection," which requires that every exposure to radiation must be kept as low as reasonably achievable, economic and social factors being taken into account.

It is clear that the introduction of these modern radiation protection concepts into national regulations and their implementation in the context of national requirements will take place gradually. It is equally clear, however, in such a process of progressive development, that a common approach prevails worldwide, facilitated to a large extent by internationally established standards and recommendations. Thus, as part of its activities to supplement the 1982 Basic Safety Standards with further guidance, the IAEA is developing guidelines for implementing the dose limitation system, for the design of radiation protection systems and occupational monitoring, and for operational radiation protection activities. An important aspect to the limitation of transboundary exposures is the determination of a minimum monetary value for the unit collective dose to be used in cost-benefit analysis for optimization of radiation protection; guidelines on this subject were issued in May 1985.[46]

Sound radiation protection programs generally have three common ingredients beyond the availability of applicable regulations: (1) capability of the management to see beyond regulatory requirements; (2) qualified staff; and (3) implementation of the optimization requirement. In order to assist member States in establishing adequate radiation protection programs, the IAEA initiated in 1984 the services of radiation protection advisory teams (RAPAT).[47] These multifold activities carried out through international cooperation and assistance are not merely aimed at increasingly harmonizing regulatory approaches to the issues involved in radiation protection, for which there is already a common basis worldwide. They further seek to ensure—as a requisite for the enforcement of applicable requirements—the availability of qualified personnel and suitable equipment; the lack of either would make any set of regulations meaningless in this area, no matter how far they are in harmony[48] with relevant international principles and commonly accepted requirements.

Conclusions

This chapter presents an overview, without entering into detailed analysis, of the issues concerning legal and technical aspects of nuclear-accident pollution. From this overview, it may be concluded that the international community has already embarked on the road to strengthening international law in order to prevent or minimize nuclear-accident pollution and to deal more effectively with post-nuclear-accident problems. In the area of post-accident questions (liability for nuclear damage), as illustrated by the checklists in the preceding section on treaty law on nuclear accidents, a network of legal instruments is already in place, while efforts to conclude new ones on specific aspects are also continuing at both the multilateral level and the bilateral level.[49]

With respect to the prevention of nuclear accidents, the experience of the IAEA, as revealed by the reaction of the member States on the question of making the NUSS codes mandatory, is instructive. Behind this remains the big question: is nuclear safety to be regarded foremost as the responsibility of individual States for the reasons explained by the IAEA, as previously noted,[50] or is it to be considered an international responsibility in the sense emphasized by the heads of major industrial nations at their 1986 Tokyo summit, also mentioned earlier? Clearly the IAEA is maintaining the momentum toward finding an appropriate approach to the question, having regard to the soft law illustrated by the checklist given earlier. Thus, it is hoped that the IAEA-expanded program for nuclear safety, which should continue to receive the full support of the member States, will maintain its target of strengthening international cooperation in this area through other activities not limited to those resulting in new multilateral legal instruments. Indeed, the February 1988 IAEA-OECD International Conference on Man-Machine Interface in the Nuclear Industry held in Tokyo was seen as part of the internationalization of nuclear safety.[51] Before that was the IAEA International Conference on Nuclear Power Performance, September 28 to October 2, 1987, which dealt with, among other things, technical aspects of nuclear safety and international cooperation in the field. Mention should also be made of IAEA's International Nuclear Safety Advisory Group (INSAG), which concluded in January 1988 its work on formulating a set of fundamental nuclear safety principles for existing and future reactor types. INSAG's report was then considered at the IAEA-OECD symposium on severe accidents in nuclear plants, held in Italy, March 21–25, 1988.

Chernobyl undoubtedly made the international community jittery about nuclear energy. Thus, while the IAEA was trying to educate the world by presenting objectively the issues through the post-Chernobyl review conference, August 25–29, 1986, and by convening the Special Session in September 1986 to review the report produced by the post-Chernobyl accident review, the press outside the U.S.S.R. was also doing its own education, making such observations as the following:

No existing nuclear power plant can ever be declared absolutely safe. What government can do is (a) ensure that the risk of such an accident happening is so small as to be negligible, and (b) make plans so that, if one does happen, the consequences can and will be controlled. Chernobyl, Three Mile Island and other, lesser, accidents have persuaded some experts that the light-water reactors in common use around the globe are insufficiently tolerant of human frailty. They rely on external safety devices supposed to spring into action when things go wrong. To achieve (a), governments and companies must now consider investing in the new generation of reactor designs—called inherently-safe reactors—that cannot melt down. The technology is available; change can be ordered better in the West; and frightened people can be persuaded of those truths.[52]

Whether or not points (a) and (b) in the above statement are readily achievable, it is clear that the IAEA, as the leading global international organization in this field, is already responding. Its expanded nuclear safety program deals with various activities including those aimed at increasing the chances of "gaining a better understanding of human performance, man's ability and limitations in complex technological environments," such as nuclear environment, while stressing the importance of the need "to find an appropriate balance between automation and human action."[53] It is true that human error—grave violation of rules and procedures—was objectively established by the IAEA as one of the factors that caused the Chernobyl accident and has now become a central issue. Thus the conduct of staff in a nuclear plant resulted recently in the shutting down of a nuclear plant in the United States, the first time as a result of a nontechnical ground. The employees of the Peach Bottom Atomic Power Station—45 miles away from TMI—were allegedly caught sleeping on the job.[54]

All these examples clearly indicate that States are determined to prevent the occurrence of another TMI or another Chernobyl and are striving to establish mechanisms for effective international cooperation in the technical aspects of nuclear safety while strengthening the legal framework for responding effectively should a nuclear accident occur. The conclusion of the two new conventions by the IAEA, in a record period of four weeks, presented an important lesson in the multilateral treaty-making process, the basic elements of which have been explained elsewhere.[55] It now remains for the IAEA to continue its work in selecting areas of international cooperation in the nuclear field in collaboration with other relevant international organizations to provide such realistic international legal instruments. In the same way, the IAEA should continue its role of providing effective international fora for exchange of views and information on nuclear safety issues through scientific conferences and meetings, which are evidently worthy of attention and full support of the international community.

In this connection, it is important to note also the initiative taken by the nuclear industries themselves to facilitate the exchange of information among utilities on matters of operational safety. Both the Institute of Nuclear Power Operation (INPO), in the United States, and the International Union of Producers and Distributors of Electrical Energy (UNIPEDE), in Western Europe, are already planning a strategy for such an exchange. Thus, at the INPO-UNIPEDE meeting of October 1987 in Paris, a proposal was made to establish a World Association of Nuclear Power Operators (WANPO).[56] As conceived, WANPO would be funded by the utilities themselves, but it would not have decision-making or regulatory powers. Its basic function would be to encourage exchange of information for the purposes of maximizing the safety and reliability of nuclear power stations. The future work of WANPO and its contributions and relation to the IAEA and NEA/OECD is clearly worth keeping in mind, as the concern with enhancing nuclear safety by building an international consensus on safety standards continues to stay at center stage.

Acknowledgments

The views expressed herein are those of the author and do not represent those of the International Atomic Energy Agency or of the United Nations. This chapter is current as of April 1988.

Notes

1. The IAEA is an autonomous intergovernmental organization established under a Statute approved on October 23, 1956, by the Conference on the Statute of the International Atomic Energy Agency, held at the headquarters of the United Nations. The Statute came into effect on July 29, 1957. The text of the Statute is in 276 U.N.T.S. 4; I.A.E.A., Multilateral Agreements, Legal Series No. 1, at 49 (1959). For a concise background of the origin and establishment of the IAEA and its relationship with the United Nations, see, *e.g.*, P. SZASZ, THE LAW AND PRACTICES OF THE INTERNATIONAL ATOMIC ENERGY AGENCY, I.A.E.A. Legal Series No. 7 (1970). 113 States (including the United States) are members of the IAEA. U.S. Dep't of State, TREATIES IN FORCE 268 (1988).

2. *See* I.A.E.A. Doc. INFCIRC/310 (Jan. 1984).

3. *See* I.A.E.A. Doc. INFCIRC/321 (Jan. 1985).

4. I.A.E.A. Doc. INFCIRC/335/GC(SPL.I)/RES(1986), at 5–11, *opened for signature* Sept. 26, 1986, *reprinted in* 25 I.L.M. 1370 (1986) (entered into force Oct. 27, 1986).

5. I.A.E.A. Doc. INFCIRC/336/GC(SPL.I)/RES(1986), at 13–22, *opened for signature* Sept. 26, 1986, *reprinted in* 25 I.L.M. 1395 (1986) (entered into force Feb. 26, 1987).

6. A.O. ADEDE, THE IAEA NOTIFICATION AND ASSISTANCE CONVENTIONS IN CASE OF A NUCLEAR ACCIDENT (1987).

7. OSART missions, initiated in 1982, are aimed at giving support to the efforts of national regulatory authorities and operating organizations by visiting nuclear installations, upon the request of a member State, to review opera-

tional practices and give plant personnel the opportunity to exchange views with the team on *all aspects of safe operation* of nuclear plants. An OSART review, let it be emphasized, does not constitute a design appraisal or a regulatory inspection to check compliance with national requirements as such. It only facilitates an intensive exchange of information for enhancing safety performance. The results of the team's visit are reported in confidence to the national authorities of the requesting State. For more on this, see, *e.g.*, Franzen, *Reviewing the Operational Safety of Nuclear Power Plants*, 29 I.A.E.A. BULL. 13, 14 (No. 4, 1987).

8. ASSET missions, distinguished from OSART, are aimed at providing the operating organizations and regulatory authorities with independent international opinion on the *causes of events* which are significant for safety operations of nuclear installations and additional concrete actions which might help prevent the occurrence of such events. Initiated in 1986, ASSET missions focus on exchange of specific information on "lessons learnt" from accidents and therefore provide, upon request of a member State, information on relevant technical disciplines, analytical techniques, and man-machine interface. *Id.*

9. OSIP began in 1985 as a program to supplement OSART by complementing the subjective judgments with objective plant-specific data aimed at helping the team experts in identifying key areas for in-depth investigation. Thus, there has been a combined OSART-OSIP mission. *See* 1 I.A.E.A. NEWS FEATURES 8 (Apr. 15, 1988).

10. INSARR is a program which has been operated by the IAEA for more than fifteen years through experts who examine both the safety aspects and radiation-protection process at nuclear facilities and advise the member State on the ways of enhancing the safety of the facilities. Its findings are submitted in an official report of the IAEA to the requesting State. *See id.* at 9.

11. Established in 1984, RAPAT is composed of experts sent, upon request of a member State, to deal with a wide range of areas from regulations to operational activities to allow for up-to-date advice on all matters involving ionizing radiation. In its missions, RAPAT includes also experts from the World Health Organization (WHO) and from the International Commission on Radiological Protection (ICRP). It should be noted, however, that RAPAT is not an international inspection authority. Its main task is to assess current situations with the host government's officials and those using radioactive materials, then to identify specific needs and priorities to ensure the safety of ongoing activities, and then finally to suggest practical long-term programs with the necessary trained personnel for a safe introduction and continuing use of radiation techniques. For more on this, see, *e.g.*, Rosen, *Adequate Radiation Protection: A Lingering Problem*, 29 I.A.E.A. BULL. 34 (No. 4, 1987).

12. Established in 1983, the IAEA-IRIS enables the organizations to collect, assess, and disseminate to participating States information on safety-significant events in the course of operation, maintenance, inspections, and testing of nuclear plants, which are selected by national authorities as being of general interest to the nuclear community. The IAEA-IRIS, using a global system which receives data also from the Eastern European countries and the developing countries, thus supplements the regional NEA-IRIS, which disseminates data from Western Europe, Canada, Japan, and the United States. *See* Franzen, *supra* note 7, at 15.

13. Introduced in 1982, INIS is a comprehensive computerized international information system in which an individual participating country can

obtain access to most of the literature on a particular nuclear subject. *See generally* INIS TODAY—AN INTRODUCTION TO INTERNATIONAL NUCLEAR INFORMATION SYSTEM (I.A.E.A. Pub. 1982).

14. NUSS currently consists of 60 documents published by the IAEA from 1979, when the number of orders for new nuclear plants increased. The NUSS documents are developed by the IAEA for the purpose of establishing an internationally agreed frame of reference for the safety of nuclear plants. As further discussed below at text accompanying note 41 and thereafter, they contain recommendations for nuclear power plant safety (*see* 50–C–G, 50–SG–G1 to 9), siting (*see* 50–C–S, 50–SG–S1 to 12), design (*see* 50–C–D, 50–SG–D1 to 14), operation (*see* 50–C–O, 50–SG–O1 to 11), and quality assurance (*see* 50–C–QA, 50–SG–QA1 to 11).

15. *See* Blix (Director General of the IAEA), *International Co-operation in the Utilization of Nuclear Energy and the Role of the IAEA*, I.A.E.A. Doc. IAEA/P.I/C.4E (1985), and especially his statement at the meeting of the Board of Governors of the IAEA, June 9, 1987, mentioning the role of WAMAP in connection with waste disposal problems for developing countries.

16. The nuclear-accident list, however, does not include, for example, the 1972 London Convention on the Prevention of Marine Pollution by Dumping of Wastes and Other Matter, Dec. 29, 1972, 26 U.S.T. 2403, T.I.A.S. No. 8165, which assigns the IAEA key responsibilities of defining the *high-level* radioactive material unsuitable for dumping, and for establishing recommendations for the issue of permits for permissible dumping of other radioactive material. It also excludes the 1979 Economic Commission for Europe Convention on Long-Range Transboundary Air Pollution, T.I.A.S. No. 10541, *reprinted in* 18 I.L.M. 1442 (1979), and its 1984 Protocol on Long-Term Financing of the Cooperative Program for Monitoring and Evaluation of the Long-Range Transmission of Air Pollutants in Europe (EMEP), Sept. 28, 1984, *reprinted in* 24 I.L.M. 484 (1985), dealing with air pollution in general, rather than specifically with pollution from nuclear accidents.

17. *See* INTERNATIONAL CONVENTIONS ON CIVIL LIABILITY FOR NUCLEAR DAMAGE, Legal Series No. 4, at 43–51 (I.A.E.A. Pub. rev. ed. 1970) [hereinafter INTERNATIONAL CONVENTIONS]. The fourteen contracting parties are Belgium, Denmark, Finland, France, Federal Republic of Germany, Greece, Italy, Netherlands, Norway, Portugal, Spain, Sweden, Turkey, and the United Kingdom. In January 1964, protocols to the Paris Convention and the Brussels Supplementary Convention, which are territorially limited to Europe, were adopted to bring the two Conventions into harmony with the Vienna Convention, *infra* note 18, which is of worldwide application. On November 16, 1982, two further protocols to the Paris Convention and the Brussels Supplementary Convention were adopted; they are not yet in force. They relate primarily to the adoption of Special Drawing Rights (SDR) of the International Monetary Fund as unit of account for the compensation amounts established by both Conventions and to an increase in the State compensation and in the aggregate compensation payable to third parties under the Brussels Supplementary Convention from 70 to 175 million SDR, and from 120 to 300 million SDR, respectively.

18. INTERNATIONAL CONVENTIONS, *supra* note 17, at 7–8. The eleven contracting parties are Argentina, Bolivia, Cameroon, Cuba, Egypt, Niger, Peru, Philippines, Trinidad and Tobago, and Yugoslavia.

19. *Id*. at 34–42.

20. The Agreement by the Nordic Countries (Denmark, Finland, Norway, and Sweden) was also signed by the IAEA, which thus became party to it. *See* I.A.E.A. Doc. INFCIRC/49 (Nov. 8, 1963).

21. INTERNATIONAL CONVENTIONS, *supra* note 17, at 55–58. The contracting parties are Argentina, Denmark, France, the Federal Republic of Germany, Italy, Liberia, Norway, Spain, Sweden, and the Yemen Arab Republic.

22. CONVENTION ON THE PHYSICAL PROTECTION OF NUCLEAR MATERIAL, Legal Series No. 12, I.A.E.A. Doc. STI/PUB/615, at 386–97 (I.A.E.A. Pub. 1982).

23. *Supra* note 4.

24. *Supra* note 5.

25. Texts in an informal collection in the author's files.

26. I.A.E.A. Doc. GOV/2326, Annex I (Sept. 1988).

27. *See* Magraw, *Transboundary Harm: The International Law Commission's Study of "International Liability,"* 80 AM. J. INT'L L. 305 (1986); *Symposium on State Responsibility and Liability for Injurious Consequences Arising Out of Acts Not Prohibited by International Law*, 16 NETH. Y.B. INT'L L. 1 (1985).

28. The equal access principle was recently recommended in article 20 of the "Principles, Rights, and Obligations Concerning Transboundary Natural Resources and Environmental Interferences," prepared by environmental law experts constituted by the World Commission on Environment and Development (WCED). The text of the article reads: "The States shall grant equal access, due process and equal treatment in administrative and judicial proceedings to all persons who are or may be affected by transboundary interferences with their use of a natural resource or the environment." WORLD COMMISSION ON ENVIRONMENT AND DEVELOPMENT, OUR COMMON FUTURE, Annex I, at 348, 351 (1986).

29. March 29, 1972, 24 U.S.T. 2389, T.I.A.S. No. 7762.

30. *Supra* note 4 (emphasis added).

31. *Supra* note 5 (emphasis added).

32. For the drafting history and commentary on the relevant articles on this point, see A.O. ADEDE, *supra* note 6, at 16–25, 35–38.

33. The usefulness of bilateral agreements such as those listed herein was considered a basic cornerstone of the Assistance Convention, *supra* note 5, as emphasized in its fourth preamble and in paragraph 2 of its first article.

34. For the controversy over the financial arrangements with respect to the Assistance Convention, see A.O. ADEDE, *supra* note 6, at 79–84.

35. *See, e.g.*, Blix, *The Next 10 Years: Major Challenge Shaping the IAEA's Future*, 29 I.A.E.A. BULL. 11, 12 (No. 3 1987). Hans Blix is the IAEA Director General.

36. *See* Tokyo Economic Summit, Statement on the Implications of the Chernobyl Nuclear Accident, *reprinted in* 25 I.L.M. 1005, 1006 (1986) [hereinafter Tokyo Statement].

37. UNSCEAR, based in Vienna and maintaining close liaison with the IAEA, submits annual reports to the General Assembly of the United Nations on this question for dissemination to member States. For the latest report submitted to the U.N. General Assembly in 1987, see U.N. Doc. A/42/210 and the relevant G.A. resolution 42/67 of Dec. 2, 1987.

38. *See* Recommendations of International Commission on Radiological Protection, 26 ANN. I.C.R.P. 1 (I.C.R.P. Pub. No. 3 1977) and 37 ANN. I.C.R.P. 10 (I.C.R.P. Pub. No. 2/3 1983). *See also* part III.B, *infra*.

39. *See* Tokyo Statement, *supra* note 36.

40. *See* Recommendations of the International Commission on Radiological Protection, I.C.R.P. Pub. 26 (1977).

41. *See supra* note 14.

42. *See* series cited *supra* note 14; *see also* in this connection views of the IAEA Board members as summarized in I.A.E.A. Doc. Gov./INF/519, para. 9 (June 1986).

43. As observed by the IAEA Director General in his statement at the 1987 June Board meeting: "[a] first look has now been taken at the need to revise the existing documents. An Ad Hoc Advisory Group came to the conclusion that no corrections to the existing NUSS codes of Practice would be needed as a result of the lessons learnt from Three Mile Island and Chernobyl, but that some complements and improvements would be desirable. The work has now started to revise the Codes. In that process all Members will, of course, be consulted. The Advisory Group concluded that the Codes should be generally acceptable to all member States and should represent standards sufficient for safety, recognizing that individual member States would have supplementary requirements. The Codes will not, of course, be transformed into international agreements binding as between parties. If the conclusion of the Advisory Group is correct that—with some variations—the Codes represent commonly accepted standards, there might be some value in registering this fact through individual, explicit notifications by member States."

44. Blix, *The Post-Chernobyl Outlook for Nuclear Power*, 28 I.A.E.A. BULL. 9, 11 (No. 3 1986).

45. In this connection, consider the recent such action following a pipe rupture in the Surry Unit 2 nuclear plant in Virginia in late 1986. *Pipe Check at Nuclear Plants*, N.Y. Times, Apr. 12, 1988, at 24, col. 4.

46. I.A.E.A., Safety Series No. 67 (1985).

47. *Supra* note 11.

48. In this connection, consider the problem faced by developing countries as described in Rosen, *supra* note 11.

49. Speaking at the Sixth (Legal) Committee of the General Assembly of the United Nations on November 18, 1987, the representative of Austria cited the bilateral agreements in nuclear field between Austria and Czechoslovakia of 1986, and those being negotiated between Austria and Poland and also one with the U.S.S.R.

50. *See supra* text accompanying note 23.

51. *Infra* note 53.

52. *Catastrophe at Chernobyl*, ECONOMIST 13, 14 (May 3–9, 1986).

53. These are some of the views expressed by Hans Blix, Director General of the IAEA, addressing the IAEA/OECD International Conference on Man-Machine Interface in the Nuclear Industry, Tokyo, Feb. 15–19, 1988. *See* 3 I.A.E.A. Newsbrief, Mar. 1, 1988, at 2.

54. *See The Peach Bottom Syndrome*, N.Y. Times, Mar. 27, 1988, sec. 3, at 1, col. 2.

55. *See* A.O. ADEDE, *supra* note 6, at 1–13.

56. *See* 1 I.A.E.A. NEWS FEATURES 9 (Apr. 15, 1988).

Chapter 7

Paying the Piper for Transboundary Nuclear Damage: State Liability in a System of Transnational Compensation

Günther Handl

Introduction

In the almost twenty years since the United Nations Conference on the Human Environment in Stockholm, the international community has made little progress toward heeding its own call for clarification of the twin concepts of international liability and compensation for transboundary environmental harm.[1] In general, pertinent State practice has tended to bypass the issue of liability (and compensation),[2] while the International Law Commission's (ILC) work on draft articles on "international liability for injurious consequences arising out of acts not prohibited by international law" has proceeded at a snail's pace.[3]

The accident at the Chernobyl nuclear power plant in 1986, however, may have marked the beginning of a process of reversal. International efforts at developing the law on transboundary environmental liability and compensation in general seem to have been gaining momentum.[4] Certainly, the issue of liability and compensation for transboundary nuclear damage has been a prominent topic of public debate ever since Chernobyl. Although accident prevention and mitigation may have topped the post-Chernobyl multilateral agenda,[5] redressing the inadequacies of existing nuclear liability/compensation systems has become as well a major objective of an international legislative reform drive.

Given the huge transboundary damages associated with the Chernobyl accident,[6] the transnational compensation issue has given rise, not surprisingly, to a veritable flood of articles and comments in legal journals.[7] Few of these, however, have paid adequate attention to an issue of fundamental importance, namely the critical role and function of source State[8] liability in any system of compensation for transboundary catastrophic accidents. Similarly, many international reform proposals presently under consideration[9] appear to give short shrift to the principles of source State liability.

Previous chapters of this book examine various aspects of State accountability in a general context. It is the purpose of this chapter to focus attention on the essential role of international State liability in minimizing the transboundary costs of nuclear accidents and thereby to contribute to a balanced discussion of transnational nuclear liability and compensation mechanisms. Such a reminder appears to be particularly appropriate at a time when several other international liability regimes are either being negotiated or under consideration.[10] The specific conclusions of this chapter, although relating to cost-internalization in the context of transboundary nuclear accidents, would be applicable *mutatis mutandis* to the setting up of international liability regimes for other transboundary risk-bearing activities.

Chernobyl as a Symbol of the Deficiencies of International Law on Transboundary Liability and Compensation?

Having dramatically highlighted the issue of liability and compensation, Chernobyl offers itself quite naturally as the point-of-departure in assessing the need for multilateral reform. Difficulties in getting access to information on diplomatic exchanges as well as in interpreting certain evidence possibly bearing on the liability/compensation issue,[11] however, suggest caution in passing judgment on the incident's international legal significance. Circumspection appears particularly warranted in viewing Chernobyl as a touchstone for the effectiveness of general international law on liability and compensation.

Nevertheless, an exploration of the incident's precedential value is essential for two reasons. First, a reasonable understanding of international diplomatic activity relating to compensation for Chernobyl-induced transboundary harm may be necessary to appreciate correctly the nature and magnitude of the task of setting up a globally effective nuclear liability and compensation regime. Second, in the international legal environment in which lawmaking is a largely decentralized and frequently informal process, public perception of a given event is likely to carry international normative implications. If this perception is factually unfounded and remains unchallenged, it may over time develop a legal significance quite independent of and separate from the underlying event.

What is striking about the "legal fall-out" from Chernobyl is the fact that despite its massive impact on the environment and the economies of neighboring countries,[12] Soviet reparation of these transboundary damages appears to be an unlikely prospect.[13] None of the affected governments formally lodged international legal claims for damages with the Soviet Union.[14] Indeed, some Western European countries[15] hinted at a lack of international legal bases for securing damages from the Soviet government. Conversely, immediately after the accident, the Soviet Union disclaimed any international obligation to make reparations for damages abroad, although it indicated its willingness to cooperate toward clarification of the international liability issue *pro futuro*.[16]

There is no denying that this state of affairs bespeaks a fundamental weakness in international nuclear liability and compensation arrangements. It would be wrong, however, to overlook certain idiosyncratic features of the incident and characterize the failure of reparation exclusively, or even primarily, as a symptomatic inadequacy of international liability and compensation norms in general. First, political expediency may well have dissuaded some affected governments from pursuing the issue of international reparation. In some cases, Western European governments appear to have been more concerned with securing Soviet cooperation in the long-term management of the risk of transboundary nuclear accidents in Europe than with obtaining compensation for economic loss ascribed to fallout from the stricken Soviet reactor. Public insistence on Soviet liability and compensation was viewed by some as prejudicing prospects for future Soviet cooperation.[17] Besides, it is plausible that some countries may have sought to avoid creating a "normative boomerang," an international legal precedent that might come to haunt them in a future transboundary accident involving their own nuclear power industry (or, for that matter, a nonnuclear activity that causes transboundary harm).[18] Second, the existence of a rather obvious causation problem[19] is likely to have discouraged States from pressing claims through official diplomatic channels.

If these incident-specific special circumstances are properly taken into account, Chernobyl is much less the damning indictment of international accident law than might appear at first sight. When approached in this fashion, Chernobyl can provide a window on contemporary general international law regarding reparation of transboundary nuclear harm,[20] and serve as a convenient signpost in reviewing its generic deficiencies and marking possible solutions to the problems.

The Principle that Transboundary Costs of Nuclear Accidents Be Fully Internalized

A first and fundamental question in connection with accidental transboundary nuclear harm is whether the maxim of "A nuclear accident anywhere is a nuclear accident everywhere" might not hold implications also for the issue of liability and compensation. Specifically, the question arises as to whether in accidents with severe consequences, the principle of a source State's full accountability for transboundary harm[21] might not give way to the idea of cost-sharing between source and victim States, or the notion that, in the face of catastrophic adversity, international solidarity should replace strict adherence to traditional allocations of international rights and obligations.

On the face of it, Chernobyl might not appear to raise the question of the justifiability of such a shift in the traditional entitlement of States. The Soviets explained their refusal to pay compensation for transboundary damage by alleging merely that there was no legal basis for such claims and, specifically, that demands for compensation were fatally blemished by a lack of a requisite causal link.[22] Nevertheless, in rejecting a priori possible claims for compensation, Soviet statements did contain references that insinuated the inappropriateness of such claims in the light of the extent and nature of the calamity suffered by the source State itself.[23]

Similarly, it would be wrong to disregard the possibility that a phenomenon which could be referred to as the "East-West factor" may have played a role in discouraging victim States from pressing international claims against the Soviet Union. Inspired by analogy to North-South relations or relations between developed and developing countries, this factor characterizes the perception that as between polluting Eastern European and polluted Western European countries, States' traditional international entitlements might be suspendable. Its premise—an international version of the "deep pocket" theory—is that economically better off victim States should contribute to the costs of reducing transnationally harmful pollution or, in the case of accidents, bear or at least share in the costs associated with the transboundary impact.[24]

Finally, at least one Western observer has called for a limit on Soviet liability "as a matter of practical politics and common sense" and the absorption, by victim countries, of part of their damage costs as an expression of international solidarity in a world that utilizes nuclear power.[25] Quite obviously, the choice between full accountability and cost-sharing, as basic international principles for allocating transboundary costs in the event of major nuclear accidents, has been at least implicitly an issue in the debates about compensation for damage allegedly caused by the Chernobyl accident.[26]

Invocation of the principle of international solidarity, for the purpose of mitigating a perceived harshness of positive international law on reparation, is unpersuasive in the context of accidental transboundary nuclear harm. To begin with, the concept of solidarity connotes social recognition of the existence of a community whose trademark is awareness of an important element of sameness among those who are considered to make up its members. To view a major nuclear accident as an event in which source State and injured neighboring States alike are victims of the age of nuclear technology, hence bound together, as it were, in a community of necessity, is to recognize correctly the state of worldwide environmental interdependence. But as a conceptual basis from which to approach the allocation of damages between source and affected neighboring States, this view is misleading. The criteria of "sameness" underlying this notion of community are irrelevant to deciding the entitlement question. Thus to somehow equate nuclear damage with harm caused by the forces of nature and then to invoke international solidarity with regard to the costs of the accident, as some might be prepared to do,[27] implies oblivion to some essential factors which are directly related to the question of cost allocation: the nature of the disaster as intrinsically a man-made one; the fact that while some States utilize nuclear power notwithstanding its obvious risks, many others do not; and the fact that, globally speaking, States' conduct lacks therefore the requisite element of "sameness" as regards the creation of transboundary nuclear risks. Given these circumstances, fairness and justice would militate against any across-the-board application of the principle of international solidarity to transboundary damage from nuclear accidents. To hold otherwise could mean to commit a victim State that has forgone the nuclear energy option domestically to subsidize foreign nuclear energy production—probably without offsetting benefits and certainly without any basis for expecting reciprocal assistance in the future.

Even as a purely subsidiary loss allocation rule, general international cost-sharing would remain objectionable. The rationale for limiting the liability of private operators of nuclear power plants[28] is not generally applicable to the process of internalizing transboundary accident costs at the international level. The consensus—frequently to be found on the national level—that encouragement of nuclear power production lies in the national interest and that, accordingly, potential liabilities exceeding a certain threshold, should be borne by the community at large rather than by the individual, private operator, has no counterpart on the international plane.[29] In sum, it is difficult to make a principled defense of replacing full accountability by a version of cost-sharing as the general international allocative principle for transboundary nuclear damages.

As a political matter, in a world divided into nuclear and nonnuclear power countries, hostile blocs, and alliances, cost-sharing is likely to prove unacceptable as the international ground rule for allocating the transboundary costs of major nuclear accidents. This assumption has been implicitly corroborated during the debates of the Special Session of the IAEA General Conference following Chernobyl. In the wake of the Soviet Union's a priori refusal to consider compensation payments, several countries felt compelled to reemphasize the basic applicability of the "polluter pays" principle to accidental transboundary nuclear harm.[30] The issue of cost-spreading was raised also indirectly during negotiations on the IAEA Convention on Assistance.[31] Several countries, foremost among them Luxembourg,[32] took strong objection to the wording of article 7 of the Convention which covers reimbursement of the costs of assistance to a requesting State. Article 7, when strictly interpreted, leaves it up to the assisting State whether or not to charge the requesting State for its costs. Controversy arose over the fact that in those exceptional situations in which the assisting State is also the source State of the accident, the wording of article 7 would not guarantee cost internalization. The only acceptable approach to allocating nuclear damages, including assistance costs, it was emphasized, was adherence to the "polluter pays" principle.[33]

While in the debates on the adequacy of article 7 the question of the basic allocative rule overlapped with the issue of what damage is compensable, there can be no misreading of the significance of the exchange among delegates: it showed vocal and broad support for retaining the principle of "full internalization" as the generally applicable rule. Indeed, in light of the preceding policy considerations, it would be surprising if States in general were to favor cost-sharing as the keystone of a future global allocative regime.

At a first glance, the 1963 Brussels Supplementary Convention on third-party liability for nuclear damage[34] might appear to contradict the proposition concerning full cost internalization just advanced. Article 3 of the Supplementary Convention introduced, among other matters, a third tier of compensation for nuclear damage, the funds for which are derived from contributions by State parties to the Convention in accordance with a formula laid down in article 12. This example of international cost-sharing, however, is of an exceptional character. It is a limited, regional arrangement among a majority of otherwise highly interdependent European countries belonging to the Organisation for Economic Co-operation and Development (OECD), all of which—except for one (Denmark)[35]—operate nuclear power or research reactors with a transboundary impact potential. Moreover, it "kicks in" only when the first two levels of compensation funds—that is, funds from the private reactor operator and from the State in which the reactor is located—have been exhausted. In short, the Brussels Supplementary Convention hardly can be viewed as a precedent for an alternative global approach to full cost internalization.

Finally, immediately after Chernobyl some countries proposed establishing a nuclear emergency assistance fund to help developing countries in cases of nuclear accidents. These proposals, however, provide no evidence of a beginning shift toward a new entitlement principle.[36] Not only did the IAEA fail to take any action, but the fund proposals also sought to establish only a special exception to the general allocative rule. They thereby indirectly confirmed that full cost internalization continued to enjoy support as the general entitlement principle.

Retention of the Principle of State Liability

A second and related issue that needs to be squarely addressed in any reform of transnational nuclear reparation arrangements is that of the specific parameters within which internalization of the costs of transboundary nuclear accidents is to take place. As international efforts at improving and harmonizing the Paris and Vienna "private law" nuclear liability conventions[37] continue,[38] and as the IAEA has begun to address the question of international liability for transboundary nuclear damage,[39] one question stands out as deserving special attention: what role, if any, is there for a source State's international[40] liability in a multilateral treaty regime that aims at global effectiveness?

The last few decades have witnessed a gradual reversal in the purely mediate position that individuals had traditionally enjoyed in international law. Private persons or enterprises have become effective, indeed formidable actors in their own right in a variety of transnational fora. The international community's response has been to strengthen the transnational accountability of these actors in general.

A telling case is the treatment of activities that pose internationally significant risks of accidental harm to human beings or the environment. State practice addressing the problem has noticeably concentrated on the private actor's transnational accountability to the exclusion of the international liability issue that might arise between source and victim States. This is true of the diplomatic handling of damage claims in connection with transboundary accidents[41] as well as treaty practice as evidenced, among others, by the Paris and Vienna Conventions on third-party nuclear liability.[42] Most recently, during the initial stages of the IAEA's review of international liability and compensation mechanisms, a number of key States indicated a strong reluctance to venture beyond the realm of the "private law" liability conventions to that of States' international liability for transboundary nuclear damage.[43]

Although recent multilateral legislative developments might yet signal a gradual reversal,[44] the conclusion appears inevitable that today there exists a strong undercurrent toward less rather than more explicitness of the international legal consequences of States' failure to prevent the occurrence of transnational environmental damage. States' reluctance to embrace the concept of States' international liability cannot fail to have a negative impact on the normative quality of the principle concerned. While it would clearly be going too far to suggest—as some have done—that the concept's traditional contents have become negotiable,[45] there is no doubt that the political climate for invoking it in a given transboundary accident may be affected. Among other things, Chernobyl testifies to this chilling effect upon victim States' willingness to press international legal claims against the Soviet Union.

In the long run, if the recent shunning of the principle of States' international liability were to take firm root, multilateral reform attempts would be seriously compromised. For no effective international prevention and compensation regime, in particular one covering nuclear accidents, can do without retaining some measure of a source State's international accountability.

First, a source State's international liability puts a hard edge on its international obligation to prevent and minimize transboundary nuclear harm.[46] This is obviously the case where liability is the consequence of a breach of an international obligation or, in other words, represents an obligation based on a secondary rule of international law.[47] But it is similarly true of liability in the sense of a primary obligation, that is, the situation in which an international duty to repair transboundary harm arises even without there having been a causally related breach of international law. Accountability in this sense is an essential complementary notion to the primary obligations of prevention and minimization of transboundary harm that source States implicitly undertake in exchange for international acceptance of their conduct of a transnationally risk-bearing activity.[48] Indeed, explicit retention of State liability is critical to optimizing primary accident cost reduction.[49]

Private law liability arrangements, such as the Brussels Supplementary Convention, may provide for a source State's financial accountability in the event of a transboundary nuclear accident. This accountability, however, hardly matches the scope of source State liability under general international law. It therefore also fails to match the latter in terms of bolstering primary accident cost reduction. As the second tier of compensation under the Brussels Supplementary Convention,[50] the State's obligation to intervene is a merely subsidiary one and is limited, among other elements, in the amount.[51] Moreover, it is subject to all the defenses to which the private operator is entitled to assert pursuant to article 9 of the Paris Convention, including that of force majeure.[52] By contrast, under general international law,[53] a source State would be fully liable for accidental transboundary harm caused by State conduct violative of an international obligation.[54] By the same token, article XII of the 1972 Convention on Liability for Damages Caused by Objects in Outer Space[55]—reflecting State liability irrespective of international wrongfulness—incorporates also a "full reparation" standard. Finally, as noted before, present sentiment among States appears to run against accepting limitation of source State liability for transboundary nuclear damage.[56] If an extrapolation from these facts were permissible, it would have to be that whenever a source State's international liability stems from an obligation based on a primary rule of international law, claims to limitation would be strongly resisted internationally.[57]

A second qualitative difference lies in the fact that exoneration of source States from liability on account of force majeure is allowed under the Paris and Brussels Conventions, but may not have a counterpart in general international law. This nonexoneration under general international law is, admittedly, not clearly established in international practice. However, there is strong supportive evidence for a presumption of nonexoneration. Nonavailability of the defense of force majeure alone would be consistent with an international liability concept that reflects international community policy on managing transboundary risks of physical harm.[58] The International Law Commission, for example, noted that a plea of force majeure as a circumstance precluding the international wrongfulness of causal State conduct would not necessarily relieve the source State of liability for any or all transboundary damages.[59] A fortiori, when an international claim for compensation is made in connection with transboundary harm caused by a recognizable, transnationally hazardous conduct[60] exoneration on the grounds of force majeure should be inconsistent with the basic concept of strict State liability.

Explicit endorsement of source State liability is also important to ensuring adequate compensation to the transboundary victims of a nuclear accident. A "private law" nuclear liability arrangement is most unlikely to satisfy this objective.

Consider, for example, the fact that the concept of "damage compensable" is circumscribed narrowly in both the Paris and the Vienna Conventions. Neither convention appears to permit recovery of evacuation costs or damage to the environment. Liability is limited to personal injury, death, or loss of property.[61] This drawback could, of course, be corrected by expanding the liability coverage of the two private law conventions. Because of the financial implications of such an extension,[62] however, it would be conceivable only if it were tied to a commensurate increase in source State exposure to liability. In other words, alternative solutions, such as simply increasing the exposure of the nuclear plant operator or pooling expanded potential liabilities among the international community, might not be achievable within the framework of a truly global liability regime. On the one hand, increased exposure for nuclear plant operators would prove impolitic because at least some States would insist on insulating private operators against potentially ruinous liability claims.[63] On the other hand, international pooling—an arrangement to spread accident costs globally among both nuclear and nonnuclear countries along the lines of the Brussels Supplementary Convention's third-tier approach—also stands little chance of realization in a multilateral regime aspiring to global effectiveness.

Neither do prospects appear promising for an international mutual insurance system exclusively among States with nuclear power industries. The persistence of differences in national nuclear safety standards and practices renders it unlikely that States in the East and West, North and South, would agree to pool among themselves the risks of worldwide nuclear power plant accidents.[64] Moreover, even if such a regime could be realized, it is unlikely that funds made available would suffice to defray the full costs of nuclear accidents. Experience with the only comparable compensation scheme, the International Fund for Compensation of Oil Pollution Damage,[65] suggests that contracting States might be willing to accept only a strictly limited fund, implying at best a limited obligation[66] to contribute to the compensation of accidental nuclear damages.[67]

In short, any attempt at widening the notion of "damage compensable" of the private law nuclear liability conventions shifts the focus back to the principle of States' international liability and, specifically, to the limitation and exoneration issue. Obviously, a broad as well as effective international compensation scheme for transboundary nuclear damage is incompatible with either the source State's privilege to limit its liability or its right to exoneration upon proving force majeure. In other words, any successful reform of the private law conventions will require a decoupling of private operator from source State liability, a clear break with present interdependencies in the multi-tier liability system of the Paris Convention. Such unrestricted source State liability in a reformed private law regime would, however, be virtually indistinguishable in scope from source State liability under general international law.

Finally, reaffirmation of the principle of source States' international liability may be essential for expediting transboundary compensation. The inordinate delay of compensatory payments to the victims of the accident in Seveso,[68] of the breakup of the Amoco Cadiz,[69] and now of the catastrophe in Bhopal[70] is indicative of the fact that, generally speaking, private recovery efforts in cases with transnational legal ramifications tend to be cumbersome, time-consuming, and expensive. A plaintiff in a nuclear accident case might be significantly better off under either of the existing Paris or Vienna Conventions than the plaintiff in the average transboundary accident case: questions regarding the proper forum and choice of defendant, as well as the choice of law, largely would be settled a priori.[71] However, the nature and possible extent of transboundary nuclear damage—for example, small impacts diffused over a wide geographical area, or injuries that may not be provable except as a statistical probability or certainty—would suggest that, at least with regard to certain compensation claims, private litigation would be an impractical recovery strategy. In those situations, and notwithstanding its own shortcomings, the international claims process might be the only reasonable avenue to a relatively expeditious compensation of transboundary victims.

Notwithstanding the ingenuity of the drafting committees concerned and even assuming unwavering support[72] among States to finding a solution to this problem within the framework of private law, it is most improbable that the international claims process could be completely and effectively replaced. The invocation of source State international liability is bound to remain an important strategy in securing compensation for transboundary nuclear harm.

In sum, in revamping present international nuclear liability arrangements, States must pay greater attention to upholding and reaffirming the principle of States' international accountability. This comment is not to suggest that the private law approach might be intrinsically flawed. On the contrary, it is eminently reasonable[73] and may well be the format of the future international compensation arrangement. Rather, this exhortation is to remind us that within such a future system, the principle of State liability will have to play an essential, complementary or subsidiary function in reallocating the transboundary costs of nuclear accidents.

The Standard of Source State Liability

Once it has been accepted that a future multilateral liability regime should incorporate the principle of source States' international liability, few would question that strict liability should be the conventional standard to be adopted. The principle of States' strict liability might be characterized as denoting a duty on the part of the source State to compensate transboundary harm which occurs despite the State's exercise of due diligence, provided that the damage sustained is typical of a recognizable, significant transboundary risk.

In the context of nuclear accidents, such a standard is intrinsically superior to traditional international liability, which is premised on the assertion that the transboundary harm sustained is the consequence of a violation of an international obligation on the part of the source State.[74] An international demand for compensation invoking the traditional standard is likely to be technically cumbersome, notwithstanding the fact that, first, source States are under a customary international obligation to give a factual account of any accident causing significant transboundary harm;[75] and second, a claimant State would be permitted "a more liberal recourse to inferences of fact and circumstantial evidence."[76] More important, compensation demands based on the traditional standard are politically awkward because of their moral connotations. A strict liability claim, by contrast, suffers from neither drawback. In addition, strict liability is clearly preferable in terms of bolstering deterrence and reparation of accidental transboundary harm,[77] as well as from an overall fairness point of view.[78]

The Paris and Vienna Conventions indirectly testify to the merits of the principle of source States' strict liability for transboundary nuclear harm. So does the work of the International Law Commission on the topic of liability.[79] Finally, there is direct and strong support among States for a global convention based on strict liability.[80] Adoption of strict liability as the eventual conventional standard for source States' international accountability might thus appear to be a readily achievable objective. Less clear, however, is whether incorporating strict State liability into a future nuclear liability convention would constitute progressive development of the international law on State liability or mere codification of a standard that is already part of general international law. The answer to this question obviously holds important implications for how the costs of nuclear accidents might be allocated internationally in the interim period until a global liability regime actually enters into force. It is also likely to affect the nature and speed of multilateral negotiations on the conventional State liability standard.

The absence of diplomatic claims for compensation after Chernobyl might easily be taken as persuasive evidence that under present international law, source States cannot be held strictly liable for accidental transboundary nuclear harm.[81] However, such a conclusion would be both simplistic and ultimately misleading. It is true that strict liability currently cannot be considered part of customary international law. There are, admittedly, indicia of a possible emergence of a customary international legal standard of strict liability for accidental transboundary harm. For example, in the second part of its decision in the *Trail Smelter* case, the U.S.-Canadian tribunal laid down a standard of strict liability for any future transboundary harm, that is, harm notwithstanding the adoption of reasonable preventive measures by Canada.[82] Some multilateral as well as bilateral agreements explicitly provide for strict source State liability.[83] Examples also exist of extraconventional practice in which States have owned up internationally to accidental transboundary damage in a way that is suggestive of strict liability.[84] Nevertheless, international practice is clearly insufficient to warrant the inference that customary international law at this time encompasses strict source State liability for abnormally dangerous activities in general or, for that matter, for transboundary risks of nuclear power production, in particular.

Strict liability for transboundary accidental nuclear harm, however, amounts to a "general principle of law" within the meaning of article 38(1)(c) of the Statute of the International Court of Justice (ICJ).[85] It, therefore, must also be considered part and parcel of the corpus of existing international law.[86]

A "general principle of law" can be said to represent a fundamental legal idea or a specific legal concept[87] that is common to all major domestic legal systems.[88] Strict source State liability for transboundary nuclear harm fully meets these dual characteristics. First, strict liability for accidental harm can be encountered in most national legal systems. Its scope of application is not limited to nuclear accidents specifically, but covers accidents involving hazardous industrial activities in general.[89] Second, strict liability is expressive of a fundamental notion of fairness, of balancing equities. It is the price for social acceptability of an activity which entails a significant, yet unavoidable risk of harm to others who, as a rule, do not partake in offsetting benefits from the risk-bearing conduct.

Transboundary risks associated with the operation of nuclear power industries raise obviously analogous distributive justice issues among States. The concept of strict liability, as evidenced in the practice of States *foro domestico*, therefore applies *mutatis mutandis* to the international allocation of damages due to transboundary nuclear accidents. This recruitment of the principle of strict liability corresponds fully to the traditional understanding of how international law borrows domestic legal ideas: not automatically, "lock, stock and barrel," as Judge Arnold McNair observed, but as an "indication of policy and principles."[90]

The logic of strict liability as part of present-day general international law is increasingly recognized in the literature.[91] It is reflected also in the reports of the International Law Commission's special rapporteurs on liability.[92] There is no denying that the extraconventional existence of strict source State liability continues to be strongly challenged. Arguments that attempt to refute its status as a general principle of law are unpersuasive, however.

A first possible objection amounts to a criticism of the traditional understanding of "general principles of law" as an expression of the domestic legal practice of States. According to socialist international legal doctrine, general principles of law—in the sense of article 38(1)(c) of the ICJ Statute—are only those that ultimately are inferable also from international treaty or international custom.[93] This view, however, is logically inconsistent with the fact that the ICJ Statute enumerates "general principles of law" as a "source" of international law separate from treaties and custom; it is, moreover, incompatible with the *travaux préparatoires* of the drafting committee responsible for the text of article 38 of the Statute.[94]

Some critics also assert that the principle of strict liability lacks a basic, unifying normative idea that is an essential characteristic of any general principle of law.[95] This objection is particularly unpersuasive in view of the well-defined and easily appreciable considerations of equity that lie at the heart of strict liability.[96]

Finally, it has been objected that a victim State could not invoke the source State's strict international liability—in the guise of a general principle of law—as a directly applicable international legal concept. It is the nature of general principles of law—so the argument runs—that they require an international judicial or arbitral imprimatur before they can be deemed as having acquired the status of general international normativity, as it were.[97] Such a formalistic view, however, hardly takes account of the very real and powerful impact that the domestic practice of States exerts in terms of creating and shaping community expectations regarding the handling of analogous problems on the international level. There is, in any event, strong support for the view that all the "sources of law" listed in article 38 of the ICJ Statute, including the general principles of law, are generally invokable in international relations.[98]

It is submitted that no legal or technical obstacles currently exist, therefore, to the assertion of an extraconventional international strict liability claim for compensation of accidental transboundary nuclear harm. In such cases, international strict liability is entirely consistent with traditional national legal expectations as to loss allocation in analogous domestic cases. Denying this consistency by emphasizing that the claims arise in formally different legal contexts—private versus international—is both legally and politically untenable. Strict liability for hazardous activities is expressive of general community expectations at both national and international levels. Much like its domestic legal counterpart, international strict liability functions as an essential corrective to the socioeconomic imbalance which inevitably arises between those States that engage in transnationally hazardous activities and those that do not yet are exposed to the risks created by others. Thus, rather than being at odds with traditional international law, strict State liability embodies the very affirmation of a fundamental order principle of the international system, the sovereign equality of States.[99]

In a large number of potential transboundary nuclear accident situations, it seems inconceivable that a source State would reject a strict liability claim for compensation simply because of its international legal foundation as a general principle of law. If publicly presented, however, such a claim might be resisted by some States exactly on the ground of an allegedly inadequate international legal basis. The most accurate characterization of the status of strict State liability, therefore, may be that it is a widely, though not universally, acceptable international standard.[100] It should be recognized, however, that resistance to the concept is likely a reflection of the sensitivity of the legal theoretical issues raised by the general-principle-of-law approach.[101] Resistance thus does not necessarily imply a rejection of the merits of strict State liability for transboundary nuclear harm, as is evident from the growing support for the principle in the literature of Socialist countries, including the U.S.S.R.[102] Indeed, the official Soviet view, for one, appears to be in favor of strict liability, albeit in the guise of a treaty-stipulated standard.[103] This merely confirms what was suggested at the outset, namely that raising strict liability to the status of a broadly based conventional standard—and thereby to assure its general effectiveness in cases of accidental transboundary nuclear harm—might be one of the easier tasks on the post-Chernobyl multilateral legislative agenda.

Notes

1. *See* Principle 22 of the Stockholm Declaration on the Human Environment, *reprinted in* 11 I.L.M. 1416 (1972).

2. Note in particular the absence of any reference to State responsibility in the U.N. Economic Commission for Europe (ECE) Convention on Long-Range Transboundary Air Pollution, Nov. 13, 1979, T.I.A.S. No. 10541, *reprinted in* 18 I.L.M. 1442 (1979). *See id.* at footnote to art. 8(f) (discussed also *infra* Chapter 12, at text accompanying notes 109 & 12–27).

3. For a review of the ILC's work on the topic, see *supra* Chapter 4; Handl, *Liability as an Obligation Established by a Primary Rule of International Law: Some Basic Reflections on the International Law Commission's Work*, 16 NETH. Y.B. INT'L L. 49 (1985); and Magraw, *Transboundary Harm: The International Law Commission's Study of "International Liability"*, 80 AM. J. INT'L L. 305 (1986).

4. *See infra* note 10.

5. For a detailed analysis of the multilateral agenda, including measures to prevent and minimize transboundary nuclear accidents, see Handl, *Après Tchernobyl: Quelques réflexions sur le programme législatif multilatéral à l'ordre du jour*, 92 REVUE GENERAL DE DROIT INTERNATIONAL PUBLIC 5 (1988), also published as *Transboundary Nuclear Accidents: The Post-Chernobyl Multilateral Legislative Agenda*, 15 ECOLOGY L.Q. 203 (1988).

6. For details, see *infra* note 12.

7. *See, e.g.*, Adede, *Toward a Convention for the Settlement of International Claims Arising from Transboundary Nuclear Pollution Damage*, [11 Current Report] Int'l Env't Rep. (BNA) 351 (June 8, 1988); Harndt, *Völkerrechtliche Aspekte des Reaktorunglücks in Tschernobyl*, BERLINER ANWALTSBLATT, Heft 6/1986, 151; Kapteyn, *Vergoeding schade Tsjernobyl—volkenrechtelijke aspecten*, 42 NEDERLANDS JURISTEN BLAD 1329 (1986); Malone, *The Chernobyl Accident: A Case Study in International Law Regulating State Responsibility for Transboundary Nuclear Pollution*, 12 COLUM. J. ENVT'L L. 203 (1987); Pelzer, *The Impact of the Chernobyl Accident on International Nuclear Energy Law*, 25 ARCHIV DES VÖLKERRECHTS 294 (1987); Rest, *Tschernobyl und die internationale Haftung—Völkerrechtliche Aspekte*, VERSICHERUNGSRECHT 1986, at 933; P. Sands, *Chernobyl: Law and Communication: Transboundary Nuclear Air Pollution—The Legal Materials* (1986); Strohl, *Tchernobyl et le problème des obligations internationales rélatives aux accidents nucléaires*, POLITIQUE ETRANGÈRE, No. 4, 1986; Uibopuu, *Tschernobyl im Lichte des Sowjetrechts*, 30 RECHT IN OST UND WEST 269 (1986); Uschakow, *Tschernobyl und das sowjetische Recht*, VERSICHERUNGSRECHT 1986, at 17.

8. "Source State", as used in this chapter, denotes a State in whose territory or under whose control transnationally harmful effects originate.

9. For a critical review, see Handl, *Transboundary Nuclear Accidents, supra* note 5, at 230–31.

10. Note, for example, the proposed separate liability protocols pursuant to article 7(a) of the 1988 Convention on the Regulation of Antarctic Mineral Resource Activities, *reprinted in* 27 I.L.M. 868 (1988), and article 12 of the 1989 Basel Convention on the Control of Transboundary Movements of Hazardous

Wastes and Their Disposal, U.N. Doc. UNEP/IG.80/3 (1989). Note also the draft ECE Code of Conduct on Accidental Pollution of Transboundary Inland Waters, U.N. Doc. ECOSOC/ENVWA/WP.3/R.1 (1988).

11. For an example of such interpretation difficulties, see *infra* note 13.

12. For example, losses alone in agriculture are said to range from several million pounds sterling in the United Kingdom (10 [Current Report] Int'l Env't Rep. (BNA) 296 (1987)) and tens of millions of guilders in Holland (*Tsjernobyl kost Nederland "enige tientallen miljoenen"*, NRC Handelsblad, Sept. 19, 1986, at 11, col. 3) to billions of schillings in Austria (Neue Zürcher Zeitung, June 20, 1986, at 2, col. 4). For very similar figures see OECD/NEA Secretariat, *The Accident at Chernobyl—Economic Damage and Its Compensation in Western Europe*, 39 NUCLEAR L. BULL. 58 (1987).

For a discussion of the issues involved in measuring damages due to radioactivity, see *infra* Chapter 8.

13. The possibility has been raised that in the case of at least one Western European country, the Soviet Union agreed to a trade deal immediately after the accident that looked deceptively like a Soviet compensatory payment. Statement of Professor Richard Lillich, 10th Sokol Colloquium, U. of Va. School of Law, Apr. 15, 1988. And it is, of course, possible that indirect compensation of Eastern European countries occurred via adjustments in their multifaceted relationships with the Soviet Union. Still, there is no hard evidence suggesting movement on the compensation issue on the part either of potential claimant States in the sense of official presentations of claims for compensation or of the U.S.S.R. in the sense of a reversal of its earlier negative stand.

14. Only the Federal Republic of Germany has raised indirectly the issue of compensation. *Sowjetunion nennt Kohls Forderung unverschämt*, Süddeutsche Zeitung, May 20, 1986, at 6, col. 3. But in its official communications to the Soviet Union, the government failed to demand compensation. *See Innenministerium nennt Kwizinski infam*, Süddeutsche Zeitung, May 17–19, 1986, at 2, col. 2.

In 1988, it was reported that the Norwegian government intended to lodge an international claim for compensation against the Soviet Union. *Schadenersatzforderung von Samit an Moskau*, Neue Zürcher Zeitung, Jan. 13, 1988, at 5, col. 1. But there is no indication that this claim has been asserted.

15. The Swedish foreign minister indicated such a belief. *See Tjernobylolyckan: Inget skadestånd*, Dagens Nyheter, May 28, 1986, at 11, col. 2. The Swiss government has taken a similar view. Statement of the Federal Council in Swiss Parliament, June 1986 (author's personal communication with Bernard Dubois, Legal Advisor to the Swiss Foreign Office).

16. *See, e.g.*, statement of the Soviet news agency TASS, *cited in Moskau weist Forderungen nach Schadenersatz zurück*, Frankfurter Allgemeine Zeitung, May 15, 1986, at 1, col. 2; statement of the Soviet delegate in the debates of the Committee of the Whole of the International Atomic Energy Agency (IAEA) General Conference's Special Session, I.A.E.A. Doc. GC(SPL.I)/COM.5/OR.1, at 4, para. 13 (1986).

17. *See, e.g.*, statement of Walter Wallmann (then West German Minister of the Environment), Süddeutsche Zeitung, Sept. 29, 1986, at 8.

As to the political sensitivity of the idea of compensatory claims within the Eastern bloc, see *Chernobyl Creates New Tightrope: Despite Economic Damage, Bloc Seeks Not to Offend Soviet*, Int'l Herald Tribune, June 9, 1986, at 1, col. 5.

18. Statement of Professor Ian Brownlie, 10th Sokol Colloquium, U. of Va. School of Law, Apr. 15, 1988; *supra* Chapter 5, at text accompanying note 10.

19. *See* Handl, *Transboundary Nuclear Accidents, supra* note 5, 242–47 (discussing the issue of whether, in the absence of generally accepted intervention levels, the costs of victim States' action to reduce the health risk to their populations could be considered damages attributable to the party responsible for the original accident, or costs due to a *novus actus interveniens*).

20. As to the need for caution in using "incidents" like Chernobyl as an epistemic unit for the assessment of international law, see M. Reisman, *International Incidents: Introduction to a New Genre in International Law*, 10 Yale J. Int'l L. 1, 13 (1984).

21. For an exposition of the traditional view, see, for example, G. Dahm, 3 Völkerrecht 238 (1961); *see further infra under* Retention of the Principle of State Liability.

22. *See, e.g., Kwizinski lehnt jede Entschädigung ab*, Süddeutsche Zeitung, May 16, 1986, at 2, col. 2.

23. *See especially* Pravda, *cited in Sowjetunion nennt Kohls Forderung unverschämt, supra* note 14; *Westen heeft zich inzake Tsjernobyl "misdragen"*, NRC Handelsblad, May 28, 1986, at 5, col. 7. Soviet anger appears to have been principally directed at what the Soviet government viewed as Western attempts to exploit the disaster for political and economic purposes. In part, however, it seemed to reflect also a Soviet view that having already incurred catastrophic losses at home, the Soviet Union should not be held accountable also for damages abroad.

24. There is evidence of the influence of such a "victim-pays" philosophy in European East-West environmental relations. For references, see Handl, *National Uses of Transboundary Air Resources: The International Entitlement Issue Reconsidered*, 26 Nat. Resources J. 405, 457 (1986); Süddeutsche Zeitung, Mar. 4, 1986, at 20, col. 4; The Economist, Mar. 4, 1987, at 45, 46. *See also* Brownlie, *A Survey of Customary Rules of Environmental Protection*, 13 Nat. Resources J. 179, 188 (1973) (raising the possibility that reducing damages because of the poverty of the tortfeasor may be a general principle of law, within the meaning of article 38(1)(c) of the Statute of the International Court of Justice).

25. Rubin, *The Soviet Nuclear Disaster and the Law*, 35 Int'l Practitioners' Notebook 8, at 9 (1986).

26. *Cf.* statement of the Soviet member of the International Law Commission, Ushakov, at the 1973rd meeting of the Commission, U.N. Doc. A/CN.4/SR.1973, at 4 (1986).

27. *Cf.* Quadri, *Cours général de droit international public*, 113 Recueil des Cours 237, 469 (1964).

28. *See infra under* Retention of the Principle of State Liability.

29. Given the threat that the use of carbon fuel consumption might pose to global climatic stability, however, *see, e.g.*, Schneider, *The Changing Climate*, 261 Sci. Am. 70 (Sept. 1989), energy conservation or alternative methods of national energy production, such as by nuclear fission, might well come to be considered in the international interest.

30. *See especially* statements of Walter Wallmann (FRG), I.A.E.A. Doc. GC(SPL.I)/OR.1, at 27–28, para. 64 (1986); and of the Swiss delegate, Schlumpf, I.A.E.A. Doc. GC(SPL.I)/OR.4, at 10, para. 37 (1986). The "polluter pays" principle was adopted by the Organization for Economic Coopera-

tion and Development in 1974. O.E.C.D. Doc. C(174)224 (1974), *reprinted in* 14 I.L.M. 242, 244 (1975).

31. For the final text, see Convention on Assistance in the Case of a Nuclear Accident or Radiological Emergency, *opened for signature* Sept. 26, 1986, I.A.E.A. Doc. INFCIRC/336, *reprinted in* 25 I.L.M. 1377 (1986) (entered into force Feb. 26, 1987).

32. *See* statements by the delegates of Luxembourg, I.A.E.A. Doc. GC(SPL.I)/OR.2, at 31–34, paras. 97–102 (1986); of Mexico, I.A.E.A. Doc. GC(SPL.I)/OR.5, at 33, para. 128; of Jordan, I.A.E.A. Doc. GC(SPL.I)/OR.7, at 23, para. 104; and of Portugal, I.A.E.A. Doc. GC(SPL.I)/OR.7, at 25, para. 112.

33. *See, e.g.*, statement of the delegate of Luxembourg, *supra* note 32.

34. Convention Supplementary to the Paris Convention of 29th July 1960 on Third Party Liability in the Field of Nuclear Energy, *reprinted in* 2 I.L.M. 685 (1963) [hereinafter Brussels Supplementary Convention].

35. As to ratifications of the Brussels Supplementary Convention, see Busek-ist, *Haftungsprobleme im Verhältnis zwischen Vertragsstaaten des Pariser und des Wiener Atomhaftungsübereinkommens*, in FRIEDLICHE KERNENERGIENUTZUNG UND STAATSGRENZEN IN MITTELEUROPA 271, 300 (N. Pelzer ed. 1986).

36. Mexico first proposed the emergency fund idea at the 1986 Special Session of the IAEA General Conference. No specific action has been taken on this matter since then, other than issuance of a tentative position paper by the IAEA Secretariat. *See Establishment of a Nuclear Emergency Assistance Fund to Help Developing Countries in Cases of Nuclear Accidents*, I.A.E.A. Doc. GOV/INF/520, at 1 (1987).

37. *See* Vienna Convention on Civil Liability for Nuclear Damage, July 29, 1960, *reprinted in* 2 I.L.M. 727 (1963); Paris Convention on Third Party Liability in the Field of Nuclear Activity, May 21, 1963, *reprinted in* 55 AM. J. INT'L L. 1082 (1961). These conventions are discussed in Chapter 6, *supra*.

38. In 1988, a "Joint Protocol Relating to the Application of the Vienna Convention and Paris Convention", to extend mutually the special liability regimes established under each convention and to prevent conflicts of law arising from the application of the conventions, was adopted by a diplomatic conference at Vienna. *Done* at Vienna, Sept. 21, 1988. Since then, efforts within the OECD Nuclear Energy Agency and the IAEA to refine the Paris/Brussels regime and to amend the Vienna Convention, respectively, have continued.

39. *See* IAEA General Conference Resolution on "Liability for Nuclear Damage," U.N. Doc. IAEA/GC(XXXII)/RES/491, 2 (1988). The first session of a recently established high-level working group that will consider, among other issues, the question of international liability, is scheduled to meet in May/June 1989. *See* 4 I.A.E.A. NEWSBRIEFS 3 (No. 4, 1989).

40. In other words, discussion will be limited to the function of the source State's international liability. Conceivably, it could, of course, be extended to include the concept of the source State's "transnational" liability, that is, its direct accountability, in its capacity as source State, vis-à-vis the private foreign claimant. As to details of such a conceivable arrangement, see Handl, *State Liability for Accidental Transnational Environmental Damage by Private Persons*, 74 AM. J. INT'L L. 525, 560–64 (1980); *see further* J. BALLENEGGER, LA POLLUTION EN DROIT INTERNATIONAL 227 (1975); Dominicé, *Observations sur la définition du droit des gens*, in FESTSCHRIFT F. RUDOLF BINDSCHEDLER 71, 89 (E. Diez, J. Monnier, J. Müller, H. Reimann & L. Wildhaber eds. 1980).

41. A recent illustration is how the issue of compensation was broached in the context of the fire that swept through the Sandoz plant in Basel and the resulting pollution of the Rhine. Thus the French government, through its environment minister, emphasized that it was Sandoz, not the Swiss government, that was responsible for indemnification: "It is the polluter who pays." Statement of Alain Carignon, Feb. 11, 1987, *cited in* [10 Current Report] Int'l Env't Rep. (BNA) 97, 98 (1987). See also the communiqué of the 7th Ministerial Conference concerning the pollution of the Rhine, Rotterdam, Dec. 19, 1986, in which the Swiss government, without acknowledging any legal obligation, simply undertook to transmit foreign claims for compensation to Sandoz. Umwelt, No. 1, at 25, 27 (1987).

42. *Supra* note 37. Both conventions contain, however, reservation clauses in which State parties' recourse to traditional international legal remedies is expressly being preserved. *See* art. XVIII of the Vienna Convention, *supra* note 37; Annex II of the Paris Convention, *supra* note 37. By contrast, neither the 1969 Brussels Convention on Civil Liability for Oil Pollution, *reprinted in* 9 I.L.M. 45 (1970), nor the (rejected) draft IMO Convention on Civil Liability and Compensation in Connexion with the Carriage of Noxious and Hazardous Substances, IMO Doc. LEG/CONF.6/3 (1984), make corresponding references.

43. For further details, see Handl, *Transboundary Nuclear Accidents*, *supra* note 5, at 230–31.

44. A more balanced focus on the liability issue might emerge as a result of various recent multilateral treaty regimes which call for separate protocols on liability and compensation. *See supra* note 10. Also the work of the International Law Commission on the State responsibility and liability topics might well make it less likely that the issue of State liability would be skirted as readily in the future as has been done in the recent past. As to the status of the ILC's work, see *Report of the International Law Commission on the Work of Its Fortieth Session*, 43 U.N. GAOR Supp. (No. 10) at 188, 220, U.N. Doc. A/43/10 (1988). The Commission's work on the liability topic is also discussed in Chapter 4, *supra*.

45. Correspondingly, the notion of "soft State liability" has been gaining currency among commentators. *See especially* Kiss, *L'état du droit de l'environnement en 1981: Problèmes et solutions*, 108 JOURNAL DE DROIT INTERNATIONAL 499, 518 (1981). For a critical view of this development, see Handl, *International Liability of States for Marine Pollution*, 21 CAN. Y.B. INT'L L. 85, 87–88 (1983).

46. *See* Brownlie, *Causes of Action in the Law of Nations*, 50 BRIT. Y.B. INT'L L. 13, 40 (1979).

47. In the ILC's parlance, which is now generally followed in international legal discourse, "primary rules of obligation"—hence also "primary obligations"—denote rules which encompass the bulk of the international obligations of States. "Secondary rules," or rules of "State responsibility" proper, are technical in nature and exclusively concerned with determining the legal consequences of a failure to fulfill obligations established by primary rules. *See Report of the International Law Commission on the Work of Its Twenty-Fifth Session*, [1973] 2 Y.B. INT'L L. COMM'N 161, 169 para. 40.

48. *See infra under* The Standard of Source State Liability.

49. On the international plane, the relationship between States' accident avoidance efforts and liability exposure is, admittedly, somewhat speculative. If domestic legal experience, in particular in the realm of products liability, can be

considered to provide an indication, however, an increase in the certainty and the amount of potential liability is likely to result in increased efforts at preventing and minimizing transboundary harm.

50. Brussels Supplementary Convention, *supra* note 34, art. 3(b)(ii).

51. Pursuant to article 3(b)(ii) of the 1982 Protocol to Amend the Brussels Supplementary Convention, the amount of reparation is limited to 175 million Special Drawing Rights. Bundesgesetzblatt 1985, II, 698. On top of that, the source State would be accountable for a fraction of an additional 125 million Special Drawing Rights whose exact amount is determined in accordance with article 12 of the Brussels Supplementary Convention.

However, the 1982 Protocol has not yet entered into force. Presently, therefore, the lower liability limits of the Brussels Supplementary Convention apply, that is, 70 million and, on a prorated basis, an additional 50 million units of account. Brussels Supplementary Convention, *supra* note 34, art. 3(b)(ii)–(iii).

52. Thus according to article 2(a)(i) of the Brussels Supplementary Convention, *supra* note 34, source State intervention is limited to the damages "for which an operator of a nuclear installation . . . is liable under the Paris Convention." Article 9 of the Paris Convention, *supra* note 37, stipulates as follows: "Except insofar as national legislation may provide to the contrary, the operator shall not be liable for damage caused by a nuclear incident due to an act of armed conflict, invasion, civil war, insurrection, or a grave natural disaster of an exceptional character." Some countries, for example, the Federal Republic of Germany, have made use of this authorization and excluded force majeure as grounds for exoneration. *See* article 25(3) of the German "Atomgesetz."

53. An exception to this rule would present itself in the situation in which payment of reparation due might endanger the very existence of the source State. *See* W. Wengler, 1 VÖLKERRECHT 514 (1964); Graefrath, *Responsibility and Damages Caused: Relationship between Responsibility and Damages*, 185 RECUEIL DES COURS 9, 92 (1984).

54. This is the clear implication of the *Chorzow Factory (Indemnity)* decision in which the Permanent Court of International Justice held that "reparation must, as far as possible, wipe out all the consequences of an illegal act and reestablish the situation which would, in all probability, have existed if that act had not been committed." 1928 P.C.I.J. (ser. A) No. 17, at 47.

The very same "full reparation" standard is also reflected in article 6, paragraph 2 of the draft articles on State responsibility submitted to the International Law Commission by Wilhelm Riphagen. Riphagen, *Fifth Report on the Content, Forms and Degrees of State Responsibility* (Part Two of the Draft Articles), U.N. Doc. A/CN.4/380, at 6 (1984); *cf.* statement of Umpire Parker in the *American-Hawaiian Steamship Company* case, *cited in* 2 M. WHITEMAN, DAMAGES IN INTERNATIONAL LAW 1245 (1937).

55. 10 I.L.M. 965 (1971).

56. *See supra under* The Principle that Transboundary Costs of Nuclear Accidents Be Fully Internalized, especially the statement of the Swiss delegate, *supra* note 30.

57. *See also infra under* The Standard of Source State Liability.

58. As to the intrinsic lack of justifiability of force majeure in the narrow sense of "Act of God", as a basis for exoneration in cases of transboundary accidents due to transnationally hazardous activities, see G. HANDL, MANAGING THE RISK OF TRANSBOUNDARY ACCIDENTS (forthcoming).

59. *See* ILC Draft Articles on State Responsibility, art. 35 ("Reservation as to compensation for damage"); the ILC commentary to draft article 31 ("Force majeure and fortuitous event"), in which the Commission endorses the view that as between innocent source and innocent victim States, it might indeed be unfair to let the transboundary loss lie with the latter completely or possibly even only in part. [1979] 2 Y.B. Int'l L. Comm'n, pt. 2, at 132, para. 39. *But see, e.g.*, Graefrath and Steininger, *Kodifikation der völkerrechtlichen Verantwortlichkeit*, [1973] Neue Justiz 225, 228.

60. *See infra under* The Standard of Source State Liability.

61. *See* Vienna Convention, *supra* note 37, art. I(k); Paris Convention, *supra* note 37, art. 3. *See also* Shapar & Reyners, *Nuclear Third Party Liability: The Challenge of Chernobyl*, 32 Nuclear Engineering Int'l 25, 26 (1987). *But see* Deprimoz, *La notion de dommage nucléaire appliquée au coût des mesures préventives en case de ménace imminente de dommages aux tiers*, in Agence de L'ocde Pour L'energie Nucléaire et Agence Internationale de L'energie Atomique, La Responsabilité Civile Nucléaire et L'assurance 215 (1985).

62. Thus a recent report of the U.S. General Accounting Office estimates that average financial consequences for a catastrophic nuclear power plant accident could range from $67 million to $15.5 billion at any one of 119 U.S. plants. U.S. General Accounting Office, *Nuclear Regulation: A Perspective on Liability Protection for a Nuclear Plant Accident*, GAO/RCED–87–124, at 18 (June 1987). These figures include evacuation and decontamination costs as well as land and farm crop values.

63. Note, in this context, the recent renewal of the Price Anderson Act, 42 U.S.C. § 2210 (1982 & West Supp. Dec. 1988), signaling the retention of a liability limit for public utilities involved in nuclear power accidents.

Even in those countries in which the operator's liability is in principle unlimited, unlimited insurance coverage is not required, nor logically speaking, is it possible. *See* N. Pelzer, Beschränkte und Unbeschränkte Haftung im Deutschen Atomrecht 57 (1982). State intervention to defray the costs of a catastrophic accident is an integral part of the national liability regime concerned. *See, e.g.*, Swiss Act of Mar. 18, 1983, on Nuclear Third Party Liability, arts. 3(1), 11, 12, SR 732.44, AS 1983, 1986.

64. For a discussion of the merits of such a fund, see *infra* Chapter 8.

65. International Convention on the Establishment of an International Fund for Compensation for Oil Pollution Damage, *reprinted in* 11 I.L.M. 284 (1972) [hereinafter Oil Fund Convention]; Protocol of 1984 to Amend the International Convention on the Establishment of an International Fund for Compensation for Oil Pollution Damage (1971), in IMO, *International Conference on Liability and Compensation for Damage in Connexion with the Carriage of Certain Substances by Sea, 1984* 26 (1985).

66. *See, e.g.*, Oil Fund Convention, *supra* note 65, arts. 4(4), 12.

67. It is true, of course, that under the Oil Fund Convention, supra note 65, only a "person" as defined in article 10 of the Convention and article I(2) of the International Convention on Civil Liability for Oil Pollution Damage, supra note 65, would be liable to contribute to the fund. However, pursuant to article 14(1) of the Oil Fund Convention, any contracting State could "declare that it assumes itself obligations that are incumbent under this Convention on any person" liable to the fund.

68. *See Nach zehn Jahren noch keine Lira*, Süddeutsche Zeitung, July 11, 1986, at 48, col. 4.

69. In Re Amoco Cadiz, 20 Env't Rep. Cas. (BNA) 2041 (1984). A decision on damages was finally handed down on January 11, 1988, after almost ten years of complex and expensive litigation. In Re Oil Spill by the "Amoco Cadiz," Findings of Fact, Conclusion of Law and Memorandum Opinion, Jan. 11, 1988 (unpublished). It has since been revised to allow for a recommended increase in damages and is, of course, still being appealed. See Amoco's Damages Raised by $30 Million in Cadiz Spill [sic], N.Y. Times, Feb. 22, 1989, at 29, col. 1. On some of the issues in the case, see Pontavice, Affaire "droit de l'environnement 'versus' droit maritime" ou la décision rendue le 18 avril 1984 concernant "l'Amoco Cadiz", 8 ANNUAIRE DE DROIT MARITIME ET AERIEN 9 (1985).

70. In February 1989, a settlement set at $470 million was reached between India and Union Carbide. See Union Carbide Corp. v. India, Order dated May 4, 1989 (Supreme Court of India); see also McCaffrey, Expediting the Provision of Compensation to Accident Victims, in TRANSFERRING HAZARDOUS TECHNOLOGIES AND SUBSTANCES: THE INTERNATIONAL LEGAL CHALLENGE 199 (G. Handl & R. Lutz eds. 1989).

71. As to jurisdictional clauses, see article 13 of the Paris Convention, supra note 37, and article II of the Vienna Convention, supra note 37; as to the "proper defendant," see articles 3 and 6 of the Paris Convention and article II of the Vienna Convention; as to the choice of law, see article 14 of the Paris Convention, and article VIII of the Vienna Convention.

72. This is clearly an overly optimistic assumption given the reservation expressed by some States with regard to the private law approach. For a representative summary of their position, see the statement of the Soviet governor at the IAEA Board of Governors' meeting of Feb. 19, 1987, I.A.E.A. Doc. GOV/OR.667, at 13, para. 31 (1987).

73. See Handl, supra note 40, at 560–64.

74. See the International Law Commission's Draft Articles on State Responsibility, Part I, art. 3, [1980] Y.B. INT'L L. COMM'N, pt. 2, at 30. For a detailed discussion of established bases of international liability of States, see Handl, supra note 3.

75. See Corfu Channel (Merits), 1949 I.C.J. Reports 4, 18.

76. Id.

77. See supra under Retention of the Principle of State Liability; Handl, supra note 45, at 98.

78. See infra text following note 89.

79. See infra note 92; statement during the debates of the International Law Commission (ILC) by the ILC's second special rapporteur on the liability topic, Julio Barboza, 1972nd meeting of the ILC, U.N. Doc. A/CN.4/SR.1972, at 12 (1986).

80. See, e.g., statement of the representative of Austria at the meeting of the IAEA Board of Governors, Feb. 19, 1987, I.A.E.A. Doc. GOV/OR.667, at 20, para. 55 (1987).

81. There is no gainsaying that uncertainty regarding extraconventional strict liability is one of the factors that may account for the dearth of diplomatic claims for compensation after Chernobyl. Note in this context that the perception of "unclear legal bases" prompted a negative assessment of prospects for compensation in the Federal Republic of Germany. Grenzüberschreitende Haftung angestrebt, Frankfurter Allgemeine Zeitung, July 3, 1986, at 2, col. 2.

82. See Trail Smelter (U.S. v. Can.), 3 R. Int'l Arb. Awards 1906, 1980 (1938 & 1941).

83. *See* further references in Handl, *supra* note 3, at 62 n. 61.

84. *See, e.g.*, U.N. Secretariat, *Survey of Practice Relative to International Liability for Injurious Consequences Arising out of Acts not Prohibited by International Law*, U.N. Doc. ST/LEG/15, at 282–89 (1984).

85. Statute of the International Court of Justice, 59 Stat. 1055, T.S. 993, 3 BEVINS 1179. Section 102 of the RESTATEMENT (THIRD) OF FOREIGN RELATIONS OF THE UNITED STATES (1987) contains a similar source of law: "General principles common to the major legal systems, even if not incorporated or reflected in customary law or international agreement, may be invoked as supplementary rules of international law where appropriate."

86. It serves us well to remember, however, that not every legal phenomenon which can be classified in terms of any one of the categories of "sources" listed in article 38(1) of the ICJ Statute, is in fact "law." *See* McDougal & Reisman, *The Prescribing Function in the World Constitutive Process: How International Law Is Made*, 6 YALE STUD. IN WORLD PUB. ORD. 249, 268 (1980). The suggestion, they argue, that "whatever emanates from these sources [is], in fact, law . . . may, in particular contexts, be belied by other communications or signals about authority and control."

87. Thus according to Sir Hersh Lauterpacht, "the recourse to and the utility of general principles of law are not confined to fundamental, or abstract, maxims of jurisprudence of a general character." H. LAUTERPACHT, 1 INTERNATIONAL LAW, COLLECTED PAPERS 70 (E. Lauterpacht ed. 1970).

88. *See, e.g.*, Vitanyi, *Les positions doctrinales concernant le sens de la notion de "principes généraux de droit reconnus par les nations civilisées"*, 86 REVUE GENERAL DE DROIT INTERNATIONAL PUBLIC 48, 90 (1982).

89. *See, e.g.*, the review in M. Arsanjani, *No-fault Liability from the Perspective of the General Principle of Law* (U.N. Codification Division 1979) (unpublished); M. WILL, QUELLEN ERHÖHTER GEFAHR (1984).

90. *International Status of Southwest Africa*, 1950 I.C.J. 128, 148.

91. *See* in particular Hardie, *Nuclear Liability: The General Principles of Law and Further Proposals*, 36 BRIT. Y.B. OF INT'L L. 223, 237 (1960); Jenks, *Liability for Ultra-Hazardous Activities in International Law*, 117 RECUEIL DES COURS 99, 105 (1966); Kelson, *State Responsibility and the Abnormally Dangerous Activity*, 13 HARV. INT'L L.J. 197, 243 (1972); Randelzhofer & Simma, *Das Kernkraftwerk an der Grenze*, in FESTSCHRIFT F. FRIEDRICH BERBER 389, 428–30 (1973); Wildhaber, *Die Öldestillerieanlage Sennwald und das Völkerrecht der grenzüberschreitenden Luftverschmutzungen*, 21 ANNUAIRE SUISSE DE DROIT INTERNATIONAL 97, 117 (1975); Cahier, *Le problème de la responsabilité pour risque en droit international*, in INTERNATIONAL RELATIONS IN A CHANGING WORLD 409, 427–28 (Geneva Ecole des Hautes Etudes Internationales 1977); Malinverni, *Surrégénérateurs et droit international du voisinage*, in LIVRE JAUNE SUR LA SOCIÉTÉ DU PLUTONIUM 187, 197 (1981); Kühne, *Haftung bei grenzüberschreitenden Schäden aus Reaktorunfällen*, 35 NEUE JURISTISCHE ZEITSCHRIFT 2139, 2146 (1986). For further references, see Handl, *supra* note 40, at 552 n. 125.

For a recent affirmation of strict liability for ultrahazardous activities as an "emerging general principle of (national) law," see WCED Experts Group on Environmental Law, *Final Report, Legal Principles for Environmental Protection and Sustainable Development*, WCDE/86/23/Add.1, comment to art. 11 (June 1986).

92. Both special rapporteurs proceed from the assumption that, in the final analysis, strict liability must be part of the existing international legal order. *See*

Quentin-Baxter, *Third Report on International Liability for Injurious Consequences Arising out of Acts not Prohibited by International Law*, U.N. Doc. A/CN.4/360, 19, para. 41 (1982); Barboza, *First Report on International Liability for Injurious Consequences Arising out of Acts not Prohibited by International Law*, U.N. Doc. A/CN.4/402, 23–30, paras. 41–57 (1986).

93. *Cf. especially*, G. TUNKIN, THEORY OF INTERNATIONAL LAW 202 (1974).

94. *See especially*, statement of Lord Philimore, P.C.I.J., Advisory Committee of Jurists, Procès-verbaux of the Proceedings of the Committee, July 17–July 24, 1920, with Annexes, 335 (1920).

95. *See* Randelzhofer, *Probleme der völkerrechtlichen Gefährdungshaftung*, in 24 BERICHTE DER DEUTSCHEN GESELLSCHAFT FÜR VÖLKERRECHT 67 (1983).

96. *See supra* text following note 89.

97. *See especially*, G. VAN HOOF, RETHINKING THE SOURCES OF INTERNATIONAL LAW 149 (1983).

98. *See* A. VERDROSS & B. SIMMA, UNIVERSELLES VÖLKERRECHT 383 (4th ed. 1984); H. LAUTERPACHT, *supra* note 87, at 71; Virally, *Cours général de droit international public*, 183 RECUEIL DES COURS 9, 172 (1983).

99. For further analysis, see Handl, *supra* note 3, at 76–78.

100. This statement is not to suggest, however, that strict liability does not represent a generally valid international legal standard. After all, effectiveness in every single case has never been and cannot be a required condition for a norm's general validity.

101. *See, e.g.*, Steinert, *Verantwortlichkeit und Haftung im Völkerrecht*, 30 WISS. ZEITSCHRIFT DER HUMBOLDT-UNIVERSITÄT ZU BERLIN, GES.-SPRACHW. R. No. 1, at 23 (1981).

102. Note, for example, the treatment of the matter in a recent Soviet manual on international law. The international liability of States arises "not only by virtue of violations of norms of international law, or by virtue of obligations from treaties, but also out of injurious consequences of lawful activities. It is incurred in case of material damage involving a source of increased danger, the utilization or application of which is not prohibited by international law (so-called responsibility for risk)." MEZHDUNARODNOE PRAVO 172 (N. Blatova ed.-in-chief 1987); *see also* S. Paskalei, OB'EKTIVNAIA OTVETSTVENNOST' GOSUDARSTV V MEZHDUNARODNOM PRAVE 116–19 (1985).

103. *See* statement of the Soviet governor, *supra* note 71, at 12–13, paras. 30–33.

Chapter 8
Measuring Liability for Damage Due to Radioactivity

Paul C. Szasz

Introduction

Any system of international accountability (whether based on State or private responsibility) involving compensation for damage caused by international pollution requires addressing the problem of assessing the injuries to individual victims and specific property and, possibly, the harm to the environment generally. However, the latter endeavor raises very difficult questions beyond the scope of this chapter, even with respect to harm due to radioactivity from nuclear accidents.

The subject of this chapter—how to ascertain the amount of damage to persons and property from radiation—is really in the first instance more of a scientific than a strictly legal one. At the very least, this subject is at the interface between the two disciplines of science, specifically medicine, and of law. This is particularly so because I do not propose to deal with the issue of the basis of liability, that is, with the questions of whether, to what extent, and to whom the State or person responsible for emitting radiation or radioactive pollution is to pay compensation.[1] Rather, I will examine only how a legal link between a given amount of radiation or pollution and any actual or potential damage to persons or property might be established.

Furthermore, it should be noted that this question, at least in the first instance, is not primarily a peculiarly international one, but is just as pertinent in the case of intra-State damage. Only in considering some of the mechanisms for paying compensation that might be necessary in light of the technical uncertainties in ascertaining damage will any international aspect of the situation make any difference. Nor are these problems entirely peculiar to the nuclear field; they also share a number of characteristics with other types of pollution.[2]

In order to analyze, clearly and usefully, the method of establishing a legal link between a particular exposure to radiation or to radioactive pollution and any damage therefrom, it is necessary to consider separately a number of different situations. These will be presented in the following order: first, physical damage to persons, considered in three, not always clearly separable circumstances—(1) persons suffering immediate injury from an exposure to a large amount of radiation, (2) persons exposed to a significant amount of radiation, but not enough to cause any immediately observable damage, and (3) persons merely exposed to some excess radiation; second, psychological damage to persons exposed, or perhaps merely possibly exposed, to radiation; and third, damage to property exposed to radiation, including both property directly destroyed or damaged and property that may have to be destroyed or at least decontaminated as a result of an exposure to radioactive pollution.

Various Situations of Actual or Potential Radiation Damage

Physical Damage to Persons

Immediate Radiation Damage to Persons

In those situations in which persons are exposed to such massive doses of radiation that they suffer immediate or almost immediate damage, such as burns or radiation sickness, there is no special problem in associating the damage with the nuclear cause. The rapidly following death or illness is clearly attributable to the radiation.[3] If death does not occur soon, the long-term effects of excessive radiation exposure, in terms of certain illnesses or of a generally reduced lifespan, are in part already well enough established[4] so that either the legal system can deal with these as it does with the multitude of more conventional traumas (such as damage to or the destruction of an organ due to a physical injury) or the problems of the long-term effects are similar to those dealt with under the next section relating to significant but nonmassive radiation exposure.

It should also be noted that situations involving massive exposures to radiation are unlikely to occur in an international context. Except possibly if an essentially mechanical explosion projects radioactive debris some distance, it would seem inconceivable for a stationary reactor, even if situated immediately on an international boundary, to cause radiation of such strength outside its site. It is, of course, possible that at the time of the accident foreigners are within the facility, including foreigners whom the State and the operator are under a special duty to protect—such as International Atomic Energy Agency (IAEA) safeguards inspectors;[5] that, however, impinges on the question of liability, which is beyond the scope of this chapter. The other possibility of substantial concentrated transboundary radioactive pollution is the crash of a satellite carrying a reactor or large quantities of radioactive materials—a subject already for some years under study by the Legal Sub-Committee of the United Nations Committee on the Peaceful Uses of Outer Space.[6]

Exposure of Persons to Significant Radiation
Not Causing Immediate Damage

The situation with respect to persons who are, or may have been, exposed to significant amounts of radiation, but not enough to cause any immediately ascertainable damage, is considerably more difficult. Again, it should be noted that such a situation is unlikely to arise on a transnational basis from a reactor accident, except for persons inside or in the immediate neighborhood of the facility or persons who handle debris from a nuclear satellite.

The difficulty in determining the damage that may be suffered by persons who were exposed to significant radiation is essentially two-fold: (1) a determination of the amount of the exposure, and (2) a conclusion as to the resulting damage. Most persons, of course, do not routinely wear dosimeters or other means of determining the amount of radiation to which they may have been exposed. Those persons who do wear dosimeters, do so normally in situations where they have reason to fear such exposure and are therefore presumably taking reasonable precautions to avoid being subjected to excessive dosages. Thus persons who are exposed unexpectedly to possibly large amounts of radiation—by being very close to a nuclear accident, or, more likely, by unintentionally handling radioactive debris—will probably not be able to prove with any certainty even the order of magnitude of their exposure.[7] Of course, if that exposure is so massive that immediate physical effects are noticeable—for example, a lowered white cell count—then the situation is that already mentioned: exposure causing some immediate damage. In other situations, a determination of the amount of exposure can only be indirect and correspondingly imprecise. Deductions might be based on the amount of time spent in certain areas as to which contemporaneous radiation measurements were made, or, more likely, as to which some later indirect calculations can be made. This, in effect, was the situation of the persons who in recent years have made claims against the U.S. government for damage to their health from the fallout from nuclear tests performed decades earlier.[8]

Again, similarly to the fallout victims, the second problem of the persons we are now considering is how to relate their exposure, whether or not ascertainable with any accuracy, to any particular damage to their health. Here we must now consider two approaches. One is to wait to learn whether such persons eventually show signs of diseases that can arguably result from excessive radiation exposure: for example, certain types of cancers that are not likely to appear for some years or even decades[9] or genetic defects in offspring, which might be observed much earlier (e.g., in a baby born soon after a parent's exposure), but, on the other hand, might only show up in later generations.[10] This is what, perforce, the fallout victims did—in part because at the time of their exposure they did not even know they had been injured, and in part because at that time experience was lacking to make any useful prediction as to their future health.[11] Gradually, however—in large part because of the experience gained with these earlier victims of the military uses of or experiments with nuclear energy,[12] including the far greater number in Japan,[13] as well as some persons who suffered industrial exposure[14]—it is, or may become possible, to use an alternative approach, based on predictions, at least statistical, about the likelihood that a given exposure will engender (or have a substantial likelihood of engendering) a particular disease,[15] or that life will in some as yet incompletely understood way be shortened as a result of that exposure.[16]

This now suggests that there may be various mechanisms whereby victims of substantial radiation exposure due to a nuclear accident might be compensated. They might be required to wait until there is some evidence of damaged health, and then make their claim—on the understanding that any statute of limitations would not run from the date of the accident or exposure, but rather from the date an illness becomes evident.[17] Alternatively, they might immediately be given a payment that would correspond, in some statistical way, to the chance of a diminished life expectancy and of increased medical expenses. As a variant of the latter approach, a payment might be made not to them but to some health or social service system, perhaps one associated with their national government,[18] which would then have the responsibility of caring for them and their dependents should a possibly radiation-related disease develop.

As we are here considering these questions in a transnational context, so that those responsible for the nuclear disaster are of a nationality, or most likely are the government, of a State other than the

State(s) of the victims, the last-mentioned mechanism would seem to be the most attractive one. It is hard to contemplate any way in which radiation victims could, or would want to be obliged to, assert claims against the perpetrator government decades after a particular incident. Much more reasonable would be some mechanism whereby the perpetrator makes, as soon as possible after the incident in question, a lump-sum payment in respect of all persons who can establish that (subject to the uncertainties already noted) they were exposed to substantial radiation, which payment would be collected by the government(s) of the victims, and would be used by it to treat or compensate the latter as and when the need arises. This mechanism would be consistent, incidentally, with the traditional international law approach concerning State responsibility for injury to aliens. Under this approach the international claim belongs to the State of which the person injured is a national, rather than to that person, and the State of nationality is not even required to pass on any proceeds received from settling such a claim—but will generally do so, of course, to the extent and in the manner that is considered justified under its internal law.[19]

In any event, unless the society to which the radiation victim belongs offers a comprehensive social protection scheme, including health care for all regardless of cause of the disease or economic circumstances, it will sooner or later be necessary to try to establish whether the health problems of that victim are due to that earlier exposure.[20] In making such a determination, it will presumably be necessary to rely on the types of principles and standards developed by U.S. federal district courts in dealing with the claims of fallout victims,[21] and by courts and administrative agencies in dealing with radiation-related worker's compensation and tort claims.[22] Such persons would thus have to establish a reasonably certain estimate of their exposure, if possible specifying to what organ(s), and show that the disease or disability they claim is consistent with such exposure, taking into account their age at the time of exposure, the length of the latency period, the frequency of the disease in the general population and any counterindications (e.g., a personal genetic predisposition to that disease).[23] Even then, no strict causal relationship can be established, but at best a statistical probability that may be expressed along the following lines: If X had not suffered the excessive radiation exposure, the probability of affliction by a certain cancer by age Y would have been A percent; the best available scientific evidence is that owing to the excess exposure that probability increased to B percent, let us say three times A; thus if X is found suffering from that cancer, it can be argued that there is a two-thirds likelihood that the disease is attributable to the radiation.[24]

The question then becomes what sort of conclusion to draw from such figures. Does one say that whoever can show a likelihood of attributability (of the disease to the supposed cause) of over 50% should recover fully, and those who are under 50% probability should not recover at all?[25] Evidently, such a rule would compensate some who theoretically should not have been, and fail to compensate others who, equally theoretically, should have been.[26] Alternatively, if someone can show a 65% or 35% probability, he could be compensated for precisely that percentage of his damage; again, however, that would only provide rough justice in a scientific guise, obviously overcompensating those who would have gotten the disease anyway, and correspondingly undercompensating those who were brought low only because of their exposure. Evidently, none of these approaches to calculating individual compensation are by any means satisfactory,[27] but at least at the present time there seems to be no scientific basis for substantially improving on them. In the long run this may not be so, perhaps when we become increasingly able to detect and count damage to individual cells and if we come to know more precisely the causes of particular cancers and of other radiation-induced diseases.[28] For the nonce, however, we are left either with some method of approximating justice for particular individuals by an extrapolation of the normal tort rules (for example, those that prevail in the United States)[29] or with dealing with such events essentially on a social basis. A possible compromise solution would be to give the affected individuals paid-up health insurance, perhaps through a special fund, in some way proportional to their radiation exposure.[30]

Finally, a suggestion made above should be recalled: in a transnational situation, all these individual calculations and compensations should be left to the national government of the victims, while the perpetrator government or facility operator should be required to make a prompt lump-sum payment to the former—the calculation of which would be based on a current measure of the total damage of this type that had been caused. In this connection, it should also be noted that to the extent that the responsible government or operator gives prompt notice of any accident and the consequent danger of exposure (as is required, for example, by the 1986 IAEA Early Warning Convention)[31] so that endangered individuals might protect themselves (by fleeing, sheltering, or cleansing), the perpetrator could reduce the estimated damage for which it must pay compensation.

Exposure of Persons to Small Amounts of Radiation

Aside from injuring particular, identifiable individuals or at least exposing some to dangerous amounts of radiation, a major nuclear disaster will also increase, to some measurable but not necessarily uniform extent, the entire background radiation of the earth, to which all humans are exposed in various degrees.[32] Current wisdom is that such an increased exposure, no matter how small, is not good for living things[33]—though it might be recalled that, not too long ago, in more naive times, exposure to some radiation, such as in thermal springs or in certain mineral waters, was eagerly sought and sometimes even falsely advertised.[34]

Although the last scientific word has evidently not yet been said on this subject, the preponderance of current expert thinking appears to be that no amount of radiation is good for the body and that consequently any increased exposure should be avoided.[35] However, as there is no reliable method of testing even this hypothesis, at least as applied to humans, it is even more difficult to establish with any certainty the quantitative effect of exposing any given individual, or even a large group, to very small doses of radiation. The best that can be done is to extrapolate backward from the reasonably known effects of large doses on a population to the small doses we are here considering—thus assuming that the same relationship continues to hold, without the introduction of any other effects that would distort it, probably downwards.[36] That such reducing effects may exist is suggested by the fact that the additional doses we are here considering are generally smaller, by an order of magnitude or more, than normal background radiation.[37] The additional doses experienced at any distance from most man-made releases thus have been compared with those received from taking a transcontinental flight[38] or from vacationing for some weeks in Denver rather than Miami.[39] As there is little evidence that even spending all one's life in Denver, or in an area where the natural radioactivity is high, results in additional radiation-related illnesses, the actual danger from very low doses remains debatable. Nevertheless, if we assume the continuity of the dosage/illness relationship into the lowest reaches, it can be asserted that the release of radioactivity during the Three Mile Island accident may have been responsible for causing—or rather for setting in motion—one additional cancer death in the communities surrounding that reactor,[40] and that the Chernobyl accident may cause thousands of premature deaths in areas far from Kiev.[41]

The problem now is whether and how to establish and quantify, on the one hand, the responsibility of those who caused the accident for these presumed additional illnesses and deaths, and, on the other hand, to perform the still more difficult task of making the presumed victims financially whole. Conceptually, the latter task is inherently impossible. For one thing, the dosage rates involved were most likely not actually measured, for even if the persons concerned—in effect, the entire population—were actually wearing dosimeters, these could not register the small exposures we are here considering. For another, even if dosages were measured, there would be no way of relating such low exposures to any eventual illness or to calculate, except in fractions with a large number of decimal places and considerably greater uncertainties, the probability of eventually becoming ill. The approaches examined in the previous section dealing with large doses thus are not at all applicable to these miniscule ones—except to conclude that no particular individual can assert any reasonable right to a measurable compensation. Even waiting a generation until any possible illness would have developed would not be useful, because the presumed increase in the number of arguably radiation-related injuries would not be statistically significant. Not only would it be impossible to identify with any certainty any particular victims, but it would even be impossible to tell how many such victims there were.[42]

If no individual can recover, does that mean that the tortfeasor need and should pay nothing? Can the sum of a lot of effective zeroes add up to something substantial? In science, of course, this phenomenon happens all the time. The gravitational force of an individual atom is negligible, indeed not directly measurable; but assembled in numbers as large as the earth or the sun, the collective force is immense. Similarly here, even if the best estimate for the number of premature radiation-related deaths from a given accident is only a substatistical one per ten million, that is, far too few to permit any individual determination and thus recovery, for the United States this would amount to approximately 25 and for the world as a whole to 500. Clearly, anyone who injured that many identifiable persons and caused their premature deaths would be held liable—and there is no really sound reason for arriving at a radically different answer just because the eventual victims are unknown and unknowable. Indeed, imposing liability furthers the goal, discussed earlier in Chapter 7, of requiring polluters to internalize all the costs of doing business, including injuries to others.

As there cannot be any individual recovery, there is no need to agonize here over the alternatives discussed in the previous section; it is evident that whatever compensation is to be made can only be to the victims' government(s). The calculation to be made, however, requires the establishment of at least three factors: (1) the exposure-disease relationship; (2) the amount of the exposure to a given population from the incident in question; and (3) the amount of compensation per presumed victim.

The first of these factors is one that in principle should be established in the abstract, that is, independently from any particular nuclear incident. Ideally this would be done by expert bodies, such as the International Commission for Radiological Protection (ICRP), working under the direction of political bodies, such as the IAEA and the World Health Organization (WHO).[43] These determinations could then be incorporated into the treaty that would presumably have to underlie the liability regime that is here tacitly assumed. Better still, such a treaty would only set out the method by which such determinations can be made and from time to time changed on the basis of new scientific evidence.[44]

The second factor is, of course, one that would have to be established for each incident and for every population. That, presumably, would be the subject of negotiation and of possible litigation between the governmental parties, in either case based on contemporaneous measurements—if possible those made by impartial international agencies, such as IAEA, WHO, or the World Meteorological Organization (WMO).[45]

The third factor is inherently a political one, as to which it is difficult to advance any proposals. The question is, can one establish an international regime that would not value every victim as deserving the same amount of compensation, when that amount would almost surely be considered outrageously low in respect of the citizens of one country but really much too high for those of others? One solution would be to provide that any compensation required in respect of a mere increase in background radiation be payable on a uniform basis not to individual governments but to some appropriate international organization, representative of the world community, such as WHO or the Office of the United Nations Disaster Relief Co-ordinator (UNDRO).

Psychological Damage

An examination of the possible damage done to persons as a result of exposing them to unwanted radiation, whether massively, substantially, or only minimally, would be incomplete without considering any psychological harm they may suffer as a result of knowing of or perhaps only assuming such exposure. The question is, should such possible damage entitle them to compensation?

In the first place, it should be noted that probably most national tort systems would not allow such recovery at all.[46] Even that of the United States, which is perhaps the most hospitable to tort claims, until relatively recently did not permit claims for mental harm not associated with some physical damage.[47] Those persons suffering immediate radiation injuries thus might have recovered additionally for their expectation of a reduced life span, and possibly even those might recover who received a dose large enough to lead them to anticipate future disability. Those persons who are merely terrified, however, could not base an actionable claim on such fear.

Why then raise the question at all? It arises in part because the issue of the psychological burden caused even by the normal operation of a reactor in a neighborhood, especially after a nuclear accident—whether related or not—has been made the subject of litigation in connection with the licensing or relicensing of reactors in the United States.[48] Presumably, if the psychic damage that might be caused by the mere operation of a reactor could prevent it from being licensed or only licensed subject to some conditions or restrictions, then such damage also has enough recognition in law to permit recovery if an accident actually occurs and some radiation is released.

There are, however, a number of reasons for rejecting psychic damage as a basis for international compensation—aside from the consideration that at best only a few national legal systems would even entertain it. The most obvious of these reasons is the subjective nature of the injury, essentially not susceptible of any objective determination.[49] The prospect of litigating tens of thousands of claims with hundreds of expert witnesses as to the psychological state of mind of more-or-less stable plaintiffs is evidently a daunting prospect and a powerful disincentive to opening this door even slightly.

Even more important is that the fear of radiation damage typically is not really caused by the exposure itself, but by what officials, experts, and especially the media say about it.[50] Perhaps because of the fortunate infrequency of serious radiation accidents, each such event is magnified by hysterical and largely uninformed speculations about actual and potential dangers. Each release of radioactive materials, no matter how slight, is heralded as a potential disaster, and because of the public's unfamiliarity with the quantities and units used, even normally sober persons may yield to the prevailing hysteria. Experience also shows that, at least in part, these uncertainties result from routine initial understatements of the danger by the authorities concerned, who—naturally wishing to avoid any excessive panic—in the long run succeed in undermining their own credibility just when they have belatedly decided that truthful, factual statements would be most useful. Other authorities, such as those of a victim country, may have other agendas, which perhaps may call for magnifying the disaster and the danger. The media may seek to inform and educate, but also to sensationalize, and in any event may be confused as to both the actual facts and generally accepted underlying scientific and medical factors.

All in all, a disentangling of these various skeins and the attribution of fault for the psychological damage that might be done to particularly susceptible individuals does not seem to be a feasible enterprise, or one really useful to achieving justice among those responsible for, and those victimized in some way by, a nuclear accident. This assessment is in spite of the fact that there is considerable evidence that psychological damage might be the most significant actual damage consequent on a nuclear accident.[51]

Compensation for Destroyed or Damaged Property and for the Costs of Decontamination

Finally, we come to the issue of compensation for damage to property. One situation is easy to deal with: if property is effectively destroyed as a result of a reactor accident, compensation should be paid in the same way it would be for destruction through any other fault. However, as pointed out in connection with the consideration of massive injuries to persons,[52] such destruction is unlikely to occur except in the most immediate vicinity of a reactor accident, or possibly through the fall of a nuclear satellite.[53] Much more difficult are the following situations: (1) the need to destroy goods, usually food, as a result of excessive contamination; and (2) the need to decontaminate property, usually premises or land, to rid these of excessive contamination. In both these situations, the problem is essentially the same: what is the proper level of purity to strive for?

When radioactive fallout descends on an agricultural region, it typically does not kill the cows or wither the grass. To the naked eye, these and other links in the food chain look, and indeed are, inherently, perfectly healthy. Yet the consumption of the ultimate food product will burden the consumer with some radioactivity which, as observed above, is detrimental—probably even in very minute quantities. In fact, ingestion of radioactive materials is particularly dangerous, for the materials may remain in the body indefinitely, radiating—and thus injuring and destroying cells—all the while.[54] Thus there are good reasons for not consuming such food, and indeed for destroying it and any sufficiently contaminated intermediate products.

The problem is one of degree. Just as we have learned that it is impossible, or at any rate impractical, to rid our food of all traces of conventional poisons, such as pesticide residues, and therefore have established permissible limits,[55] it is also necessary to do so with respect to radioactive contamination. But what should those limits be, and who should establish them? Unfortunately, the first question is not, in spite of superficial appearances, a purely scientific one. As already mentioned,[56] no amount of radioactivity is good for anyone, though the evidence for the danger of very small quantities is at best indirect. Consequently, the setting of permissible limits is ultimately a mixed economic and political question. If the costs of maintaining a particular limit are to be borne by the domestic economy of the consumers—that is, in effect by the consumers themselves—then these consumers, or at least all but the most finicky of them, will perforce come to terms with limits that do not price the food out of their reach. If, however, the cost of maintaining the limit is to be assumed by the perpetrator of the pollution, then the victim society, through its political processes, is apt to set limits arbitrarily lower and correspondingly more expensive to maintain.

This reflection brings us then to the second question: who is to establish these limits when they are to constitute the basis for international compensation?[57] Evidently, if left to the domestic processes of the victim country, the limits would be set very low—though whether this would be too low is a matter for judgment. Equally, if the setting of limits were to be left to the government responsible for the disaster, these might be set much higher—though again, whether this would be objectively too high cannot be said outright.[58] One control might be that the limit set in respect of foreign claims may not be higher than that actually used for domestic purposes in the country of the nuclear incident. Such a "national treatment" rule, however, would by no means always be satisfactory, particularly if the perpetrator country generally fails to maintain acceptably high health standards. Thus, here again, the solution would appear to be an impartial international standard—if possible one set in advance so as to provide immediate guidance in case of need.[59] In addition, it would be useful to have an impartial mechanism for determining, on the spot, what items fall above the set limits, and thus need be destroyed, and which ones meet the limit and may therefore be maintained—or at least may not be destroyed at the cost of the perpetrator of the contamination.

The rule of compensation would thus be that the perpetrator State is responsible for the cost of disposing of all contaminated products that exceed, in accordance with impartial measurements, the internationally set limits. If the country concerned wishes to maintain stricter limits, it must, of course, always be free to do so, in protection of its own citizenry; but the additional costs of doing so would have to be met from its own resources. It should be pointed out that ultimately both States concerned should find it in their interest to be, at all times, completely honest in their public utterances. To fail to do so, as apparently repeatedly happened in connection with the Chernobyl incident (which constitutes so far the only large-scale international nuclear disaster), is to risk making the public suspicious of even honest determinations and announcements, given that certain interests and publicists will inevitably cry alarm and insist on the futile or rather the unreachable goal of total purity.

The approach to *decontamination* of property, such as land and premises, should be essentially the same: an internationally agreed-upon standard, applied, if necessary, with the assistance of international supervision. The cost of achieving the agreed standard would have to be borne by the State responsible for the contamination; any additional cleansing would be at the cost of the government or individual concerned.[60]

Summary and Conclusions

It is apparent that the measurement of the amount of liability due to radioactive exposure or pollution is neither simple nor susceptible of any overall solution. Rather, the approach used must depend both on the type of damage in question, whether to persons or to property, and particularly on the intensity and amount of the exposure, which determines whether the damage is immediate and manifest or only future and speculative.

In the former situation, that is, when persons are injured or property is damaged or destroyed, there is no conceptual difficulty about measuring liability, and the normal mechanisms for international dispute resolution should suffice to help resolve any factual disagreements. When the exposure or pollution is slight or entirely minimal, however, more complicated mechanisms must be relied on for evaluating, or rather estimating, any liability and for allocating compensation.

First of all, it would be useful if, independent of any particular incident or accident and of the resulting disputes, some generally accepted standards were to be established for estimating the likely injury in the long run to individuals from significant (even though not precisely determinable) amounts of radiation; for estimating the injury to populations from different levels of fallout or other low-level exposure; and for determining the maximum levels of radioactive pollution that will leave various products consumable or otherwise usable, without further cleansing or other processing. Such standards, or preferably the methods for establishing and refining them from time to time, should be incorporated into any treaty regime that is to govern transnational liability in this area. Several international organizations might be entrusted with such standard setting, such as the ICRP, IAEA, WHO, and Food and Agriculture Organization of the United Nations (FAO).

Second, it would be useful if such a treaty regime also provided for resort, on a facultative or even a compulsory basis in the course of dispute resolution, to mechanisms for the impartial determination of any disputed radiation values, such as the exposure that may have been suffered by particular individuals, the amount of fallout affecting given populations, and the amount of contamination of products (such as items in the food chain) or buildings. Such impartial assistance would help the governments concerned to resolve the factual bases of claims resulting from a nuclear accident for which one of them is potentially liable, and would be particularly valuable for countries not in a position to make such reliable measurements themselves, so as to guide both their protective measures and the claims they assert. Again, such tasks might be assigned to the IAEA and WHO.

So far, in spite of one known massive accident, several quite limited ones, and some near-accidents, the peaceful uses of nuclear energy have proven to be relatively safe, if compared to the injuries and illnesses resulting from the utilization of other forms of energy. Naturally, it is hoped that this record will improve rather than worsen. But in view of the steadily expanding use of nuclear power—in spite of the accidents that have occurred—it is too much to hope that Chernobyl will have been the last nuclear disaster with transboundary effects. As further accidents may, indeed are almost bound to happen, it behooves us to establish, aside from technical and managerial devices designed to prevent such accidents and to mitigate their ill effects, international legal mechanisms to assist in the swift, practical, and fair resolution of any resulting claims and disputes.

Acknowledgments

The views expressed herein are purely my own, and do not necessarily reflect those of the United Nations or of the International Atomic Energy Agency, which I served earlier (UN, 1971–89; IAEA, 1958–66). I would like to acknowledge here the assistance of Ned Greenberg, then a student at the American University, Washington College of Law, in preparing the annotations to this chapter.

Notes

1. For international standards governing civil liability for nuclear damage, see Convention on Third Party Liability in the Field of Nuclear Energy, July 29, 1960, 956 U.N.T.S. 251 (1974); Convention on Civil Liability for Nuclear Damage, May 21, 1963, 1063 U.N.T.S. 265, *reprinted in International Conventions On Civil Liability for Nuclear Damage*, I.A.E.A. LEGAL SERIES No. 4, at 7

(1976); Convention on the Liability of Operators of Nuclear Ships, May 25, 1962, *id.* at 36, *reprinted in* 57 Am. J. Int'l L. 268 (1963). For an analysis of common law liability for damage due to radiation exposure, see Stason, *Tort Liability for Radiation Injuries*, 12 Vand. L. Rev. 93 (1959).

2. Analogous problems of legal causation are present when establishing the link between exposure to toxic chemicals or chemical wastes and individual injury. *See* Note, *The Inapplicability of Traditional Tort Analysis to Environmental Risks: The Example of Toxic Waste Pollution Victim Compensation*, 35 Stan. L. Rev. 575 (1983).

3. The time it takes for tissue damage to appear varies, depending upon the type of effect and the characteristics of the particular tissue, but such damage can manifest itself within a few hours of exposure. *See* Report of the United Nations Scientific Committee on the Effects of Atomic Radiation (UNSCEAR), 37 U.N. GAOR Supp. (No. 45), U.N. Doc. A/37/45 (1982) [hereinafter 1982 UNSCEAR Report], at 50; *see also* United Nations Environment Programme (UNEP), *Radiation: Doses, Effect, Risks*, diagram 5.2, at 51 (1985).

4. An increased incidence of particular illnesses—such as leukemia, breast, thyroid, and rectal cancer, fibrosis, chronic nephritis and various central nervous system disorders, to name a few—has been clearly established as a long-term effect of excess radiation exposure. 1982 UNSCEAR Report, *supra* note 3, at 51–53.

5. *See* P. Szasz, The Law and Practices of the International Atomic Energy Agency § 21.8 (1970).

6. *See* Szasz, *Report on the 28th Session of the Legal Sub-Committee of the UN Committee on the Peaceful Uses of Outer Space (COPUOS)*, 17 J. Space L. 41 (1989); Szasz, *Report on the 27th Session of COPUOS*, 16 J. Space L. 57 (1988); Szasz, *Report on the 26th Session of COPUOS*, 15 J. Space L. 50 (1987); Szasz, *Report on the 25th Session of COPUOS*, 14 J. Space L. 48 (1986).

7. Even if an individual is wearing a dosimeter or film badge at the time of exposure, entirely accurate radiation measurement is unlikely. An error in measurement of plus or minus 30 to 40% has been called normal, and this error may rise to 500% or more. O'Toole, *Radiation, Causation, and Compensation*, 54 Geo. L.J. 751, 758 (1966) (citing a representative of the American College of Radiology, Hearings on H.R. 1267 Before Select Sub-Committee of the House Education and Labor Committee, 87th Cong., 2d Sess. [1962]).

8. A district court in Utah recently struggled with the problem of estimating the radiation dosage received by 24 sample plaintiffs (selected from 1,192 in a class action) who alleged that atmospheric testing by the government prior to 1963 had exposed them to large doses of radiation. The judge finally approximated the dose amounts by amalgamating the few exposure estimates the government had made at the time with a single test contemporaneously done in the area by a Utah official, limited film badge data taken from two of the atomic tests, testimony from witnesses who observed events and remembered symptoms, present studies of trace amounts of radioactive residue in the soil, and expert witness testimony that sought retrospectively to project the exposure levels and which the judge termed "educated guesses." Allen v. United States, 588 F. Supp. 247, 427 (D. Utah 1984), *rev'd on other grounds*, 816 F.2d 1417 (10th Cir. 1987), *cert. denied*, 484 U.S. 1004 (1988). *See* Swartzman & Christoffel, *Allen v. The United States of America: The "Substantial" Connection Between Nuclear Fallout and Cancer*, 1 Touro L. Rev. 29 (1985). *But cf.* Johnston

v. United States, 597 F. Supp. 374, 390 (D. Kan. 1984) (where the court rejected similar evidence because the defendant's experts reconstructed a dose of 7 rems or less, while the plaintiff's experts reconstructed doses of hundreds or thousands of rems). Congress finally cut through this Gordian knot in the Radiation Exposure Compensation Act, P.L. 101–426 (signed into law on Oct. 15, 1990, while this volume was in page proof), doing at best rough justice by granting "partial restitution" of $50,000 to "down-winders" and $100,000 to uranium miners through conclusive presumptions of injury or lack thereof depending on the disease, a minimum length of presence in designated areas during designated periods, age at first exposure, and other factors (e.g., alcohol use). For a somewhat similar approach by Congress, see the Radiation-Exposed Veterans Act of 1988, 38 U.S.C. § 312(c).

9. For instance, leukemia has a minimum latency of 2 to 3 years, while the minimum is 9 years for rectal cancer, and 10 years for lung and thyroid cancer. *See* Advisory Committee on the Biological Effects of Ionizing Radiation, BEIR, Report, National Academy of Sciences (1980) (cited in Johnston v. United States, 597 F. Supp. at 426).

10. The great majority of harmful genetic mutants that would be produced would not be phenotypically expressed in the first generation. Estep & Forgotson, *Legal Liability for Genetic Injuries from Radiation*, 24 LA. L. REV. 1, 50 (1963). *See also* Report of the United Nations Scientific Committee on the Effects of Atomic Radiation (UNSCEAR), 43 U.N. GAOR Supp. (No. 45), U.N. Doc. A/43/45 (1988) [hereinafter 1988 UNSCEAR Report], at 45–57 and Table 7; *Radiation: Doses, Effects, Risks, supra* note 3, at 58–59.

11. Although it has been known for decades that radiation caused cancer and genetic damage, see Martland, *The Occurrence of Malignancy in Radioactive Persons*, 15 AM. J. CANCER 2435 (1931); Muller, *Artificial Transmutation of the Gene*, 66 SCIENCE 84 (1927), no statistical pool or long-term study has established accurate predictive patterns for radiation-induced illnesses.

12. This not only includes residents near the Nevada Test Site (*see supra* note 8) and the Pacific Test Site, but also some eighty thousand U.S. troops who participated in maneuvers during, and moments after, nuclear detonations. *See* Note, *Radiation Injury and the Atomic Veteran: Shifting the Burden of Proof on Factual Causation*, 32 HASTINGS L.J. 933 (1981).

13. Compilation and analysis of data on the increased incidence of leukemia among survivors of the atom bomb began in the early fifties. *See* Folley, Borges & Yamawaki, *Incidence of Leukemia in Survivors of the Atomic Bomb in Hiroshima and Nagasaki, Japan*, 13 AM. J. MED. 311 (1952).

14. *See* Waggoner, Archer, Carroll, Holaday & Lawrence, *Mortality Patterns Among United States Uranium Miners and Millers 1950–1962*, 6 ATOMIC ENERGY L.J. 1 (1964).

15. These statistical predictions, however, are subject to manipulation by expert witnesses with differing agendas or different clients. *See* Jose, *U.S. Court Practice Concerning Compensation for Alleged Radiation Injuries*, in STATUS, PROSPECTS AND POSSIBILITIES OF INTERNATIONAL HARMONIZATION IN THE FIELD OF NUCLEAR ENERGY LAW (1985). In Johnston v. United States, 597 F. Supp. at 412, one expert testified that the probability that radiation caused the plaintiffs' cancers ranged from 76.7% to 99.7%, while another expert, using the exact same formula, testified that the probabilities were from .01% to 3%. *See generally* Tribe, *Trial by Mathematics: Precision and Ritual in the Legal Process*, 84 HARV. L. REV. 1329 (1971) (describing the limitations of statistical evidence).

16. That there is a general, long-term life-shortening effect of radiation appears to be sufficiently well established. *See* 1982 UNSCEAR Report, *supra* note 3, section III.C.3, paras. 207–21, at 54–57.

17. *See* Allen v. United States, 588 F. Supp. at 340–47.

18. A national contingent injury fund based on the statistically increased probability of acquiring a radiation injury such as leukemia has been proposed for the United States. *See* Estep, *Radiation Injuries and Statistics: The Need for a New Approach to Injury Litigation*, 59 MICH. L. REV. 259 (1960). Including radiation injury in welfare coverage has also been suggested. *See* O'Toole, *supra* note 9, at 776 (citing Plaine, *Legal Aspects of Radiation Injuries and Compensation*, 9 HEALTH PHYSICS 7–12 [1963]).

19. *See generally*, E. BORCHARD, THE DIPLOMATIC PROTECTION OF CITIZENS ABROAD (1915). *See* RESTATEMENT (THIRD) OF THE FOREIGN RELATIONS LAW OF THE UNITED STATES § 721 Reporters' Note 8 (1987).

20. Making the legal connection between health problems and radiation exposure is necessarily difficult due to the scientific uncertainties; it is still impossible to differentiate between cancer caused by a specific radiation exposure and naturally occurring cancer. Jose, *supra* note 15, at 346.

21. About three thousand lawsuits have been filed against the United States by persons claiming injury from fallout. Although this large body of cases could provide an opportunity to develop standards for litigating such claims, the dozen or so personal injury or wrongful death radiation cases actually tried on the merits have applied diverse standards and reached divergent conclusions. *Id.* at 337–42. *Compare* Allen v. United States, 588 F. Supp. at 428 (holding that a legally sufficient causal link was established in the case of ten plaintiffs who "substantially" demonstrated a "reasonably exclusive factual connection" between their exposure and subsequent illness), *with* Johnston v. United States, 597 F. Supp. at 412 (holding that plaintiffs failed to maintain the burden of proving causation "to a reasonable degree of medical certainty").

22. It is estimated that there are around 400 radiation lawsuits presently filed against private defendants. Jose, *supra* note 15, at 338.

23. *See* Dennis, *The Philosopher, the Model, and the Monitor: Who Wags the Dog?*, in ASSESSMENT OF RADIOACTIVE CONTAMINATION IN MAN, I.A.E.A. SM–276/14, at 59 (1984). Because the etiology of certain diseases is unknown even to medical practitioners, an extensive review of causal agents and personal characteristics will still not produce an unassailable determination. A court's finding of legal causation, therefore, may not be the result of a neutral weighing of facts. *See* O'Toole, *supra* note 7, at 771.

24. *See* Tribe, *supra* note 15, at 1353–54. This type of statistical probability of causation was rejected by the court in Johnston v. United States, 597 F.Supp. at 394, as being "speculation based upon other speculation." *See also* Brennan, *Causal Chains and Statistical Links: The Role of Scientific Uncertainty in Hazardous-Substance Litigation*, 73 CORNELL L. REV. 469 (1988).

25. This is in essence the traditional rule for causation; the plaintiff must prove that the defendant's conduct more likely than not caused the injury. W. PROSSER, LAW OF TORTS 241 (4th ed. 1971). The causal indeterminacy inherent in radiation cases, however, presents a significant obstacle to achieving this level of proof. Swartzman & Christoffel, *supra* note 8, at 54–55.

26. Estep & Forgotson, *supra* note 10, at 46–47.

27. Hearings on H.R. 1267, *supra* note 7, at 238: "Trying to prove for legal purposes the biological connection of irradiation with a particular nonspecific,

latent injury under existing rules makes the 'correct' result theoretically impossible. . . . [The] results reached in radiation cases under normal proof rules could best be described as a lottery. . . . Compensation will be granted to some unnecessarily and full recovery unjustly denied to others."

28. In just the last few years, advances in recombinant DNA technology and the convergence of ideas and techniques from viral oncology, cell genetics, and molecular biology have imparted a level of precision hitherto unknown for unravelling the action of specific genes and the genetic bases of several spontaneously arising and mutagen-induced cancers. See Report of the United Nations Scientific Committee on the Effects of Atomic Radiation (UNSCEAR), 41 U.N. GAOR Supp. (No. 16), U.N. Doc. A/41/16 (1986) [hereinafter *1986 UNSCEAR Report*], at 3.

29. U.S. tort law has previously grappled with the problem of compensation for injuries with multiple causative factors. See, e.g., Basko v. Sterling Drug, Inc., 416 F.2d 417 (2d Cir. 1969) (holding that plaintiff, blinded by one of two drugs administered, could recover on the basis that either was the cause of the harm); McAllister v. Workmen's Compensation Appeals Board, 69 Cal. 2d 408, 445 P.2d 313, 71 Cal. Rptr. 697 (1968) (holding that a plaintiff who developed lung cancer after 32 years of firefighting and 42 years of smoking cigarettes established a sufficient factual connection to receive workers' compensation).

30. *See supra* note 18.

31. Convention on Early Notification of a Nuclear Accident, I.A.E.A. document INFCIRC/335 *reprinted in* 25 I.L.M. 1370 (1986) (entered into force Oct. 27, 1986). See A.O. Adede, The IAEA Notification and Assistance Conventions in Case of a Nuclear Accident (1987).

32. Natural background radiation contributes almost 76% of the collective human dose of radiation; medical uses account for some 24%; test explosions account for .34%; occupational exposure accounts for .07%; and nuclear power production accounts for .01%. *Nuclear Safety: An International Perspective*, 1 I.A.E.A. News Features 4 (Apr. 15, 1988) (based on preliminary UNSCEAR data). *See also* 1988 UNSCEAR Report, *supra* note 10, Table II, at 63, from which it appears that even in 1986 the total global effect of Chernobyl fallout was only some 5% of the natural background radiation. In addition, it should be noted that recent U.S. Environmental Protection Agency studies indicate that, in addition to previously considered sources of background radiation, account should be taken of even more massive human exposure to accumulations of radon gas within buildings, which more than double the previous estimates of total radiation burden and may result in 5–20,000 additional cancer deaths per year. N.Y. Times, Nov. 20, 1987, at A14, col. 5; N.Y. Times, Apr. 11, 1988, at B7, col. 1; 134 Science News 180 (1988).

33. The existence of a radiation threshold—below which exposure is safe—has never been scientifically substantiated. The great weight of evidence, in fact, is to the contrary, and it is current medical practice to assume that such a threshold is absent. 1986 UNSCEAR Report, *supra* note 28, at 12.

34. *See* F. Soddy, 2 British Med. J. 197–99 (July 25, 1903); *Old Age May Be Stayed*, Salt Lake City Telegraph, Nov. 6, 1903, *cited in* S. Weart, Nuclear Fear: A History of Images 37 (1988); *see also Facts About Low-level Radiation* 8 (IAEA Dep't Pub. Info. Aug. 1988).

35. There is indeed some evidence that, in respect of certain pathological effects, relatively lower doses may in fact be more hazardous. Some radiation has been shown to be far more carcinogenic at repeated lower levels than at

higher levels. A therapeutic effect on cancer development at higher dose levels is a possible explanation. *See* O'Toole, *supra* note 7, at 762–63.

36. UNSCEAR, however, has determined that a strict linear extrapolation from high to low dose levels could overestimate risk by a factor of five. The susceptibility of a human population to tumor induction has instead been assumed to follow a bell-shaped form. To predict the incidence of cancer at doses lower than those at which direct observations of humans are available, UNSCEAR combined empirical data on the incidence of various forms of malignancy at relatively high doses where observations have actually been made, with informed assumptions about the form of the relationships linking the incidence of cancers with the radiation dose. 1986 UNSCEAR Report, *supra* note 28, at 11–13. *See also Facts About Low-level Radiation*, *supra* note 34, at 9, 12–14; *Radiation: Doses, Effect, Risks*, *supra* note 3, diagram 5.5, at 55.

37. Bauser, *Through the Looking Glass and Back Again: The PANE Case, A Rebuttal*, 9 HARV. ENVTL. L. REV. 211, 215 (1985) ("The maximum off-site radiation dose received by any individual [during the Three Mile Island accident] was less than the annual natural background radiation in the area. The average dose to a person within five miles of the plant was probably less than ten percent of annual background radiation") (citing Report of the President's Commission on the Accident at Three Mile Island, *The Need for Change: The Legacy of Three Mile Island* [Oct. 1979]). The latest UNSCEAR figures (*see* 1988 UNSCEAR Report, *supra* note 10, paras. 174–85 and figures 1 and 2, at 41–44) show that for the most affected countries (Bulgaria, Austria, Greece, Romania), the first-year "Committed effective dose equivalent" from the Chernobyl accident was estimated at some 30% of natural background radiation, while for most Western European countries the ratio was 5–10%; in comparison with the "30-year effective dose equivalent" from natural sources, the Chernboyl accident burdened South-East, North and Central Europe with about a 1.5% additional dose, and Western Europe with about 0.2%.

38. Bauser, *supra* note 37, at 215 (citing National Council on Radiation Protection and Measurements, Report No. 45, *Natural Background Radiation in the United States* 21 [1975]).

39. Bauser, *supra* note 37, at 215 (equating radioactive release at Three Mile Island with vacationing for two months in Denver rather than Pennsylvania, citing U.S. Environmental Protection Agency, *Radiological Quality of the Environment in the United States*, Table 2–2, EPA 520/1–77–009 [Sept. 1977]).

40. Jordan, *Psychological Harm after PANE: NEPA's Requirement to Consider Psychological Damage*, 8 HARV. ENVT'L L. REV. 55, 84 n. 202 (1984) (citing the President's Commission Report, *supra* note 37, as estimating a 35% chance that even *one* individual will die of cancer as a result of accident).

41. Initial estimates of expected cancer deaths from Chernobyl ranged from five to forty thousand for the Soviet Union and from two to six thousand for elsewhere in Europe. N.Y. Times, Aug. 31, 1986, § 4, at 1, col. 1. Some later reports greatly reduced these numbers, but quite recently official sources in Byelorussia have hinted at much larger losses in lives, health, and property in quite extended areas around the site of the accident, and the Soviet, Bielorussian, and Ukranian governments have officially requested both the United Nations and the I.A.E.A. to organize international studies on the consequences of the accident. *See* I.A.E.A. Press Release PR 90/9 (May 7, 1990); U.N. Doc. E/1990/64; Ilyin & Pavlovskij, *Radiological Consequences of the Chernobyl Accident in the Soviet Union and Measures Taken to Mitigate Their Impact*, in 3 NUCLEAR

POWER PERFORMANCE AND SAFETY, I.A.E.A. STI/PUB/761 (1988); Anspaugh, Catlin & Goldman, *The Global Impact of the Chernobyl Reactor Accident*, 242 SCIENCE 1513–19 (1988), *summarized in* N.Y. Times, Dec. 27, 1988, at C4, col. 1. *But see* a study by Dr. Robert P. Gale cited in the N.Y. Times, May 23, 1988, at A7, col. 1. It should also be noted that recently Jay M. Gould, a fellow of the Institute of Policy Studies in Washington, advanced a thesis, based on a statistical analysis of death rates in the months immediately following the Chernobyl accident (i.e., for May–August 1986), that the fallout therefrom may have caused some 20–40,000 additional deaths in the United States. *See* Graham, Wall St. J., Feb. 8, 1988, at 6, col. 1, based on an unpublished letter Mr. Gould had addressed to *The Lancet* and copies of which he distributed widely. Most scientists seem to have difficulty in accepting his *post hoc ergo propter hoc* reasoning in the absence of some suggestion of a plausible mechanism whereby almost undetectably slight radioactive contamination could almost immediately cause such a massive number of deaths.

42. Estep & Forgotson, *supra* note 10, at 35 (regarding small percent increased chance of genetic injury); *see* Allen v. United States, 588 F. Supp. at 418 (concluding that the scientific measure of "statistical significances" used to determine increased injury to a population from radiation exposure was too stringent a standard to satisfy legal needs).

43. The IAEA and WHO are currently cosponsors of a long-term epidemiological investigation of as many as 135,000 people who were evacuated from the regions surrounding Chernobyl. This study, which includes the International Agency for Research on Cancer (IARC), could derive important information for setting internationally agreed-upon exposure/disease ratios. I.A.E.A. Press Release PR 87/14 (May 22, 1987).

44. A similar provision for updating standards was included in the Resolution of the IAEA Board of Governors Concerning the Establishment of Maximum Limits for the Exclusion of Small Quantities of Nuclear Material from the Application of the Vienna Convention on Civil Liability for Nuclear Damage, adopted Sept. 11, 1964, INTERNATIONAL CONVENTIONS ON CIVIL LIABILITY FOR NUCLEAR DAMAGE, I.A.E.A. Legal Series 4, at 19 (1976).

45. The IAEA is already in a position to be making contemporaneous determinations of exposure levels. The Convention on Early Notification, *supra* note 31, provides that the IAEA is to act as an information clearinghouse in the event of any future nuclear accident. Article 5 provides that the IAEA maintain and relay information such as the location and nature of the accident, the cause and foreseeable development of transboundary release, the results of environmental monitoring, and the predicted behavior over time of the radioactive release. This information is all directly relevant to determining the extent and intensity of human exposure.

46. *See* 11 INT'L ENCYCLOPEDIA OF COMPARATIVE LAW: TORTS, pts. I & II (1983).

47. *See* Kaufman v. W. Union Tel. Co., 224 F.2d 723 (1955), *cert. denied*, 350 U.S. 947 (1955) (holding that action governed by federal law cannot be maintained to recover damages for mental suffering alone); Chesapeake & Potomac Tel. Co. v. Clay, 194 F.2d 888, 90 U.S. App. D.C. 206 (1952) (holding that mental anguish alone is not compensable in damages).

48. *See* Jordan, *supra* note 40, at 65 (arguing that Court's holding in Metropolitan Edison Co. v. People Against Nuclear Energy (PANE), 460 U.S. 766 (1983), requires federal agency to consider probable impacts of starting nuclear power plant operation). *Contra* Bauser, *supra* note 37, at 211.

49. Bauser, *supra* note 37, at 234; *see also* Willmore, *"Cancerphobia": A Toxic Tort Time Bomb*, Wall St. J., Sept. 14, 1988, at 34.

50. Bauser, *supra* note 37, at 216. *See generally* S. Weart, *supra* note 34.

51. *See* S. Weart, *supra* note 34, at 372. *Contra* Bauser, *supra* note 34, at 217 (stating that all comprehensive psychological studies agree that psychological stress from the Three Mile Island accident was short-lived).

52. *See supra* text accompanying notes 5–6.

53. Compensation for damage due to the fall of a nuclear satellite could be governed by the Convention on International Liability for Damage Caused by Space Objects, March 29, 1972, 24 U.S.T. 2389, T.I.A.S. No. 7762. U.N. General Assembly Resolution 2777 (XXVI) of Nov. 29, 1971, which was at least a factor in causing the Soviet Union to settle a claim by Canada when a Soviet satellite scattered radioactive debris on northern Canada. *See* correspondence concerning the claim reproduced in 18 I.L.M. 899 (1979); Protocol of Settlement of April 2, 1981, 20 I.L.M. 689 (1981). *See also Soviets Ready to Discuss Liability Pact for Nuclear Mishaps*, L.A. Times, Oct. 6, 1986, at 12, col. 1.

54. *See* Hague, *Radioactivity in the Food System: Lessons from Chernobyl*, 20 CERES: The FAO Review 29 (1987).

55. *See* PESTICIDE RESIDUES IN FOOD: REPORT OF THE 1980 JOINT MEETING OF THE FAO PANEL OF EXPERTS ON PESTICIDE RESIDUES IN FOOD AND THE ENVIRONMENT AND THE WHO EXPERT GROUP ON PESTICIDE RESIDUES, FAO Plant Production and Protection Series, No. 26 (1981).

56. *See supra* text accompanying note 35.

57. It should be evident that it is not practicable, and in any event not satisfactory, to leave such limits to be set by market forces—for the same reason that countries able to do so prescribe maximum limits for other types of contaminants. In the first place this is not a decision most consumers are capable of resolving intelligently on their own; furthermore, it would tend to victimize the poorer consumers who might be unable to afford uncontaminated food or be tempted to buy contaminated products if available on the market.

58. That such conflicts are indeed likely to arise appears from the Soviet assertions that property damage abroad from the Chernobyl accident "resulted from action taken by authorities overanxious to protect their populations against overestimated risks of radiation exposure," Handl, *Transboundary Nuclear Accidents: The Post-Chernobyl Multilateral Legislative Agenda* 15 ECOLOGY L.Q. 203, 242–43 (1988); *see also id*. at 245 n. 203.

59. *See Proposal for Action by the Codex Alimentarius Commission in Relation to Radionuclide Contamination of Food: Proposed FAO/WHO Levels for Radionuclide Contamination for Food in International Trade* (Agenda Item 5), CX/EXEC 88/35/4 (1988). The objective is to develop "Guideline Values on Derived Intervention Levels" (DILs) to "represent levels of radioactivity in food (and possibly other media) below which intervention was not justified," taking "into account not only the cost to society from the health risk, but also from the imposition of counter measures." Report of the Seventeenth Session of the Codex Alimentarius Commission, Rome, June 29–July 10, 1987, paras. 34–53, at 5–8, 11; *see also* Handl, *supra* note 58, at 245–47.

60. *See supra* text accompanying notes 55–59.

Chapter 9
Pollution from Nuclear Accidents

L.F.E. Goldie

Introduction

At the present time, man-made disasters involving international liability and responsibility are arising with increasing frequency in disparate technological and scientific contexts and in terms of very different legal relations or regimes. One example involved the Soviet nuclear satellite Cosmos 954, which reentered and disintegrated in the earth's atmosphere, scattering radioactive debris over large portions of Canadian territory and eventually crashing near the Great Slave Lake. (Fortunately there were only a few inhabitants in that wilderness.) The negotiation of the subsequent issues of State responsibility and liability appeared to have been handled in a traditionally diplomatic manner.[1] Thus, for example, Bryan Schwartz and Mark Berlin[2] examined the issues arising from that crash in the Canadian Northern Territories in light of the famous *Trail Smelter*,[3] *Lac Lanoux*,[4] *Nuclear Tests*,[5] and *I'm Alone*[6] cases and with reference to a U.S. Senate committee staff report[7] on the Convention on International Liability for Damage Caused by Space Objects (the Space Liability Convention).[8] The authors presented their analysis of customary international law in terms of "Trespass by Mere Fact of Entry," "Claims for Violation of Sovereignty," "Damage to Persons and Property," "Psychological Harm as Material Damage," "Prevention of Future Damage," "Interference with the Sovereign Rights of Canada," and the possible "Emerging Right of Entry." They then revised these same topics in light of the Space Liability Convention. All in all, however, these writers tend to proceed with the traditional models and modes of analysis of liability for transfrontier harms.

This chapter analyzes several aspects of determining international accountability and achieving appropriate compensation with respect to mass transboundary disasters, such as are likely to be caused by pollution from nuclear accidents. The discussion begins with an examination of some inadequacies of the traditional State responsibility approach to such disasters, using the 1985 tragedy at Bhopal, India, as an example. An alternative approach to determining liability and compensation regarding such accidents—nuclear or otherwise—is then outlined, drawing on the concepts of special community, special regimes, amenities rights, and preemption, and using the 1986 Rhine chemical spill, the earlier Sevesco chemical accident, and a New York pollution/servitude case as examples. The 1986 accident at the nuclear power plant in Chernobyl, U.S.S.R., and the international response it has prompted, including the possibility of establishing a regime to determine liability, are then examined. Finally, issues related to the timing of asserting, assessing, and compensating for claims are addressed.

Do Traditional Theories of Responsibility Respond to Mass Injuries Due to Catastrophic Disasters?

A threshold problem of the traditional approach via the norms of State responsibility is that harms may be so diffuse that the traditional approach of predicating responsibility on the establishment of an injury due to a breach of obligation or "illicit act," for which some form of compensation or indemnification is necessary, may not be possible. The world community may well find, through the inadequacy of the contemporary law governing State responsibility, that there is a need for developing international and transnational[9] law—which would be applicable, for example, to claims for compensation and indemnification for transfrontier nuclear injuries—in such a manner that the law can encompass cases where there may not be any specifically identifiable party or item of property with a concrete injury within the traditional meaning of individual claims.[10]

Increasingly, situations arise involving harm to a highly populated and industrialized urban area, such as the Soviet Union's disaster at Chernobyl.[11] In relation to such cases, one might well argue that international law could, or even should, begin to develop transnational legal regimes focusing on ideas of mutual responsibilities. These responsibilities should be seen as arising from inherent principles reflecting the values on which social relationships among the States concerned should be predicated. Should one argue that such a form of responsibility calls for the recognition of a need to formulate a concept of a "wrongful act"?

These issues could have been presented in the aftermath of the

Bhopal disaster[12] in terms, not so much of traditional ideas of tortious action, as of the values of the responsibility which should prevail in relation to the transfer of technology from a rich to a poor country. In such circumstances, a web of interacting concerns should prevail over traditional ideas. Indeed, in such a context the notion of "wrongful act" becomes crass. Furthermore, the need exists for a definitive articulation of reciprocating scales of unequal responsibilities that are predicated on unequal capabilities to control, or alternatively to ignore, the possibilities of exposure to harm. Such an articulation should include doctrinal guides, or legal rules if possible, for bringing such values to bear within the context of a given disaster.

In the Bhopal case, a special regime of such reciprocal responsibilities should have been articulated but never was. Unfortunately, the resolution of the modalities of a regime governing the post-disaster attempts at amelioration and compensation for the victims was grossly clouded by the tasteless antics of members of the U.S. plaintiffs' bar who traveled to India. Their methodology, namely of finding individual plaintiffs and then earning money from sharing the proceeds (via contingent-fee arrangements) that they might milk from each plaintiff's lawsuit, ran counter to the need for a collective claim to be made in terms of the articulated collectivity (the "special community") of the injured. They thus diverted attention from the larger issues of who is responsible, and to what extent, in cases where values of advancing human well-being (e.g., the "green revolution") perhaps overleap human capability and bring disaster to the vulnerable (e.g., by leaking chemical fertilizers into waters that support extensive fisheries).

Through the attendant disappointments and frustrations, the Bhopal litigation has tended to undermine any articulation of a special regime based on the principal of good neighborliness and on the treatment of all individuals within the special community to which any catastrophic disaster establishes, as entitled to respect, participation, and recognition as ends in themselves as fellow human beings. The need to recognize a special community is further evident from the long-term destructive effects of the catastrophe on the social framework which gave meaning, roles, and structure to the lives of all the victims of the catastrophe. All such persons within that special community created by the physical event and by their factual and involuntary inclusion in the disaster should have been entitled to participate autonomously and collectively in the terms of compensation for being brought within the zone of risk. Claims derived from the victims' exposure to risk should be balanced commensurately with the benefit that society as a whole gains from the risk-creating enterprise (in this case, needed fertilizers for the "green revolution") and the degree of control of the situation enjoyed by the victim and the operator.

Elements of an Alternative Approach

Stipulating the "Special Community" and the "Special Regime"

The concept of "special regimes"[13] operating to identify and confer value on specific claims and entitlements within the limits of each of the special communities created by a catastrophic event can be developed further: the community may also receive from the continuing society which embraces it a system of concrete values providing content to the formal framework established by the participants' claims to rights of recognition, respect, and participation. An example of this heuristic device can be found in the story of the "Rhine Spill" of November 1, 1986, at the Sandoz chemical plant warehouse near Basel, Switzerland.[14] Prior to this event, the European Community had promulgated the Sevesco Directive.[15] Although not a treaty, the Directive formulates concepts for the way in which treaties may be drafted or, alternatively, reciprocating legislative transnational regimes may evolve.

The Directive was a formulated response to the notorious catastrophical accident at the Swiss-owned Inmesa chemical plant (a subsidiary of Hoffman-LaRouche) at Sevesco, Italy, which contaminated some 10,000 acres of a valley. (All the people and livestock living in the 10,000-acre area had to be removed because of the severity of degradation.) The Directive was designed to correct two broad categories of problems. Previously, member States of the European Community had, in their domestic laws and administrative procedures, divided the regulation of chemical plants into two distinct administrative compartments: worker safety and environmental protection. Second, among the member States there was a considerable disparity of standards. This disparity had the side effect of creating unequal competitive conditions within the Common Market, thereby giving the European Community authority under articles 100, 189, and 235 of the Treaty of Rome to promulgate the Directive and so eliminate such inequalities.[16]

The Directive prescribed a rigorous common standard for the States of the Community. Its fifth preambulatory paragraph provided that:

Whereas, for every industrial activity which involves, or may involve, dangerous substances and which, in the event of a major accident, may have serious consequences for man and the environment, the manufacturer must take all measures to prevent such an accident and necessary to limit the consequences thereof.[17]

Although, in general, the Directive was addressed to States and called upon them to adopt the administrative structures, guidelines, and controls it outlined and prescribed, its article 3 formulated a standard of protection:

Member states shall adopt the provisions necessary to ensure that, in case of any of the industrial activities specified in Article 1, the manufacturer is obliged to take all the measures necessary to prevent major accidents and to limit their consequences for man and the environment.[18]

The Directive then established a two-tier regulatory regime based on the nature of the chemicals handled, their quantity, and the use to which the plant put them. The substances involved were classified as "dangerous" and "particularly dangerous" (defined by toxicity) and assigned two categories of activity—storage and other.[19]

Although this two-tier classification may not be immediately germane to the nuclear catastrophe problem, the issue of notification by means of a continuous dialogue between the operator, the workers, and the community or the communities included in the area of potential major hazard provides an all-important model. Indeed, the issue of distance, bearing in mind other physical factors such as prevailing winds and general air mass conditions, might well provide a substitute (in the nuclear context) for the Sevesco dichotomy of substances. Underlying both location (for nuclear harm) and the character of the potentially harmful substance (for widespread chemical disasters) are the common characteristics of the vulnerability and helplessness of the population of the surrounding community and of downwind communities that may be affected (for whose vulnerability and helplessness I have stipulated the term of "exposure").[20] The interactive dialogue of the Sevesco model has further value, moreover, in that it looks to the observance of preventive measures as well as the participation in them by those whose specific interest in protection brings them within the special community that the potentiality for harm also creates.

As an aftermath of the Sevesco disaster, and occurring after the promulgation of the Sevesco Directive, the 1986 Rhine spill provides an interesting example of how a protective regime's scope may fall short of covering the full range of the special community of the injured, or of all those who may run the risk of being exposed to a disaster caused by the operation of a risk-creating enterprise. Thus, while all the member States of the European Community had adopted the Directive and were applying it within their administrative and legal systems, Switzerland—which is not a member of the European Community—continued to operate at a lower, and less costly, level of safety regulation and of environmental protection. In so doing, of course,

Switzerland was able to obtain competitive advantages for its chemical products over those produced by the Community's members. Yet the Swiss chemical plant that was the origin of the disaster was located in the upper reaches of the river Rhine. This river is a natural resource toward which Switzerland, being upstream and so geographically placed to be able to inflict greater environmental harm on the lower riparian States than it could itself suffer, owed at least an equal moral duty, as a "good neighbor," to protect its neighbors from major environmental harm.[21] Ideally, Switzerland's chemical industry should have been regulated to achieve a level of concern equal to that established by the Sevesco Directive for the member States of the European Community. Had that been the case, the Rhine spill would not have occurred. In that accident, chemicals (consisting of some thirty different agents that were subsequently found to have compounded their deleterious impacts through having become synergistically fused into new compounds) were poured accidentally into the Rhine river. This accident effectively undid a decade-long and dedicated effort to rehabilitate the historic stream. Instead, it reinforced and restored the Rhine's appellation of the recent past, "Europe's Sewer." Very serious harm was caused to 185 miles of the river from Basel to Mainz and further serious injury from there through the Netherlands to the North Sea. The spill's toxic effects compounded the environmental disaster.

After the disaster, Switzerland took responsibility and, belatedly, brought its safety measures and administration into line with its neighbors.[22] In so acting, Switzerland accepted the Sevesco Directive's standards, and thus effectively subscribed, by its domestic unilateral, but reciprocal, legislation, to the values of the European Community's transfrontier regime for the control of pollution. This stance was established by the legislative adoption of the same system of equal respect and concern, interaction, participation, and mutual flow of essential information as had been established for the European Community and its member States by the Sevesco Directive.

Amenities Rights and Special Regimes

Amenities Rights in the Domestic Arena

My second theme is that of the formal concept of "amenities rights,"[23] with changing contents depending on the value systems of the regimes within which those rights are articulated. The contents of those rights are to be seen as provided by the prevailing values of the social and ideological systems in which they exist. Recognition of amenities rights in each society requires that the State or individual utilizing a resource will not impair others' enjoyment of their legally assured amenities. Thus, whereas Günther Handl, in Chapter 7, emphasizes the sword of entitlement and its limits, this chapter stresses the shield of the protection of the autonomy and liberty of others to enjoy what they have and what the law allows to them.

True, Handl limits the sweep of his sword of entitlement by prohibiting it from inflicting "substantial" injury.[24] Within the area of entitlement (or, to change the metaphor, below the threshold of substantial harm), the territorial State is free to act as it pleases. Above that threshold it must respect its neighbors' right not to be made to suffer substantial injury. On the other hand, the concept of the shield of amenities rights limits other States' entitlements in terms of the regime of shared values which may arise once the activity of the entitled party includes within its scope both (or more) parties, all of whom share values that provide the content of the concrete and specific amenities rights.

The supervening regime that gives a legal dimension to the special community created by the physical harm involves the injurer and the injured together. It looks, in a relativistic manner, to the basic rights to amenities of all that are caught within the network of relations shared by the participants or the regime. These ensure the individual's effective participation in the community so created and his or her entitlement to recognition and acceptance as an equally autonomous fellow creature. In the international arena, the conflicts of amenities rights may be more variable than in the domestic scene.

Be that as it may, some 16 years or so ago, I offered a tentative and provisional definition of my then-emerging view of amenities rights.[25] At that time, amenities rights were formulated only in terms of domestic law, that is, of the individual citizen's enjoyment of the amenities of a protected environment within a State. Amenities rights were also seen as dependent on the value system in the State or legal order where they had been recognized and established. The following description was offered:

[Amenities rights] would appear to be emerging as enforceable claims for the protection of rights to health, by preventing the pollution of the air by chemicals and by noise, and rights to vindicate individuals' stake in the community's heritage of a beautiful landscape. There also appears to be a right of recreation in quiet places or in areas of dramatic and unspoilt grandeur. Property and community values of a novel kind seem not to be excluded. They include claims to prevent erosion of the countryside and blight of the cities. Procedurally the vindication of such types of personal and property claims as these could well be undertaken by groups or communities, or by representative suits, as well as by individuals acting to vindicate rights which are specifically their own.[26]

This theory, it is suggested, is, *mutatis mutandis*, relevant to the international arena and applicable as future transnational regimes of shared values emerge among States, individuals, and corporate entities.

Amenities Rights Taking Effect Transnationally

With regard to "amenities rights" on the transnational plane, it must be stressed that the observer or investigator should not expect to see one standard and one prescriptive regime. The content of transnational amenities rights in any specific case may well depend on the transnationally held extralegal, "higher law" principles held in common among a group of States. These principles influence decision-making and depend, as Savigny pointed out (when referring to the seminal role of common beliefs and values in the mutual recognition of rights and decisions among the sovereign States of the fragmented Germany of his time),

on an international common law of nations having intercourse with one another; and this view has in the course of time always obtained a wider recognition, under the influence of a common Christian morality, and of the real advantage which results from it to all concerned.[27]

This community of beliefs, within the system of European (and especially German) sovereignties, provided the answer to the conundrum that Savigny had previously posed when he wrote:

(1) Every state is entitled to demand that its own laws only shall be recognized within its bounds;
(2) No state can require the recognition of its law beyond its bounds.
I will not only admit the truth of these propositions, but even allow their extension to the utmost limits; yet I believe that they afford little help to the solution of our problem.[28]

The "strict rule of sovereignty," that is, the rule that no sovereign is bound to recognize foreign laws, was to Savigny, and remains for publicists in the fields of transnational law, private international law, and conflict of laws, of little help. In Savigny's eyes, this is so because it is "not to be found in the legislation of any known state."[29] He saw, instead, the operation of a very different principle, namely, that of the recognition and application of foreign laws in appropriate cases.

Hence a common expectation may well be that a case should receive "the same decision, whether the judgments are pronounced in this state or that."[30] The existence, then, of transnationally held "higher law" or political-moral values independent of legal order is the necessary precondition of a transnationally or even an internationally operating regime. For it is not enough that there should be agreement across borders for individuals' rights of recognition, respect, and participation to exist. These concepts—recognition, respect, and participation—are merely formal. To be operative, they require concrete definition to provide the major premise of a decision.

The existence of concrete metalegal or higher law premises of decision derived in this manner can also be exemplified in a wider context. They may provide the norms underpinning special, nontreaty regimes arising from the mutual recognition of rights, or treaty regimes recognizing, for example, shared values and traditions among the participating States. An example of the latter type of regime was provided by the agreement between the United States and Canada entitled "Convention for Settlement of Difficulties Arising from the Operation of the Smelter at Trail, B.C." Article 4 provides the following:

> The Tribunal shall apply the law and practice followed in dealing with cognate questions in the United States of America as well as international law and practice, and shall give consideration to the desire of the high contracting parties to reach a solution just to all parties concerned.[31]

This theory of special regimes is not proposed as an explanation of all the modalities of the recognition of common values in the transnational effectiveness of claims. Indeed, such a reading would completely contradict the purpose of this chapter, which merely proposes an additional heuristic tool for the study of some of the variables relevant to determining the effectiveness of finding transnational responsibilities, or transnationally recognized amenities rights, in specific situations—including those involving accidental nuclear pollution—and as between specific communities and States. In particular, however, this thesis is offered as a justification for viewing, as between certain legal orders, metalegal or legal propositions or legal doctrines having effective transnational operation among participating States, despite the fact that such propositions need not be shown as governing generally, let alone universally, in the relations of all States or legal systems.

In any given case the theory of special regimes may be of use as an alternative to saying that there is no general customary obligation or claim, or no treaty regime, governing generally all similar situations of a given class. But a rule of decision, reflecting the special and common value systems, or metalegal ideas of right or wrong, within each regime—for example, a common acceptance of the content of commonly held notions of entitlements to amenities—may emerge as a result of the common values, principles, and practices of the States concerned. Alternatively, the regime may be viewed as providing a "higher law" or metalegal prescriptive set (i.e., a set of common values) which may not be, in itself, or in themselves, immediately and mandatorily applicable. Identifying the metalegal function of common values in such regimes may bring with it the advantage of the individualization of justice in a set of situations involving transnational harms calling for a transnational and common resolution. Furthermore, in preserving a principled means of resolving issues crossing the boundaries of States, such an analysis as that proposed may circumvent the difficulties of proving the existence of customary law rule that is universally viable in the modern world, in order to establish the responsibility of the State whose operations have caused injury.[32] Although the "acceleration of history"[33] and the individualization of justice may have brought about contemporary situations not conducive to the development of customary international law in its classic sense, these very factors may create a focus on special cultural or local factors that may well provide for legal solutions and settlements among the States directly concerned. These States, and only these States, or some of them, appear apt for transnationally operative legal change, or as pressing for a commitment to a new and common basis for a rule more adequately reflecting the needs of the victims of risks created by current advances in technology and innovations in the applied sciences.

In the context of amenities rights, the term "special regime" thus operates to regulate the relations of the States enmeshed within the factual network of a special community arising out of the immediate situation calling for legal adjustment; the common acceptance of the higher law or metalegal values or inwrought inherent rules and values is made applicable within the special community through the regime's operation. It also puts forward the possibility that legal obligations may be perceived as regulating special relations even though such obligations may not be appropriate under general international law. A matter of definition is that the special community is seen as the factual, physical grouping of the operator causing an injury and those transnationally exposed to the risk created by the initiation of the operation and who have been injured in the event of a transnational catastrophic accident. A special regime regarding amenities is the source for finding applicable transnationally effective values for defining and applying the values of the operator's responsibilities and those of the State that licensed him in terms of the ideas of right and wrong common to the

States concerned. A concrete example of this thesis is provided by the discussion of the Sevesco Directive and the aftermath of the Rhine spill in the foregoing section.[34]

Risk-Creation and Preemption as Expropriation

To the theory of special regimes, a notion of preemptive conduct is offered in counterpoint. This latter term is postulated to indicate acquisitive first come, first served, winner take all, or shut-out behavior or policies. Preemptions may be of diverse kinds. First, there is the zero-sum game type of preemption. This type is illustrated by the policy choice of a society that treats as beneficial, or socially tolerable, those enterprises or activities that may, at the same time, be stigmatized as ultrahazardous. That is, with regard to those enterprises or activities, social utility is held to outweigh argument that, in terms of the hazards they may entail, would otherwise justify their prohibition.[35] On the other hand, when their hazardous qualities do result in injury, they must pay their way. That is, should their operations cause injury or contamination despite their observance of due care, and indeed all necessary safety features, such enterprises are held liable for the harm that they bring about. To undertake the ultrahazardous activity is itself to create the possibility of risk. I have suggested that a connection between strict liability and risk-creation as expropriation may be discerned:

> Perhaps a principle may be seen as emerging whereby an enterprise which, in the course of its [ultrahazardous] business, engenders the possibility of injuries to the members of the public who consume its wares or come into contact with its operations, is liable for damage arising from the risk it creates. To [impose on] an enterprise [mere fault liability] would have the effect of enabling it to conduct its operations at the expense of others and to throw a valid operating cost onto the shoulders of its neighbors, or onto those of the ultimate consumers of its products or services. Professor Cowan has aptly called the emerging judicial policy which gives recovery under these conditions "the policy of [viewing a] deliberately created risk as [an] expropriation."[36]

The corollaries to this proposition are (1) that choices, decisions, and policies having expropriatory effects—actually, by creating injuries to others, or potentially, by creating risks for others—should be adjusted so as to coexist with the decisions, choices and interests of those others; and (2) that the decisions, choices, and interests of those others, in their turn, should also be adjusted in their operations so that they all can be made compatible with one another in a common set of legal relations.

The courts should not assume, as New York State's highest appellate court did in *Boomer v. Atlantic Cement Co.*,[37] that there is no possibility of accommodation between different activities and that such cases inevitably involve zero-sum games. In *Boomer*, an enterprise opened a cement plant in an upstate New York area whose main traditional activities had long been apple-growing and dairying. The dust and smoke from the manufacturing process had a deleterious impact on the surrounding orchards, poisoning the trees, impairing the crops, and blighting the dairy pastures. The apple growers and dairy farmers of the region sought to enjoin the cement manufacturing activity—or at least its deleterious consequences. The court confirmed the lower court's refusal[38] to grant the injunction the farmers sought, on the ground that the manufacturing process brought considerably more employment and prosperity to the region than did the main agricultural activities. On the other hand, the court called upon the cement manufacturer to compensate the farmers and apple-growers in a sum representing the rental or usable value of their lands.[39]

The theory underlying that grant was that the cement plant, creating employment and economic benefits in general, should not be the subject of a permanent injunction: "The total damage to the plaintiffs' properties is, however, relatively small in comparison with the value of the defendant's operation and with the consequences of the injunction which the plaintiffs seek."[40] Judge Bergen concluded his opinion with the following analogy with a "servitude on land":

Thus it seems fair to both sides to grant permanent damages to plaintiffs which will terminate this private litigation. The theory of damage is the "servitude on land" of plaintiffs imposed by defendant's nuisance. (See *United States v. Causby*, 328 U.S. 256, 261, 262, 267, where the term "servitude" addressed to the land was used by Justice Douglas relating to the effect of airplane noise on property near an airport.) The judgment, by allowance of permanent damages imposing a servitude on land, which is the basis of the actions, would preclude future recovery by plaintiffs or their grantees.

This should be placed beyond debate by a provision of the judgment that the payment by defendant and the acceptance by plaintiffs of permanent damages found by the court shall be in compensation for a servitude on the land.[41]

On the other hand, Judge Jasen in his dissent argued against the majority's formulation of its judgment in terms of an "inverse condemnation." This measure, he believed, should not be invoked for the "private gain or advantage" of a private person.[42] He stated:

In sum, then, by constitutional mandate as well as by judicial pronouncement, the permanent impairment of private property for private purposes is not authorized in the absence of clearly demonstrated public benefit and use.

I would enjoin the defendant cement company from continuing the discharge of dust particles upon its neighbors' properties unless, within 18 months, the cement company abated this nuisance.

It is not my intention to cause the removal of the cement plant from the Albany area, but to recognize the urgency of the problem stemming from this stationary source of air pollution, and to allow the company a specified period of time to develop a means to alleviate this nuisance.[43]

Clearly, unlike his brethren, Judge Jasen did not believe that the nature of cement manufacturing inevitably entailed a zero-sum game posing, in contradictory postures, the plant's expected economic bene-fits for the region against the amenities rights of the farmers. He perceived the possibility of mutual accommodations being worked out between the farming and cement manufacturing pursuits that would result, possibly, in reduced levels of the cement manufacturing activity, or at least in improving the cement plant's environmental protection procedures, thus enabling the continued preservation of both dairy farming and apple-growing. The majority's solution, namely that of imposing a "servitude on land without consent of the owner by pay-ment of damages where the continuing impairment of the land was for a private use"[44] was unnecessary and, being a public condemnation of property for a private purpose, unconstitutional under the constitu-tion of New York State. Unfortunately, neither counsel for the farmers nor the dissent argued for an injunction that would establish a mutu-ally viable cooperative regime between the two interests set in opposi-tion in *Boomer*, as the arbitrators achieved in the *Trail Smelter* arbitra-tion.[45] It would appear that the dissent failed to grasp the creative implication of its insight.

The foregoing criticism of *Boomer* aptly leads to the second type of legal relationship in the context of apparently incompatible uses, that is, the possibility that incompatible uses of the environment may lead to the beginning of a mutually acceptable regime that permits both sides to coexist, possibly at reduced levels for one or other or possibly both, but that still provides for the survival of both. Although the gains of any one participant may be achieved at the expense of the others, those other parties do not need to suffer a total loss, only a partial deprivation. Such a policy of imposed deprivation may be either di-rectly equal to the amount gained by the preemptive actor, or, alter-natively, merely proportional to that gain. The determinative factor whereby the outcome may be characterized as one rather than the other is constituted by the degree of opposition of the interests in play—the angle of attack, as it were. Unlike the zero-sum game type of the preemptive situation, both of these situations are open to preliminary negotiations and to compromise settlements. They may also be amenable to settlement by reference to equitable principles of distributive justice.

This chapter has not been written in order to participate in the debate that has led to a veritable "Battle of the Books" and a contention of law review articles and symposia[46] over the role of economic efficiency versus values in tort lawyers' quest for social justice. The preceding paragraphs, however, obeyed the need to expose the *Boomer* model, in which a zero-sum game result was brought about by the use of a damages judgment to effectuate an "inverse condemnation" that should not be invoked for the "private gain or advantage of a private person"[47] (private law expropriation).[48] The proponents of the view that damages awards are conducive to wealth maximization in society characterize such awards as imposing a rational and efficient allocation of the costs of accidents in society. They argue that those costs, arising from courts' and juries' appraisals, in the light of prevailing values, of the injured parties' needs, are distributed on a rational basis conducive to overall efficiency. The faith that these advocates hold has been, one would think, tested from time to time. A concerned friend may point, with some delicacy perhaps, to the purported award of $986,000 to a woman for loss of her psychic powers—that loss being ascribed to her undergoing a brain (C.A.T.) scan.[49] To characterize this award as the datum point for a rational and efficient distribution of society's resources could cause raised eyebrows in some learned circles.

Be that as it may, one commentator on the damages-as-efficiency school has inquired whether pecuniary awards may, in a *Boomer*-like situation, "reduce pollution and enhance business" and has suggested that the injunctive alternative "may be less flexible than monetary relief."[50] Implicit in this comment on my view of *Boomer* is the appraisal that an injunction would provide a less desirable outcome because the parties might well "be locked into court ordered behavior."[51]

In response, one may point out the possibility of the injunction being formulated in a flexible and contingent mode. On the other hand, the "pay now, adjust later" mode of damages awards imposes a *fait accompli*. Such an award, moreover, may impose even more limiting and handicapping restraints on the possibility of the development of flexible market responses. The cost of damages, or of insurance against them, may well drive otherwise thriving enterprises out of business, or cripple their operations.[52] The majority in *Boomer* should have seen more in the case than an economic contest of apples versus cement. Contextual, aesthetic, and environmental interests should have been perceived as relevant. They should have been balanced with the other and more direct interests of the parties in a more inclusive regime. In the *Trail Smelter* case, more than merely the pecuniary interests of smelting lead and zinc (creating sulphur dioxide smoke) versus dairy farms, apple orchards, and fisheries were involved; the Tribunal considered economic, aesthetic, and environmental issues holistically.[53] In contrast with *Boomer*, *Trail Smelter* illustrates how, in a non-zero-sum game situation, damages also may become relevant to supplement and reinforce, but not supplant, the regime which was established in an award analogous to a domestic law injunction. This, again, contrasts with the "private expropriation" that the damages award in *Boomer* impelled.

A further consideration is that the contest leading to a damages result may leave out of account the important facts that the resource itself may not be wholly within the field of action and interaction of the participants, or that there may be natural environmental changes. This last possibility, too, provides a situation of shareable resources and responsibilities. Here, typically, a gain by one party leaves the others in their former positions. In such cases, the resource itself accommodates any unilateral act that is not classifiable as exclusively preemptive. This chapter, however, is not so much concerned with preemptions of resources, such as attempts to appropriate the flow of a stream, for example, or to capture exclusively the mineral resources of a region. Rather, the type of preemptive conduct reviewed critically here relates to the establishment of a socially desirable enterprise that involves concomitantly the creation of risks and potential deprivations for others in a manner that may limit or even interdict the autonomous action of those others; examples include the conduct of the Sandoz company of Switzerland leading to the Rhine spill of 1986 and the actions leading to the Chernobyl disaster, discussed later in this chapter.

An earlier example of preemptive activity reflecting a zero-sum game model is provided by some States' raising the level of radioactive fallout by nuclear bomb tests in the atmosphere to such an extent that they greatly escalate the risk that other States would incur if they were to engage afterwards in nuclear activities of their own. Indeed, such nuclear testing may have the additional effect of intensifying the risk of other States' engaging in the peaceful employment of nuclear resources, as in the generation of power, medical diagnosis, and industrial uses of all kinds. Such nuclear activities indeed do constitute zero-sum game preemptive acts. In such circumstances as those where the "stake" is a resource that can be won only once, or the performance of an activity which can be safely carried out only under certain given conditions (which may never recur), the preemption becomes total. These activities may be viewed as lawful only when either lacunae in international law[54] or high political tensions exist to create extremely permissive situations for the preemptive actor.[55] There, indeed, we may perceive that the law is treated, or condemned, as irrelevant or as out of keeping with the situation, or is rejected as inexpedient or totally ineffective.

Regimes Protecting Amenities and Countering Preemptions

A tentative basis for distinguishing among the many types of special regimes restraining preemptive activities may now be suggested. Although regimes may be distinguished in terms of many criteria, the present comparison relates to specific situations of State responsibility. For example, in the context of transnational pollution, the existence of a governing special regime may be identified by several criteria: (1) The group of States concerned may accept a community of laws and legal ideas. They may also subscribe to a common set of metalegal ideas and values. The *Trail Smelter* arbitration and the Sevesco Directive provide eloquent examples of such communities of transnational legal and metalegal ideas. (2) Certain States may accord mutual respect and recognition to the unilateral policies of others acting in substantial conformity with their own, enmeshing all the States concerned in a regime reflecting those policies. An example may be found in the Swiss legal and administrative reforms following the Rhine spill disaster when Switzerland, a non-member, but enjoying similar legal traditions to those of the European Community countries and being geographically located so as to render their environmental protection laws comparatively ineffective, brought its policies and procedures into line with those of the Community member States. (3) There may be a common loyalty among a group of States to standards of regulation and responsibility, as well as a common understanding that a problem can be mutually and equitably administered in the light of scientific knowledge so that there exists among them a mutual understanding. A regime of this kind most clearly illustrates the possibility of precluding preemptive acts as between the participants which might otherwise be permitted under general international law among the generality of States. (4) Specific asymmetries deriving from discrepancies of exposure to injury and risk-creation may give rise to equities deriving from a need to correct "imbalances," to quote Aristotle's vision of equity.[56] Furthermore, the greater the imbalance in a given legal community between risk-creation on the one hand and exposure to risk on the other, the greater is the need for the legal community, the regime, to compensate in terms of adjusting against expropriation or preemption, on the one hand, and the unjust enrichment[57] arising from risk-creation on the other.

The Chernobyl Disaster: Exposure Without Recourse

Summary of the Disaster

The conduct of the Soviet Union for a while after the disaster at the nuclear power plant at Chernobyl,[58] which began on April 26, 1986 (the errors leading to the disaster started and became compounded on April 25), illustrated the lack of any special regime of common values of mutual respect, recognition, and equal participation between the Soviet Union and the countries (at least those outside the Warsaw Pact) where clouds of radioactivity had a baleful and widespread effect. Water and grass were contaminated; fruit, vegetables, milk, and meats were destroyed over wide areas; and populations will live for coming years under the fear of leukemia and other radiologically caused, irreversible, or almost irreversible, ailments. In regard to this latter aspect, a problem of time as well as a causality in any immediate sense, is present. Instead of giving an immediate warning, as would be called for under the Sevesco Directive[59] or the European conventions on liability for nuclear harms,[60] for some days the Soviet Union denied the event altogether, then minimized the danger, then attacked the media in Western countries for exaggerating the seriousness of the event.

After some delay following research by Swedish meteorologists, the Swedish Embassy in Moscow made some low-keyed diplomatic representations, and a Moscow newscaster read a statement from the Soviet Council of Ministers as follows:

An accident has taken place at the Chernobyl power station, and one of the reactors was damaged. Measures are being taken to eliminate the consequences of the accident. Those affected by it are being given assistance. A Government Commission has been set up.[61]

In the meantime, however, the U.S. spy satellite systems gave an early warning of the explosion. A spy satellite was maneuvered to take pictures of the burning reactor. Its first pictures were sent to earth on the same day as the terse Soviet announcement. Contrary to the official Soviet bulletin, photographs of the disaster indicated: "The image was of a serious accident, getting worse, and being disregarded by an unsuspecting public."[62] As late as Wednesday of that week, Dan Rather reported on CBS television that U.S. intelligence took the view that the adjoining reactor might be melting down.[63]

Absence of Any Regime of Mutual Participation, Respect, and Reparation

Although the second reactor did not melt down, the disaster should not be understated. It was the greatest peacetime nuclear disaster, exceeded only by the wartime disasters at Hiroshima and Nagasaki. During the week following the Chernobyl catastrophe, millions of Europeans were exposed to varying doses of radiation. Many did not dare go swimming, drink milk, or buy or consume garden produce. They gulped iodine solution, dusted their clothes, and stayed indoors as much as possible. Indeed in some areas, especially in Italy, the government impounded a vast quantity of vegetables and created a brief artificial scarcity. But, almost inevitably, different countries followed different polices of prophylaxis, frequently owing to their own domestic policies regarding nuclear power. Thus, for example:

On one side of a Rhine bridge, at Kehl, in West Germany, the children were forbidden to play on the grass and the lettuces sat uneaten in the ground. On the French side of the bridge, around Strasbourg, very similar lettuces were declared harmless. . . . One French ecologist said sarcastically that the fall-out cloud which covered the rest of Europe seemed to have decided to omit France from its itinerary.[64]

Paradoxically enough, however, rather than the Soviet Union's taking action to ensure payment of reparations to the States and individuals who suffered or were exposed to harm as a result of the Chernobyl catastrophe, that country (the Soviet Union) itself was the recipient of some marginal help from other countries. That assistance came from the U.S. medical profession through physicians Robert Gale and Israeli citizen Yair Reisner and their teams, as well as from other countries in the form of various kinds of rescue and rehabilitation services. Does this positive reaction of support, sympathy, and cooperation from Western countries perhaps testify to the emergence of a nascent sense of a legal community between the Soviet Union and Western Europe and the United States?

Clearly, the nuclear disaster at Chernobyl and the radioactive cloud it spread over Europe created a classic example of the special legal community between source of the injury and the injured. Because the Soviet Union has never admitted liability or sought to make reparations on the basis of any sense of moral good neighborliness, however, the questions arise as to whether and, if so, what kind of, regime exists that may reciprocally testify to, and provide values for, the mutual recognition of entitlements to respect and participation and reparation for harm inflicted by the disaster. As has been pointed out, the spontaneous reaction of support and assistance tends to run counter to the evidence which the Soviet negativism may seem to provide against the idea of a legal community embracing both sides of the "European Divide." Possibly a further step toward such a common regime may have been tentatively initiated by Chairman Mikhail Gorbachev's speech on May 14, 1986. He said—after describing the Chernobyl disaster's impact within the Soviet Union and after expressing appreciation for the work, sympathy, and support from other socialist countries and Western political figures, businessmen, scientists, and doctors—that the Soviet Union highly appreciated "the sympathy of all those people who have responded with open hearts to"[65] the Soviet Union's misfortune. He then proposed that States should, on the basis of cooperation through the International Atomic Energy Agency (IAEA), establish measures for the "safe development of nuclear power engineering" and within the framework of such measures he called for

a system of prompt notification and provision of information in the case of breakdowns and defects. Equally, an international mechanism needs to be arranged with a view to the quickest possible rendering of mutual assistance when dangerous situations arise.[66]

Post-Chernobyl—The IAEA Acts

The 1986 Conventions

From July 21 to August 15, 1986, a group of governmental experts from 62 countries and 10 international organizations met in Vienna in pursuance of a decision taken by the Board of Governors of the IAEA.[67] They formulated two draft conventions, one on Early Notification of a Nuclear Accident (the Notification Convention)[68] and the other on Assistance in the Case of a Nuclear Accident or Radiological Emergency (the Assistance Convention).[69] The Notification Convention had as its object the creation of a duty incumbent upon a State in which an accident occurs to give prompt and effective warning to other States which may be affected through a transboundary movement of the ionized material and so avoid the crucial 60-hour delay that existed before the Soviet Union admitted to the world the major disaster that the word "Chernobyl" now stands for had occurred. This obligation of warning is by no means onerous. Indeed, the Chernobyl disaster showed that early warning of a nuclear accident within a State's border was less injurious to that State's credibility than letting other countries discover it for themselves through satellite signals and telltale radiation. At the IAEA subsequent conference, the Soviet Union gave its full support to the Notification Convention, reversing its former policy of not giving its neighbors an early warning of the Chernobyl accident.

The Chernobyl disaster pointed up a second major deficiency in international legal relations. As has been pointed out earlier, no international regime and no international framework existed whereby nations could promptly assist each other in the event of a nuclear accident. The Assistance Convention established by the IAEA created a formal legal structure to ensure prompt and effective international assistance of the type that was forthcoming, at least to a limited extent and largely on an *ad hoc* and voluntary basis, after the Chernobyl catastrophe. The Chernobyl experience showed that both nations from whom the voluntary help had come, as well as those who might well suffer a Chernobyl-like accident themselves, could easily and promptly agree to this Convention.

The Notification and Assistance Conventions have been criticized as inadequate on several grounds. First, the Notification Convention leaves to the country concerned the decision as to whether the accident is likely to cause transboundary pollution.[70] It thus provides countries that fail to notify their neighbors with a ready-made excuse that they did not immediately realize the gravity of the situation. The critic who raised this difficulty added:

And if one could prove culpability [i.e., failure to give prompt warning]— what then? There are few sanctions the IAEA can impose, except for withdrawing technical assistance, but whereas this can reasonably be imposed if a country is thought to be diverting IAEA-provided technology to non-peaceful ends, to withdraw help in matters of safety, just when the country in question had proved, in the clearest way possible, that it was in urgent need of such help, would prove counter-productive.[71]

It should be pointed out that the Convention does include, in article 11, a procedure for dispute settlement which would be available in situations where a failure to notify of the danger had caused transfrontier injury or other basis for controversy or confrontation, although both the United States and the Soviet Union have made a reservation to article 11. Third, and most important, the IAEA conventions do not address the basic and all-important question of nuclear safety: they make no effort to set binding minimum safety standards or otherwise reinforce international safety regulations, and there are no provisions in either convention imposing liability on a State that fails to meet certain safety requirements and causes a nuclear accident.[72]

Drafting the IAEA Liability Regime—Two Possible Approaches

Since the drafting of the two IAEA conventions on notification and assistance, the IAEA has begun work on its own civil liability convention. This is intended to make provision for damages arising from a nuclear accident. Thus, at its special session in December of 1986, the IAEA Board of Governors requested the Secretariat to prepare a compilation and analysis of relevant treaty law and other international instruments, international case law, and authoritative writings regarding international liability for nuclear damage.

The Secretariat's work was considered at the General Conference's special session in February 1987. Two views arose at this meeting. First, certain States thought that, if harmonized and simultaneously applied, the 1960 Paris Convention on Third Party Liability in the Field of Nuclear Energy[73] and the 1963 Vienna Convention on Civil Liability for Nuclear Damage[74] would be sufficient and preferable to the creation of a new convention.[75] A second group rejected this approach because both of these nuclear conventions limit "themselves to the liability of individuals or judicial persons for damage resulting in loss of life or for damage to the property of individuals."[76] This latter group believed that a new convention, encompassing the broader question of international liability for the injurious consequences of activities attributable to States in the context of their relations among themselves and formulating relevant principles of responsibility as well, should be created.[77]

Thus the IAEA Secretariat observed:

> From the texts of the two Conventions set out above it can be seen that the damage for which liability and compensation are envisaged is directly linked to that suffered by individuals or their property. Thus the consequences of a nuclear accident resulting in damage to the general environment (water, air, the soil, etc.) are not within the scope of the regime of either the Paris or the Vienna Convention.[78]

Recognizing that the consequences of a nuclear accident may result in general damage to the environment as a whole, or to States both in their territorial and in their governmental policymaking public functions, and hence not fall completely within the scope of either convention, the proponents of the joint application thesis attempt to compensate for this shortcoming by extending the special liability regimes of both the Vienna and the Paris Conventions to provide for the wider protection of victims. This extension surely does not fill the lacuna perceived by the second group who are proposing a new, comprehensive regime.

In addition, the existing liability regimes of the two presently existing nuclear liability conventions provide for the absolute and exclusive
liability of the operator of a nuclear installation (on the principle of
"channeling").[79] They also make provision for the limitation of the
operator's liability in amount and time, the operator's obligation to
carry liability insurance, and the guarantee of State intervention to
meet compensation needs exceeding the operator's financial security.
Other measures advocated by the joint application ("Joint Protocol")
group concern the elimination of problems of simultaneous application. These conventions do not go far enough, however, in indicating
which parties carry the primary liability.

The second group of States advocates the creation of a new liability
regime based on the customary international law of State responsibility. The thesis of this group is based on the proposition that principles of State responsibility for transboundary harm are drawn from
international case law such as the *Trail Smelter*,[80] *Corfu Channel*,[81] *Lac
Lanoux*[82] cases. They conclude, from these authorities, that "[o]ne
aspect of the duty a state may be said to have . . . is . . . to protect other
states and their nationals from serious transboundary effects."[83] Similarly, this group argues that international instruments, such as Principle 21 of the Stockholm Declaration[84] and the Charter of Economic
Rights and Duties of States,[85] provide guides for supporting the notion
that all States have the responsibility to ensure that activities within
their jurisdiction or control do not cause serious damage beyond the
limits of national jurisdiction.[86]

With regard to the measure of damages in cases of nuclear injury, the
second group points to the rule in the *Chorzow Factory* case, which holds
that reparations should "insofar as possible wipe out all the consequences of the illegal act and reestablish the situation which would, in
all probability, have existed if the act had not been committed."[87] In
general, they point to Principle 21 of the Stockholm Declaration,[88]
article 235(3) of the United Nations Convention on the Law of the
Sea,[89] the draft principles for the World Commission on Environment
and Development (WCED),[90] and the draft rules on international law
and transfrontier pollution of the International Law Association.[91]
From these sources, this second group of States asserts the existence of,
or the need to create by a convention, the general principle that there is
a duty to cooperate in formulating appropriate methods for assessing
damage and determining payment procedures in matters of compensation for transboundary harm.[92]

On the matter of procedures for the settlement of disputes arising
from claims of damage due to nuclear harms, this second group of the
IAEA member States (i.e., those advocating a convention spelling out

the relevant rules of State responsibility and applying them to nuclear catastrophes) support existing international bodies (for example, the Organization for Economic Cooperation and Development [OECD] and the WCED group of experts) that advocate the concept that equal rights of access to dispute settlement forums should open not only to States but also to individual and juridical persons subjected to such harms.[93] Indeed the WCED group of experts has stressed the importance of such a right of access. To this end they drafted a provision (article 20) stating:

> States shall provide remedies for persons who have been or may be detrimentally affected by a transboundary interference with their use of a transboundary natural resource or by a transboundary environmental interference. In particular, states of origin shall grant those persons equal access as well as due process and equal treatment in the same administrative and judicial proceedings as are available to persons within their own jurisdiction who have been or may be similarly affected.[94]

The Two Approaches Distinguished

In summary, there are certain key distinctions between the two groups of advocates of their own perceptions of the relevant liability regime for the IAEA to sponsor. First is the issue of acceptability. The States that advocate a joint protocol harmonizing the Paris and Vienna Conventions[95] (mostly European States that are currently parties to one or both conventions) recognize that for such a protocol to be effective, more States must become parties to both of the conventions, and participation in the agreements should be expanded from its European context to a broad international regime.[96] This first group of States also believes that the creation of a new convention based on State responsibility would not be prudent at this time, owing to a lack of consensus among States on the matter of liability for general environmental damages.[97] This consideration is particularly pertinent when we recall the Soviets' reaction to the claims of compensation arising from the Cosmos 954 nuclear incident, and the diplomatic settlement for a considerably smaller sum than that assessable under such damage claims in international law as allowed in the *Factory at Chorzow*[98] case, where damages were assessed as including *lucrum cessans*.[99]

States advocating the creation of a new multilateral instrument operate on the famous remark of Dr. Samuel Johnson, "Depend upon it Sir, when a man knows he is to be hanged in a fortnight it concentrates his mind wonderfully."[100] They believe that any lack of consensus on State responsibility for transnational nuclear damage that may have existed before the Chernobyl accident would be more easily overcome in the wake of the international concern which arose over the possibility of uncompensated damages after that disaster.[101] Generally, States willing to support a new multilateral instrument (notably the Soviet Union) believe that the alternative—that is, the joint protocol approach—would be an unacceptable solution since the lack of wide acceptance of the Paris and Vienna Conventions prior to Chernobyl would hardly qualify them as the bases for a generally applicable international liability regime in the wake of the accident.[102]

A second fundamental distinction between the two approaches relates to the desire of some States to have an international regime based on the civil liability of individuals and juridical persons versus those who believe that such a regime should be based on the principles of State responsibility. The States supporting the joint protocol believe that the existing civil liability regimes of the Paris and Vienna Conventions are adequate to ensure compensation to victims of nuclear harm when combined with government commitments to ensure judgments against civil nuclear operators.

The IAEA representative from the United States expressed the view that the IAEA should not involve itself in drafting a new convention based on State responsibility, since this was properly the realm of "other fora"[103] (presumably the International Law Commission, U.N. General Assembly, general conferences called by the U.N. General Assembly, or other drafting sources). States advocating a new multilateral instrument rejected the limitation of the liability question within the framework of civil law on the grounds that such a regime would be concerned only with damage caused to private individuals and organizations. A regime based on State responsibility would, on the other hand, deal with questions concerning relations between States, including liability for damage to the environment.[104] As of this writing, the IAEA had not resolved its dilemma whether to go with the joint protocol or to establish a new liability regime based on principles of state responsibility.

Modes of Protection Other Than by Means of Liability Regimes

It should be noted here, before concluding this section, that many outside observers have criticized both groups of IAEA negotiators and criticize equally the notion of responding to the Chernobyl accident through the establishment of a liability regime, whether it be in terms of a new convention applying the principles of State responsibility or of one based on existing international agreements. These observers believe that increased safety programs are more likely to prevent future Chernobyls than is the fear of potential liability. Although the IAEA has responded to the Chernobyl accident with a program of expanded nuclear safety activities,[105] many argue that this should be the exclusive area of its attention, rather than focusing on liability as well. Bennett Ramberg, writing in *Foreign Affairs*, has suggested several multilateral alternatives to current IAEA regulatory programs.[106] He proposed "several multinational alternatives" which he denominated "international nuclear reviews" (INRs).[107] He proposed that they should be characterized by a formal structure and incrementally increasing authority that address the whole range of nuclear risks. Ramberg believes that this would provide "a comprehensive approach,"[108] the diverse elements of which could mutually reinforce one another better to ensure a benign nuclear regime. He opened his explanation of his concept of the INRs with the following observation:

> The most elementary form would require the IAEA to publish a set of guidelines, portions of which would be relevant to exporters, importers and domestic manufacturers. These guidelines would require definition of the contemplated nuclear project, its economics, the operator's disposition toward nuclear weapons, the facility's vulnerability to sabotage and military attack, safeguards against diversion of sensitive nuclear materials, and the operator's ability to run the plant and to manage materials safely.[109]

Ramberg also perceives there should be some system of sanctions and incentives to ensure compliance with the INR guidelines. These he calls "action options." Unfortunately, he does not define what these may specifically be. Ones that spring into my imagination tend, on reflection, to be counterproductive or inhumane. On the other hand, his ideal, which we all share, namely, that the IAEA would come to "license all nuclear facilities, whether imported or domestically produced,"[110] would not seem to be politically feasible at this time. Ramberg concludes his suggestion, however, on an upbeat note, writing:

> Would such an incremental but comprehensive approach work? Certainly all the stages of INRs are more comprehensive, and most are more authoritative, than the institutions addressing nuclear risks today. In Chernobyl the most powerful INR might have prevented the accident by, at a minimum, requiring installation of quick-starting emergency diesel generators (which are available in other countries), thereby eliminating the rationale for the ill-fated "safety" test in the first place. Efforts of this sort are not cost-free. Nations would have to accept greater international scrutiny of their nuclear programs. But this burden is not entirely foreign to today's nuclear regime, which embraces IAEA and NPT nuclear safeguards. Considering the dangers now evident, it is reasonable to argue that the cost involved is nominal compared to the consequences of another Chernobyl—or worse.[111]

We have seen, in the post-Chernobyl world of tentative and incipient nuclear disarmament, a greater propensity of States to agree to standards of thorough inspection, at least in some sectors of nuclear weapon deployment and manufacture.[112] Accordingly, strict inspection might well be supplemented and enforced today by vesting in the IAEA, or other international agencies charged with the management of inspections, a power to require all States to refuse to supply nuclear materials to a State resisting such inspections. It is also clearly in the common interests of nuclear States to ensure that inspections can effectively prevent the development of black markets in stolen fissionable materials. Finally, powers of inspection should have sanctioned support in cases where offending nations develop a capability of manufacturing their own nuclear fuels. Other observers have advocated the installation of automatic monitoring systems to warn of radiation hazards at various nuclear facilities.[113] Another option is expanding IAEA safety review teams that can investigate a nuclear power plant from all safety aspects, from management procedures to radiological protection for the workers, and including an examination of the operating records of the reactor itself.[114]

The Temporal Dimension

Introduction

As Paul Szasz describes earlier, in Chapter 8, harm from nuclear accidents may not appear—indeed, typically does not appear—immediately after exposure; in such cases, it is usually not possible to determine conclusively whether the exposure actually caused the injury or illness when it does appear. The preliminary issue for a discussion of questions of time in the context of the liability of nuclear operators—as in all cases of liability for injuries that may not be immediately apparent (as, for example, various industrial ailments due to the employees' exposure to deleterious substances)—is whether the compensation due should be paid immediately, and its quantum predicated on the degrees of the probability that the victim may become afflicted thereby. This approach has the effect of giving the operator an early repose from claims for latent damage, despite the fact that such damage may eventually become fatal, or at least debilitating, while being, at the time of settlement, statistically negligible. This section will review what I perceive to be the premises of the highly sophisticated statistical and socially oriented model based on probabilities that Szasz has so carefully and persuasively articulated, and will then outline some possible alternative methods employing concepts of time to indicate some equitable bases for claims arising from latent injuries.

One implication of assessing compensation in terms of measured probabilities, rather than awaiting the event, is whether the chosen treaty regime should give nuclear operators early repose from answering claims for latent injuries by extinguishing those claims before the injuries on which they are predicated become patent, that is, before they become undeniable as their symptoms begin to appear. Alternatively, should that repose be deferred? The earlier the repose, the greater will be the protection of the operator from diverting costs from investment to compensation. Society, in the form of those exposed to uncompensated harm, is thus asked to bear costs that some would argue should be internalized as a cost of the nuclear operator's doing business. Early repose is thus a subsidy paid by the injured parties to the operation, for example, of a nuclear power facility.

On the other hand, it may be argued that the operators' repose should be deferred, and criteria in terms of a time dimension should be formulated that would defer the operators' repose. Such temporal criteria should be developed as alternative concepts to those formulated in terms of the probability, here and now as it were, of harms which would cause a number of later and valid claims to be "too late." On this basis, furthermore, treaty negotiators, arbitrators, judges, or legislators could have recourse to a further possible choice between the three following alternatives: (1) the equitable model of "laches";[115] (2) a prescriptive period after which rights are extinguished as in civil law systems;[116] or (3) causes of action being terminated only after a given period, as in the Anglo-American common law system's statutes of limitations.[117] Choice among these three models should be preceded by a discussion of the time when rights to make claims accrue. This issue of accrual, in its turn, leads to an analysis of the applicability of the concepts of the critical date and intertemporal law.

Time and the Right to Claim

Accrual

The object of this section has been stated in the Introduction, namely, to suggest an alternative to a theory of measuring compensation in terms of probability. The objection to this latter form of compensation is due to its resulting in a once-and-for-all time payment to be made on the basis of the degree of probability that a potential harm will become actual, that is to be assessed in terms of predicating the amount paid on the actuarially established probability of the victims' expectations of suffering and death in the future. The degree of probability of suffering gives the proportion of the amount that is seen as payable. When the improbability of harm replaces its probability, nothing would appear to be due. Because problems of time, on the other hand, have not been thoroughly or systematically worked out in public international law,[118] theories regarding accrual as developed in the Anglo-American common law—especially those evolved in the courts of the United States with regard to nuclear harms and to industrial injuries such as, for example, asbestosis—will be taken, by and large, as offering useful and possibly persuasive precedents.[119] In aid of this analysis, moreover, two established international law concepts will be employed, namely, the critical date[120] and the intertemporal law.[121]

The Time Bar and Theories of the Accrual of Rights

When an injury may remain latent in the victim's body for a considerable period, the issue does not relate so much to the period of limitation or prescription as to the selection of the appropriate criterion for establishing when the period begins to run, that is, the point of time of the accrual of the claim or right of action.

The courts of the United States have employed three different theories in determining when latent injuries due to scientific and technological innovations have occurred and thus have created three possible times of accrual for a given cause of action. These theories are the discovery test, the time of exposure test, and the medical evidence test. Of these three tests, the discovery criterion has become pervasive in asbestos cases.[122] It has been formulated in the following terms: "the cause of action accrues when the plaintiff knows or through the exercise of due diligence should have known of the injury."[123] Application of the test may differ, however, because courts disagree about what facts constitute discovery. Accrual and discovery might coincide, for example, with one or more elements: knowledge of the injury, its cause, the identity of the defendant, and the existence of a legal claim. The judicial trend has been to trigger the statute of limitations at the point where the plaintiff gains awareness of the injury and causation.[124]

The time of exposure test holds that the statute of limitations begins to run when the plaintiff comes in contact with the harmful material. This point of time may be appropriately designated as the "time of exposure." The New York courts have followed this rule and employed it to bar claims for asbestos-caused injuries. Critics of the time of exposure test argue that a statute of limitations should not bar a plaintiff's recovery before he or she learned, or could have learned, of having sustained the injuries that are the subject of complaint. For example, the dissent in *Steinhardt*[125] maintained that because asbestos particles have no immediate effect at the time of exposure, no real injury occurs at that moment. Moreover, because not every person exposed to asbestos will eventually contract asbestosis, the time of development for those who suffer the malady is unpredictable.

The medical evidence test, an alternative to the discovery test, makes the accrual of a cause of action dependent upon the medical evidence in each case. Under this test the statute begins to run at one of two possible times: when the injury is diagnosable or when medical evidence fixes the time of injury. The medical evidence rule was applied in *Newbauer v. Owens-Corning Fiberglass Corp.*[126] This case arose out of exposure to asbestos, but it provides an analogy with exposure to nuclear radiation. There the court held that, since asbestosis and mesothelioma are impossible to diagnose at the time of exposure, exposure and accrual of the statute of limitations should not be treated as simultaneous. Instead, the limitations period was held to begin when the injury was diagnosable without regard for any noticeable impairment to the plaintiff. Two problems have been pointed out with regard to the medical evidence test: (1) since determination of accrual is made without consideration of plaintiff's knowledge, even a reasonably diligent plaintiff may not have investigated a possible cause of action before the running of the statute; and (2) the scientific evidence necessary to determine a time of accrual cannot be relied upon to pinpoint an exact date of injury since the rate of bodily deterioration in nuclear- as in asbestosis-related diseases varies from person to person.[127]

Each of the three preceding tests attempts to strike an equitable balance between injured victims of defectively dangerous products and the operators of nuclear plants or producers of other products that may injure workers or members of the consuming public faced with defending legal actions. The discovery test, the most pro-plaintiff of the three, was created to give plaintiffs an opportunity to state a claim that is inherently unknowable within the ordinary statutory period. The original test presumed that a reasonably diligent plaintiff's right to a remedy outweighs an operator's interest in absolute repose from legal actions. Delaying accrual of the plaintiff's cause of action, by tolling the statute until the plaintiff discovers the factual (medical) basis of his or her claim, has shifted the balance heavily in favor of plaintiffs, possibly having a crippling impact on an industry that, on balance, society might perhaps prefer to see remaining viable and productive. The time of exposure test, the most pro-defendant of the three, places an almost absolute value on repose for operators from legal actions and virtually ignores the plaintiff's interest in recovering for wrongfully caused injuries. The medical evidence test represents a compromise between the discovery and time of exposure tests: in latent disease and injury cases, medical evidence would not show harm or diagnosability until some time after the last exposure, but it almost always would establish accrual before the reasonably diligent plaintiff could discover the injury and the injurious act.

Although these three tests represent the current judicial methods for determining when statutory accrual occurs in cases of latent damage, there are alternative theories regarding limitations on actions that could potentially resolve some of the problems that arise under each of the three current rules. It can be said, for instance, that the problem of leaving some victims of latent damage uncompensated is not completely resolved by any of the three rules. For example, under the discovery rule, even in its most liberal form, plaintiffs with knowledge of their injury, its cause, the identity of the defendant, and the existence of legal recourse can be denied compensation if they do not act upon their rights quickly enough. This delay may be simply the result of a failure to select the particular triggering event. Of course, the usual situation is that victims of latent damage do not have the benefit of such knowledge until a considerable amount of time has passed. On the other hand, once they have knowledge of the disease, its cause, and the means of obtaining compensation, and still do nothing, they are "sleeping on their rights" and equity would see the possibility of their being estopped through laches.[128]

One line of legal thought that obviates the need for selecting a particular event that triggers the statute of limitations is the concept of the continuous injury. The continuous injury doctrine involves the situation where harm is inflicted at one moment but is disclosed to the injured party or is discovered by the damaged plaintiff at some time beyond the statutory period for bringing a cause of action concerning that injury. By utilizing the continuous injury concept, courts could perceive an injury as occurring, or accruing, each time damage relating to that injury is sustained. Viewing an injury as "continuing" allows courts to toll a statutory time period until the aggrieved party awakens to his ability to seek legal redress. The concept of the continuous injury arose in early Anglo-American cases involving suits for nuisance. Despite the fact that the original causal conduct or occurrence had ceased, actions could be maintained for the continuing effects.[129]

Later medical malpractice decisions adapted the view of the continuous tort.[130] This was premised on the theory that an ongoing relationship that is the source of continuing injury will toll the statute of limitations until the relationship pertaining to that injury is no longer in force (such as the doctor-patient relationship that would otherwise have barred certain actions). The continuous tort doctrine encompasses the principle that an injury continues beyond the initial causal event until a time when the harm is discovered. At that time, the injured party's cause of action accrues. In this sense, the discovery test plays a part in the development of the continuous tort doctrine. The set limitation of the discovery rule is thus avoided by identifying the triggering event and then perceiving it as continuous. The statute would run only when the continuing situation ceases. Such an extension could be achieved by allowing victims of latent damage to undertake legal action at any point in time as long as physical injury can be shown. The theoretical justification for this extension is that a physical injury is an ongoing event. As such, it constantly renews the time at which the statute of limitations begins to run.

The continuous tort doctrine has the advantage, for victims of latent injury, of being able to claim when the harm is discovered. The statute of limitations becomes effective only in cases in which, after the injury ceases to be latent, the victim still fails to act. A disadvantage of this extension is that defendants can never be at repose since their potential for liability into the future remains uncertain. The policy underlying statutes of limitations is to allow defendants to allocate their resources and plan their business activities without a threat of legal liability stretching into the indefinite future. Thus, a determination of whether the continuous tort doctrine should be thus extended rests upon a comparison of the value society places on the compensation of victims of latent damage and that placed on providing defendants with a means, after a reasonable period of time, of continuing with their business activities and allocating assets to enhance productivity rather than keeping them as reserve or paying them to insurers for adequate coverage.

A second approach to the time bar problem in cases of latent damage is the relation back doctrine. Although this doctrine has not been employed in domestic U.S. cases concerning latent damage, treaty negotiators and arbitrators on the international plane might consider reviewing it as a possible source of ideas. The doctrine, which in current practice is found in a civil procedure context where statutes of limitations might otherwise bar a plaintiff from amending a complaint to add or substitute new defendants after the limitations period has run, is here suggested as an analogy in cases of latent harm where, possibly, remedies to vindicate substantive rights would become time-barred. Adapting this analogy to the present problem, a plaintiff might become entitled to bring a fresh claim arising out of the later discovery of what had previously been entirely latent and, given the current level of scientific knowledge, unknown harm, by attaching the subsequent claim for that freshly discovered harm to an earlier claim (provided such did exist) arising out of the catastrophe or emergency. Part of this adaptation would be the requirement that the later claim arose out of the same "conduct, transaction, or occurrence" as the initial claim and, further, that the earlier or initial claim was not itself statute-barred. Here a caveat should be stated. Adopting such a theory might have the effect of allowing a party to defer indefinitely his or her compliance with the statutes of limitations. This effect would bring the doctrine into direct conflict with the policies behind those statutes that implement the idea that, at some point of time, there has to be an end to litigation and that the defendant should be freed of the expectations and uncertainties of litigation—that he or she eventually should be given repose.

Utilizing the relation back doctrine, as adapted and redefined in these paragraphs, in cases of latent damage would involve similar policy choices as between the interests of injured plaintiffs and defendants to those considered in the context of the continuous tort theory. Although it would be possible to extend the continuous tort concept to allow injured plaintiffs to circumvent the statute of limitations completely, courts have limited its application by identifying an explicit time that triggers the statute, namely, the moment of the discovery of the injury. Similarly, it would be possible to allow the claims of plaintiffs suffering latent damage to "relate back" to the initial undetected injury such that the time at which legal remedy is sought would be deemed to be the same time at which the injury complained of was sustained. Use of this legal fiction would, for statute of limitations purposes, allow a court action to proceed as if the time interval between the infliction of the latent injury and legal claim did not exist.

The advantage of the relation back doctrine over the discovery test is that the statute of limitations trigger remains tied to the time of injury. Under the discovery rule, courts have abandoned the time of injury and gone in search of other time criteria to serve as the statutory trigger (these include the time of the physical discovery of the injury, time of identification of a particular culpable defendant, and time of awareness of a legal remedy).[131] Under the relation back principle, the statute of limitations is always triggered as at the time of injury. The court is not required to search for other events such as those indicated in some of the other doctrines. Instead, all legal claims would be deemed to relate back to the time of injury so that, in effect, the intervening period of time between the injury and the claim is suspended.

A disadvantage of the relation back doctrine is that it has the possibility of eliminating the statute of limitations altogether. Whereas the discovery rule maintains a limit on when an injured plaintiff can bring legal action (the trigger is the point of time when the plaintiff becomes aware of his legal rights—this point of time being viewed in its most liberal terms), the relation back principle contains no such moderating mechanism. When an injured plaintiff can assert his claim against a defendant at any time chosen by the claimant, because the claim can be related back to the initial injury, the defendant cannot anticipate repose no matter how long the time may be from the initial injury. This situation clearly would impose a crippling burden on nuclear power development, for example, because the operator would have continuously to divert resources from capital investment to the reserves (or insurance premiums) he must maintain to meet future claims. Because the liabilities against which those resources are to be held would remain, for an indefinite period, an unknown quantity, the operator would have to keep them burdensomely large.

The "Critical Date"[132]

In international law, the point (or, possibly, points) of time falling at the end of a selected period (or span or spans of time) within which the material facts of a dispute are said to have occurred are usually called the "critical date." This point of time is also the date after which the actions of the parties to a dispute can no longer independently affect the issue[133] except, possibly, in an explanatory, clarificatory or auxiliary way.[134] It is exclusionary, and it is terminal. Hence it is most frequently resorted to in territorial disputes to indicate the period within which a party should be able to show the consolidation of its title or its fulfillment, for example, of the requirements of the doctrine of occupation. In other legal situations, it provides the point of time when the parties' rights may be said to have crystallized. The traditional use of the term "critical date" may sometimes appear to import little more than the point of time in the course of an international dispute when the parties reject other possible means of resolving their differences and, defining them in terms of legal dialectic, reduce these differences to "objects of litigation."[135] At other times, however, the points, or potential points, of future contention will have crystallized long prior to the time the concrete issues will have presented themselves. This point is clearly illustrated by Judge Jules Basdevant's designation of the critical date in the *Minquiers and Ecrehos* case.[136]

In international relations, of course, many differences are never reduced to a "legal dialectic," but remain refractory to reasoning and can only be characterized by "unbridled dynamism."[137] As such they cannot be subjected to such a cutoff point of time, which may well trigger the regime of legal reasoning and dialectic, as the critical date. The trigger of the critical date for an issue may well be some legal restatement of the parties' claims in terms of the applicable dialectic. Judge Basdevant found the critical date in that dispute to have been October 24, 1360, the date of the Treaty Bretigny (Calais).[138] Prior to that treaty, the dispute between England and France had been characterized by "unbridled dynamism" (including two famous battles— Crécy and Poitiers). The effect of the treaty, insofar as it was relevant to the reefs, was to reduce those States' relations to "legal dialectic." Hence, centuries later, it could provide guideposts in reviewing the legal issues involved with the post–Treaty of Bretigny separation of English from French Normandy. Judge Basdevant's judgment is also instructive from the viewpoint of this discussion for its imaginative use of "subsequent facts." Although the critical date of 1360 provided the triggering facts on which the rights of the parties were said to depend, and so led to the exclusion of subsequent facts, those subsequent facts were nevertheless permitted to have a utility that rendered them admissible or applicable.

To restate that formulation: Events occurring before the critical date have substantive value. They are right-creating facts.[139] Events occurring after the critical date have only an evidentiary and probative value, and that of a narrow and dependent category. Their admissibility is dependent on whether they are in continuation of, or may effectively throw light on, the substantive, right-creating events anterior to the critical date. Hence subsequent facts are admissible—but only in the subordinate and contingent capacity just indicated. They do not create or perfect title; nor may they be adduced directly in proof of title, but only indirectly and to corroborate and explain the probative events occurring before the critical date. For example, in the *Island of Palmas* case,[140] single Arbitrator Hans Max Huber, after determining that 1898, the date of the Treaty of Paris, was the critical date in the case before him, said:

> The events falling between the Treaty of Paris, December 10, 1898, and the rise of the present dispute in 1906, cannot in themselves serve to indicate the legal situation of the island at the critical moment when the cession of the Philippines by Spain took place. They are however indirectly of a certain interest, owing to the light they might throw on the period immediately preceding.[141]

Judge Basdevant's generosity with subsequent facts in the *Minquiers and Ecrehos* case (spread as they were over almost six centuries and over two long, protracted contests, each of which has been designated as a "Hundred Years War," namely those of 1337–1453 and 1689–1815) illustrates their function as not having independent probative value, but serving merely to resolve matters of detail and to throw further light on issues of detail that may be appropriately seen as relating back to the crystallizing facts. The central argument of this section is that the critical date may be generally defined as the temporal element in the point of convergence of distinct sets of facts or concatenations of events, each of which are put forward in the same dispute. This convergence occurs when both parties to a legal dispute submit distinct sets of facts and series of events and distinct theories of the case for the characterization or definition of the issues.

The *Eastern Greenland*[142] case illustrates the relevance of the convergence of distinct facts or series of facts as giving rise to the critical date of that case, namely July 10, 1931, when Norway promulgated its decree annexing the area in dispute. Regarding this crystallizing event the Court pointed out, "It must be borne in mind, however, that . . . the critical date is July 10th 1931."[143] That is, the critical date was seen as the point of time when the long-standing Danish claim converged with the freshly asserted Norwegian claim. This convergence occurred when the latter claim was officialy announced.

Disputes of this type are not the commonest as, most usually, both in international disputes and in contests in municipal courts, the plaintiff's claim may provide the basis for the definition of the issues. When each of the parties adduces its own facts and arguments for the characterization of the issues, neither party can unilaterally conclude the matter. On the other hand, a legal dispute can only exist if a common juristic definition can be offered. For before a dispute can be the subject of adjudication, the separately characterized right-creating facts in the dispute must be brought to a common ground: their convergence must necessarily be effectuated.

The critical date arises when questions of time form a necessary element in the point of convergence. That convergence may only come to operation when two or more of the right-creating or perfecting facts or concatenations of events converge in a state of dialectical conflict or contradiction. A dispute in which such a convergence arises cannot be made an object of litigation until the conflicts or contradictions within it are articulated in terms of legal argument, or one set of these facts is selected as controlling.[144] The doctrine provides a point of time as the touchstone for resolving or selecting the operative facts, and hence for characterizing the appropriate case. In this way the doctrine effectively brings the whole legal relation into focus. Once determined or manifest, the critical date sets limits to the period within which the definitive facts can be seen as having taken place. This defining of limits in turn leads to the casting of the issues of the dispute into a concrete, legal form.

How, then, does the critical date set a term to a period in which rights or claims become manifest, or are consolidated, or can adequately provide an object of litigation? The date in question is to be found at the point of convergence already stressed. This criterion can be clarified, further, by the uses to which the critical date doctrine was put by Judge Basdevant and Sir Percy Spender in the *Minquiers and Ecrehos* and *Rights of Passage* cases, respectively. These judgments also demonstrate the utility of that doctrine in giving a hard cutting edge to the consolidation of historic titles. The convergence of separate activities, which is inherent in the notion of the critical date as discussed in the preceding paragraphs, provides the means of determining the period over which the claimant may be said to have consolidated its title to sovereignty, or failed in that enterprise. The argument here is that, since general international law sets no fixed period for the consolidation or perfection of titles, the relevant aspect of the critical date doctrine provides a functional terminating point to a period over which a State may consolidate or perfect its title to a disputed territory or to a right similar to an easement or servitude or any other substantive right that can be perfected by the lapse of time. It does not follow from this line of reasoning, however, that the decision on whether a good root of title has come into being lies in the court's discretion, for the critical date doctrine comes into operation when a catalytic event which, converging as it were with a series of acts constituting a State's inchoate relation to a territory, crystallizes that relation and presents it for decision as to whether the acts in question have consolidated the title claimed, or have failed.

Because no international legal disputes arising from transfrontier environmental harms have been published as having been resolved in terms of temporal (and especially of critical date) issues, territorial disputes involving key issues of time have been resorted to. More specifically, it is necessary to extract relevant general principles from those decisions resolving territorial disputes, and to relate them to international claims arising from man-made pollution disasters. In terms of these occasions for disputes, it may be necessary, quite frequently, to think in terms of injuries that begin as latent mischief and only grow over time into the kind of conspicuous catastrophes that beget international disputes. The relevance of the critical date concept is that it indicates the operative facts around which the dispute crystallizes so as to form the necessary legal dialectic that is essential to the legal, as distinct from the political, aspects of a dispute.[145] Only when the operative facts have so crystallized can the injured State assert its legal claim.

Adapting from the territorial disputes already cited, the analysis proposes that all facts prior to the critical date may potentially be germane (insofar as they relate to the operative facts when these latter occur subsequently). At the time of their occurrence they were legally inchoate; subsequently, however, they could become characterized in terms of the later crystallizing circumstances. Given this caveat, prior facts may participate in the formulation of the injured State's claim. On the other hand, events occurring after the critical date may be treated as relevant only to the extent that they may explain or throw light on the crystallizing facts or relevant facts anterior to them.

A clear-cut example of the foregoing generalization is the Chernobyl nuclear catastrophe. The critical date for States' asserting claims against the Soviet Union would clearly be the moment when the injury impacted and caused harm on their territories, that is, when the nuclear fallout became overwhelming and unavoidable and brought with it inevitable harm to individuals and destruction to property—including rendering the property hazardous to human use or consumption. A more perplexing illustration of critical date issues would be that of an accumulation of injurious factors over a period of time, for example, the transnational pollution of waters through deleterious substances such as carcinogenic compounds, nuclear wastes and leaks from oil refineries or tank farms leaching through adjacent ground, or the pollution of the common transnationally flowing air through the emission of industrial and chemical smokes of various kinds and degrees of harmfulness. With such slowly accumulating pollution agents—which, over a lengthy period, can accumulate in the water, soil, and vegetation of a country, and in the bodies of its citizens—the critical date crystallizes the operative facts, as they flow through time, at the point when discovery reveals the prior-existing situation of injury.

Discovery might be due to the emergence of statistical anomalies among a population, or to the discovery of new and more accurate instruments of detection. Thus presented, the critical date doctrine may appear, at first blush, as resembling the discovery test, already discussed, that has been developed to indicate a possible point of time when the statute of limitations may be thought to begin running. The critical date does not look to the starting point of the statute's running, however. It serves a very different purpose. It looks to the identification of the transactions and events that thereafter define the legal dialectic, the identification of the concrete object in dispute, for the purpose of its subsumption under an objective value judgment made by applying existing norms.

The Intertemporal Law

In the *Island of Palmas* case the single Arbitrator, Max Huber, stated his famous definition of the intertemporal law:

As regards the question which of different legal systems prevailing at successive periods is to be applied in a particular case (the so-called inter-temporal law), a distinction must be made between the creation of rights and the existence of rights. The same principle which subjects the act creative of a right to the law in force at the time the right arises, demands that the existence of the right, in other words its continued manifestation, shall follow the conditions required by the evolution of law.[146]

This formulation has not gone without criticism, however. As stated by Huber, the title would have to satisfy two criteria: (1) there must be title under the original regime in force when that title was acquired (e.g., discovery as a source of title in the sixteenth century); and (2) the original title's continued validity by satisfying changes in the law from the date of the original title down to the critical date (i.e., the nineteenth-century requirement of the manifest exercise of sovereignty and control and a clear intention to engage in that exercise).

Judge Philip Jessup has commented on that twofold set of criteria, as follows:

Under the theory of the "intemporal law" as expounded, it would appear that A would no longer have good title to Island X but must secure a new title upon some other basis or in accordance with the new rule. Such a retroactive effect of laws would be highly disturbing. Every State would constantly be under the necessity of examining its title to each portion of its territory in order to determine whether a change in the law necessitated, as it were, a reacquisition. If such a principle were applied to private law and private titles, the result would be chaos. Title insurance would be an impossibility.[147]

Judge Jessup then added:

It seems doubtful whether Judge Huber intended to sanction the theory that land titles, valid under pre-existing national laws, can be wholly disregarded (*i.e.*, confiscated) if a new system of land tenures is instituted by the State. Such, however, would be a logical corollary of the theory of intertemporal law as applied in the award.[148]

Judge Jessup also pointed out that Judge Huber's formulation of the second step of the intertemporal law was not essential to his ultimate conclusions.[149] In Judge Jessup's view, the facts of the case showed that Spain's title to Palmas Island had not crystallized in the period when discovery was thought to confer title, but had remained inchoate during that period and down to the critical date, namely 1896.[150]

Taking this observation as a starting point, one may restate the theory of the intertemporal law as operating upon the critical date in a fact-value context. The law governing the situation in issue is triggered by the critical date finding. That legal rule so triggered characterizes the facts and ascribes legal consequences to them. Indeed, one may see the critical date as not only selecting and targeting the operative facts, but also as establishing the time when the controlling rule of law applies. Hence it also serves to identify that controlling rule and its specific legal content as operative at the time so established.

Thus modified, the concept of the intertemporal law is germane to the problem of time in the application of the international law of State, corporate, and enterprise responsibility for transnational harms and, more particularly, for transnational nuclear harms. A basis for a claim may arise when either one or both parties consider the law to be unclear and their rights and obligations unresolved. The intertemporal law leaves such claims as may exist in an inchoate and undefined condition. Upon the crystallization of the operative facts through the agency of the critical date, however, the intertemporal law operates to ascribe legal consequences to those operative facts and to the parties' relations in connection therewith.

In the *Minquiers and Ecrehos* case, the Court (despite a variety of critical dates having been identified by different judges) refused to regard French title to the islands founded on the feudal relationship (enfeoffment) of the Norman dukes as vassals of the French kings (who were termed their suzerains), because, prior to the critical date, the intertemporal law witnessed the sweeping away of the concept of feudal suzerainty and its replacement by territorial sovereignty. Hence Judge Basdevant's choice of the Treaty of Brétigny (Calais) as providing the critical date has so much appeal to this writer. The watershed this Treaty established was in terms of State sovereignty. By virtue of this Treaty, the French lands of the English king, for which previously he had owed homage and fealty to his suzerain, the French king, were to be held by him, thenceforth, in full sovereignty. The Treaty liberated him from the obligations of homage and fealty to those lands' previous suzerain. It also terminated the old, feudal, regime and replaced it by a new international one. Today, of the extensive territories so wrested from French sovereignty by that Treaty, only the Channel Islands and the Ecrehos and Minquiers reefs remain under English sovereignty. But the critical date of 1360, according to Judge Basdevant's most persuasive thesis, was determined by the crystallization of the legal dialectic between the two States (Great Britain, as the successor of England, and France) that were parties to the dispute, and was characterized under the legal regime which the intertemporal law designated as the Treaty of Brétigny.

Thus, just as the relevance of the critical date doctrine to issues of claims arising out of transnational nuclear disasters, such as that at Chernobyl, was shown to be identified by the "triggering" mechanism of the system of accrual of rights chosen by legislators, courts, negotiators, and treaty draftsmen, so the intertemporal law, operating on that trigger ensures that the body of law, on which the facts identified by the critical date are predicated, remains both effective and determinative. In cases giving rise to international responsibility for transfrontier nuclear harms, the intertemporal law excludes a regime of liability from governing the situation until the critical date is triggered through the crystallizing events, the intersecting factors, which precipitated that point of time as operating to define the parties' legal relations. Thereafter, whatever theory of temporal determination is chosen (i.e., laches, prescription, or limitations periods), time will, together with the criteria or fixed periods so chosen, run against the injured party until he or she takes the necessary definitive step to toll the passing of time.

Review of the Proposals Prescribing the Availability of Claims for a Time (or Times)

All the foregoing alternative proposals are predicated on the basis that inequities might well arise if latent injuries are converted into probabilities with compensation payable, soon after the disaster, in terms of the degrees of probability of various categories of people in the total class of persons exposed to the potentially dangerous or debilitating amounts of nuclear radiation or dust. The degree of probability of injury, under this theory, is seen as providing the measure of damages to be paid. The higher the risk of harm, the more the compensation. There is the further category of persons who are reduced, by the probability tables, to a class of persons being entitled to a contingent right of medical attention and public care.

On the other hand, I agree with Szasz's employment of probability criteria for evaluating compensation to individuals' home States' public medical organization. Nevertheless, the argument in this section is that the probability tables should not be used to identify a class of individuals and to deny all of its members access to compensation other than through the medical or social service system of their home State. This method of identifying the degree of the probability or improbability of that class should only be used to identify the lump sum to be paid to the medical services of that State which has undergone nuclear contamination. That is, statistical units may provide the means of measuring the amount to be paid to health services; but they should not be used to identify a class of living human beings that the operators might otherwise seek to establish in terms of probability statistics in order to exclude them from making any direct, adequate, and effective compensatory payments on specific and no doubt varying individual claims.

Notes

1. On the history of the diplomatic handling of this event and for a legal analysis in traditional terms, see Schwartz & Berlin, *After the Fall: An Analysis of Canadian Legal Claims for Damage Caused by Cosmos 954*, 27 McGill L.J. 676 (1982) [hereinafter Schwartz & Berlin].

2. *Id.* at 679–91.

3. Trail Smelter (U.S. v. Can.), 3 R. Int'l Arb. Awards 1905, 1938 (1938 & 1941).

4. Lac Lanoux (Fr. v. Spain), 24 I.L.R. 101 (1957) (English), 12 R. Int'l Arb. Awards 281 (1957) (French), *reprinted in* 53 Am. J. Int'l L. 156 (1959).

5. (a) Request for the Indication or Interim Measures of Protection (Austl. v. Fr.), 1973 I.C.J. Pleadings, vol. I (Nuclear Tests), at 43 (May 9, 1973); (b) Nuclear Tests (Austl. v. Fr.), Merits, 1974 I.C.J. 253 (Judgment of Dec. 20, 1974); (c) Request for the Indication of Interim Measures of Protection (N.Z. v. Fr.), 1973 I.C.J. Pleadings, vol. II (Nuclear Tests), at 49, 135 (May 14, 1973); and (d) Nuclear Tests (N.Z. v. Fr.), Merits, 1974 I.C.J. 457.

6. 2 R. Int'l Arb. Awards 1609 (1935); 2 Hackworth, International Law 703–8 (1941).

7. Staff of Senate Comm. on Aeronautical and Space Sciences, The Convention on International Liability for Damage Caused by Space Objects: Analysis and Background Data, 92d Cong., 2d Sess. (Comm. Print May 1972).

8. Convention on International Liability for Damage Caused by Space Objects, Nov. 29, 1971, 24 U.S.T. 2389, T.I.A.S. No. 7762, *reprinted in* 66 Am. J. Int'l L. 702 (1972).

9. For a discussion of the concept of transnational in the context, *inter alia*, of nuclear disasters, see Goldie, *Liability for Damage and the Progressive Development of International Law*, 14 Int'l & Comp. L.Q. 1189 n. 1 (1965) [hereinafter Goldie, *Liability for Damage*].

10. For a discussion of this phenomenon, see *supra* Chapter 8.

11. The accident at Chernobyl is discussed *supra* in Chapter 6 and *infra under* The Chernobyl Disaster: Exposure Without Recourse.

12. For a discussion of the factual background of the Bhopal tragedy, see, *e.g.*, W. Moorehouse, The Bhopal Tragedy: What Really Happened and What it Means for American Workers and Communities at Risk (1986). Note: I have a bibliography of some six pages and the above book is cited simply as an example. In that bibliography the articles in various issues of The Economist in 1984–85 (vols. 294–96) are particularly well-balanced and informative.

13. I have disparately and possibly fragmentarily expressed the main theses adumbrated here in, *inter alia*, the following articles: (i) *Concepts of Strict and*

Absolute Liability and the Ranking of Liability in Terms of Relative Exposure to Risk, 6 NETHERLANDS Y.B. INT'L L. 175 (1985) [hereinafter Goldie, *Concepts*]; (ii) *Equity and International Management of Transboundary Resources*, 25 NAT. RESOURCES J. 665 (1985), *reprinted in* TRANSBOUNDARY RESOURCES LAW 102 (A. Utton ed. 1986); (iii) *The Nuclear Tests Cases: Restraints on Environmental Harm*, 5 J. MAR. L. & COM. 491 (1974) [hereinafter Goldie, *Nuclear Tests*]; (iv) *International Impact Reports and the Conservation of the Ocean Environment*, 13 NAT. RESOURCES J. 256 (1973); (v) *Amenities Rights—Parallels to Pollution Taxes*, 11 NAT. RESOURCES J. 274 (1971) [hereinafter Goldie, *Amenities Rights*]; (vi) *International Principles of Responsibility for Pollution*, 9 COLUM. J. TRANSNAT'L L. 283 (1971) [hereinafter Goldie, *Principles of Pollution*]; (vii) Goldie, *Liability for Damage, supra* note 9; (viii) *The Critical Date*, 12 INT'L & COMP. L.Q. 1251 (1963) [hereinafter Goldie, *Critical Date*]; and (ix) *Special Regimes and Pre-emptive Activities in International Law*, 11 INT'L & COMP. L.Q. 670 (1962).

14. *See infra* text accompanying notes 21–22.

15. European Communities Council Directive of June 24, 1982, on Major-Accident Hazards of Certain Industrial Activities, 85/501/EEC, 25 O.J. EUR. COMM. (No. L 230) 1 (1982) [hereinafter Sevesco Directive].

16. Treaty to Establish The European Economic Community, March 25, 1958, 298 U.N.T.S. 3.

17. Sevesco Directive, *supra* note 15.

18. *Id.*

19. *Id.* arts. 2–4.

20. The term "exposure"—which was throughout this paper in counterpoint to the concept of "amenities rights," which it is the responsibility of a risk-creating enterprise to vouchsafe—was defined in Goldie, *Concepts, supra* note 13, at n. 1, as follows: "The term 'exposure,' which appears in the title and in the article that follows, is the term which J. R. Commons substituted for Hohfeld's 'no-right' and is used in that sense. *See* J. R. COMMONS, LEGAL FOUNDATIONS OF CAPITALISM 97–98 (1924). Both 'exposure' and 'no-right' indicate the legally unprotected, factual, relations epitomized in Hohfeld's adaptation of John Chipman Gray's famous shrimp salad illustration. *See* W. HOHFELD, FUNDAMENTAL LEGAL CONCEPTIONS 41–42 (1919). In the ensuing pages the term 'exposure' will be used since it has a more descriptive significadon than the approximately synonymous term 'no-right' as evolved by Hohfeld."

21. In Goldie, *Concepts of Strict and Absolute Liability and the Ranking of Liability in Terms of Relative Exposure to Risk*, 6 NETH. Y.B. INT'L L. 211–12, n. 103, 213–17 (1985) [hereinafter Goldie, *Ranking*], I suggested that "good neighborliness" arose as a legal duty among the participants in a "special community." This latter concept was presented as a relativistic model based on Stammler's concept of such a community in which the voluntary and involuntary participants become enmeshed as a result of their participation together in a factual event situation or transaction, for example a tort injury, a contract, or a transnational (*see supra* note 9) catastrophic disaster. *See* R. STAMMLER, THE THEORY OF JUSTICE 215 (Husick trans., MODERN LEGAL PHILOSOPHY SERIES 1925), quoted in *id.* at 211 n. 103.

22. *Swiss Give Pledge of Tighter Control on Toxic Chemicals*, The Times (London), Nov. 13, 1986, at 11.

23. For an adumbration of this concept and its significance for the law of responsibility for environmental protection, see Goldie, *Amenities Rights, supra* note 13, at 275–76.

24. *See supra* Chapter 7.

25. Goldie, *Amenities Rights*, *supra* note 13, at 275–76.

26. *Id.*

27. Friedrich Karl von Savigny, Private International Law 27 (W. Guthrie trans. 1869).

28. *Id.* at 26.

29. *Id.*

30. *Id.*

31. Trail Smelter (U.S. v. Can.), 3 R. Int'l Arb. Awards at 1907.

32. De Visscher, Theory and Reality in Public International Law 152–55 (P. Corbett trans. 1957). *See also id.* at 194–97 (2d ed. in original French 1955).

33. De Visscher, *supra* note 32, at 156.

34. *See supra* third section on stipulating the "special community" and the "special regime."

35. *See, e.g.*, Boomer v. Atlantic Cement Co., 26 N.Y.2d 219, 257 N.E.2d 870, 309 N.Y.S.2d 312 (1970). For a discussion of this case, see *infra* notes 37–45 and text accompanying.

36. Goldie, *Liability for Damage*, *supra* note 9, at 1212–13; *see also* Goldie, *Principles of Pollution*, *supra* note 13, at 283.

37. 26 N.Y.2d 219, 257 N.E.2d 870, 309 N.Y.S.2d 312 (1970).

38. 55 Misc. 2d 1023 (N.Y. App. Term. 1968).

39. *Boomer*, 26 N.Y.2d 219 (1970)(Judge J. Bergan).

40. *Id.* at 223.

41. *Id.* at 228 (citation omitted).

42. *Id.* at 230 (Jasen, J., dissenting).

43. *Id.* at 232 (footnotes omitted) (Jasen, J., dissenting).

44. *Id.* at 231.

45. *See infra* third section on regimes protecting amenities and countering preemptions.

46. *See, e.g.*, *Symposium on Efficiency as a Legal Concern*, 8 Hofstra L. Rev. 485 (1980) [hereinafter *Symposium*].

47. Judge J. Jasen dissenting in Boomer v. Atlantic Cement Co., 26 N.Y.2d 219, at 230, 257 N.E.2d 870, at 876, 309 N.Y.S. 312, at 321 (1970).

48. Goldie, *Ranking*, *supra* note 21, at 185–87.

49. An exhaustive scan of "Westlaw" and "Lexis" has failed to produce a law report citation to this case. One may assume, accordingly, that it remains unreported in the legal sense. On the other hand, it is mentioned in The Economist. *See Product Liability in America: Damage Limitation*, 313 The Economist 84 (Dec. 2–8, 1989). This award has, however, been the topic of interviews and newscasts on the major television networks.

50. Written comment on this chapter by an editorial reviewer [hereinafter editorial letter]. Not all the proponents of this Posnerian school have remained totally faithful and wedded to it. For example a chronological scale of Guido Calabresi's books dealing with the topic is instructive: (1) The Cost of Accidents: A Legal & Economic Analysis (1970); (2) Tragic Choices (1978); and (3) Ideals, Beliefs, Attitudes and the Law (1985). One may also note, with interest, Calabresi's concessions to those writers who are oriented to values in the law in his defensive piece, *About Law and Economics: A Letter to Ronald Dworkin*, in *Symposium*, *supra* note 46, at 559–61 (1980), where he argues that

there is room for both efficiency and distribution (as instruments or "signposts") and justice (the goal) in the operation of the legal system.

51. Editorial letter, *supra* note 48.

52. Of course, a business enterprise does not make the same claims on one's humanity as a fellow human being does. But human tragedies may result from the demise, bankruptcy, or debilitation of enterprises. The implicit Malthusianism (in terms of an enterprise's "fitness" to "survive" litigation and insurance costs) of the efficiency advocates may remind one of the unregenerate Ebenezer Scrooge's condemnation of Tiny Tim as being part of "the surplus population."

53. Trail Smelter (U.S. v. Can.), 3 R. Int'l Arb. Awards 1905 (1938 & 1941).

54. *See* Goldie, *Legal Pluralism and "No-Law" Sectors*, 32 AUSTL. L.J. 220 (1958), and the authorities therein cited.

55. *See* DE VISSCHER, *supra* note 32, at 75–88.

56. *See* GOLDIE, RECONCILING VALUES OF DISTRIBUTIVE EQUITY AND MANAGEMENT EFFICIENCY IN THE INTERNATIONAL COMMONS (WORKSHOP, NOVEMBER 8–10, 1982), Hague Acad. Int'l L. 335 (1983).

57. *Id.* at 348–49.

58. For a brief outline of the events leading up to, and flowing from the Chernobyl disaster, see HAWKES, LEAN, LEIGH, MCKIE, PRINGLE & WILSON, CHERNOBYL: THE END OF THE NUCLEAR Dream (1986) [hereinafter CHERNOBYL].

59. *See supra* notes 17–18 and text accompanying.

60. *See, e.g.,* the treaties indicated in Goldie, *Concepts, supra* note 13, at 195–97; *see also* Goldie, *Liability for Damage, supra* note 9, at 1216–18, 1242–44.

61. CHERNOBYL, *supra* note 58, at 118.

62. *Id.* at 123; *see* 122, 127–28. This book has quite a comprehensive statement regarding the role of the U.S. spy satellite systems.

63. *Id.* at 127–28.

64. *Id.* at 154.

65. *Id.* at 190.

66. *Id.* at 191–92.

67. Szasz, *Introductory Note to International Atomic Energy Agency Conventions on Nuclear Accidents*, 25 I.L.M. 1369 (1986).

68. I.A.E.A. Doc. INFCIRC/335, *opened for signature* Sept. 26, 1986, *reprinted in* 25 I.L.M. 1370 (1986) (entered into force Oct. 27, 1986) [hereinafter Notification Convention].

69. I.A.E.A. Doc. INFCIRC/336, *opened for signature* Sept. 26, 1986, *reprinted in* 25 I.L.M. 1395 (1986) (entered into force Oct. 27, 1986).

70. Notification Convention, *supra* note 68, arts. 1 & 2.

71. Rich, *Chernobyl: The International Dimension*, 42 WORLD TODAY 186, 187 (No. 11, Nov. 1986).

72. *Id.*

73. Paris Convention on Third-Party Liability in the Field of Nuclear Energy, July 29, 1960, as amended in 1964 and 1982, INTERNATIONAL CONVENTION ON CIVIL LIABILITY FOR NUCLEAR DAMAGE, Legal Series No. 4, at 43–51 (IAEA Pub. rev. ed. 1970).

74. Vienna Convention on Civil Liability for Nuclear Damage, May 21, 1963, INTERNATIONAL CONVENTIONS ON CIVIL LIABILITY FOR NUCLEAR DAMAGE, Legal Series No. 4, at 7–8 (IAEA Pub. rev. ed. 1970).

75. *See* Goldie, *Liability for Damage, supra* note 9, at 1216–20, 1242–44; Goldie, *Concepts, supra* note 13, at 195–97.

76. Note by the Director General, IAEA Board of Governors, *The Question of International Liability for Damage from a Nuclear Accident* 2, I.A.E.A. Doc. GOV/ INF/509 (mimeo Jan. 26, 1987) [hereinafter *Question of International Liability*].

77. *Id.*

78. *Id.* Annex 2. *See also id.* at 15, where both the OECD study and the WCED group of legal experts were taken to task in the IAEA Secretariat's working paper (mentioned above) for failing to consider the question of compensation for damage in the context of the "relations of States *inter se* involving claims against States."

79. *See* Goldie, *Liability for Damage, supra* note 9, at 1216–20, 1242–44; Goldie, *Concepts, supra* note 13, at 195–97.

80. *Supra* note 3.

81. Corfu Channel (U.K. v. Alb.), 1949 I.C.J. 4 (Judgment of Apr. 9).

82. *Supra* note 4.

83. *Question of International Liability, supra* note 76, Annex, at 7. In its discussion, for example, of the Lac Lanoux arbitration the IAEA Board of Governors pointed to the old Roman maxim, *sic utere tuo ut alienum non laedas. Id.*

84. Declaration of the United Nations Conference on the Human Environment, prin. 21, REPORT OF THE STOCKHOLM CONFERENCE, U.N. Doc. A/ CONF.48/14 & Corr. 1, at 7 (1972), *reprinted in* 11 I.L.M. 1416 (1972) [hereinafter 1972 Stockholm Declaration].

85. G.A. Res. 3281 (XXIX), 29 U.N. GAOR Supp. (No. 31) at 50, U.N. Doc. A/9631 (1975), *reprinted in* 14 I.L.M. 251 (1975).

86. *Question of International Liability, supra* note 76, Annex, at 9.

87. Factory at Chorzow (Ger. v. Pol.), 1929 P.C.I.J. (Ser. A) No. 17, at 47 (Sept. 13). *But see id.* at 73 (dissenting opinion of Lord Finlay). *Question of International Liability, supra* note 76, Annex, at 11.

88. 1972 Stockholm Declaration, *supra* note 84, prin. 22.

89. United Nations Convention of the Law on the Sea, Dec. 10, 1982, art. 235(3), *reprinted in* 21 I.L.M. 1261 (1982).

90. *Question of International Liability, supra* note 76, Annex, at 12, 14.

91. *Id.* at 13–14.

92. *Id.* at 13.

93. *Id.* at 14.

94. *Id.*

95. *Supra* notes 73 & 74.

96. This discussion is to be found at *Question of International Liability, supra* note 76, at 15.

97. *See, e.g.*, Comments of the Swedish representative to the IAEA Board of Governors, Provisional Record of the Sixth Hundred and Sixty-Seventh Meeting, Held at Headquarters, Vienna, Feb. 19, 1987, at 3–4, I.A.E.A. Doc. GOV/OR. 667 (mimeo Mar. 6, 1987) [hereinafter GOV/OR. 667].

98. Factory at Chorzow (Ger. v. Pol.), 1929 P.C.I.J. (ser. A) No. 17, at 47–63. In this case the Court applied the Lex Aquilia as it had survived for some two thousand years so as to stress the responsibility of Poland for illegal ("noxal") conduct.

99. *Id.* at 47; *see also id.* at 73 (Lord Finlay); H. Lauterpacht, *Private Law Sources and Analogies of International Law* 149 n. 1 (1927); I. L. OPPENHEIM, INTERNATIONAL LAW 352–53 (esp. 353 n. 1) (H. Lauterpacht ed., 8th ed. 1955)

[hereinafter Lauterpacht's OPPENHEIM]; 3 M. WHITEMAN, DAMAGES IN INTERNATIONAL LAW 2256–60 (1937, reprinted 1976).

100. J. BOSWELL, 3 LIFE OF JOHNSON 167 (Sept. 19, 1777) (G. Hill ed. 1977) (L. Powell rev. ed. 1934).

101. *See, e.g.*, comments of the Federal Republic of Germany's representative to the IAEA, GOV/OR. 667, *supra* note 97, at 5.

102. *See, e.g.*, Comments by the representative of the Soviet Union to the IAEA, GOV/OR. 667, *supra* note 97, at 13.

103. GOV/OR. 667, *supra* note 97, at 11.

104. *See* Comments by the representative of the Soviet Union to the IAEA, GOV/OR. 667, *supra* note 97, at 13.

105. *See* IAEA, General Conference, *The Agency's Program and Budget*, I.A.E.A. Doc. GC(XXX)/777/Add.1 (Sept. 24, 1986) (containing the Agency's Programme and Budget for 1987 and 1988, wherein the expansion of such activities as evaluation of technical and economic performance of nuclear power, reactor design evaluation, and radiation protection is discussed).

106. Ramberg, *Learning from Chernobyl*, 65 FOREIGN AFF. 304 (1987).

107. *Id.* at 327.

108. *Id.*

109. *Id.*

110. *Id.* at 328.

111. *Id.*

112. *See supra* note 86 and text accompanying.

113. *See, e.g.*, Rich, *Chernobyl: The International Dimension*, 42 WORLD TODAY 186 (No. 11, Nov. 1986).

114. *See, e.g.*, Aherne, *Implicating of the Chernobyl Nuclear Accident*, RESOURCES 10, 12 (Winter 1987).

115. Laches indicates an estoppel in pais arising from delay in asserting or enforcing a right. The Anglo-American equitable doctrine states that equity aids the vigilant and not the indolent. As Lord Camden said: "A Court of equity has always refused its aid to stale demands, where a party has slept on his rights and acquiesced for a great length of time." Smith v. Clay, 29 Eng. Rep. 742, 3 Bro. C. C. 640, n. (Ch. 1767). *See also* Allcard v. Skinner, 36 Ch. D. 145 (1887). This doctrine is a species of equitable estoppel.

As BLACK'S LAW DICTIONARY points out, failure to claim or enforce a right or do something which should have been done at a proper time will bar that party from subsequently asserting his or her claim when the other party (the defendant, for example) can show that he or she altered his or her position for the worse in reliance upon the claimant's inaction. *See* BLACK'S LAW DICTIONARY 787 (5th ed. 1979) and the cases therein cited. The estoppel element arises, of course, from silence or inaction inducing the other party's reliance and alteration of position for the worse. Ashburner tells us that the importance of the lapse of time varies with: (1) the nature of the claim; (2) the character of the claimant; and (3) the subject matter with which the claim deals. *See* ASHBURNER, PRINCIPLES OF EQUITY 516 (D. Browne 2d ed. 1933). Ashburner also tells us, in cases where a statute of limitations may also be relevant, that "Where a statute of limitation imposes a bar, or where equity imposes a bar by analogy to a statute mere inaction by the claimant within the time allowed by the statute cannot be treated as evidence that he has waived or abandoned his rights. On the other hand, where a claimant knows that the party against whom he has a claim is altering his position on the faith that the claim has been abandoned, or would not enforce his claim, and the claimant does nothing, his inaction may bar his claim even within the period which the statute allows for prosecuting it." *Id*. at 57. The laches concept is also recognized in admiralty where it closely follows equity. But in 1980 Congress enacted Pub. L. No. 96–382 which set a three-year statute of limitations period for "a suit for recovery of damages for personal injury or death, or both, arising out of a maritime tort." 94 Stat. 1515, 46 U.S.C. § 763a. In cases not covered by the statute, the traditional admiralty doctrine of laches still applies. This doctrine, similarly to equity, requires proof of unreasonable delay and reliance thereon leading to an alteration of the other party's position in the worse. On the confusion in the application of the doctrine as a background of the statute, see G. GILMORE & C. BLACK, THE LAW OF ADMIRALTY 772–74 (2d ed. 1975). For a general discussion of the concept in admiralty, see *id*. at 774–76.

116. In Roman Law and in modern civil law systems, the doctrine described in the text involves the vesting of a right through lapse of time. This vesting has both an affirmative and a negative aspect since rights may also be divested. For Roman law definitions, see A. BERGER, ENCYCLOPEDIC DICTIONARY OF ROMAN LAW, 45 TRANSACTIONS OF THE AMERICAN PHILOSOPHICAL SOCIETY 645–46 (N.S. pt. 2, 1953, reprinted 1980). *See also* definition of "usucapio," *id*. at 752–53. This double aspect of Roman law has carried over into public international law. *See, e.g.*, Johnson, *Acquisitive Prescription in International Law*, 27 BRIT. Y.B. INT'L L. 342 (1950). *See also* DE VISSCHER, *supra* note 32, at 208–9, 321, 328; Lauterpacht's OPPENHEIM, *supra* note 99, at 349–50, 575–81. *See especially id*. at 349 n. 4, where the author writes of extinctive prescription's remaining flexible and without fixed time limits: "Thus it resembles the laches, or acquiescence, of English Equity rather than the statutory limits governing Common Law claims." It should also be pointed out that a similar point of view—namely, that delay equals acquiescence, equals reliance, equals estoppel—provided an underlying premise of the International Court of Justice's judgment in the Fisheries Case. *See* Fisheries Case (Gr. Brit. v. Nor.), 1951 I.C.J. 116.

In conclusion, it should be noted that extinctive and acquisitive prescription are substantive. That is, the rights to which they apply are created or extinguished as the case may be and is not merely procedural—i.e., extinctive merely of causes of action.

117. In Anglo-American "common law" the temporal dimensions of rights have been the creation of legislation which prescribe the time period within which proceedings to enforce the rights to which they refer must be taken. These statutes are of two kinds: (1) where, upon the expiration of the statutory period, the right itself is barred as in the case of a person with a title to real estate but who has been out of possession of it for the statutory period (which varies with the legislatures of the law districts involved); and (2) where the remedy, but not the right, is barred by the lapse of the prescribed period of time. Here a right may continue to exist, but its vindicating cause of action vanishes. This distinction may not be theoretical because such a right may still be protected by a lien (but not a cross-action or counterclaim). *See* BLACK'S LAW DICTIONARY 835 (5th ed. 1979).

118. An example of the difficulties of articulating a theory of the lapse of time as affecting claims in international law is to be found in the Pious Fund case (The Religious Properties Arbitration, 1876) (U.S. v. Mex.), 2 J. MOORE, INTERNATIONAL ARBITRATIONS 1348–52 (1898), J. SCOTT, HAGUE COURT REPORTS (1916). Lauterpacht commented on this case as follows: "The apparent

rejection of the principle of extinctive prescription by the Hague Court of Arbitration in the Pious Fund case in 1902 . . . has not been generally followed." Lauterpacht's OPPENHEIM, *supra* note 99, at 349 n. 3.

119. Reliance in presenting this argument is upon article 38(1)(c) and (d) of the Statute of the International Court of Justice as discussed in De Visscher, *supra* note 32, at 403.

120. This doctrine has become well established in the jurisprudence of the International Court of Justice and of arbitral tribunals. *See, e.g.*, Minquiers and Ecrehos (U.K. v. Fr.), 1953 I.C.J. 47 (especially the separate opinion by Judge Basdevant, *id.* at 74); Nottebohm (Liech. v. Guat.) (Preliminary Objection), 1955 I.C.J. 4, 111, 122; Right of Passage (Port. v. India), 1960 I.C.J. 4, 100 (dissenting opinion of I.C.J. President Spender); Legal Status of Eastern Greenland (Den. v. Nor.), 1933 P.C.I.J. (ser. A/B) No. 53; Island of Palmas (U.S. v. Neth.), 2 R. Int'l Arb. Awards 829, 845 (1928). For scholarly writings on this topic, see I. BROWNLIE, PRINCIPLES OF PUBLIC INTERNATIONAL LAW 133–34 (3d ed. 1979); R.Y. Jennings, *General Course in International Law*, 121 HAGUE ACAD. INT'L L., Collection of Courses 327, 423–27 (1967) [hereinafter Jennings, *General Course*]; R.Y. JENNINGS, ACQUISITION OF TERRITORY IN INTERNATIONAL LAW 31–35 (1963); Goldie, *The Challenge of Transnational Expectations and the Recognition of Foreign Bankruptcy Decrees—The United States Adjustment*, 58 BRIT. Y.B. INT'L L. 303, 338–43 (1988); S. ROSENNE, THE TIME FACTOR IN THE JURISDICTION OF THE INTERNATIONAL COURT OF JUSTICE 13–16 (1960); G. Fitzmaurice, *The Law and Procedure of the International Court of Justice 1951–54: Points of Substantive Law, Part II*, 32 BRIT. Y.B. INT'L L. 20 (1955–56); Goldie, *Critical Date*, *supra* note 13.

121. *See infra* text accompanying note 113 (the famous quotation from Huber, Palmas Island case, 2 R. Int'l Arb. Awards 829, 845 (1928)).

122. *See* Wilson v. Johns-Manville Sales Corp., 684 F.2d 111 (D.C. Cir. 1982).

123. *Id.* at 116.

124. Thus, under McDaniel v. Johns-Manville Sales Corp., 542 F. Supp. 716 (N.D. Ill. 1982), the injured parties bore the responsibility of discovering their claims.

125. Steinhardt v. Johns-Manville Corp., 54 N.Y.2d 1008, 430 N.E.2d 1297, 446 N.Y.S.2d 244 (1981). There the court found that the cause of action accrued at the moment the offending substance invaded the plaintiff's body. New York courts also apply the time of exposure rule to cases of injury due to the pregnancy drug DES, Rheingold v. E.R. Squibb, Inc., No. 74 Civ. 3420 (S.D.N.Y. 1975), and cases of radiation-induced injuries, Schwartz v. Heyden Newport Chem. Co., 12 N.Y.2d 212, 188 N.E.2d 142 (1963).

126. Neubauer v. Owens-Corning Fiberglass Corp., 686 F.2d 570 (7th Cir. 1982).

127. *Id.*

128. *See supra* note 94 and text accompanying.

129. *See* Reed v. State, 15 N.E. 735 (N.Y. 1888).

130. By a "continuous" or "continuing" tort in this context is meant such harms as those occasioned, day after day over a substantial period of time, by a victim's exposure to a slow but relentless accumulation in his or her system of harmful or noxious substances, for example asbestos fibers. The injury due to such an accumulation may, moreover, be unknown to the victim, as may also be his or her legal right, over a long span of time. Given the present state of the law in many States (and apart from statutory reform) such a victim's legal claim

could become statute-barred before a remedy might be sought. *See*, *e.g.*, White v. Schnoebeler, 91 N.H. 273, 18 A.2d 185 (1945); *see generally*, W. PROSSER & W. KEETON, TORTS 165 (5th ed. 1984), and especially nn. 9–12 and the authorities cited therein.

131. Each of these "triggering" events could, of course, provide the "critical date" (see next subsection) of the cause of action or basis of claim.

132. *See supra* the authorities cited in note 120 and accompanying text. Much of the text is either extracted from or a summary of Goldie, *Critical Date*, *supra* note 13, at 1251–53, 1255–57, 1264–73 & 1283–84.

133. *See* Johnson, *supra* note 116, at 342 n.4; *see also* Sir Lionel Heald's submission to a similar effect before the International Court of Justice in the Minquiers and Ecrehos case, *supra* note 120, [1953] 2 I.C.J. Pleadings (Minquiers and Ecrehos) 46 (Sept. 18).

134. *See* Goldie, *Critical Date*, *supra* note 13, at 1252–53 and the authorities there cited, especially nn. 3–9.

135. DE VISSCHER, *supra* note 32, at 79.

136. Minquiers and Ecrehos case, *supra* note 120, at 74.

137. DE VISSCHER, *supra* note 32, at 79.

138. *Id.* at 76.

139. Examples of this view of the relevant facts may be found in Judge Huber's formulation of the "inter-temporal law" in the Island of Palmas case (U.S. v. Neth.), 2 R. Int'l Arb. Awards 829, 845 (1928). *See also* Sir Percy Spender's dissenting opinion in the Right of Passage case (Port. v. India), [1960] I.C.J. 4, 100.

140. SCOTT, HAGUE COURT REPORTS (SECOND SERIES) 83 (1932).

141. *Id.* at 83, 125.

142. 1933 P.C.I.J. (ser. A/B) No. 53.

143. *Id.* at 45.

144. *See*, for a presentation of the difference, for the purpose of this chapter, between political and legal disputes as depending upon the amenability of the latter to definition as "objects of litigation" and hence appropriate for casting into "terms of legal dialectic," *supra* text accompanying note 135; DE VISSCHER, *supra* note 32, at 79, 331–33, 351–55.

145. The leading authorities on this topic are those already cited, *supra* note 112. In addition, however, the following authorities, who did not cover the critical date issue, are relevant to that of the international law: P. Jessup, *The Palmas Island Arbitration*, 22 AM. J. INT'L L. 735, 739–40 (1928); T. Elias, *The Doctrine of Intertemporal Law*, 74 AM. J. INT'L L. 285 *passim* (1980).

146. Island of Palmas (U.S. v. Neth.), 2 R. Int'l Arb. Awards 829, 845 (1928).

147. Jessup, *Palmas Island*, *supra* note 145, at 740.

148. *Id.*

149. *Id.*

150. 1896 is the date of the Treaty of Paris, under article III of which the Philippine Archipelago was surrendered by Spain to the United States and was delineated, as far as the claims of the parties *inter se* were concerned.

Part III:
Acid Deposition:
Regional and Bilateral
Approaches

Chapter 10
Acid Deposition: Policies, Politics, and Practicalities

Daniel Barstow Magraw

Acid deposition, more commonly referred to as acid rain, involves the deposition of acids from the atmosphere to the earth's surface.[1] Acid deposition frequently involves transboundary harm; that is, emissions of sulphur dioxide and nitrogen oxides in one State often result in acid deposition and corresponding injury in another State. It has become increasingly evident over the past two decades that acid deposition is causing significant damage to surface waters and aquatic life.[2]

Acid deposition occurs throughout the inhabited portions of the world.[3] The major control efforts have occurred and continue to occur in Europe and North America, principally between Canada and the United States. The remaining chapters of this book focus on the science of acid deposition (Chapter 11) and on the European and Canada–United States experiences (Chapters 12 to 16).

Europe presents the interesting situation of horizontally and vertically multilayered activities occurring simultaneously. At the international level, parallel but nonidentical efforts have taken place in the European Economic Community (EC), the Organisation for Economic Co-operation and Development (OECD), and the United Nations Economic Commission for Europe (ECE).[4] In various ways, those three international governmental organizations—of which only the ECE currently has any involvement of Eastern European countries—have served to stimulate, supplement, and reinforce each other's pollution-control efforts. Some global environmental efforts, such as the 1979 Convention on Long-Range Transboundary Air Pollution (the LRTAP Convention)[5] and the 1987 Montreal Ozone Protocol,[6] have involved participation both by one of those organizations (the EC in the case of the LRTAP Convention and the Montreal Protocol) and by member

States of that organization.[7] At the national level, obligatory or hortatory directives of those institutions are implemented by municipal regulations.[8] Furthermore, some countries have independently motivated regulations at the national or subnational level.[9]

This complex situation, discussed in detail later in Chapter 12, is still evolving. The more effective involvement of Eastern European countries, apparently made possible by the sweeping political changes in autumn 1989, will undoubtedly be especially interesting and important. Those countries reportedly are characterized by severe environmental problems—problems that can have transboundary repercussions in Eastern and Western Europe—and their new leaderships face strong pressures to provide more consumer goods and otherwise to achieve rapid economic growth.[10] Regardless of how the European situation develops, it should prove to be instructive for other regional attempts to deal with transboundary acid deposition.

In North America, bilateral efforts to control transboundary acid deposition have been made by Mexico and the United States[11] and by Canada and the United States.[12] There have been no trilateral acid deposition negotiations among those countries.

Chapters 13 to 16 focus on the acid deposition controversy between Canada and the United States. That dispute, which has lasted more than 20 years, has taken place in the context of what is probably the world's most successful bilateral environmental relationship.[13] The dispute has developed in several phases.[14] The first phase was the period during the late 1960s and early 1970s, when scientific and political awareness grew, including the enactment of the U.S.[15] and Canadian[16] Clean Air Acts. Among other things, it was realized that emissions in Canada were leading to acid deposition in northeastern United States and that emissions in the United States were leading to acid deposition in eastern Canada. Second was the period of diplomatic and legal offensive between 1977 and 1985, which included the signing in 1980 of a Memorandum of Intent between the two countries about acid deposition[17] and the issuance of a Joint Report of the Special Envoys on Acid Rain prepared by envoys from the two countries.[18] Canada's claim, in brief, was that it was taking unilateral action to reduce sulphur dioxide emissions in eastern Canada by approximately 50% and to reduce the transboundary flux from Canada to the United States by at least 50% and that the flux of sulphur dioxide from the United States to Canada was injuring lakes and streams in eastern Canada, among other natural resources, and should be reduced.[19] The Joint Report supported Canada's position.[20] Canada demanded that the flux from the United States to Canada be cut by 50%.[21] This period also witnessed negotiations between Canada and Quebec and between Ontario and New York.

The remaining years of President Ronald Reagan's Administration (1986–88) comprised the third phase. During that phase, the U.S. position was dominated by the claim that there needed to be more information before the United States would commit to reduce the transboundary flux.[22] The governors of New York and Ohio also negotiated during this period.

The fourth stage began in January 1989, when President George Bush took office. Most significantly, in summer 1989, President Bush proposed major changes in U.S. air quality policy that apparently would meet Canadian demands for a 50% decrease in the transboundary flux of sulphur dioxide.[23] Even in this stage, however, the United States has continued to argue that a high level of uncertainty impedes the ability to make policy decisions, at least in the context of a lawsuit seeking to force the Environmental Protection Agency to take steps to control emissions leading to acid rain.[24]

The Canada–United States acid deposition controversy is interesting for several reasons. The role that scientific uncertainty and knowledge have played involves a set of issues that is inevitable in most international environmental disputes: what do we know with a reasonable amount of certainty about a particular situation (e.g., acid deposition), and how much do we need to know in order to make policy changes? At a more abstract level, the questions are how science and politics should relate on a given issue, and how scientists and politicians should relate.[25]

As noted above and in Chapters 13 to 16, the United States has taken the position that too little is known to warrant substantial U.S. action to reduce the transboundary flux of sulphur dioxide from the United States to Canada. The Federal Republic of Germany (until acid-deposition-caused damage was discovered in the Black Forest and other West German forests) and the United Kingdom (until more recently) have taken similar positions with respect to European acid deposition. The same issue has arisen with respect to the possibility of global warming[26] and has been used by some countries (including Japan and the United States) to justify delay.[27]

There may, of course, be sufficient uncertainty in a given situation to make informed decision-making impossible. But it is also possible to exaggerate either the degree of uncertainty or the need for greater certainty in order to fabricate a rationale for maintaining the status quo. Human nature (presumably as well as State nature, if there is such a thing) is not immune to the temptation to engage in such exaggeration. James N. Galloway addresses this set of questions in Chapter 11 and concludes that, although some uncertainties exist, we know—and have known for some time—enough about transboundary acid deposition to justify action.[28]

Canada argues, in effect, that politics has affected science, or at least the expression and interpretation of scientific conclusions, pointing specifically to the controversial Executive Summary of the National Acid Precipitation Assessment Program (NAPAP).[29] Galloway apparently would agree.[30] For its part, Canada mounted a substantial public relations campaign, complete with polished brochures;[31] but the contents of the campaign (including the brochures) appear to be consistent with established science.

The U.S. government's reluctance to take major preventive action has resulted in large part from the high costs of prevention.[32] But the problem is more complicated. It was not only the Reagan Administration, which presumably was concerned about the *net* national costs of prevention, that blocked progress. Congress was unable to overcome the opposition of powerful members of Congress from states that would be disproportionately burdened by preventative measures, for example, Senator Robert Byrd from West Virginia (which contains large deposits of high-sulphur coal) and Congressman John Dingell from the coal-burning Midwest. This opposition thus stemmed primarily from the fact that costs and benefits of proposed actions are not evenly distributed within the country that is the source of the transboundary flux. Again, such a distributional imbalance is not unusual in the pollution context.

The U.S. government has not defended its position solely on the grounds of the high cost of prevention, or at all on the fact that, internally, costs of prevention would be geographically lopsided.[33] Rather, as indicated above, the United States has relied in large part on assertions of scientific uncertainty. Those assertions, and thus that defense, are subject to attack, of course, if their methodology, facts, or logic is flawed or if new, contradictory scientific evidence accumulates. The Canadians have followed that approach.[34] Significantly, not even the Reagan Administration could withstand it entirely: the Administration's policies did respond to scientific arguments and joint fact-finding, though at a far slower pace and in a somewhat different direction from what Canada desired or thought was required by international law.[35] This process thus demonstrates the importance of efforts to establish a commonly accepted factual basis for environmental negotiations—a technique that has been used to great advantage regarding international watercourses by the Canada–United States International Joint Commission.[36]

A second fascinating facet of the Canada–United States acid deposition dispute concerns the role, articulation, and manipulation of international law. The negotiations between the two countries have expressly included assertions and counterassertions about the international legal aspects of the dispute.[37] Moreover, both countries agree that international agreements and customary international legal principles exist and apply to the dispute;[38] both invoke substantially the same set of case law and State practice to establish those principles;[39] and both even articulate those principles in the same terms, that is, in terms of the famous quote from the *Trail Smelter* case, the principle of good neighborliness, and Principle 21 of the 1972 Stockholm Declaration on the Human Environment.[40] In fact, both countries seem to consider those three expressions to be parts of one overarching standard.[41]

An example of the legal argumentation is that, relying on the *Trail Smelter* case,[42] the United States has argued that Canada must prove its injury by "clear and convincing" evidence, and that this test is not met because of the alleged uncertainty discussed above.[43] It is not at all clear that the *Trail Smelter* tribunal was correct in imposing such a criterion.[44] In any event, even that standard would be met at this stage, at least in Canada's (and my own) judgment.[45]

Another interesting example concerns the content and application of Principle 21. It is arguable that Principle 21's prohibition against transboundary pollution is absolute,[46] that is, that the State in which the pollution originates (the "source State") is internationally accountable to the State in which the pollution causes harm once that harm becomes sufficiently large to become legally recognizable.[47] That approach is consistent with the United Nations International Law Commission's approach to international liability (which would involve a balancing test, however, regarding the amount of reparations to be paid)[48] and with the Commission's approach to pollution of international watercourses (harm to a downstream State cannot be an equitable use, although some accommodation may be required).[49]

In contrast, it is apparently the United States' position that Principle 21 contains a balancing test, rather than being an absolute prohibition as described above; that the balancing involves on one side a source State's right to exploit its own natural resources; and that the United States meets that test.[50] This position is supported by the view that the relevant standard of care regarding transboundary harm (except possibly for a strict liability standard for ultrahazardous activities) is due diligence, which involves a balancing test,[51] and by the use of a "reasonableness" standard in cases such as *Lac Lanoux*.[52]

As indicated above, it is not clear that the relevant standard of care contains a balancing test. Moreover, if a balancing test is involved, it is not clear what factors are relevant to the balancing or that U.S. activities satisfy the standard with respect to acid deposition. What is important as a general matter in this formulation and application of Principle 21 as a balancing test is the indeterminacy it creates where, as in most international situations, there does not exist a mandatory dispute-settlement mechanism. A balancing test in such a situation provides the terms for a dialogue, but it also allows States deniability within a wide range of behavior.

A third intriguing aspect of the Canada–United States acid deposition dispute concerns the use, or nonuse, of impartial dispute-settlement mechanisms. As mentioned above, the two countries did appoint a joint fact-finding body, composed of one person appointed by the chief executive of each country, and that body issued its report and recommendations.[53] But the dispute has not been submitted for binding adjudication or arbitration, even though similar disputes have been so submitted by these two countries. The *Trail Smelter* arbitration,[54] for example, is widely viewed as a very successful instance of environmental dispute settlement. Moreover, the *Gulf of Maine* case in the International Court of Justice, which delimited the northeastern maritime boundary between the two countries, involved environmental arguments.[55] Altogether, Canada and the United States have submitted approximately twenty disputes of various types to binding arbitration.[56] Yet the current dispute continues to be approached via negotiation. One question is whether Canada ever officially requested that the dispute be settled by binding arbitration. When asked that question (by this author) in August 1988, Canada's Legal Advisor Edward Lee stated that Canada had not done so, that Canada preferred to settle the matter amicably by a negotiated agreement, and that Canada was waiting to see what the then soon-to-be-elected Administration's position would be.[57]

The final point concerns a nonlegalistic approach to this dispute. The political impasse that existed at the end of the Reagan Administration led at least one Canadian, Brian Flemming, to argue for innovative policy responses that do not embody a pure polluter-pays principle, such as the "absolute" version of Principle 21, but rather take account of the practicalities of the situation in a manner that reflects the benefits that Canada will receive if the acid deposition situation is remedied.[58] Flemming cites as an example the 1987 arrangement by which the federal government of Canada, the provincial government of Quebec, and the company Noranda, Inc., each agreed to contribute one-third of the $125,000,000 necessary to reduce the sulphur dioxide emissions at a major Noranda plant in Quebec by 50% by 1990.[59] He urges a renewed effort at the multilateral level to improve pollution-control standards, especially via a holistic approach, and also new bilateral attempts to make atmospheric environmental improvement both economic and palatable to politicians, scientists, Rust Belt industries, and utility companies. One possibility, he suggests, might be for the Canadian government to offer to deliver cheaper power to the Rust Belt on a long-term, guaranteed basis to replace the coal-fired power generated there.

Flemming's suggestions are reminiscent of several environmental protection programs in other contexts. The Chinese, in order to improve and protect the quality of Beijing's water supply, provided economic benefits to villagers whose activities had polluted the water, effectively in exchange for the cessation of those activities. As one Chinese official explained, the villagers could not be expected to cooperate unless they somehow benefited from the change.[60] Several riparian States (e.g., the Netherlands) on the Rhine River pay France to dispose of chlorides from a French potash plant in ways other than dumping them in the Rhine,[61] and West Germany reportedly has paid the cost of installing scrubbers in Eastern European plants in order to reduce the transboundary flux into West Germany. In both situations, the downstream States were presumably responding to the fact that it was less expensive to reduce or eliminate the pollution than to bear the effects of the pollution. A different example involves private contributions in the United States to pay for debt-for-nature swaps in developing countries:[62] the motivation in such cases is much closer to altruism. In any event, Flemming argues that Canada and the United States need to approach the acid deposition situation open to innovative and flexible solutions.[63]

Such an approach is always helpful, of course. President Bush's air quality policies seem much more consistent with the scientifically established factual reality and with the United States' obligations under international law than were those of the previous Administration. In addition, on July 8, 1990, as this book was being prepared for the typesetter, President Bush and Prime Minister Mulroney announced that the two countries "have agreed to begin negotiations for a practical and effective air quality accord."[64] Considerable ground for optimism thus exists that this dispute will be resolved quickly and equitably. Even if this story's almost ineluctable "happy ending" comes sooner rather than later, however, the story itself is still of great interest—both procedurally, as an example of international negotiation, and substantively, as an instance of State practice.

Notes

1. For a more complete description of acid deposition, see *infra* Chapter 11.
2. *See id.*
3. *See, e.g.*, Clark, *Managing Planet Earth*, Sci. Am., Sept. 1989, at 47, 51.
4. These organizations are described in Chapter 12, *infra*, at notes 4 (EC), 5 (OECD), & 3(ECE). The United States takes part in the OECD and ECE, but not in the EC. For a summary of the EC's environmental activities, see Haigh, *The Environmental Policy of the European Community and 1992*, [12 Current Report] Int'l Env't Rep. (BNA) 617 (Dec. 13, 1989). At least two other European organizations are active in the environmental area. The Council of Europe has 23 member States and is drafting a treaty on compensation for pollution damage. *See* [13 Current Report] Int'l Env't Rep. (BNA) 21 (Jan. 10, 1990). The Conference on Security and Cooperation in Europe (CSCE) has 35 participating States—all the European States except Albania, plus Canada and the United States—and has existed since 1973. The Final Helsinki Act, concluded by the CSCE in 1975, has four chapters, one of which includes the environment. *See* Conference on Security and Cooperation in Europe: Final Act, ch. 2, Aug. 1, 1975, *reprinted in* 14 I.L.M. 1292 (1975).
5. Nov. 13, 1979, T.I.A.S. No. 10541, *reprinted in* 18 I.L.M. 1441 (1979).
6. Protocol on Substances that Deplete the Ozone Layer, Sept. 16, 1987, *reprinted in* 26 I.L.M. 1541 (1987).
7. For a description of so-called mixed treaties, to which both the EC and individual member States of the EC belong, see Van der Mensbruggle, *How Is the EC Commission to Control Obligations of Member States in the Framework of Environmental Conventions at World, Regional Levels*, [10 Current Report] Int'l Env't Rep. (BNA) 464 (Sept. 9, 1987).
8. *See, e.g.*, *Water Fight: British Spat with EC Over Pollution Shows What 1992 May Bring*, Wall St. J., Dec. 14, 1989, at 1, col. 1 (western ed.). Harmonization of national regulations is especially important in the EC, of course.
9. An example of a controversial local environmental protection action is the 1988 cancellation by Mayor Rolfe Böhme and the City Council of Freiburg of the West German auto race, Schauinsland Rennen, which had run through the Black Forest since 1925.
10. *See, e.g.*, *Eastern Bloc Seeks U.S. Aid to Clean Up*, Boulder Daily Camera, Jan. 6, 1990, at 3B, col. 1; *Starting Over: Romanians Address an Economy that Left Their Lives Threadbare*, Wall St. J., Jan. 2, 1990, at 1, col. 1 (western ed.); Denver Post, Dec. 10, 1989, at H1, col. 2. As reported by the Wall Street Journal (*supra* this note): "Romania's frenzied industrialization ran roughshod over the landscape, transforming many rural towns into Dickensian hells of slag heaps, foul-smelling smokestacks and smudged gray factories. An ink factory near the city of Sibiu has so polluted the atmosphere that surrounding trees and houses are black. In a town called Turda, a cement works expels a beige mist from a forest of smokestacks. Strip-mining has ripped up much of the rural landscape and polluted waterways.

"There's scant hope of quick improvement in this. 'The environment here is a national disgrace,' says Alina Toma, a biology teacher in Turgu Mures. 'But we have so many other problems to get over that I don't think cleaning up the air will be a high priority.'"
11. *See, e.g.*, Agreement of Cooperation Regarding Transboundary Air Pol-

lution Caused by Copper Smelters Along Their Common Border, Jan. 29, 1987, United States-Mexico, *reprinted in* 26 I.L.M. 33 (1987).

12. These efforts date back at least to the 1920s, with the dispute that led to the famous Trail Smelter arbitration (U.S. v. Can.), 3 R. Int'l Arb. Awards 1905 (1938 & 1941).

13. For a description of that relationship, see *infra* Chapter 14; Magraw & Nickel, *Can Today's International System Handle Transboundary Environmental Problems?* at text accompanying notes 31–52, in UPSTREAM-DOWNSTREAM: ISSUES IN ENVIRONMENTAL ETHICS (D. Scherer ed. forthcoming).

14. The first three of these phases were described in comments at the April 1988 Sokol Colloquium on International Law and Pollution at the University of Virginia, by Brian Flemming, C.M., Q.C., who is Chairman and Chief Executive, VGM Capitol Corp., Nova Scotia. Mr. Flemming formerly was advisor to the Canadian Government on marine and environmental conferences (1970–76) and Assistant Principal Secretary and Policy Advisor to Prime Minister Pierre Trudeau (1976–79).

15. Clean Air Act of 1970, Pub. L. No. 91–604, 84 Stat. 1676.

16. Clean Air Act, ch. 47 (Can. 1971).

17. Memorandum of Intent Between the Government of Canada and the Government of the United States Concerning Transboundary Air Pollution, Aug. 5, 1980, Canada-United States, 80 U.S. Dep't St. Bull. 21 (1980).

18. D. LEWIS & W. DAVIS, JOINT REPORT OF THE SPECIAL ENVOYS ON ACID RAIN, U.S. Dep't of State, Washington, D.C. (Jan. 1986) [hereinafter JOINT REPORT].

19. *See infra* Chapter 13, at text accompanying notes 46–48. The Canadian government's view, based on research done in Canada, is that the acid rain problem in Canada is a sulphur-driven phenomenon, rather than one dependent on nitrogen oxides (which also flow from the United States to Canada), at least in part because the soil in eastern Canada is nitrogen-deficient.

20. *Supra* note 18, at 5.

21. *See infra* Chapter 13, at text accompanying note 37.

22. *See infra* Chapter 13, at text accompanying notes 25–26.

23. President Bush's proposals were introduced in Congress as H.R. 3030, 101st Cong., 1st Sess. (introduced July 27, 1989) and S. 1490, 101st Cong., 1st Sess. (introduced Aug. 3, 1989). For the probable effect of those proposals if enacted, see *infra* Chapter 13, at text accompanying note 55. In late October 1990, when this book was in page proof, Congress passed Clean Air Act amendments mandating a 10 million ton reduction in U.S. sulphur dioxide emissions by the year 2000, which apparently will meet Canada's demands. President Bush signed that legislation into law on Nov. 15, 1990. Pub. L. No. 101–549.

24. *See* U.S. EPA Brief in Ontario v. EPA, CA DC, No. 88–1788 (Nov. 22, 1989), *quoted in* [12 Current Report] Int'l Env't Rep. (BNA) 597 (Dec. 13, 1989).

25. For a discussion of the relation between science and politics, see D.K. PRICE, THE SCIENTIFIC ESTATE (1965).

26. For examples of differing views of the likelihood that human-induced global warming will occur, see Ramirez, *A Warming World*, FORTUNE, July 4, 1988, at 102; Schneider, *The Changing Climate*, SCI. AM. Sept. 1989, at 58; Brookes, *The Global Warming Panic*, FORBES, Dec. 25, 1989, at 96.

27. *E.g.*, Raloff, *Governments Warm to Greenhouse Action*, 136 SCI. NEWS 394

(Dec. 11, 1989); [12 Current Report] Int'l Env't Rep. (BNA) 580 (Dec. 13, 1989).

28. *See infra* Chapter 11, at text following note 11.

29. NATIONAL ACID PRECIPITATION ASSESSMENT PROGRAM, INTERIM ASSESS-MENT ON THE CAUSES AND EFFECTS OF ACID RAIN (U.S. Gov't Printing Office 1987); *infra* Chapter 14, at text accompanying notes 23–29.

30. *See infra* Chapter 11, at text accompanying notes 9–11.

31. *See, e.g., Canada-United States Acid Rain* (Can. Gov't, Rev. July 1989).

32. *See, e.g., infra* Chapter 15, at text following note 6; Chapter 13, at text following note 20.

33. The latter consideration is irrelevant from an international-law perspective.

34. *See, e.g.,* Federal/Provincial Research and Monitoring Coordinating Committee (RMCC) for the National Acid Rain Research Program, Environment Canada, *A Critique of the U.S. National Acid Precipitation Assessment Program's Interim Assessment Report* (Dec. 1987), *reprinted in* 1 INT'L ENVTL. AFF. 57 (1989).

35. Consider, for example, the United States' response to the JOINT REPORT, *supra* note 18, which is described in Chapter 15, *infra*, at text accompanying notes 8–13. The U.S. response, among other measures, was to institute a five-year, $5 billion emission control technology demonstration program, rather than to agree to reduce the transboundary flux of sulphur dioxide.

36. For a description of the International Joint Commission, see R.B. BILDER, WHEN NEIGHBORS QUARREL: CANADA-U.S. DISPUTE-SETTLEMENT EX-PERIENCE 54–60 (Inst. for Legal Studies, Univ. of Wis.-Madison Law School May 1987) (The Claude T. Bissell Lecturer, Univ. of Toronto 1986–87. Disputes Processing Research Program, Working Paper Series 8).

37. *See, e.g., infra* Chapter 14, at text accompanying note 1.

38. *See, e.g., id.; infra* Chapter 16, at text accompanying notes 4–23.

39. *See, e.g., infra* Chapter 14, at text accompanying notes 1–8; Chapter 16, at text accompanying notes 13–23.

40. *See* sources cited in note 39.

41. *Compare* Lammers, *"Balancing the Equities" in International Environmental Law* 153, 154, in THE FUTURE OF THE INTERNATIONAL LAW OF THE ENVIRON-MENT (R. J. Dupuy ed. 1985) (proceedings of the Nov. 12–14, 1984 Hague Workshop) (containing a list of 25 "principles or concepts" that have been used to establish or deny the (in)admissibility of instances of transboundary pollution).

42. *Supra* note 12.

43. *See supra* text accompanying notes 14–15.

44. *See* Kirgis, *Technological Challenge to the Shared Environment: United States Practices*, 66 AM. J. INT'L L. 290 (1972).

45. *See infra* Chapter 14, at text following note 32.

46. By "absolute" in this context, I do not mean that there can be no excuses under international law. For example, one can imagine tranboundary pollution excused by necessity or self-defense (although reparations might be required).

47. There is an active debate among international lawyers about how that level of injury should be defined. Terms such as "significant," "appreciable," "substantial," and "non-*de minimis*" have been proposed. To my knowledge, the United States has not defended itself by arguing that Canada's injury from transboundary acid deposition is too trivial to be legally recognizable.

48. The International Law Commission appears to be leaning toward adopting a strict liability standard for determining reparations in the context of "international liability." *See supra* Chapter 4, at text accompanying note 35.

49. *See id.* at text accompanying notes 75–78.

50. *See infra* Chapter 15, at text following note 35; Chapter 16, at text accompanying notes 23–26 & Part IV.

51. *See, e.g., supra* Chapter 3, at text following notes 24 & 34; *cf. id.* at text accompanying note 72 (regarding duty to cooperate).

52. Lac Lanoux (Fr. v. Spain), 24 I.L.R. 101, 140 (1957) (English), 12 R. Int'l Arb. Awards 281 (1957) (French).

53. *See* JOINT REPORT, *supra* note 18.

54. Trail Smelter (U.S. v. Can.), 3 R. Int'l Arb. Awards 1905 (1938 & 1941).

55. Delimitation of the Maritime Boundary in the Gulf of Maine Area (Can. v. U.S.), 1984 I.C.J. 246 (Judgment of Oct. 12). The United States argued that the Georges Bank, the richest fishery at issue in the delimitation, was a single ecosystem that can be adequately protected only by being located entirely within one nation. The court split the Georges Bank, noting that there was no reason to conclude that the long history of environmental cooperation between the two countries would not continue with respect to managing the Georges Bank fisheries.

56. R.B. BILDER, *supra* note 36, at 43.

57. Comments of Edward G. Lee, Aug. 7, 1988, Toronto, Canada, at a panel on the Canada–United States Acid Rain Dispute at the Annual Meeting of the American Bar Association.

58. Comments by Brian Flemming, *see supra* note 14, April 16, 1988, Charlottesville, Virginia, at Sokol Colloquium on International Law and Pollution.

59. *See also infra* Chapter 13, at text accompanying note 32.

60. Private discussion between the author and a Chinese official. One might argue, perhaps oversimplistically, that this approach involves an appropriate symmetry: if it is desirable that actors internalize all the costs (including externalities) of their activities, is it not also desirable that they receive compensation (or at least an offset) for any benefits that result from their activities or from changes in those activities? For related discussions, see Coase, *The Problem of Social Cost*, 3 J.L. & ECON. 1 (1960); *supra* Chapter 7, at text accompanying notes 40–73; Handl, *National Uses of Transboundary Air Resources: The International Entitlement Issue Reconsidered*, 26 NAT. RES. J. 405 (1986).

61. *See* J. LAMMERS, POLLUTION OF INTERNATIONAL WATERCOURSES 176–77, 181 (1984).

62. For a discussion of debt-for-nature swaps, see CONSERVATION INTERNATIONAL, THE DEBT-FOR-NATURE EXCHANGE: A TOOL FOR INTERNATIONAL CONSERVATION (1989).

63. *See supra* note 58.

64. Joint Statement by President George Bush and Prime Minister Brian Mulroney (July 8, 1990), *reprinted in* BNA Env't Daily (July 9, 1990). The Joint

announcement continued: "U.S. Environmental Protection Agency Administrator William K. Reilly and Canadian Environment Minister Robert de Cotret will discuss this issue when they meet in mid-July in Ottawa. We expect to begin negotiations shortly thereafter.

Chapter 11
Introduction to the Scientific Aspects of Acid Deposition

James N. Galloway

Introduction

In this chapter, I describe the general scientific background of one type of international pollution—the phenomenon commonly called acid rain or, more accurately, acid deposition. The latter term is more accurate because the deposition process involves not only rain, but also snow, clouds, fog, and material contained in gases and aerosols. They all bring acids to the surface of the earth. Both wet and dry deposition—dry being the type that falls out of the atmosphere when it is not raining or snowing—are instrumental in transferring acids of sulphur and nitrogen from the atmosphere to receiving ecosystems.

For the legal community to take action on an environmental issue— in this case, acid deposition—scientists ideally must provide information on three areas: (1) the degree of change in the composition of the atmosphere or the environment caused by sulphur and nitrogen emissions; (2) the degree to which this change in composition causes an impact on ecological systems; and (3) the extent to which these impacts are reversible, or in other words, the extent to which some benefit results from a change in policy to control emissions. Once these three scientific areas are addressed, policymakers can determine whether environmental changes are severe enough to take political or legal action.

In assessing proposed answers to those questions, it is necessary to keep in mind the nature and great complexity of the physical system, that is, the environment, in which acid deposition occurs. The emissions of sulphur and nitrogen to the atmosphere have substantially increased as a result of fossil fuel combustion and mineral ore smelting. To understand the environmental consequences of these increased emissions, processes in several linked systems must be examined. The first process is, of course, the emission process, because it determines the injection rate of sulphur and nitrogen to the first environmental reservoir—the atmosphere. Within the atmosphere there are several processes (transport and chemical and physical transformations) that control the deposition rate to the next environmental reservoir—the soils. Then, within the soils, there are again processes that control the injection rate of sulphur and nitrogen to the third, and final, reservoir—the surface waters. Once the chemical and physical changes in the atmosphere, soil, and surface water reservoirs are understood, the biological changes can be addressed.

Thus, in their natural order, the topics of concern are the atmosphere, the soils, the surface waters, and the biological communities living in these environmental reservoirs. The scientist's task is to determine the magnitude and rate of the chemical, physical, and biological changes occurring within these reservoirs.

In this chapter, I first present my views on each of the three relevant reservoirs—atmosphere, soils, surface waters—with respect to the current state of scientific knowledge: what we know and what we do not know. I then describe the conclusions of one other study about the state of scientific knowledge.

The Atmosphere

We know that the human emission of sulphur and nitrogen into the atmosphere of industrialized or heavily populated regions overwhelms the natural atmospheric emissions. Those human emissions are orders of magnitude larger than sulphur and nitrogen emissions from natural processes. In eastern North America, if one were to capture the sulphur and nitrogen in a box of the atmosphere, greater than 95% of that sulphur would be from human origin, less than 5% from natural origin.[1] Owing to these emissions and others, the atmospheric deposition of sulphur and nitrogen has increased by factors of ten, over natural conditions, in regions of North and South America, Europe, Asia, and Africa.[2]

Both wet and dry deposition are important. Near sources, dry deposition is greater than wet; far from sources, wet deposition is more important than dry. Cloud water deposition is also an important vector for sulphur and nitrogen.

There is large-scale transport of anthropogenic sulphur and nitrogen through the atmosphere—not only from the United States to Canada but also from the United States to Europe, Africa to South America and North America, Asia to North America. Quite apart from harm to biological resources, the increased concentrations of sulphur and nitrogen species in the atmosphere have decreased visibility and increased the corrosion of structures. Acid deposition is a local problem, a regional problem, and a continental problem. To a lesser degree (because sulphur and nitrogen are deposited from the atmosphere relatively rapidly), it is also a hemispheric and a global problem.

On a more positive note, we know that if emissions of sulphur and nitrogen to the atmosphere are decreased, the deposition of sulphur and nitrogen will correspondingly decrease. Therefore, if a control policy is instituted that reduces emissions by 50%, there will be an equivalent reduction in deposition.

What are the uncertainties about the atmosphere? There is a large amount of missing scientific knowledge, especially in the area of chemical transformations: how fast do the reactions occur, and what are the exact reaction mechanisms, for example, the specific pathway of sulphur dioxide to sulfate? Although those are interesting scientific questions, they are unimportant when the issue is the effect of environmental acidification, because generally the effects on ecosystems are not dependent upon the species of sulphur or nitrogen deposited from the atmosphere. Any type of sulphur or nitrogen deposition causes harm.

In summary, our knowledge of effects on the atmosphere is relatively complete. We know there are higher concentrations of sulphur and nitrogen owing to human activities, that the material can and is transported long distances, that there are high deposition rates, and that reductions in emissions cause reductions in deposition.

The Soils

The soils are important reservoirs for three reasons. First, they host the forests and other biological communities. Second, they host the microorganisms that control the availability of nutrients for all terrestrial and many aquatic communities. And third, they can eliminate or enhance the potential for acidification of surface waters.

In regard to the soils as hosts for biological communities, the changes that can occur in the soils as a result of acid deposition are an increase in toxicity and a decrease in nutrients. Acidification of soils has been shown to occur and to produce both types of change.

What are the uncertainties? We know that over the last few decades forests are growing slower than before in portions of North America, Asia, and Europe, including Scandinavia. We do not know why. Scientists suspect that there are a variety of causes for this, but there is no smoking gun. And there will not be for a while, in part because forests grow very slowly. It is going to take years, perhaps decades, before we know exactly why forests are becoming less productive. By that time, the patient may have died.

I believe it is time now for what William Ruckleshaus, when he was Administrator of the Environmental Protection Agency (EPA), called "prudent judgment." That is, phrased differently, what would a scientist say is the best explanation of the decrease in forest productivity?

It is a consensus of a majority of the scientific community that the decrease in forest productivity is due to some combination of natural and human causes. Fossil fuel combustion is certainly an important factor. Whether it is a combination of sulphur, nitrogen, and ozone, or just sulphur or just ozone or just nitrogen, or some other combination, we do not know. But certainly there is a human impact through combustion of fossil fuels on the growth of forests in North America and Europe.

Surface Waters

The effects of acidification are the least controversial with respect to this reservoir. We know that there are thousands of lakes and streams in North America and Europe that are sensitive to acidification. We know that a large number—thousands, in fact—have acidified, and we know that their biological populations are extremely sensitive. Once pH decreases below 6—just slightly acidic—biological damage begins to occur.[3] Moreover, even if acid deposition does not increase, there are thousands of streams that will be acidified owing to the phenomena of delayed acidification. For example, in the mountains of Virginia, it is estimated that in the next few decades, a large portion of the native trout streams will be acidified.[4]

One of the uncertainties about surface-water acidification is the rate of continued acidification. Although systems all over the world will continue to acidify, there is as yet no way to predict the exact rate, for example, whether systems are going to double acidity in two years or ten years.

What about recovery? Suppose the fossil-fuel switch was turned off and the emissions of sulphur and nitrogen into the atmosphere were eliminated? How would acidified freshwaters respond? Undoubtedly, they would recover. Freshwaters in some areas of the world—north of about 40 degrees latitude—would recover very quickly. Freshwaters in other parts of the world, because of differences in the soil composition, would recover very slowly. Whether "slowly" means decades or centuries, though, remains uncertain.

Other Studies

The preceding material is a thumbnail presentation of the current state of scientific knowledge. There are a number of other summaries as well, some compiled by people who have other opinions. I briefly discuss one other document below.

In 1985, the Ad Hoc Committee on Acid Rain, Science and Policy was formed. The result of that committee was a document titled "Is There a Scientific Consensus on Acid Rain?"[5] To prepare that document, the Committee asked four questions: What are the sources of acid deposition? How extensively has acid deposition damaged the environment? What would happen if we reduced the emissions of sulphur dioxide? And what is the relationship between scientific information and public policy? The Committee, with those four questions and a series of subquestions in each of these major areas, examined six publications that had addressed those issues, then compared the answers. It is especially interesting for comparative purposes to note that three of the documents were from the National Academy of Sciences,[6] one document was from the Environmental Protection Agency,[7] one document was from the Congress' Office of Technology Assessment,[8] and one document was from the White House Office of Science and Technology Policy.[9] Thus the six documents represented a variety of political flavors, if you will.

For all the documents reviewed, substantial consensus existed on the sources of acid deposition, on the effects of acid deposition, especially with respect to freshwaters and material damage, and on the likely effects of reducing emissions responsible for the acidity. The document concluded that adequate information existed to select emission-reduction strategies to reduce acid deposition efficiently.

There is another document that recently appeared: the 1985 Assessment from the National Acid Precipitation Assistance Program, which is commonly known as NAPAP.[10] Note that although this is an assessment for 1985, it appeared only in September 1987, two years later. The statements in the 1985 NAPAP Assessment generated substantial controversy; for example, a congressional committee held hearings about what was wrong with the document.[11]

Conclusion

Because of the nature of their studies, most scientists can go their entire lifetimes making contributions to the state of knowledge—valuable contributions to society—and never have to interact with lawyers and policymakers. Scientists who are involved in studying acid deposition—as I am—have the opportunity for that nónscience interaction. It is a challenge. Something that I find especially frustrating in this interaction is that we can have consensus in the scientific community about an impact, in this case the impact of acid deposition on the environment, and yet the policymakers say either that there is not an impact or that more research is needed before we find an impact. In the area of acid deposition, there are still unanswered questions. The extent of our knowledge is certainly great enough, however, to say that delay of action in response to acid deposition is due not to lack of scientific knowledge but rather to lack of political courage.

Notes

1. Galloway & Whelpdale, *An Atmospheric Sulphur Budget for Eastern North America*, 14 Atmos. Env't 409 (1980).
2. *Id.*
3. Schnidler, *Effects of Acid Rain on Freshwater Ecosystems*, 239 Science 149–56 (1988).
4. Webb, Cosby, Galloway & Hornberger, *Acidification of Native Brook Trout Streams in Virginia*, 25 Water Resources Rev. 1367 (1989).
5. Ad Hoc Committee on Acid Rain, Science and Policy, Is There a Scientific Consensus on Acid Rain? (1985).
6. National Academy of Sciences, Acid Deposition: Processes of Lake Acidification (1984); National Academy of Sciences, Atmospheric Processes in Eastern North America; A Review of Current Scientific Understanding (1983); National Academy of Sciences, Atmosphere-Biosphere Interactions: Toward a Better Understanding of the Ecological Consequences of Fossil Fuel Combustion (1981).
7. CARP, Environmental Protection Agency, The Acidic Deposition Phenomenon and Its Effects: Critical Assessment Review Papers, vols. I & II, USEPA Rep. EPA–600/8–83–016A (July 1984).
8. Office of Technology Assessment, Acid Rain and Transported Air Pollutants: Implications for Public Policy, Rep. OTA-O-204 (June 1984).
9. Office of Science and Technology Policy, Report of the Acid Rain Peer Review Panel (July 1984).
10. National Acid Precipitation Assessment Program, Interim Assessment on the Causes and Effects of Acid Rain (U.S. Gov't Printing Office 1987).
11. *Acid Rain Oversight: Hearings Before the Subcomm. on Energy and Power of the House Comm. on Energy and Commerce*, 100th Cong., 2d Sess. 1 (1988).

Chapter 12
The European Approach to Acid Rain
Johan G. Lammers

Introduction

This chapter discusses and analyzes the practice of the European States with regard to the phenomenon commonly known as acid rain, by which is meant the problem of the acidification of the environment, resulting in harm to human health, aquatic ecosystems, soil, ground water, and vegetation (especially forests). As has been explained in greater detail in Chapter 11, acid rain is caused mainly by the discharge into the air of sulphur and nitrogen compounds from stationary combustion sources, industrial noncombustion processes, nonindustrial and domestic activities (including residential heating), and mobile sources.

The harm caused by acid rain usually results from the emission of sulphur and nitrogen compounds taking place at such a distance that it is not generally possible to distinguish the contribution of individual emission sources or groups of sources. In view of the political configuration of Europe, it is understandable that the origin of such emissions is often located outside the country where the harm is sustained. Acid rain henceforth often constitutes a form of "long-range transboundary air pollution," which has been defined in article 1(6) of the 1979 Convention on Long-Range Transboundary Air Pollution as "air pollution whose physical origin is situated wholly or in part within the area under the national jurisdiction of another State and which has adverse effects in the area under the jurisdiction of another State at such a distance that it is not generally possible to distinguish the contribution of individual emission sources or groups of sources."[1] The political configuration in Europe entails not only that acid rain is usually, at least in part, of a transboundary nature, but also that often more than two countries are involved, considering the place of origin of the pollutants and the place where the harm is caused. Statistics regarding sulphur dioxide (SO_2) and nitrogen oxides (NOx) emissions on a country-by-country basis in Europe (and in Canada and the United States) have been compiled by the Secretariat of the United Nations Economic Commission for Europe on the basis of information provided by the parties to the 1979 Convention on Long-Range Trans-boundary Air Pollution.[2]

This discussion and analysis of the approach taken by European States with regard to acid rain will be limited, in general, to the approach taken by those States with regard to their *substantive* rights and duties under international or regional European law concerning acid rain, that is, with regard to their rights not to be detrimentally affected by acid rain and to their duties to prevent or abate acid rain. It is evident that this approach must, in principle, be induced from the practice (conduct and statements) of the European States relating to the phenomenon of acid rain, either specifically or among other matters.

At the international or regional European level, such practice has mainly taken shape and is still taking shape within the framework of the United Nations Economic Commission for Europe (UN ECE)[3] and the European Economic Community (EEC).[4] Also relevant, however, are certain developments in the Organisation for Economic Co-operation and Development (OECD).[5]

Because the emphasis in this chapter is on the approach taken by European States with regard to their *substantive* rights and duties concerning acid rain, rights and duties of *cooperation* to counteract acid rain and also aspects of *international responsibility or liability* for unlawful conduct or damage involving acid rain are not discussed. A discussion of those matters—various aspects of which are covered in preceding Chapters 3 and 4—would considerably exceed the necessarily limited scope of this chapter.

Developments Within the United Nations Economic Commission for Europe (UN ECE)

The Conference on Security and Co-operation in Europe, which took place from July 1973 to August 1975 and in which almost all European States participated, together with the United States and Canada, dealt with environmental problems in addition to vital security questions in Europe. In the chapter of the Final Act of the Conference relating to the environment, the participating States, for instance, acknowledged

that each of the participating States, in accordance with the principles of international law, ought to ensure, in a spirit of co-operation, that activities carried out on its territory do not cause degradation of the environment in another State or in areas lying beyond the limits of national jurisdiction.[6]

One of the fields in which the participating States were to cooperate in the future was the control of air pollution, in particular:

[d]esulphurization of fossil fuels and exhaust gases; pollution control of heavy metals, particles, aerosols, nitrogen oxides, in particular those emitted by transport, power stations, and other industrial plants; systems and methods of observation and control of air pollution and its effects, *including long-range transport of air pollutants*.[7]

The participating States were to develop their cooperation in the environmental field, among others, by

promoting the progressive development, codification and implementation of international law as one means of preserving and enhancing the human environment, including principles and practices, as accepted by them, relating to pollution and other environmental damage caused by activities within the jurisdiction or control of their States affecting other countries and regions.[8]

In view of its composition, the UN ECE constituted the natural framework for East and West European States to promote in the field of acid rain "the progressive development, codification and implementation of international law"; and it is within that framework that in 1979 in Geneva the Convention on Long-Range Transboundary Air Pollution[9] (1979 LRTAP Convention) and in 1985 in Helsinki the Protocol to the 1979 Convention on Long-Range Transboundary Air Pollution on the Reduction of Sulphur Emissions or Their Transboundary Fluxes by at Least 30 Per Cent[10] were concluded. Moreover, since early 1987 efforts have been undertaken with the UN ECE to develop a protocol concerning the reduction of the emission of nitrogen oxides—efforts that were successful in November 1988.[11] In the future, moreover, work may start on a protocol concerning volatile organic compounds (VOCs), also known as hydrocarbons. These must be reduced, along with nitrogen oxides, if secondary pollutants such as ozone are to be controlled.

The 1979 Long-Range Transboundary Air Pollution Convention

The 1979 LRTAP Convention[12] was concluded by 32 European States (including the Byelorussian SSR and the Ukrainian SSR), the European Economic Community, Canada, and the United States during a High Level Meeting concerning protection of the environment held from November 13–16, 1979, in Geneva within the framework of the

UN ECE. It entered into force on March 16, 1983. In spite of the official title of the Convention, which refers to "transboundary" air pollution only, many of its provisions deal with "air pollution, including transboundary air pollution."[13] While this category may not be restricted to acid rain, it can be safely said that the wish to cope with long-distance acid rain constituted the main reason for concluding the Convention. Because practically all European States—whether State of origin of acid rain or victim thereof (if not both) and whether located in East or West Europe—took part in the negotiations for the Convention and eventually ratified the Convention,[14] the Convention gives a clear indication of what written international obligations for preventing and abating acid rain appeared to be generally acceptable for European States in 1979.

Substantive obligations—or rather obligations prescribing the development of policies and strategies—are to be found in articles 2, 3, and 6 of the 1979 LRTAP Convention. Articles 2 and 3 contain fundamental principles of the Convention. Article 2 provides:

The Contracting Parties, taking due account of the facts and problems involved, are determined to protect man and his environment against air pollution and shall endeavour to limit, and, as far as possible, gradually reduce and prevent air pollution, including long-range transboundary air pollution.[15]

Article 3 provides:

The Contracting Parties, within the framework of the present convention, shall by means of exchanges of information, consultation, research and monitoring, develop without undue delay policies and strategies which shall serve as a means of combating the discharge of air pollutants taking into account efforts already made at national and international levels.[16]

Article 6, concerning air quality management, provides:

Taking into account Articles 2 to 5, the ongoing research, exchange of information and monitoring and the results thereof, the cost and effectiveness of local and other remedies and, in order to combat air pollution, in particular that originating from new or rebuilt installations, each Contracting Party undertakes to develop the best policies and strategies including air quality management systems and, as part of them, control measures compatible with balanced development, in particular by using the best available technology which is economically feasible and low- and non-waste technology.[17]

An important feature of the quoted provisions is their very comprehensive scope. They do not purport to protect merely certain specific interests against air pollution, but in fact all interests which could possibly be detrimentally affected by such pollution. Moreover, the provisions apply to "air pollution, including long-range transboundary air pollution,"[18] "air pollutants,"[19] or "air pollution";[20] that is, they do not apply to *transboundary* air pollution *only*, so that their application is not made dependent on proof of such pollution. As far as transboundary air pollution is concerned, this may be of a short- or a long-range nature. Moreover, as has already been noted, the quoted provisions cannot be deemed to apply to acid rain only, even though acid rain has beyond any doubt been the major *ratio concludendi* of the Convention. It is further noteworthy that the quoted provisions apply in principle to air pollution as defined in the Convention without any qualification as to the seriousness of the harm caused, so that, strictly speaking, proof of substantial harm is not required to be able to invoke the provisions.

The scope of the quoted provisions of the 1979 LRTAP Convention is thus extremely broad, a welcome feature from an environmentalist point of view. A close reading of the quoted provisions, however, makes clear that there is in fact very little reason for satisfaction.

Because of the many qualifications to which the obligation to prevent or abate air pollution has been subjected, the quoted provisions are characterized by a considerable lack of real commitment on the part of the parties to prevent or abate air pollution. The term in article 2 "taking due account of the facts and problems involved"[21] is singularly vague and ambiguous; depending on the circumstances, it may serve to strengthen or weaken the obligation to prevent or abate air pollution. Apart from that, the parties shall only "*endeavour* to limit, and, *as far as possible, gradually* reduce and prevent" air pollution.[22] The verb "endeavour" implies that there is not even a firm obligation on the part of the parties to prevent an *increase* in the amount of air pollution originating in their territory. More stringent verbs, however, such as "make every effort" or "undertake," were not generally acceptable to the negotiating States. Also, as has been noted, there is an obligation only to "gradually reduce" the air pollution. Given the cost and the technical problems involved in such an effort, this limitation is understandable. But even that obligation is weakened because there is an obligation only to reduce air pollution gradually "as far as possible."

The lack of real commitment to control air pollution is also apparent from articles 3 and 6. Those articles, in fact, only impose on the parties a duty to "*develop*"[23] air quality management policies and strategies, not to *implement* such policies and strategies. As to the *means* to develop those policies and strategies at the *international* level, the parties have committed themselves in article 3 only to "exchanges of information, consultation, research and monitoring."[24] The obligation in article 6 is further circumscribed by the general reference to article 2 with its noted weak elements and by its permitting the parties to take into account "the cost and effectiveness of local and other remedies" and speaking of "control measures compatible with *balanced development*, in particular by using the best available technology which is *economically feasible*."[25] The restriction that the control measures must be "compatible with balanced development" was inserted to cover the situation of certain less-developed European countries—for example, Romania, Spain, and Ireland—which feared that their industrial development would be unduly hampered in the future. The insertion of the restriction was a condition for those countries in order to be able to accept article 6.

The previously mentioned restrictive elements in article 6 may be deemed, in fact, to give a more specific meaning to the verb "endeavour" in article 2. Although it is true that article 6 puts some additional emphasis on the prevention of pollution from *new* or *rebuilt* installations, one should not lose sight of the fact that the qualifications mentioned earlier apply in principle also to pollution originating from such installations. In fact, this point only confirms that the Convention does not even contain a firm commitment of the parties to prevent an *increase* of the existing air pollution originating in their territory.

A proposal made by the Nordic countries during the negotiations to the effect that the parties would agree in the Convention to give highest priority to the conclusion in 1981 of an annex on sulphur compounds containing strategies and policies for the prevention of an increase in, and subsequently a progressive reduction of, long-range transboundary air pollution according to a timetable to be agreed on, appeared unacceptable to the pollution-exporting countries. The noncommittal provisions in articles 2, 3, and 6 as eventually adopted reflect the reluctance, at least in 1979, by the COMECON countries[26] and such other pollution-exporting West European countries as the United Kingdom and the Federal Republic of Germany to accept legally binding obligations to take meaningful air pollution control measures.

As has already been noted, the 1979 LRTAP Convention entered into force on March 16, 1983. In a resolution adopted on the occasion of the opening of the Convention for signature, however, the signatories declared that they would initiate as soon as possible and on an interim basis the *provisional* implementation of the Convention and carry out the obligations arising from it to the maximum extent possible pending its entry into force. This resolution had been proposed by the Nordic countries after it had become clear that the Convention would contain obligations which were considerably less stringent than those proposed by the Nordic countries.[27] Adoption of the resolution was, in fact, considered by the Nordic countries as a sine qua non for their signing of the Convention.

It is evident that the 1979 LRTAP Convention constitutes above all a vehicle for promoting exchange of information, consultation, research, and monitoring necessary for the development of policies and strategies to combat air pollution. The task of promoting and reviewing the implementation of the Convention has been entrusted to the so-called Executive Body for the Convention, which consists of representatives of the parties operating within the framework of the UN ECE and the Senior Advisers to ECE Governments on Environmental Problems. The provisional implementation of the Convention pending its entry into force was promoted and reviewed by an Interim Executive Body, which met for the first time in November 1980.

The 1985 Sulphur Protocol

As aptly stated by Hendrick Vygen, the 1979 LRTAP Convention "can only be judged fairly if it is not seen as a static event but as a point of departure for a dynamic negotiating process in pursuit of a better air quality in the ECE region."[28] This process was to take place through the establishment of an Executive Body for the Convention that would meet at least once a year.

During the Ministerial Conference on Acidification of the Environment, which took place from June 28–30, 1982, in Stockholm following two expert meetings on the effects of acidification and on control strategies, it was agreed that

The acidification problem is serious and, even if deposition remains stable, deterioration of soil and water will continue and may increase unless additional control measures are implemented and existing control policies are strengthened.[29]

The Conference henceforth agreed that further concrete action was needed within the framework of the 1979 LRTAP Convention.[30] Noteworthy in 1982 was also the new strong involvement of the Federal Republic of Germany after reports had shown considerable damage to the German forests as a result of acid rain.

During the first session of the Executive Body for the LRTAP Convention in June 1983, Sweden, Norway, and Finland proposed that the parties to the Convention agree to a 30% reduction of their national sulphur emissions by 1993, using 1980 as a basis for calculation. This proposal was supported by Switzerland, Austria, the Federal Republic of Germany, Canada, Denmark, and the Netherlands. Agreement (with the exception of the United States) in the Executive Body, however, could only be reached on "the *need* to decrease effectively [without quantitative specification] the total annual emissions of sulphur compounds or their transboundary fluxes by 1993–*1995*, using 1980 emission levels as the basis for calculations of reductions."[31] At the Canada-Europe Ministerial Conference on Acid Rain held in Ottawa on March 21, 1984, the 30% club was enlarged by the addition of France.[32] A further step was taken during the Multilateral Conference on the Causes and Prevention of Damage to Forests and Waters held in Munich from June 24–27, 1984, when a total of 18 countries—now including the U.S.S.R. and a number of other East European countries—agreed to reduce their annual sulphur emissions *or their transboundary fluxes* by at least 30% as soon as possible and at the latest by 1993, using 1980 as the base year.[33] It was then also recognized that the contribution to air pollution by certain countries, in particular some of the smaller South European countries and Ireland, was of little significance.[34]

At the request of the Munich Conference, the text of a formal international agreement embodying the political agreement reached at the Ottawa and Munich Conferences was elaborated within the Executive Body for the 1979 LRTAP Convention, resulting eventually in the adoption on July 9, 1985, in Helsinki of the Protocol to the 1979 Convention on Long-Range Transboundary Air Pollution on the Reduction of Sulphur Emissions or their Transboundary Fluxes by at Least 30 Per Cent (the Sulphur Protocol).[35] Article 2 of the Protocol contains the basic substantive provision: "The parties shall reduce their national annual sulphur emissions or their transboundary fluxes by at least 30 per cent as soon as possible and at the latest by 1993, using 1980 levels as the basis for calculation of reductions."[36] Article 10(3) contains a special arrangement for States that accede to the Protocol after its entry into force. Such a State shall nevertheless implement article 2 at the latest by 1993. If the Protocol is acceded to after 1990, however, article 2 may be implemented later than 1993, but not later than 1995. The possibility of accession enables States that were not willing to sign the Protocol—for example, the United Kingdom, the United States, Spain, and Poland—to become parties to the Protocol at some appropriate moment in the future after the closing of the very short period reserved for signing it (i.e., July 5–12, 1985).[37]

For a number of the signatories, it was clear that the Protocol constituted only a first step toward the abatement of acidification of the environment by sulphur compounds and that a much bigger reduction in emissions would be needed in the long run if a suitable decrease in acid deposition were to be achieved. This realization was expressed as follows by the Netherlands on the occasion of the signing of the Protocol: "based on a number of assumptions . . . only a reduction of SO_2 emissions by a factor of 3.5 and a reduction of NOx emissions by a factor of 1.5 would result in an acceptable level of deposition in Western Europe."[38]

Yet, as to further reductions, the parties were able to agree in the Protocol only on a very noncommittal text. Instead of providing that "The parties shall study at the national level the necessity for further reductions," or even better "shall endeavour to effect further reductions," article 3 of the Protocol merely provided:

The Parties recognize the *need* for each of them to *study* at the national level the necessity for further reductions, beyond those referred to in Article 2, of sulphur emissions or their transboundary fluxes *when environmental conditions warrant.*[39]

On the opening day for signature, the Sulphur Protocol was signed by 21 out of the then 30 parties to the 1979 LRTAP Convention. On September 2, 1987, following ratification by 16 States, the Sulphur Protocol entered into force. For Luxembourg, Switzerland, and Belgium, the Sulphur Protocol entered into force later.[40]

Notable absentees are Greece, Iceland, Ireland, Poland, Portugal, Romania, Spain, Turkey, the United Kingdom, the United States, and Yugoslavia. Of these, Romania (as of December 31, 1987) had not yet become a party to the 1979 LRTAP Convention. Among the other countries, the absence of Poland, Spain, the United Kingdom, and the United States is to be especially deplored because of the very substantial amount of SO_2 emissions caused by those countries.

Poland refused to become a party to the Sulphur Protocol because it did not have adequate modern technology to reduce its SO_2 emissions. The United States stated that since 1970 it had already considerably reduced its SO_2 emissions, and in its view these pre-1980 reductions should have been taken into account in the Protocol. Moreover, according to the United States, further SO_2 emission reductions should only be undertaken after new scientific information had been acquired indicating the need to make such reductions and if such reductions appeared to be justified by cost-benefit analyses.[41] Also, the United Kingdom pointed to the fact that it had already considerably reduced its SO_2 emissions since 1970. It intended to reduce its emissions further after 1980, but uncertainty in the development of its (nuclear) means of energy supply made it uncertain whether the timetable imposed by the Sulphur Protocol could be met. As stated more specifically in a major speech on U.K. environmental policy by William Waldgrave, the U.K. Minister of State at the Department of Environment:

The decision not to join the "30% Club" was not an easy one; we realise how important the 30% protocol is as a symbol of nations' concern to act on acid rain, and we thought about the issue extremely carefully before we took the position we did at the recent Helsinki meeting. To explain that position, I must mention . . . a specific difficulty. . . .

The specific difficulty arose from domestic circumstances in the past twelve months in the UK and our projection of energy requirements towards the end of the century. I mentioned earlier the enormous improvements in air quality that we have achieved in the United Kingdom. Our emissions of sulphur dioxide have been declining steadily since 1970: they now stand some 42% below the level in that peak year. Since 1980, they have fallen by about 25%.

This trend began before a number of our European partners began to move on the downward path, and has been caused by a combination of factors, some of which I have already mentioned. The use of lower sulphur fuels, more efficient use of energy and industrial modernization have also played a substantial part.

We expect that the further development of nuclear power; continued improvements in energy efficiency; and, in the longer term, the development of new and cleaner combustion technologies will all help to ensure that this downward trend continues.

However, we currently face an unusual degree of uncertainty. Our figures for 1984, in particular, are not a reliable guide, because last year industrial action compelled us to burn an atypical mix of fuels in our power stations and elsewhere. We also await the outcome of a major public inquiry into a new nuclear power station. While the Government's long-term plans indicate an increasing proportion of nuclear as a source of electricity, this depends on decisions which may have to be the subject of further detailed public enquiries.

For all these reasons we cannot be absolutely certain about the change in our sulphur dioxide emissions over the next decade, and we decided that we should not sign the protocol unless we were sure that we would meet its conditions in all respects. However, it *is* my government's policy to achieve further reductions in the emission of sulphur dioxide—we are aiming to get these down to 30% of 1980 levels, by the end of the 1990s. We have little reason to doubt that we shall achieve our aim, although possibly in a slightly longer timescale than envisaged in the protocol; but we do not believe that we would be justified in taking specific and costly action to meet the timetable laid down in the protocol.[42]

Unlike the 1979 LRTAP Convention, the Sulphur Protocol entailed for the parties a highly definitive and concrete commitment to reduce their national sulphur emissions: *"shall* reduce . . . *30 per cent* . . . at the latest by *1993*, using *1980* levels as the basis for calculation."[43] The sources from which and the measures by which the 30% reduction was to be achieved were not specified in the Protocol, however. Apart from a very general obligation in article 6 to the effect that "the parties shall . . . develop without undue delay national programmes, policies and strategies which shall serve as a means of reducing sulphur emissions or their transboundary fluxes,"[44] freedom of choice of sources and measures was in fact left to the parties in achieving the required reduction of sulphur emission. Another important aspect of the Sulphur Protocol was that by accepting 1980 as the base year for calculation of the reduction of the sulphur emissions, the parties to the Protocol implicitly also accepted a ceiling for sulphur emissions. As is noted above,[45] such a ceiling was neither explicitly nor implicitly provided for in the 1979 LRTAP Convention.

While the obligation laid down in article 2 of the Protocol is clear and straightforward and for that reason must be preferred over the vague and noncommittal obligations contained in the 1979 LRTAP Convention, a few critical observations should nevertheless be made. Why was the year 1980 and not another year chosen as the base year for calculating the 30% reduction in sulphur emissions? A quick look at the survey of national SO_2 emissions compiled by the Secretariat of the UN ECE[46] shows that for most of the parties to the Sulphur Protocol the total national emission of sulphur dioxide in 1984 or 1985 (July 9, 1985, being the date of adoption of the Protocol) was already lower—for some countries, considerably lower—than in the agreed base year 1980. For example, for France the total SO_2 emission was 3,558,000 tons in 1980 and 1,845,000 tons in 1985; for the Federal Republic of Germany these figures were 3,200,000 tons in 1980 and 2,400,000 tons in 1985; for Italy 3,800,000 tons in 1980 and 3,150,000 tons in 1983; for the United Kingdom (not a party to the Protocol) 4,670,000 tons in 1980 and 3,540,000 tons in 1984; and for the U.S.S.R. 12,800,000 tons in 1980 and 11,100,000 tons in 1985. Thus, even before the Sulphur Protocol had become binding on the parties, a clear downward trend in the total emission of SO_2 was already taking place and was perceivable in most of the major SO_2-emission-producing countries.

To a large extent, this downward trend may probably be attributed to a shift in the use from relatively high SO_2-emission-producing fuels to less- or non-SO_2-emission-producing fuels (such as, for example, the use of hydropower, geothermal energy, and nuclear energy). The energy-consumption (10^6 tons of oil equivalent [toe]) and energy-mix (in percent of gross energy consumption) data for the European Economic Community (all figures for 12 member States of the EEC) and the U.S.S.R. presented in Table 12.1 are relevant in this respect.[47]

While the downward trend in SO_2 emissions has greatly facilitated the conclusion of the Sulphur Protocol, this does not mean that the Protocol is only of minor relevance. The Sulphur Protocol will remain important, among other reasons, in that it constitutes a legal bar against a reversal of the SO_2-emission trend when economic conditions or energy consumption patterns tend to lead again to an increasing use of relatively high-SO_2-emission-producing fuels.

Apart from the question whether there is an upward or downward

TABLE 12.1. Energy Consumption and Energy Mix for EEC and
U.S.S.R.

EUROPEAN ECONOMIC COMMUNITY*					
YEAR	1980	1984	1985	1990	1995
Gross Energy Consumption	*1053*	*1041*	*1055*	*1116*	*1159*
Solid fuels	23%	22%	23%	23%	25%
Liquid fuels	54%	47%	45%	43%	41%
Gaseous fuels	17%	19%	18%	18%	17%
Hydro and geo	2%	1%	2%	2%	2%
Nuclear	4%	11%	12%	14%	15%
Other sources					
U.S.S.R.					
YEAR	1980	1984	1985	1990	1995
Gross Energy Consumption	*1294*		*1585*	*1840*	
Solid fuels	31%		24%	14%	
Liquid fuels	21%		14%	9%	
Gaseous fuels	29%		32%	27%	
Hydro and geo	15%		16%	50%	
Nuclear	5%		14%		
Other sources					

*ALL FIGURES FOR 12 MEMBER STATES OF EEC.

trend in the use of fossil fuels after the selected base year—and this
may not be the same for all countries—there also is the fact that certain
countries may have already effected considerable cuts in SO_2 emissions
before the base year, while others have not. Accordingly, a 30% cut as
provided for in the Sulphur Protocol will have the result that country A
that already undertook considerable cuts in SO_2 emissions before the
base year will in the end be obliged to reduce its sulphur emissions to a
considerably larger extent than country B that only started to take
control measures after the base year. This finding follows clearly from

the following example in which it is assumed that countries A and B emitted the same amount of sulphur dioxide in 1970 (100 units), but country A reduced its emissions by 30% before 1980, whereas country B did not.

	1970	*1980*	*1993*
Country A:	100	70	49
Country B:	100	100	70

Another aspect of the 30% cut in the Sulphur Protocol is that it applies to all parties regardless of the size of the population and the level of industrial development. Consider the following hypothetical situation: a less developed country L having a population of, for instance, 1,000,000 inhabitants will have to reduce its SO_2 emissions, for example, from 20 to 14 units, while a more developed country M having the same population but a much higher level of economic development will have to reduce its SO_2 emissions, for example, from 100 to 70 units. Although the reduction for country M is considerably greater than for country L, it is also true that country M may still continue to emit considerably more sulphur dioxide than country L should no further control measures be taken in the future. Given the need for drastic SO_2 emission reductions from an environmental point of view, equity would seem to require that country M be obliged to achieve a considerably higher percentage of SO_2 emission reductions than country L. It is further clear that if country M had already achieved considerable SO_2 emission reductions before the base year it would not be entitled, or in any event would be entitled much less, to invoke that fact vis-à-vis country L. As the Sulphur Protocol did not take account of considerable differences in industrial development and the resulting considerable differences in amounts of SO_2 emissions caused, this aspect could in fact be dealt with only by not putting pressure on less developed countries to become a party to the Sulphur Protocol. This solution is not an ideal one, of course, because at present no SO_2-emission limits are imposed on less developed countries that are not parties to the Sulphur Protocol. In light of this situation, the following statement by the U.K. Minister for Environment in his speech to the German Foreign Policy Society is critical:

This brings me to the more fundamental difficulty which my government also faced—the arbitrary nature of the protocol itself. If the proposition had been a 40% reduction from the year of peak emissions, the UK would have already met that condition. If the protocol had been based on a figure for emissions per head of population, its impact on the countries concerned would also have been quite different. And if the protocol had been designed as a first step toward reducing deposition to a level tolerable by the environment in the most vulnerable areas, it would have gained in logic and, again, been different in format.

In short, my government sees the protocol as arbitrary in its approach, and only one of several ways in which a common will to reduce emissions can be demonstrated. But I stress here that, even though we were not able to sign the protocol, we believe that our actual performance will be equal to—or better than—that of a number of countries who did. The Swedish Government, amongst others, recognizes this; in a recent assessment of the efforts being made in a number of European countries to reduce sulphur emissions, they estimated that the UK would achieve a cut of 50% between 1970 and 1995; a figure which is not dissimilar from the 55% they recorded for the Federal Republic.[48]

A major factor to be kept in mind, of course, is the fact that in spite of the considerable reduction in SO_2 emissions already achieved before 1980, the United Kingdom was in 1980—as it was in 1985—still the greatest SO_2 emitter in Western Europe. In that year it emitted 4,670,000 tons per year compared with 3,558,000 tons for France; 3,200,000 tons for the Federal Republic of Germany; 3,800,000 tons for Italy; and 3,200,000 tons for Spain (not a party to the Protocol).[49]

What has been said above amply illustrates that the 30% reduction clause in article 2 of the Sulphur Protocol was a substantive provision of a very general, simple, and straightforward nature that did not take account of any special conditions possibly existing in the member States of the UN ECE. Among the other special conditions that were not taken into account are the nature and the extent of the harm caused by sulphur compounds in each State.

As has already been noted, the Sulphur Protocol formed in the eyes of a number of its signatories only a first step toward the abatement of the acidification of the environment by sulphur compounds. Nevertheless, pleas made by the Nordic countries, Austria, Switzerland, the Federal Republic of Germany, and the Netherlands to develop a second stage to the Sulphur Protocol that would lead to a further tightening of the sulphur emission abatement goals remain so far without success.

The NOx Protocol

At its fourth session in November 1986, the Executive Body for the LRTAP Convention expanded the mandate of its Working Group on Nitrogen Oxides, allowing it to elaborate a draft protocol to the LRTAP Convention concerning control of emissions of nitrogen oxides or their transboundary fluxes. The resistance on the part of the East European countries to elaborating such a protocol—which still existed during the third session of the Executive Body in July 1985—had ceased. The

East European countries, however, made their cooperation dependent on the willingness of the Western countries to agree on provisions in the future NOx Protocol obliging the parties to facilitate the transfer of technology to reduce emissions of nitrogen oxides.

The NOx Protocol eventually concluded on November 1, 1988, at Sofia, envisages a two-stage approach with regard to the substantive or basic obligations of the parties "to control and/or reduce national annual emissions of nitrogen oxides or their transboundary fluxes."[50] As a first step, the parties shall arrive at a *stabilization* of the levels of NOx emissions or the transboundary fluxes thereof. In particular, they shall as soon as possible take effective measures to control and/or reduce their NOx emissions or transboundary fluxes so that these—at the latest by December 31, 1994—do not exceed the level of emissions or transboundary fluxes in the year 1987 or in any previous year to be specified by a State upon signature of, or accession to, the Protocol, provided that in addition with respect to any Party specifying such a previous year, its national average transboundary fluxes or national annual average emissions of nitrogen oxides for the period from January 1, 1987, to January 1, 1996, do not exceed its transboundary fluxes or national emissions for the year 1987.[51]

Contrary to the 1985 Sulphur Protocol, the NOx Protocol thus does not oblige the parties to achieve certain quantified reductions of the NOx emissions or transboundary fluxes from the 1987 level or level of a previous year of such emissions or transboundary fluxes. Reductions of NOx emissions or transboundary fluxes are only required to the extent that such emissions or transboundary fluxes have increased after 1987 or after a selected previous base year. It follows that the stabilization provision envisaged in the Protocol does not preclude increases in NOx emissions or transboundary fluxes over present levels, provided that at the target date the level of emissions or transboundary fluxes does not exceed the level in 1987 or in a selected previous base year.

The fact that the NOx Protocol entitles the parties to select the year 1987 *or any previous year* as the year of reference for their duty to stabilize their NOx emissions or transboundary fluxes thereof,[52] allows a party to select a year in which the level of its national annual NOx emissions or transboundary fluxes thereof was higher than in the year 1987. The possibility for each party to the Protocol to select the base year most suitable to it introduces in the basic obligations of the parties a flexible element that is not to be found in the 1985 Sulphur Protocol. Moreover, this possibility permits taking into account NOx emission reductions resulting from antipollution measures taken by a State before 1987 or to ignore possible reductions resulting from decreasing economic activities. However, as has been indicated above, the right to select a previous year is not unqualified. A State selecting such a previous year will be obliged to make sure that its national *average* annual transboundary fluxes or national *average* annual emissions for a period from January 1, 1987, to January 1, 1996, do not exceed its transboundary fluxes or national emissions for the year 1987. It was hoped that by means of this flexible element certain States, such as the United States, which were not able to adhere to the 1985 Sulphur Protocol, would be able to sign and ratify the NOx Protocol.

The NOx Protocol envisages the stabilization of NOx emissions or transboundary fluxes only as one, albeit very important, *part* of the measures to be taken in the short term. The parties shall *furthermore* (i.e., not *merely* with a view to achieve the *stabilization* of NOx emissions or transboundary fluxes at the agreed target date and thus involving in certain countries the possibility of NOx emission *reductions*), at the latest two years after the date of entry into force of the protocol, apply *national emission standards* to major *new or substantially modified stationary* sources and *new mobile* sources based on *the best available technologies which are economically feasible*, taking into account the Technical Annex and, in respect of mobile sources, also the relevant decisions taken within the framework of the Inland Transport Committee of the UN ECE.[53] With regard to major *existing stationary* sources, the parties are obliged to introduce gradually and without a final deadline control measures, taking into consideration the Technical Annex mentioned earlier, the characteristics of the plant, its age, its rate of utilization, and the need to avoid operational disruption.[54] The Technical Annex is of recommendatory nature only; its purpose is to provide guidance for the parties in identifying economically feasible technologies they can use to effect the obligations of the Protocol.

While the measures discussed above are all short-term and first-stage, the NOx Protocol also contains provisions on measures to be taken in its second stage. Those provisions, however, are only programmatic and cooperative. No later than six months after the date of entry into force of the Protocol, the parties shall commence negotiations on further steps to reduce NOx emissions taking into account, among other factors, the best available scientific and technical developments and internationally accepted critical loads. To that end the parties shall cooperate to establish (1) critical loads, (2) NOx emission reductions required to achieve agreed objectives based on critical loads, and (3) measures and a timetable commencing no later than January 1, 1996, for achieving such reductions.[55]

The critical loads approach plays an important role in the second stage of the NOx Protocol. By a "critical load" is meant a quantitative estimate of an exposure to one or more pollutants (i.e., nitrogen oxides in the case of the NOx Protocol) below which significant harmful long-term effects on specified sensitive elements of the environment do not occur according to present knowledge. The development and application of the critical loads approach is hence an effect-related approach designed to determine on a scientific basis necessary reductions of NOx emissions taking account of the sensitivity of the receptor and the impact of the pollutant on the receptor.

It follows from the foregoing that, according to the present Protocol, *major* reductions of NOx emissions or transboundary fluxes from the level in 1987 or a selected previous year will in all probability be realized only in the second half of the 1990s. In this connection, it is important that the NOx Protocol explicitly leaves open the possibility for parties to take more stringent measures than provided for in the Protocol.[56] Indeed, a number of European States—in particular Austria, Belgium, Denmark, the Federal Republic of Germany, Finland, France, Italy, Liechtenstein, the Netherlands, Norway, Sweden, and Switzerland—consider the obligations envisaged in the Protocol as too weak and declared themselves prepared to accept an obligation to reduce NOx emissions by at least 30% by the year 1998 at the latest, using the levels of any year between 1980 and 1986[57] as the basis for calculating the reduction. The refusal of other States to commit themselves already in the first stage of the Protocol to substantial NOx emission reductions is mainly based on the grounds that, in their view, the necessary scientific, ecological, geophysical, and economic substantiation for such reductions is still lacking as the critical load approach referred to above has not yet been sufficiently developed and that, in their view, the causal relationship between NOx emissions and damage has not yet sufficiently been demonstrated.[58] According to those States, the first stage of the Protocol should be used not only to stabilize NOx emissions but also to develop scientifically substantiated targets for NOx emission reductions.

In addition to the substantive or basic obligations to control NOx emissions, the Protocol also includes a provision specifically dealing with unleaded fuel. The parties shall as soon as possible, and no later than two years after the date of entry into force of the Protocol, make unleaded fuel sufficiently available, in particular cases as a minimum along main international transit routes, to facilitate the circulation of vehicles equipped with catalytic converters.[59] The attenuating qualification, "in particular cases as a minimum along main international transit routes," was inserted to meet the concern of the Soviet Union, where unleaded fuel is expected not to be generally available for a long time.

Developments Within the European Economic Community

Introduction

Directives of the Council of Ministers of the European Economic Community (the Council) are an important legal instrument for the prevention or abatement of long-distance transfrontier air pollution and are also the main instrument with which the European Economic Community (EEC) must give effect to the obligations assumed by it by becoming a party to the 1979 LRTAP Convention. Moreover, in relation to third States, the practice of the EEC and its member States along the lines of the EEC directives constitutes a substantial part of the total practice of States now involved in long-distance transfrontier air pollution, as either States of origin, victim States, or both. Accordingly, it is not only appropriate but also inevitable to take into account the developing law and practice of the EEC in a study dealing with the European approach to acid rain.

Measures taken unilaterally by member States of the EEC for the protection of the environment may differ in form and stringency. If the member States are left entirely free on this point, new trade barriers and unequal conditions of competition may arise between the member States which would subsequently lead to an improper functioning of the Common Market. This consideration and the need to protect the environment have already, in a rather early stage, led the EEC to adopt directives for the approximation, that is, the harmonization, of laws of member States relating to measures to be taken against air pollution.

Emissions from Motor Vehicles

As early as March 1970, the Council adopted the Directive on the Approximation of the Laws of the Member States relating to Measures to be Taken against Air Pollution by Gases from Positive-Ignition Engines of Motor Vehicles.[60] The objective of this directive was to formulate permissible limits for the emission of carbon monoxide and unburnt hydrocarbons from passenger cars with this type of engine. To keep pace with technical progress in the construction of these engines and with the increasing concern for the requirements of public health and protection of the environment, the directive has been regularly amended. The permissible emission limits were made more stringent, and new emission limits were set for other air pollutants such as nitrogen oxides.

In December 1987, the Council formally adopted a new directive substantially amending the directive of March 1970 concerning air pollution caused by gases from passenger cars.[61] In the 1987 directive, new limit values are set for emissions of carbon monoxide, combined emissions of hydrocarbons and nitrogen oxides, and emissions of nitrogen oxides, which vary according to the engine capacity of the vehicle. The 1987 directive distinguished three categories of cars: a first category of large cars with an engine capacity of more than 2 liters; a second category of middle-class cars with an engine capacity of 1.4 to 2 liters; and a third category of small cars, which accounts for more than half of the cars in the European Economic Community, with an engine capacity of less than 1.4 liters.

New *models* of the first category, as from October 1, 1988, must meet limit values that are adapted to European conditions but are equivalent in their effect on the environment to standards for vehicle emissions in force in the United States. Those limit values must be met by all new *cars* of the first category as from October 1, 1989. Somewhat less stringent European limit values apply to the middle-class cars (the second category). These limit values will apply to new models of middle-class cars as from October 1, 1991, and to all new middle-class cars as from October 1, 1993. New models of middle-class cars with diesel engines must comply with new limit values as from October 1, 1994, and all new middle-class cars with diesel engines must comply with those limit values as from October 1, 1996. Only slightly lowered European limit values will apply during a first stage to cars of the third category. Those limit values will apply from October 1, 1990, to new models of the third category and from October 1, 1991, to all new cars of that category. Limit values of increased stringency, which in principle had to be fixed by the Council before the end of 1987, would apply in a second stage as from 1992 and 1993 for new models and all new cars of the third category, respectively. Those limit values of increased stringency, however, were formally adopted only in a directive of the Council of July 18, 1989, and will apply from July 1, 1992, to new models of the third category and from December 31, 1992, to all new cars of that category.[62]

The new European limit values are optional in that member States *may* refuse approval or *may* prohibit the entry into service of motor vehicles which do not meet the new limit values.

Council negotiations on the 1987 amending directive started shortly after the Commission introduced its first proposal for the amending directive in June 1984. Adoption of the amending directive was considerably delayed because of diverging views of the member States as to (1) the stringency of the new limit values (the Federal Republic of Germany, the Netherlands, and Denmark being in favor of more stringent limit values and the United Kingdom, France, Belgium, and Italy being in favor of less stringent limit values); (2) the timetable for the introduction of the new limit values; (3) the question whether only a specific emission control technology (namely, the catalytic converter) should be possible or whether car manufacturers should be left a real choice of emission-control technologies that would also permit, for instance, the use of lean-burn engines (the latter approach was taken); and (4) the conditions under which member States would be entitled to provide for fiscal incentives to promote the introduction and sale of clean cars.

Agreement of principle on the content of the amending directive was already reached in the Council in March and June 1985, except for a general reservation by Denmark, which considered the limit values too weak and held the view that all limit values should in principle be equivalent to those applicable in the United States. As a result of persistent Danish opposition, the amending directive could not be formally adopted by the Council because under then-prevailing Community law, adoption of the amending directive required a unanimous decision by the Council. The Danish opposition against the amending directive was eventually circumvented after the entry into force of the European Single Act,[63] by which the EEC Treaty was amended. On the basis of the new article 100 A of the amended EEC Treaty,[64] the amending directive could be, and was, adopted by the Council by a qualified majority vote in spite of Danish and, later, Greek opposition.

Together with the adoption of the 1987 amending directive concerning new limit values for the gaseous emissions from passenger cars, the Council also formally adopted a new directive setting limit values for the first time for the gaseous emissions from heavy commercial motor vehicles with diesel engines.[65]

Emissions from Industrial Plants

In June 1984, the EEC Council adopted the Directive on the Combating of Air Pollution from Industrial Plants.[66] According to this directive, the member States are obliged to subject the operation or substantial alteration of certain industrial plants (as defined in Annex I to the directive) not yet in operation or built before July 1987 to the requirement of prior authorization. Those plants comprise the energy industry, production and processing of metals, manufacture of non-metallic mineral products, the chemical industry, waste disposal, and certain other industries. Plants serving national defense purposes were explicitly excluded.

According to article 4 of the directive, authorization may be granted only when the competent authority is satisfied that

1. All *appropriate* preventive measures against air pollution have been taken, including the application of the best available technology, *provided that the application of such measures does not entail excessive costs*;

2. The use of plant will not cause *significant* air pollution particularly from the emission of substances referred to in Annex II;

3. None of the emission limit values applicable will be exceeded;

4. All the air quality limit values applicable will be taken into account.[67]

The pollution substances mentioned in Annex II are sulphur and nitrogen compounds, carbon monoxide, organic compounds (in particular hydrocarbons), heavy metals and their compounds, dust, asbestos, glass and mineral fibres, chlorine and its compounds, and fluorine and its compounds. According to article 5, member States *may* fix emission limit values—that is, the concentration and/or mass of polluting substances in emissions from plants during a specified period which is not to be exceeded[68]—more stringent than those referred to in article 4 in the case of particularly polluted areas. In respect of areas which need special protection, they also *may* fix air quality limit values and emission limit values more stringent than those referred to in article 4. The directive provides further (in article 8) that the Council, acting *unanimously*, shall *if necessary* fix emission limit values based on the best available technology not *entailing excessive costs*.

Member States must follow developments as regards the best available technology and the environmental situation. In light of this examination, they must "if necessary" impose appropriate new or more stringent conditions on plants that have already been authorized in accordance with the directive.[69] The member States must thereby not only take account of developments regarding the best available technology or the environmental situation but also "the desirability of avoiding excessive costs for the plants in question, having regard in particular to the economic situation of the plants belonging to the category concerned."[70] The latter qualification implies that for "weak" plants in a generally economically strong branch, there is only little excuse for not taking protective measures.

While the preceding obligations relate to plants not yet in operation or built before July 1987, the directive also imposes certain less stringent obligations in respect of existing plants, that is, plants already in operation or built or authorized before that date. In view of an examination of developments as to the best available technology and the environmental situation, member States must take measures for *gradually* adapting such plants to the best available technology, taking thereby into account the following factors: the plant's technical characteristics; its rate of utilization and length of its remaining life; the nature and volume of polluting emissions from it; and the desirability of not entailing excessive costs for the plant concerned, having regard in particular to the economic situation of undertakings belonging to the category in question. The directive purports to lay down only minimum requirements, because member States may adopt provisions that are stricter than those provided for in the directive in order to protect public health and the environment.

The directive does not impose very stringent obligations on the member States to combat air pollution from industrial plants. With regard to *existing* plants, there is only a duty *gradually* to adapt the plants to the standard of the best available technology and this requirement only under a number of important reservations. Not only with respect to existing plants, but also with regard to new plants, the economic and financial cost involved in taking protective measures remains an important qualifying factor. It also appears to be clear, however, that an authorization to a *new* plant may not be given if the use of the plant will cause "significant" air pollution.[71] Significant air pollution, however, may be the combined result of the emissions from a great number of plants, and the directive may not provide adequate protection against that type of air pollution as it prescribes in such cases only the application of the best available technology, provided this does not entail excessive costs. Moreover, the emission and air quality limit values referred to in article 4 constitute so far but a limited bar to air pollution, as such limit values have come into being at Community level for a few air pollutants only.

Emissions from Large Combustion Plants

In December 1983, the EC Commission submitted a proposal for a Council Directive on the Limitation of Emissions of Pollutants into the Air from Large Combustion Plants.[72] The Commission regarded this proposal, together with its proposal for a Council Directive on the Combating of Air Pollution from Industrial Plants, as an important means to combat acid rain and to implement the 1979 LRTAP Convention[73] to which the Community is a party.

The proposed directive was intended to apply to combustion plants whose rated thermal output, including that of ancillary plants, was equal to or greater than 50 megawatts (MW) irrespective of the type of fuel used (solid, liquid, or gaseous). "Combustion plant" was defined as "any technical apparatus designed to run on one or more fuels for the purpose of producing energy by burning the fuel, with the exception of units driven by diesel engines." The Commission proposed two main strategies to reduce the air pollution caused by combustion plants. First, by overall reductions of total annual emissions from existing and new combustion plants, in the amount of 60% for sulphur dioxide, 40% for dust, and 40% for nitrogen oxides, taking 1980 as the base year and to be achieved by December 31, 1995. To that end, member States would be obliged to draw up before December 31, 1986, appropriate programs with timetables and implementing procedures. Second, as from January 1, 1985, member States would be required to impose on *new* combustion plants *emission limit values* set out in an annex in respect of sulphur dioxide, dust, and nitrogen oxides. For installations below 100 MW, this obligation would be deferred by five years. Annex I to the proposed directive specified two sets of emission limit values for sulphur dioxide and nitrogen oxides, namely, a first set of emission limits applicable from January 1, 1985, until December 31, 1995, and a second set of more stringent values applicable after December 31, 1995.

Temporary exemptions from one of the provisions of the directive could be granted by the Commission in certain cases under certain conditions. These four situations are (1) if the energy production in a member State would be largely based on the use of *indigenous* solid fuel containing a very high sulphur content, so that compliance with the emission standards could only take place at disproportionate costs; (2) if the total annual emissions of a member State in the base year 1980 would be considerably lower than the levels in other member States; (3) in the case of a breakdown of a purification facility; and (4) if an operator of a plant which normally used low-sulphur fuel would be unable to meet the emission limit values because of a serious shortage of low-sulphur fuel.

Since the first exchange of thoughts in the Council in March 1984, member States have held considerably diverging positions on various issues, such as on the power threshold of the combustion plants to be covered by the directive, the proposed overall reductions of SO_2, NOx, or dust emissions, the emission limit values for new plants, and the permissible exemptions.

Proposed Overall Emission Reductions

From the beginning some member States—and among the major polluting States, in particular the United Kingdom—opposed the overall emission reductions proposed by the Commission. The main obstacles were the extent and timing of the reductions and the fact that *equal* reduction targets would apply to all member States regardless of special circumstances in those States. During the March 1986 session of the Council, nine of the (then) ten member States were able to agree on a statement setting forth the following framework for future work on the directive:[74] the regulation of emissions from all new plants on the basis of standards related to the best available technology not involving excessive cost; a two-stage approach for overall reductions in emissions; the setting of a Community target for an overall reduction in SO_2 emissions—this would need to be substantial, where "substantial" meant an improvement on the reduction envisaged by the 1985 Sulphur Protocol; the setting up of appropriate programs, member State by member State, for achieving the overall reduction—programs that would take account of the scale of the emissions from different member States, their contributions to overall pollution in Europe, special situations (related to their stage of economic development, the nature of locally available fuels, and the overall effort involved), and other relevant criteria; and comparable action in relation to emissions of NOx.

The United Kingdom was unable to accept this framework for future action and reserved its position. It appears from the statement that considerable uncertainty continued to exist as to the targets and target dates of the overall emission reductions. The statement also makes clear, however, that the idea of *equal* reduction targets for all member States was generally rejected.[75] Yet, although there was a growing feeling that member States with a relatively small energy-generating capacity in 1980[76] and hence contributing relatively little to the overall pollution in Europe should be required to achieve less stringent reduction targets, considerable controversy continued to exist as to the mode and extent of the differentiation of the individual reductions to be achieved by each member State.

Subsequent proposals made by the Netherlands Presidency of the Council involved an overall *Community* reduction of 60% SO_2 and 40% NOx emissions in two stages, that is, 45% SO_2 and a still-unspecified percentage of NOx emission reduction in 1995 and a total of 60% SO_2 and 40% NOx emission reduction in 2005—to be achieved by differentiated contributions of member States based on what each member

State already planned to do, rather than on criteria such as those contained in the stated framework for future action mentioned above. No proposal was made with respect to dust. Agreement could not be reached, however. While the approach was in principle acceptable to France, Italy, Belgium, Luxembourg, and Portugal, some other countries (the Federal Republic of Germany and Denmark) and the Commission regarded the proposal as too weak, and other countries (the United Kingdom and Spain) reserved their positions.

After an even weaker proposal made by the United Kingdom during the British Presidency, the Belgian Presidency proposed a new approach which the Council during its session in March 1987 was prepared to accept as a useful framework for further deliberations. In this approach, the 60% SO_2 and 40% NOx emission reduction requirements would apply only to emissions caused by existing plants and not, as had been the case in the Commission proposal, to emissions from existing and new plants. The SO_2 emission reduction was in principle to be achieved by each member State in two stages, that is, 40% in 1993 and 60% in 1998, subject, however, to exemptions in certain special cases. No specific proposals were developed for nitrogen oxides. The Belgian Presidency eventually proposed specific differentiated SO_2 emission reduction targets and target dates for existing plants, which each member State was able to accept in respect to itself, but which could not all (in particular not those claimed by the United Kingdom and Spain) be accepted by the other member States.

Taking the proposals made by the Belgian Presidency as a starting point, the subsequent Danish Presidency proposed in the autumn of 1987 a *three*-stage approach to solve the problem. SO_2 emission reductions up to a maximum of, in principle, 80% for each member State were now to be achieved in three phases—1993, 1998, and 2010. Lower reduction target figures were proposed for Greece, Ireland, Luxembourg, Portugal, and Spain. No figures were proposed for NOx emissions, but an approach similar as for SO_2 emissions was proposed for such emissions. The Danish Presidency proposals, however, were not generally acceptable.

In January 1988, the German Presidency proposed another *reduced* three-stage approach, namely, 1993, 1998, and *2003* for overall reductions of SO_2 emissions from existing plants—in principle, 40% in 1993, 60% in 1998, and 70% in 2003. The targets for each individual member State, however, were to be adjusted, taking into account technical and economic feasibility, the principle of comparable efforts under comparable conditions, as well as other significant special circumstances in the member States. The figures thus established for phases I and II appeared now to be generally acceptable, except for a reservation on the part of the United Kingdom. Although the concept of a third phase appeared to be generally acceptable, member States differed considerably on the acceptability of the reduction targets proposed by the Presidency for phase III. NOx reduction targets in two phases (1993 and 1998) were also proposed by the German Presidency, but these appeared to be acceptable to only half of the member States.

Emission Limit Values

While the overall reduction targets for sulphur dioxide, nitrogen oxides, and possibly dust aim at securing a major decrease in the overall emission of sulphur dioxide, nitrogen oxides, and possibly dust in the *short* term, emission limit values for *new* plants are intended to ensure—as existing plants become redundant and are replaced by new ones—that emissions in the *long* term fall to only a fraction of present day levels. As set forth above, the draft directive proposed by the Commission would oblige member States to impose, as from January 1, 1985, on *new* combustion plants, emission limit values with respect to sulphur dioxide, dust, and nitrogen oxides. Two sets of emission limit values were envisaged for sulphur dioxide and nitrogen oxides. A first set applicable from January 1, 1985, until December 31, 1995, and a second set of more stringent values applicable after December 31, 1995. The emission limit values proposed by the Commission also gave rise to considerable controversy among the member States. As we have already seen, during the March 1986 session of the Council, nine of the (then) ten member States were able to agree on a statement setting forth a framework for future action which envisaged the imposition of emission limit values on new plants based on "the best available technology not involving excessive cost."[77] Earlier proposals by the Federal Republic of Germany and the Netherlands to develop emission limit values also for *existing* plants appeared to be wholly unacceptable to some other member States, in particular the United Kingdom.

After the adoption of the proposal by the Belgian Presidency to limit the application of the overall reductions of SO_2 and NOx emissions to emissions from *existing* plants,[78] the question of the stringency of the emission limit values for *new* plants gained considerably in importance.

Other Controversial Issues

Other controversial issues which formed the subject of deliberation were the following:

1. the definition of a combustion plant and the threshold for the capacity of the combustion plant to which the directive is to apply at all (50 MW as proposed by the Commission or 100 MW as proposed by some member States);
2. possibly a special regime for combustion plants with a capacity between 50 and 100 MW using a certain type of fuel and/or producing a certain type of pollutant; and
3. the nature and extent of derogations from the otherwise applicable emission limit values—
   a. in the case of use of indigenous solid fuels of a high and considerably fluctuating sulphur content, high moisture content, high ash content, and therefore low calorific value,
   b. in the case of use of peak load installations, and
   c. in the case of plants burning lignite.

The Agreement Eventually Reached

During the session of June 28–29, 1988, the Council of Ministers eventually reached agreement on the substance of the directive. The directive in its final form, carrying the date of November 24, 1988,[79] remains in principle applicable to combustion plants of 50 or more MW irrespective of the type of fuel used (solid, liquid, or gaseous),[80] whereby "combustion plant" has now been defined as "any technical apparatus in which fuels are oxidized in order to use the heat thus generated."[81] Certain specified types of plants, however, are now excluded from the scope of the directive.[82] Moreover, plants powered by diesel, petrol, and gas engines or by gas turbines, irrespective of the fuel used, are also not covered by the directive.[83] Whether a plant is to be regarded as an "existing" or "new" plant depends on whether the original construction license, or in the absence of such a procedure, the original operating license, was granted *before* or *on or after* July 1, 1987.[84]

With respect to existing plants, member States must not later than July 1, 1990, draw up appropriate programs containing timetables and implementing procedures for the progressive reduction of the total annual emissions of such plants.[85] These programs must be drawn up and implemented with the aim of complying at least with emission ceilings and corresponding percentage reductions laid down for sulphur dioxide in Annex I, to be realized in three phases (1993, 1998, and 2003), and for nitrogen oxides in Annex II, to be realized in two phases (1993 and 1998). Taking the 1980 level of the annual emission of sulphur dioxide or nitrogen oxides expressed in kilotonnes (a "tonne" is a metric ton, equivalent to 1.102 "short" tons) as the base level, the member States are obliged to realize different reduction targets. Thus, for example, by 1993 (phase I), 1998 (phase II), and 2003 (phase III), respectively, the prescribed sulphur dioxide reduction targets are (taking the emissions in 1980 as the base level) for Denmark −34%, −56%, and −67%, for Germany and the Netherlands each −40%, −60%, and −70%, and for Spain 0%, −24%, and −37%; but an extension is permitted for Ireland, namely, +25%, +25%, and +25%, and for Portugal, namely, +102%, +135%, and +79%. Annexes I and II contain, in addition to real figures of 1980 emission levels, adjusted 1980 emission levels. These adjusted levels include the additional net energy-generating capacity for which in the period 1980–87 a license has been given. Taking these adjusted 1980 emission levels for sulphur dioxide as the base level, the reduction targets are—for 1993, 1998, and 2003, respectively—for Denmark −40%, −60%, and −70%, for Germany and the Netherlands each again −40%, −60%, and −70%, but for Ireland −29%, −29%, and −29%, and for Portugal −25%, −13%, and −34%. The differentiation in reduction targets between the various member States of the Community is justified by differences in development, technical, and economic feasibility or other significant special circumstances in the individual member States.

It should, however, be noted that the reduction targets are not fixed once and for all. On the basis of (summary) reports to be provided by the member States, the Commission will in 1994 make a report to the Council on the implementation of the reductions prescribed by the directive, accompanied where necessary by proposals for a revision of the phase III reduction targets and/or date for sulphur dioxide and the phase II reduction targets and/or date for nitrogen oxides. The Council shall then decide upon such proposals by unanimity. Moreover, the Commission is in certain cases entitled to modify the reduction target and/or date for a certain member State "if a substantial and unexpected change in energy demand or in the availability of certain fuels or certain generating installations creates serious technical difficulties for the implementation by a Member State of its programme." There is, however, a certain danger here that the directive might be undermined; thus the Council acting by a qualified majority, at the request of any member State within three months, may make a different decision.[86]

Although with respect to existing plants progressive reductions of total annual emissions are to take place designed to reach in phases certain emission ceilings, new plants will have to comply with certain emission *limit values* fixed in Annexes III to VII regarding sulphur dioxide, nitrogen oxides, and dust. These limit values are subject to change by a unanimous decision of the Council on the bases of proposals to be submitted by the Commission before July 1, 1995.[87]

The directive, however, allows for a considerable number of exceptions from the emission limit values. First of all, the Council will only in 1990 make a decision on the limit values for combustion plants between 50 and 100 MW. With respect to those plants, therefore, no limit values exist until 1990.[88] Furthermore, derogations from otherwise applicable emission limit values for sulphur dioxide emitted by new plants using solid fuels have been allowed for (1) new peak load plants meeting certain requirements; (2) new plants that burn *indigenous* solid fuel which, instead of complying with limit values will have to comply with certain desulphurization rates laid down in Annex VII; and (3) on the persistent insistence of Spain, certain new plants in Spain meeting certain requirements.[89] Derogation from otherwise applicable emission limit values for sulphur dioxide, nitrogen oxides, and dust are further allowed for plants burning *indigenous* lignite "if, notwithstanding the application of the best available technology not entailing excessive costs, major difficulties connected with the nature of the lignite so require and provided that lignite is an essential source of fuel for the plants."[90]

A temporary derogation from the emission limit value for nitrogen oxides is also allowed "in the event that monitoring reveals that due to unforeseen reasons, the emission limit value is not being complied with." The operator shall in that case be required to take all appropriate primary measures to achieve compliance as soon as possible and in any case within one year. This form of derogation is also subject to revision by the Council on the basis of a proposal to be submitted by the Commission before July 1, 1995.[91] Certain temporary derogations are further under certain strict conditions allowed in the case of (1) the malfunction or breakdown of abatement equipment; (2) a plant which normally uses low-sulphur fuel, but is unable to comply with the emission limit values because of an interruption in the supply of low-sulphur fuel resulting from a serious shortage; or (3) a plant which normally uses only gaseous fuel, but has to resort exceptionally, and for a short period, to the use of other fuels because of a sudden interruption in the supply of gas.[92]

The regime for existing plants (progressive reductions of annual emissions) and new plants (emission limit values) laid down in the directive is supplemented with provisions concerning monitoring and measuring methods and/or equipment,[93] reporting duties of the operators of the plants vis-à-vis the competent authorities of the member States,[94] and reporting duties of the member States vis-à-vis the Commission.[95]

The Composition of Fuels Used in Particular in Motor Vehicles or for Heating Homes

The EEC has also attempted to counteract air pollution through directives dealing with the composition of fuels. Thus, in November 1975, the Council adopted the Directive relating to the Sulphur Content of Certain Liquid Fuels, obliging member States to reduce progressively the sulphur content in that type of fuel.[96] A more stringent directive was adopted in March 1987 obliging member States to ensure that gas oils can be marketed in the Community only if their sulphur compound content does not exceed 0.3% by weight as from January 1, 1989.[97] Member States may even require the use of gas oils with a sulphur content equal to 0.2% in zones where a considerable increase in pollution is foreseeable in the wake of urban or industrial development or in zones that should be afforded special environmental protection. The same applies where damage to the environment or to the national heritage caused by total sulphur dioxide emissions requires the sulphur content of gas oil to be fixed at a lower value than 0.3%. The mentioned directives relate mainly to gas oil used for heating homes or for motor fuel, in order to curb the emissions of sulphur dioxide arising from such uses. They do not apply to gas oils in the refining industry, in marine vessels, or in the fuel tanks of inland waterway vessels or motor vehicles *crossing a frontier* between a third country and a *member State.*

The preoccupation of the EEC with pollution caused by motor vehicles has further led to restrictions on the lead content of petrol. According to a Directive concerning the Lead Content of Petrol adopted by the Council in June 1978, the lead content of petrol placed upon the Community market was fixed at a *maximum* of 0.40 g Pb/l (grams of lead per liter) as from January 1, 1981, in order to protect public health and the environment.[98] Member States, however, were *entitled* to prescribe a lower maximum lead content for petrol placed on their national market, albeit not lower than 0.15 g Pb/l.

According to a new directive adopted in March 1985, member States were obliged to *continue* to ensure the availability and balanced distribution of leaded petrol within their territories.[99] They were now *exhorted*, however, to reduce "as soon as they consider it appropriate" the permitted lead content to 0.15 g Pb/l. Most important, the new directive also obliged the member States to ensure the availability and balanced distribution of unleaded petrol as from October 1, 1989, while opening the possibility of an even earlier introduction of such petrol. Moreover, the benzene content of leaded petrol or of unleaded petrol was not to exceed 5.0% by volume as from October 1, 1989, or even earlier parallel to an introduction of unleaded petrol before that date. The new directive also provided that the unleaded petrol must have the quality of "premium" petrol (i.e., have a minimum motor octane number [MON] of 85.0, and a minimum research octane number [RON] of 95.0 at the pump). Member States were free to introduce in addition another unleaded "regular" petrol (with lower octane ratings).

In a more recent directive adopted in July 1987, a further step was taken.[100] Individual member States were given a right to *prohibit* the marketing in their territory of leaded "regular" petrol (at six months' notice to the EEC Commission and to the public), provided they accelerated the introduction and distribution of unleaded petrol in their territory before its mandatory introduction in 1989. Indeed, the effective availability of unleaded petrol throughout the EEC before 1989 became increasingly necessary because of the steadily increasing number of cars that require unleaded petrol (those equipped with catalytic converters) that are being sold in the EEC and also because of the application of new emission standards for cars with an engine capacity of over 2 liters by October 1, 1988, which imply the use of catalytic converters as of that date.

Ambient Air Quality Standards

Ambient air quality standards have so far only been adopted at the EEC level for a few pollutants. In July 1980, the Council adopted the Directive on Air Quality Limit Values and Guide Values for Sulphur Dioxide and Suspended Particulates;[101] in December 1982, the Directive on Air Quality Limit Value for Lead in the Air;[102] and in March 1985, the Directive on Air Quality Standards for Nitrogen Dioxide.[103]

The three directives prescribe *limit* values for the concentration of the pollutant concerned in the atmosphere (usually specified in one or more annexes of the directive), which, in order to protect in particular human health, must not be exceeded throughout the territory of the member States during a specified period. According to the directives, the limit values must, in principle, be reached within a certain period: for sulphur dioxide and suspended particulates, in principle, April 1, 1983, or in certain zones, by way of exception, April 1, 1993, at the latest; for lead, seven years after notification of the directive to the member States; and for nitrogen oxide, in principle, July 1, 1987, or in certain zones, by way of exception, January 1, 1994, at the latest.

In addition to limit values for air quality, the directive on sulphur dioxide and suspended particulates and the directive on nitrogen dioxide prescribe so-called guide values, by which are meant concentrations of sulphur dioxide and suspended particulates or of nitrogen dioxide that are intended to serve as reference points for establishing specific schemes in special zones to be determined by member States. In zones in which a member State considers it necessary to limit or prevent a foreseeable increase in pollution in the wake of urban or industrial development, the member State shall (in the case of sulphur dioxide and suspended particulates) or may (in the case of nitrogen dioxide), taking the *guidelines* as a reference point, fix values which are lower than the previously mentioned limit values. In zones which the *member State considers* should be afforded *special environmental protection*, however, the member State shall (in the case of sulphur dioxide and suspended particulates) and may (in the case of nitrogen dioxide) fix values that are generally lower than the guide values. The directive on nitrogen dioxide provides explicitly that member States may at any time fix values more stringent than those laid down in the directive.

Application of the measures taken pursuant to the directives must not bring about a significant deterioration in the quality of the air where the level of pollution by sulphur dioxide and suspended particulates or, in respect of zones outside urban areas, the level of nitrogen dioxide at the time of the implementation of the directives is low in relation to the limit values. Thus, application of the directives may not lead to a shift of air pollution to other relatively "clean" areas.

Of the three directives mentioned, only the directive on sulphur dioxide and suspended particulates and the directive on nitrogen dioxide deal explicitly with the case of transfrontier air pollution. They merely provide on this point, however, that the member States concerned shall consult with a view to remedying the situation. In a separate Council Resolution on Transboundary Air Pollution by Sulphur Dioxide and Suspended Particulates, which was adopted on the same date as the directive on sulphur dioxide and suspended particulates, it was, however, stated that "the member States will *endeavour* in accordance with the objectives of the above-mentioned Council Directive . . . to limit and as far as possible gradually reduce and prevent transboundary air pollution by sulphur dioxide and suspended particulates."[104]

It is important to keep in mind that the limit values in the three directives were established to protect human health in particular, whereas at the time of the adoption of the directives insufficient technical and scientific information was available to the Council to enable it to lay down limit values specifically designed to protect the environment generally. The adoption of limit values for the protection of human health, however, may be expected to contribute to the protection of the environment as well.

It will be further noted that the directives for sulphur dioxide and suspended particulates and for nitrogen dioxide leave open the possibility for important derogations from the time schedule within which the limit values must, in principle, be met. According to the preamble of the directives, the measures to be taken in pursuance of the directives must be economically feasible and compatible with balanced economic development. Furthermore, the directives do not even provide for a standstill with respect to pollution levels that, at the time of the implementation of the directives, are low in relation to the applicable limit values and possibly do not even provide for such a standstill with respect to pollution levels that at that time exceed the applicable limit values.

Developments Within the Organization for Economic Cooperation and Development (OECD)

Work done within the framework of the OECD is also relevant to the European approach to acid rain. Reference should first be made to the principles contained in the 1974 OECD Council Recommendation on Principles Concerning Transfrontier Pollution, which, however, concerns transfrontier pollution in general.[105]

Measures specifically concerning air pollution were recommended in 1974 by the OECD Council in its Recommendation on Guidelines for Action to Reduce Emissions of Sulphur Oxides and Particulate Matter from Fuel Combustion in Stationary Sources[106] and in its Recommendation on Measures Required for Further Air Pollution Control.[107] According to the first recommendation, which in its preamble explicitly recognized the responsibility of States to ensure that no damage is caused to the environment of other States, member States should with respect to stationary emission sources, among other measures, encourage the use of clean fuels, limit the maximum sulphur content of fuels, and encourage the efficient use of fuels. The second recommendation was not limited to emissions from stationary sources and urged the member States, among other things, to strive "with all practicable speed" to reduce emissions of sulphur oxides and particulate matter by applying "the best available abatement techniques" for those pollutants and to develop and apply measures reducing emissions of other air pollutants, namely, nitrogen oxides and hydrocarbons. Another early recommendation is also relevant. In its Recommendation on Reduction of Environmental Impacts from Energy Production and Use, the OECD Council recommended that member States, regarding sulphur dioxide emissions, "accept the view that the effects resulting from long-range transport of pollutants should be taken into due account by Member countries, so that activities within their jurisdiction or control do not cause damage to the environment of other countries."[108]

In the more recent Council Recommendation on Control of Air Pollution from Fossil Fuel Combustion, considerably more specific recommendations were made to member States in order to cope with air pollution. The Council recommended that member States, among other things,

(a) should pursue policies to control more effectively air pollution resulting from emissions of oxides of sulphur and nitrogen, hydrocarbons, and particulate matter, from stationary and mobile sources in their countries in order to achieve environmentally acceptable levels of ambient air quality and deposition of pollutants;
(b) should achieve this objective by an appropriate combination of some or all of the following means:
—more efficient use of energy;
—the use of less-polluting fossil fuels;
—increased use of non-fossil energy sources, to the extent that these are compatible with other policy goals;
—the use of new and environmentally more benign combustion technologies;
—stricter control of air pollutant emissions.[109]

In an annex to the recommendation, a number of specific guiding principles were set out which member States should take into account in furthering their air pollution control policies. Some of those guiding principles relate specifically to large stationary installations and mobile sources and are quoted here in full:

3. Large Stationary Installations
(a) Implementation of emission standards by an effective programme of control measures for large stationary installations, consistent with the use of the best available and economically feasible technologies, and with the target, through national policies and programmes, of achieving the reduction of total national emissions required to reach environmentally acceptable air quality and deposition levels, and where appropriate with a transitional regime for existing plants.
(b) Encouragement or incentives (*e.g.* tax, investment, loan or grant) for timely retirement or modernization of older, more polluting installations, to the extent that this does not conflict with other economic policies.

4. Mobile Sources

(a) Implementation as soon as practicable of internationally harmonized emission standards by category for major air pollutants from vehicles, implying for many countries substantive reduction of pollutant emissions by using the best available and economically feasible technology.

(b) Encouragement and incentives for the development of less polluting and more efficient engines and vehicles.

(c) Promotion of good vehicle maintenance.

(d) Encouragement and incentives for the use of less polluting fuels for transportation (for example, liquified petroleum gas and compressed natural gas), where technologically and economically feasible.

(e) Regulations or other incentives to ensure the availability and use of unleaded gasoline as soon as possible and to phase out leaded gasoline as a long-term goal.

(f) Encouragement and incentives for the use of public transportation where appropriate.

(g) Setting and enforcement of speed limits for driving, especially on highways, if such limits contribute to a relevant reduction of air pollution.

(h) Traffic management in urban areas.

In view of the composition of its membership,[110] the OECD can play an important, but at the same time also only a limited, role in the control of acid rain. On the one hand, the OECD counts among its member States most of the major polluting countries as well as major affected countries. On the other hand, the East European polluting countries are not member States of the OECD. It is for that reason that the UN ECE eventually provides a more appropriate framework for further action in order to give effect to the goals of environmental cooperation proclaimed in the Final Act of the Conference on Security and Co-operation in Europe.[111]

Conclusion

Within the framework of the U.N. Economic Commission for Europe, East and West European States with a few notable exceptions have thus far only been able to commit themselves firmly to a 30% reduction of annual emissions of sulphur dioxides or their transboundary fluxes.[112] A NOx Protocol stabilizing NOx levels in the early 1990s and prescribing the application of national emission standards on the basis of the best available technologies which are economically feasible for new sources and a gradual and conditional introduction of control measures for existing sources and envisaging further reductions commencing in the second half of the 1990s which must still be agreed upon, on the basis of as yet undeveloped so-called critical loads, was concluded in November 1988.[113]

Within the smaller framework of the European Economic Community, it has appeared somewhat easier to arrive at international agreement on air pollution prevention and abatement measures; but here,
too, firm commitments on such measures can be agreed on only with
great difficulty. Only recently could agreement on motor vehicle emissions be reached; likewise, only after many years of negotiations has it
been possible to reach agreement on a restriction of the air pollution
caused by large combustion plants.

It appears to be extremely difficult to reach international agreement
on the level of stabilization and the measure of emission reductions to
be achieved within a given period of time by more than thirty European States, which show great differences in location, size, population,
economic development, use of various forms of energy sources, and
consequently also in their level of contributing to the problem of acid
rain in Europe. These differences also call for a differentiation of the
burden of each State in reducing and eventually eliminating the problem of acid rain in Europe. Thus, apart from the problem of reaching
agreement on the level of stabilization and reduction of the overall
emission of the pollutants causing acid rain, there also remains the
intricate problem of the equitable apportionment of the burden of the
necessary reduction of the overall emission or how to share equitably
the overall emission that may still be permitted without giving rise to a
significant extraterritorial environmental interference. Through all
this also plays the problem of the availability or nonavailability of
pollution prevention or abatement technology and the economic feasibility of applying this technology. The element of the economic feasibility in itself also permits a certain differentiation in the burden of
countries to prevent and abate acid rain. However, in certain matters
differentiation is hardly possible, that is, with regard to substances and
objects which form part of the trade or traffic between European
States, such as fuels and cars.

In principle, general international law leaves to States freedom of
choice of measures to prevent or abate transboundary air pollution,
provided the States apply measures which are adequate to prevent or
abate the infliction of substantial harm to areas beyond the limits of its
national jurisdiction. In order to coordinate and strengthen these efforts to counteract transboundary air pollution and to avoid obstacles
to international trade or unwarranted shifts in competitive positions,
however, States may agree on specific measures in international agreements or decisions. Within the framework of the UN ECE, this has,
however, hardly been the case. As we have already seen, the 1985
Sulphur Protocol only prescribed a certain emission reduction result to
be achieved within a specific time period. Within the UN ECE frame-

work, the use of specific measures has so far only been agreed on in the NOx Protocol[114] in the form of national emission standards based on the best available technologies which are economically feasible taking into account a recommendatory technical annex. It is further in directives of the EEC that specific measures to counteract air pollution have to some extent been internationally agreed on.

Whether or not compelled by substantive obligations flowing from international agreements or decisions, European States have, albeit to varying degrees, taken a variety of measures to prevent or abate air pollution. These measures have included legislation and regulatory provisions by which ambient air quality standards, fuel quality standards, emission standards, licensing of potentially polluting activities (e.g., certification of mobile sources or licensing of stationary sources), physical planning and zoning, or other regulatory measures (e.g., speed limits) were prescribed. In a number of countries, use has been made of economic incentives and disincentives, such as subsidies, fuel tax measures, emission charges and fines, or emission credits and quotas. Many countries, moreover, prescribed the use of appropriate control technology by requiring the use of the so-called best practicable means or best available technology. Such technology requirements may have been prescribed in environmental legislation or in permits or licenses. In various countries, the best practicable technology has formed the basis for prescribing emission standards. Within the framework of the Executive Body of the 1979 LRTAP Convention, these national measures have formed and will form in the future the subject of regular review in order to ascertain the extent to which the objectives and fundamental principles laid down in articles 2, 3, 4, and 5 of the LRTAP Convention have been met.[115]

Trends in national emissions of sulphur dioxide and nitrogen oxides have also been followed. According to a survey made by the Executive Body for the 1979 LRTAP Convention, most parties to the convention had reported reduced emissions of sulphur dioxide. Of the 27 parties for which data had become available both for 1980 and a more recent year (1983, 1984, or 1985), 23 had reduced sulphur dioxide emissions compared with 1980. Ten parties had reduced their emissions by 30% or more. Overall emissions of sulphur dioxide in Europe had decreased from 51.3 million tons in 1980 to 44.7 million tons in 1985 (i.e., down 12–13%).[116]

The estimate of *future* SO_2 emissions submitted by 20 parties reflected the signing of the 1985 Sulphur Protocol.[117] Signatories to that protocol estimate their 1995 emissions to be 30% or more below the 1980 level. Eleven parties forecasted a reduction by about 50% or more before 1995, four of them even more than 65%.[118]

Although these reductions of SO_2 emissions achieved and projected are in themselves not insignificant, certain caveats must in my view be made. First, among the European countries which contribute substantially to the total SO_2 emission in Europe, for example, those that in 1980 emitted more than 1,000,000 tons sulphur dioxide per year, there are some that have not yet become a party to the 1985 Sulphur Protocol, namely, the United Kingdom, Italy, Spain, the German Democratic Republic, Poland, and Yugoslavia. While the United Kingdom may achieve a 30% reduction in SO_2 emissions at a somewhat lower speed than the European countries that have become a party to the 1985 Sulphur Protocol,[119] this may not be expected from, or may at least be considerably more doubtful for, the other mentioned countries.

Second, given the available data concerning projected SO_2 emission reductions and the uncertainties that still persist with regard to the future SO_2 emission reductions of a number of major polluting States, it remains to be seen whether the total SO_2 emission reduction in Europe in 1995 will considerably exceed the 30% which must be achieved at the end of 1993 according to the 1985 Sulphur Protocol. Such a reduction, albeit not insignificant, may not be adequate in order to prevent significant harm to the environment. Certainly, it would not be sufficient for the Netherlands, for example, for which only a reduction of SO_2 emissions by a factor of 3.5 would result in an acceptable level of SO_2 deposition in Western Europe.[120]

According to the survey made by the Executive Body for the LRTAP Convention, the emission data on nitrogen oxides submitted by 27 parties generally showed a nearly constant level or a slight reduction over the period 1980–1983/85. Future estimates were available from 15 parties. The estimated trends from 1980 to 1995 varied considerably, from an increase by 50% to a decrease by 50%.[121] However, it should be borne in mind that projections on future NOx emission reductions from many major NOx emitting countries were still lacking and that the negotiations on the NOx Protocol indicate that in the early 1990s in Europe not much more than a stabilization of the overall emission of nitrogen oxides at the level of 1987 or a selected previous year may be expected.

The foregoing implies that an overall SO_2 emission reduction considerably exceeding 30% of the 1980 level and a significant overall NOx reduction may only be realized in the second half of the 1990s and during the first decade of the twenty-first century. While it is clear that the European States take action to stabilize and reduce the emission of pollutants causing acid rain, it is at the same time also clear that this is a very slow process.

At this point, the question may be raised how the practice of the European States with regard to the prevention and abatement of acid rain relates to the principles or rules of general international law concerning transboundary environmental interferences. Should this practice of the European States, as it develops on the basis of international agreements and decisions, be regarded as a *deviation* from the principle of general international law providing that *States shall observe due care in that no significant harm is caused to other States or to areas beyond the limits of national jurisdiction*? That is, should European State practice be considered a deviation in the sense that in the case of acid rain, the prevention and abatement of significant extraterritorial harm may take place at a slower speed than required under the previously mentioned principle or in the sense that the development or the continued existence of significant extraterritorial harm might even be permitted? And, if the practice of the European States with regard to acid rain is to be looked upon as a deviation, is it then a deviation which can be justified only on the basis of special written international law; or are we facing a special practice which the European States apply in the case of acid rain and which they consider lawful even in the absence of special written international law? Or, could it be said that there is no question of a deviation from the general principle of international law mentioned earlier, but that, regarding the complexity and scope of the problem of acid rain, the rather slow and possibly inadequate measures taken to prevent or abate acid rain may be regarded as a not improper application of the duty imposed by the principle of general international law to observe due care in preventing and abating significant extraterritorial harm?

It seems that before an attempt could be made to answer these questions, still another question could be raised, namely, whether vis-à-vis the victim States the duty to prevent or abate significant extraterritorial harm must be deemed to rest upon the *collectivity* of States which contribute to the acid rain or on each *individual* contributory State on behalf of the collectivity of contributory States *regardless of the size of the contribution made by that State* or whether this duty may be deemed to rest upon each *individual* State in respect of its individual contribution, in which case perhaps some States may be deemed to deviate from the principle of general international law while other States do not. Taking into account the fact that individual contributions to acid rain in Europe can be approximately established through the Co-operative Programme for the Monitoring and Evaluation of Long-Range Transmission of Air Pollutants in Europe (EMEP),[122] an individualized or State-by-State application of the principle of general international law remains, in principle, possible. Its application will also depend, however, on the possibility to solve, *as between the States which contribute to the pollution*, the intricate problem of the equitable apportionment[123] of the burden to effect necessary reductions of the overall emission, or to share the overall emission which may be regarded as permissible, as not giving rise to significant extraterritorial harm. Depending on the outcome of this equitable apportionment, it may then be established which European States must be deemed to deviate from the principle of general international law which obliges polluting States to observe vis-à-vis potential victim States due care in preventing and abating significant extraterritorial harm.

Due to the lack of adequate data and the time limits inherent in preparing this chapter, most of the questions raised here can only be raised in theory and not answered *in concreto*.

If the slow and possibly inadequate process of measures to prevent and abate acid rain—whether on the part of the polluting European States considered as a collectivity or on an individual State basis—must be regarded as not fully compatible (in the case of the individualized approach, perhaps only on the part of some States) with the principle of general international law prohibiting the infliction of significant extraterritorial harm, the question arises whether the States causing that harm must be deemed to incur international responsibility vis-à-vis the victim States or whether they may be considered excused to the extent that their practice is in conformity with less demanding international agreements or decisions with respect to victim States that have participated in those international agreements or decisions. Here, it may be noted that the agreements concluded within the UN ECE may be and, in fact, are in the eyes of a number of European States basically to be regarded as a "first step" and not intended to settle definitively the admissible extent of the pollution.[124]

It is also relevant that the parties to the LRTAP Convention, in a footnote to article 8 of that Convention, declared, "The present Convention does not contain a rule on State liability as to damage."[125] In view of the content of the LRTAP Convention, this footnote only states the obvious. The intent of the footnote, however, was probably to make clear that any question of international responsibility or liability was to remain unaffected by the LRTAP Convention. If this assumption is correct, claims based on a breach of the principle of general international law prohibiting the infliction of significant extraterritorial harm caused by acid rain may likewise not have been affected by the LRTAP Convention or, it is assumed, by its implementing protocols, unless the contrary has been clearly indicated. This fact also implies that for the States participating in the international agreements and decisions concerned, the principle of general international law has not been set aside by those international agreements and decisions.

Notes

1. Convention on Long-Range Transboundary Air Pollution, Nov. 13, 1979, T.I.A.S. No. 10541, *reprinted in* 18 I.L.M. 1442 (1979) [hereinafter 1979 LRTAP Convention].

2. *See* U.N. Economic Commission for Europe, *National Strategies and Policies for Air Pollution Abatement*, U.N. Doc. ECE/EB.AIR/14 (1987) [hereinafter UN ECE Report].

3. The United Nations Economic Commission for Europe was created by a decision of the Economic and Social Council, Res. 35/IV (Mar. 1947), following a recommendation by the U.N. General Assembly. It has 34 members, including Canada and the United States. E.J. OSMANCZYK, THE ENCYCLOPEDIA OF THE UNITED NATIONS AND INTERNATIONAL AGREEMENTS 826 (1985).

4. The EEC is a customs union composed of 12 European countries: Belgium, Denmark, Federal Republic of Germany, France, Greece, Ireland, Italy, Luxembourg, the Netherlands, Portugal, Spain, and the United Kingdom. Its founding document is the Treaty to Establish the European Economic Community (often referred to as the "Treaty of Rome" or the "Rome Treaty"), March 25, 1957, 298 U.N.T.S. 3.

5. The OECD is an economic policymaking organization composed primarily of industrialized countries. Its 24 members are Australia, Austria, Belgium, Canada, Denmark, the Federal Republic of Germany, Finland, France, Greece, Iceland, Italy, Ireland, Japan, Luxembourg, the Netherlands, New Zealand, Norway, Portugal, Spain, Sweden, Switzerland, Turkey, the United Kingdom, and the United States.

6. Conference on Security and Co-operation in Europe: Final Act (Aug. 1, 1975), *reprinted in* 14 I.L.M. 1292, 1307 (1975).

7. *Id.* at 1308 (emphasis added).

8. *Id.* at 1309.

9. 1979 LRTAP Convention, *supra* note 1.

10. Protocol on the Reduction of Sulphur Emissions or Their Transboundary Fluxes by at Least 30% (entered into force Sept. 2, 1987), *reprinted in* [1 Ref. File] Int'l Env't Rep. (BNA) 21:3021 (1989) [hereinafter 1985 Sulphur Protocol].

11. Protocol to the 1979 Convention on Long-Range Transboundary Air Pollution Concerning the Control of Emissions of Nitrogen Oxides or Their Transboundary Fluxes, Nov. 1, 1988, U.N. Doc. ECE/EB.AIR/18, Annex 1 (1988), *reprinted in* [1 Ref. File] Int'l Env't Rep. (BNA) 21:3041 (1989).

12. 1979 LRTAP Convention, *supra* note 1.

13. *See, e.g., id.* art. 2.

14. As of 1988, the parties to the 1979 LRTAP Convention were Austria, Belgium, Bulgaria, Byelorussian Soviet Socialist Republic, Canada, Czechoslovakia, Denmark, European Economic Community, Federal Republic of Germany, Finland, France, German Democratic Republic, Greece, Iceland, Ireland, Italy, Liechtenstein, Luxembourg, Netherlands, Norway, Poland, Portugal, Spain, Sweden, Switzerland, Turkey, Ukrainian Soviet Socialist Republic,

Union of Soviet Socialist Republics, United Kingdom, United States, and Yugoslavia. U.S. DEP'T OF STATE, TREATIES IN FORCE 343 (1988).

15. 1979 LRTAP Convention, *supra* note 1, art. 2.

16. *Id*. art. 3.

17. *Id*. art. 6.

18. *Id*. art. 2.

19. *Id*. art. 3.

20. *Id*. art. 6.

21. *Id*. art. 2.

22. *Id*. (emphasis added).

23. *Id*. art. 3 (emphasis added).

24. *Id*.

25. *Id*. art. 6 (emphasis added).

26. COMECON, the Council of Mutual Economic Assistance, was organized in 1949 by the U.S.S.R. in response to the Marshall Plan. Cuba, Mongolia, and all East European communist countries except Albania are members.

27. For the proposals of the Nordic countries, see 4 ENVTL. POL'Y & L. 191–93 (1978).

28. Vygen, *Urging for a Firm Clean Air Policy Across National Borders*, 11 ENVTL. POL'Y & L. 34 (1983).

29. For the Conclusions and Recommendations of the Stockholm Conference, see 9 ENVTL. POL'Y & L. 101 (1982).

30. *Id*.

31. *See* 11 ENVTL. POL'Y & L. 46 (1983) (emphasis added).

32. *See* 23 I.L.M. 662 (1984), *also in* 12 ENVTL. POL'Y & L. 86 (1984).

33. *See* letter from the Netherlands Government to the Second Chamber of the Netherlands Parliament (Staten-General), in *Bijlagen tot het Verslag der Handelingen van de Tweede Kamer der Staten-Generaal*, 1985/86, -19423, No. 1.

34. *Id*.

35. 1985 Sulphur Protocol, *supra* note 10.

36. *Id*. art. 2.

37. *Id*. art. 10(3).

38. Statement made by the Netherlands delegation at the Third Session of the Executive Body for the 1979 LRTAP Convention, *supra* note 1, held in Helsinki, July 8–12, 1985.

39. 1985 Sulphur Protocol, *supra* note 10, art. 3.

40. Luxembourg ratified the Sulphur Protocol on August 8, 1987, Switzerland on September 21, 1987, and Belgium on June 9, 1989.

41. Statement made by the Netherlands delegation in its (unpublished) report on the Third Session of the Executive Body for the 1979 LRTAP Convention, *supra* note 1, held in Helsinki, July 8–12, 1985.

42. Speech by William Waldgrave to the German Foreign Policy Society in Hamburg, F.R.G., 15 ENVTL. POL'Y & L. 112 (1985).

43. 1985 Sulphur Protocol, *supra* note 10, art. 2 (emphasis added) (quoted in full *supra* at text accompanying note 36).

44. *Id*. art. 6.

45. *See supra* text accompanying notes 21–25.

46. *See* UN ECE Report, *supra* note 2.

47. *Id*. at 46.

48. Speech by William Waldgrave, *supra* note 42.

49. *See* UN ECE Report, *supra* note 2.

50. Protocol to the 1979 Convention on Long-Range Transboundary Air Pollution Concerning the Control of Emissions of Nitrogen Oxides or Their Transboundary Fluxes, art. 2 (Nov. 1988) [hereinafter NOx Protocol], *reprinted in* 28 I.L.M. 214 (1989).

51. *Id.* art. 2.

52. *Id.*

53. *Id.* art. 2(2).

54. *Id.*

55. *Id.* art. 2(3).

56. *Id.* art. 2(4).

57. Declaration on the 30 Per Cent Reduction of Nitrogen Oxide Emissions, at Sofia on October 31, 1988.

58. Stated by the Netherlands delegation in the (unpublished) Report on the Third Session of the Executive Body for the 1979 LRTAP Convention, *supra* note 1, held in Helsinki, July 8–12, 1985.

59. NOx Protocol, *supra* note 50, art. 4.

60. 13 O.J. Eur. Comm. (No. L 76) (Apr. 6, 1970).

61. Directive Amending Directive 70/220/EEC on the Approximization of the Laws of the Member States Relating to Measures to be Taken Against Air Pollution by Gases from the Engines of Motor Vehicles, 31 O.J. Eur. Comm. (No. L 36) 1 (Feb. 9, 1988).

62. 32 O.J. Eur. Comm. (No. L 226) 1 (Aug. 3, 1989).

63. Single European Act, Feb. 17, 1986, 30 O.J. Eur. Comm. (No. L 169) 1 (1987), *reprinted in* 25 I.L.M. 503 (1986).

64. Treaty to Establish the European Economic Community, Mar. 25, 1957, art. 100A, 298 U.N.T.S. 3, as amended by *id.*

65. *Supra* note 62.

66. 27 O.J. Eur. Comm. (No. L 188) 20 (July 16, 1984).

67. *Id.* art. 4 (emphasis added).

68. *Id.* art. 2(5).

69. *Id.* art. 12.

70. *Id.*

71. *Id.* art. 4.

72. 27 O.J. Eur. Comm. (No. C 49) 1 (Feb. 21, 1984).

73. 1979 LRTAP Convention, *supra* note 1.

74. *See* report of the Netherlands Permanent Representative to the European Communities in Brussels, to the Netherlands Ministry of External Affairs on the outcome of the 1065th meeting of the Council of Ministers on March 6, 1986, in Open (telex) Bericht NL BUZ 213 BRE 933 of March 7, 1986, at 6.

75. *Id.*

76. These States include Greece, Ireland, Luxembourg, Portugal, and, to a lesser extent, Spain.

77. *Supra* note 74 and text accompanying.

78. *See supra* text following note 76.

79. Directive on the Limitation of Emissions of Certain Pollutants into the Air from Large Combustion Plants, Nov. 24, 1988, 31 O.J. Eur. Comm. (No. L 336) 1 (Dec. 7, 1988), *reprinted in* [2 Ref. File] Int'l Env't Rep. (BNA) 141:3901.

80. *Id.* art. 1.

81. *Id.* art. 2(7).

82. *Id.* The following are excluded: (1) plants in which the products of combustion are used for the direct heating, drying, or any other treatment of

objects or materials, e.g., reheating furnaces and furnaces for heat treatment; (2) post-combustion plants, i.e., any technical apparatus designed to purify the waste gases by combustion which is not operated as an independent combustion plant; (3) facilities for the regeneration of catalytic cracking catalysts; (4) facilities for the conversion of hydrogen sulphide into sulphur; (5) reactors used in the chemical industry; (6) coke battery furnaces; (7) cowpers.

83. *Id.*

84. *Id.* art. 2(10).

85. *Id.* art. 3.

86. *Id.*

87. *Id.* art. 4.

88. *Id.* footnote to Annex III.

89. *Id.* art. 5.

90. *Id.* art. 6.

91. *Id.* art. 7.

92. *Id.* art. 8.

93. *Id.* art. 13.

94. *Id.* art. 14.

95. *Id.* art. 16.

96. 18 O.J. Eur. Comm. (No. L 307) 22 (Nov. 27, 1975).

97. Directive on the Sulphur Content of Fuels, 30 O.J. Eur. Comm. (No. L 91) 19 (Apr. 3, 1987). Article 1(1) of the 1987 Directive defines "gas oil" as "any petroleum product falling under subheading 27.10 C I of the Common Customs Tariff (10 December 1984 edition) or any petroleum product which, by reason of its distillation limits, falls into the category of middle distillates intended for use as fuel and of which at least 85% by volume, including distillation losses, distills at 350° C."

98. 20 O.J. Eur. Comm. (No. L 197) (July 22, 1978).

99. Directive on Lead Content of Petrol, 28 O.J. Eur. Comm. (No. L 96) 25 (Apr. 3, 1985).

100. 30 O.J. Eur. Comm. (No. L 225) 33 (Aug. 13, 1987), *reprinted in* [2 Ref. File] Int'l Env't Rep. (BNA) 141:1405.

101. 23 O.J. Eur. Comm. (No. L 229) 30 (Aug. 30, 1980), recently amended by the Council directive of June 21, 1985, 32 O.J. Eur. Comm. (No. L 201) 53 (July 14, 1989), which laid down provisions for harmonization of measuring methods.

102. 25 O.J. Eur. Comm. (No. L 378) 15 (Dec. 31, 1982).

103. 28 O.J. Eur. Comm. (No. L 87) 1 (Mar. 27, 1985).

104. 23 O.J. Eur. Comm. (No. C 222) 1 (Aug. 30, 1980) (emphasis added).

105. OECD Council Recommendation C(74)224 (Nov. 1974), *reprinted in* OECD, Legal Aspects of Transfrontier Pollution 11 (1977) and 14 I.L.M. 242, 244 (1975).

106. OECD Council Recommendation C(74)16 (Final) (June 1974).

107. OECD Council Recommendation C(74)219 (Nov. 1974).

108. OECD Council Recommendation C(76)162 (Final) (Oct. 1976).

109. OECD Council Recommendation C(85)101 (June 1985).

110. OECD member States are listed *supra* note 5.

111. *Supra* note 6.

112. 1985 Sulphur Protocol, *supra* note 10.

113. *See supra* text following note 50.

114. *See supra* note 50.

115. 1979 LRTAP Convention, *supra* note 1, arts. 2, 3, 4 & 5.
116. *See* UN ECE Report, *supra* note 2, at 2, 37.
117. 1985 Sulphur Protocol, *supra* note 10.
118. *See* UN ECE Report, *supra* note 2, at 37.
119. *See supra* text accompanying note 48.
120. *See supra* note 38.
121. *Supra* note 116 and text accompanying.
122. *See* 1979 LRTAP Convention, *supra* note 1, art. 9; 1984 EMEP Protocol to the 1979 LRTAP Convention, U.N. Doc. ECE/EB AIR/11 (1984).
123. Determination of whether an apportionment is "equitable" requires an examination of all the facts and circumstances of the situation. *See*, *e.g.*, North Sea Continental Shelf (W. Ger. v. Den.; W. Ger. v. Neth.), 1969 I.C.J. 3, 50 (Judgment of Feb. 20); Case Concerning the Continental Shelf (Tunisia v. Libyan Arab Jamahiriya), 1982 I.C.J. 18, 60.
124. *See supra* text accompanying note 38.
125. 1979 LRTAP Convention, *supra* note 1, art. 8, n. 1.

Chapter 13
Acid Rain: A Canadian Policy Perspective

Ross Glasgow

Background

The United States in 1970[1] and Canada in 1971[2] enacted Clean Air Acts designed to improve ambient air quality. Although not identical, the standards established under these Acts to control sulphur dioxide, nitrogen dioxides, particulants, oxidants, and carbon monoxide are equivalent. Between 1970 and 1984, Canada reduced sulphur dioxide emissions by approximately 41%, and during the same period, the United States reduced emissions by approximately 24%.[3] These reductions had a dramatic positive effect on ambient air quality near the sources of the emissions.

The provisions of neither Clean Air Act, however, were designed to address the problem of long-range transport of pollutants. Indeed by leading in some cases to the construction of tall stacks that disperse pollution over great distances, these efforts to improve local air quality unintentionally exacerbated the problem of long-range transport of pollutants.

An increasing awareness of the impact of acid rain on the Canadian environment led to growing concern among Canadians. As the scientific understanding of the physical properties of acid rain, and in particular the role played by long-range transport of sulphur dioxide, expanded, it became increasingly clear in Canada that acid rain is a North American problem requiring a North American solution. Public awareness of the dangers posed by acid rain is very high in Canada, and it has erased party and intergovernmental differences that are commonplace with virtually any other issue in Canada. Every political party in Parliament, every provincial government, and every shade of Canadian public opinion are part of the consensus demanding action to control acid rain.

The Bilateral Dimension

As a bilateral issue between Canada and the United States, acid rain is at least a decade old. In July 1978, recognition of the international dimension of the acid rain problem led Canada and the United States to establish a Bilateral Research Consultation Group (BRCG) on the long-range transport of airborne pollutants (LRTAP) with a mandate to facilitate information exchanges, to coordinate research activities between the two countries, and to develop an agreed scientific data base from which Canada and the United States could develop solutions to this problem.[4]

That same year in response to increasing concern in the United States about the impact of Canadian-generated acid rain on the environment of the United States, the Congress of the United States passed a resolution calling upon the President to initiate discussion with Canada in order to negotiate a cooperative agreement to protect the air quality of North America.[5] In December 1978, Canada agreed to such discussions and emphasized the important role of LRTAP in the acid rain issue. The BRCG was specifically requested to investigate the transboundary pollution caused by Canada and the United States.[6] The BRCG's report confirmed that the principal source of emissions affecting eastern Canada originated in the Ohio Valley.[7]

In July 1979, Canada and the United States jointly announced their intention to develop a cooperative agreement on transboundary air quality, which was followed on August 5, 1980, with the signature of a Memorandum of Intent on Transboundary Air Pollution.[8] In the Memorandum, the two countries stated their intention to enforce existing air pollution laws vigorously and to work toward the development of a bilateral agreement on air quality. The Memorandum established five joint Work Groups to investigate various aspects of the problem. The Work Groups were to study, among other things, the impact of air pollutants on sensitive areas, and how atmospheric pollutants are transformed and transported from where they are emitted to where they fall.

On June 23, 1981, Canada and the United States began formal negotiations to develop a bilateral agreement on transboundary air pollution, and on February 21, 1983, the technical and scientific Work Groups established under the Memorandum of Intent released their final reports and referred them for peer review to the Royal Society of Canada and the United States Office of Science and Technology Policy.[9] On June 28, 1983, the U.S. Peer Review Panel issued an interim report followed by a final report which called for reductions in acid emissions and rejected the argument that more research is needed before control action is taken.[10]

On June 30, 1983, the United States National Academy of Sciences released its study confirming a link between sulphur dioxide emissions and acid deposition.[11] This study was followed by the July 27 release of the Canadian Peer Review report concluding that the scientific evidence was sufficient to warrant the prompt introduction of abatement measures.[12]

On January 25, 1984, President Ronald Reagan, in his State of the Union address, indicated that the United States would not take action to reduce emissions. Instead, the United States would intensify its research into the causes and effects of acid rain.[13]

In an effort to restart the bilateral dialogue on this issue, on March 17, 1985, Prime Minister Brian Mulroney and President Reagan appointed Special Envoys on Acid Rain. The Envoys' mandate was to consult on each country's legal and regulatory approach to pollutants linked to acid rain, enhance research cooperation and information exchange between Canada and the United States, and identify methods of improving the environment of both countries.[14]

In January 1986, the Special Envoys released their report. It concluded that acid rain is not only a serious environmental hazard in both the United States and Canada but is also a serious transboundary problem.[15] In their annual Summit meeting held in March, President Reagan and Prime Minister Mulroney endorsed the Special Envoys' Report.[16] This was the first time that the U.S. Administration formally acknowledged these realities and was therefore a significant step forward.

Following from the recommendations of the Special Envoys, Canada and the United States established a Bilateral Advisory and Consultative Group to oversee the implementation of the envoys' recommendations and to serve as a vehicle for consultations between the two countries.[17] The Group also agreed to prepare a report to update the scientific work undertaken under the 1980 Memorandum of Intent[18] and to review opportunities available under existing legislation for emission reductions.[19] The United States also agreed to establish a five-year $5 billion control technology commercial demonstration program that would demonstrate retrofit technologies designed for existing facilities, especially those using high-sulphur coal.[20] The object of this program, which became known as the Clean Coal Technology Program, was to develop alternative technologies to remove sulphur from coal, which is the chief fuel source for electric thermal plants in the northeast and midwest United States as well as the chief source of U.S. acidic emissions into Canada. Alternative technologies were felt by some to be necessary because existing methods of removing sulphur were either inadequate, in the case of coal cleaning, or extremely expensive, in the case of scrubbers, hundreds of which were installed at immense expense, as a result of the U.S. Clean Air Act. The program was also intended to result in some near-term reductions in emissions from the United States that affect Canada.

President Reagan announced on the eve of his April 8, 1987, summit with Prime Minister Mulroney that he would seek full funding to satisfy the envoys' report. He also asked the Vice-President's Task Force on Regulatory Reform to prepare a report within six months on the regulatory impediments to action by the United States on acid rain.[21]

At the summit, Prime Minister Mulroney supported the President's initiative but reiterated Canada's need for emission reductions. President Reagan, in his address to the Canadian Parliament, said he would consider the Prime Minister's suggestion to develop a bilateral acid rain accord.[22]

On April 8, 1987, Canadian and U.S. scientific organizations issued a joint report on the state of scientific knowledge on the long-range transport of airborne pollutants and acid deposition.[23] Canadian officials believe the report confirmed Canadian views on the serious, widespread, and worsening acid rain damage in eastern Canada.

On May 23, 1987, the two sides met to follow up on the President's April commitment to consider a Canadian proposal for an acid rain accord. Canada presented to the United States a concept paper setting out the major principles that Canada believed must form the core of any such accord.[24] Central to Canada's position is the need for both countries to agree on specified reductions in sulphur dioxide emissions and a timetable for achieving these reductions.

Eight months later, on January 25, 1988, the United States responded to the Canadian proposal by indicating that the United States would, among other things, be prepared to negotiate a limited air-quality agreement under which Canada and the United States could carry out further joint monitoring, research, and evaluation of the acid rain problem.[25] The U.S. response did not include any provision for a commitment to agreed reductions and a timetable to achieve these reductions. Canada provided to the United States at the same time a further elaboration of Canadian views in the form of a draft text for an accord.[26]

Canadian Program

In Canada, the provinces have responsibility for environmental matters within their jurisdiction, including air pollution, while the federal government is responsible for environmental matters that are interprovincial or international in nature. The Canadian Clean Air Act as amended authorizes the Canadian Minister of the Environment to regulate, if necessary, air pollutants (1) to prevent harm to another country, (2) to enforce the conditions of an international obligation, and (3) where emissions constitute a significant danger to public health.[27]

In light of the impact of acid rain on the Canadian environment and increasing public opinion pressure, the federal and provincial governments discussed for some time what action should be taken in Canada to deal with this serious problem. Following intensive scientific research, Canadian scientists concluded that to halt the process of acidification and prevent further damage to the Canadian environment, acid deposition must be reduced to no more than 20 kilograms per hectare (18 pounds per acre) per year in all vulnerable areas.[28] The establishment of this critical loading level was an essential step in the development of the Canadian acid rain program, and it was the basis for determining what reductions in emissions were necessary.

On March 6, 1984, the federal and provincial environment ministers agreed to reduce annual sulphur dioxide emissions in eastern Canada to 2.3 million metric tons (one metric ton—also referred to as "tonne"—is equivalent to 1.102 "short"—or "U.S."—tons) by 1994.[29] This reduction represents a 50% cut from 1980 allowable levels. Eastern Canada in this case is defined as those provinces east of the Saskatchewan-Manitoba border and includes Manitoba, Ontario, Quebec, New Brunswick, Nova Scotia, Prince Edward Island, and Newfoundland. These provinces contain areas that are highly vulnerable for two basic reasons: first, because of the amount of acid rain deposited on them, and second, because their capacity to neutralize acid is limited.

On February 5, 1985, the federal and provincial environment ministers established specific emission ceilings for each participating province.[30] On March 6, 1985, the Canadian Minister of the Environment announced a comprehensive acid rain action plan, which in addition to the reduction of sulphur dioxide emissions, also included tough new automobile emission standards, financial assistance for the development of control technologies, and a scientific research and monitoring program.[31]

It is important to understand that the major sources of sulphur dioxide emissions in Canada are nonferrous smelters rather than coal-fired thermal electric power plants as in the United States. The Canadian program is therefore focused on the nonferrous smelting industry while ensuring that Ontario Hydro also severely reduces emissions from its thermal power plants. The Canadian program does not prescribe specific control strategies but rather is designed to let the private sector and provincial utilities choose the most cost-effective means of achieving the required emission reductions. Canada has also set aside funds to share with the private sector the cost of commercial technology demonstration at smelters and of developing clean coal technologies. In addition, Canada has agreed to help with smelter modernization and the pollution abatement measures.[32]

While it took some time to develop a consensus in Canada on the need for action and to reach agreement on what should be done, the program came together quickly once these principles were agreed to. Regulatory and pollution control program measures to achieve more than 90% of the emission reductions required are now in place and have been ratified in binding agreements between the federal government and all seven participating provinces.[33] Significant reductions have been achieved since the control program was initiated,[34] and Canada is well launched on its goal of meeting the 1994 target of 2.3 million metric tons. This level of emissions represents an absolute cap on emissions and requires offsets in existing sources for any additional emissions from new sources.

The International Dimension

On the basis of extensive scientific research into the long-range transport of air pollutants, it is clear that on average 50% of the acid deposition which falls in Canada is caused by emissions generated in the United States.[35] In some particularly vulnerable areas in Canada, up to 75% of the acid deposition originates in the United States.[36] This means that the planned reductions in eastern Canadian emissions cannot by themselves reduce acid deposition to or below the critical load level of 20 kilograms per hectare or 18 pounds per acre.

To reduce emissions to or below the critical loading level, it will be necessary to reduce the transborder flow of sulphur dioxide to 2 million metric tons per year, which represents a reduction of approximately 50% of the 1980 transborder flow.[37] If this reduction does not take place, the Canadian environment will continue to receive more acid deposition than it can tolerate and the damage caused by this deposition will mount.

The circumstances indicate that the United States has a clear responsibility to take action to deal with acid rain. The United States and Canada are obliged by international law and neighborly precedent to reduce the transborder flow of air pollution where such pollution causes damage in the territory of the other. The Boundary Waters Treaty of 1909 between Canada and the United States established the principle that neither country should pollute boundary waters to the injury of the other and called for an end to transboundary pollution.[38]

The *Trail Smelter* decision of 1941 established the principle that neither country should pollute the atmosphere to the injury of the other.[39] The arbitration tribunal held Canada liable for emissions flowing south of the border into the state of Washington. The tribunal held, "No state has the right to use or permit the use of its territory in such a manner as to cause injury by fumes in or to the territory of another."[40] This declaration was a historic turning point in the development of international environmental law and a giant step forward in the recognition by Canada and the United States of their international environmental obligations. Under the terms of the decision, Canada agreed to control sulphur dioxide emissions from the smelter. Canada also paid compensation for damages caused by emissions from the smelter.

Principle 21 of the United Nations Conference on the Human Environment, reflecting the *Trail Smelter* decision, holds in part that all nations have "the responsibility to ensure that activities within their jurisdiction or control do not cause damage to the environment of other States or to areas beyond the limits of national jurisdiction."[41] Many nations, including Canada and the United States, have endorsed this principle. It is a basic element of the 1987 United States–Mexico agreement on transboundary air pollution.[42]

The United Nations Convention on Long-Range Transboundary Air Pollution of 1979, which both Canada and the United States have signed, expressed a determination to reduce and prevent long-range transboundary air pollution.[43] Twenty-three European countries and Canada have further signed a protocol under the Convention to reduce their sulphur dioxide emissions by at least 30% by 1993.[44]

The Science of Acid Rain

In the name of scientific uncertainty, insufficient attention is being paid to the extent and seriousness of the acid rain problem. This problem was compounded by the release in September 1987 of the Interim Assessment of the National Acid Precipitation Assessment Program (NAPAP), the Executive Summary of which suggested that the acid rain problem was not serious or getting worse.[45]

As is discussed in greater detail in Chapter 11, while there are some remaining uncertainties, there is much that is known about the problem. First, the effects of acid rain are already widespread and serious. Approximately 700,000 lakes in eastern Canada receive acid deposition at a rate greater than 20 kilograms per hectare per year of wet sulphate. Approximately 14,000 of these lakes have acidity or pH levels of 5.0 or less, and there are approximately 150,000 lakes with a pH less than 6.0, the acidity level at which detrimental biological effects begin to occur.[46] In addition, analysis of surface water chemistry based on data from about 8,000 lakes shows extensive reduction in the ability of these lakes to neutralize the acid being deposited on them. This change is occurring most seriously in areas of greatest sulphate deposition caused by the long-range transport of air pollutants. Large areas of southcentral Ontario, southern Quebec, New Brunswick, Nova Scotia, and Newfoundland already suffer serious and widespread effects as a result of acid rain.[47]

Second, the effects of acid rain are worsening. A study by the Ontario Ministry of the Environment of Plastic Lake in southcentral Ontario, a lake representative of tens of thousands of sensitive lakes in eastern Canada, shows that over a seven-year period from 1979 to 1986, sulphate deposition dropped by 25%. However, acidity increased by 67% and alkalinity decreased by 300% in this period.[48] Taken together, this information means that many thousands of sensitive lakes in Canada are not in chemical equilibrium at current emission and acid deposition levels. Damage in these lakes will continue to occur until acid deposition is reduced to environmentally tolerable levels.

Third, the acid rain problem is worse and more serious than was anticipated ten years ago. The current and potential damage to the environment is much more widespread and serious than expected at that time. Damage to sensitive lakes is occurring more rapidly than originally predicted and at much lower levels of acidity. Effects on forests, groundwater, soils, and materials are emerging as areas of concern as well as the potential effect on human health.

Finally, what is known about the nature, causes, and effects of acid rain is sufficient to design effective abatement programs. It is clear that sulphur is causing damage in aquatic and terrestrial systems, materials, and perhaps human health. Canadian studies have shown that reducing sulphur dioxide emissions will result in a proportional reduction in sulphur loading over large areas. One thirteen-year study found that total sulphur dioxide emissions from sources within 1,000 miles of southern Nova Scotia decreased by 25% over the period between 1971 and 1983. Sulphate deposition in the area decreased by almost one-half, and many of the lakes and streams are showing chemical recovery.[49] Biological recovery, unfortunately, is lagging far behind, reinforcing the need to take prompt action to reduce emissions.[50]

A North American Solution

It is necessary to establish a program to reduce sulphur dioxide emissions designed to address the acid rain problem. Such a program is in place in Canada and will be fully implemented by 1994, at which time

Canadian emissions will be 50% of base 1980 levels. Not only will this benefit the Canadian environment, but it will also significantly reduce the flow of acid rain from Canada into the United States.[51]

On January 25, 1988, the United States recommitted itself to fulfilling the recommendations of the Joint Envoys and agreed to negotiate a limited Air Quality Accord with Canada.[52] The Accord would provide for monitoring, investigating, and evaluating the problem of acid rain. The U.S. negotiators indicated their expectation that acid rain would be reduced through a series of regulatory and deregulatory reforms.[53]

The U.S. decision to negotiate an acid rain agreement is welcomed. The decision is deficient, however. It does not commit the United States to targeted reductions over a specified time period. In light of the impact of acid rain on Canada and the extensive scientific information provided by Canada to the United States on this issue, this decision is difficult to understand.

The Clean Coal Technology Program, recommended by the Special Envoys, has been launched. A panel has been established to recommend projects for funding. The criteria to be used include those of the Special Envoys' Report. Two Canadians have been invited to participate in the panel, as advocated by the Envoys.[54] But the Program is a means to an end, not the end itself. For Canada, the end remains an agreement between Canada and the United States that will cut in half acid rain crossing the border into Canada by 1994. Canadian scientific calculations indicate that such a reduction, together with Canada's own program, will permit the Canadian environment to recover.

Canada's position is clear, simple, and reasonable. Canada is already taking action to clean up its own house, and it wants the United States to do likewise. What is being asked for is not easy or cheap. Delay will not, however, make it any less expensive for either country. Indeed, it will add to the expense.

The United States has a legal obligation to act. It also has a neighborly duty to do so. No amount of protestations of uncertainty or nitpicking of a Canadian program that has no counterpart in the United States can change these two facts.

Canada will keep on trying until the United States joins with Canada to help solve the acid rain problem. Canada is asking the United States to do no more than it is doing itself. When the United States acts, both the United States and Canada will be the beneficiaries.

Postscript

Several developments have occurred since this chapter was originally written in April 1988. In June 1989, the Administration of President

George Bush proposed legislation that would reduce U.S. domestic emissions of sulphur dioxide by 10 million short tons.[55] Other bills introduced separately in Congress share that common feature, that is, a reduction of U.S. domestic sulphur dioxide emissions by 10 million short tons. The Canadian Government—whose policy position has remained essentially unchanged—has determined that a 10 million short ton reduction in the United States would be sufficient to achieve the Canadian objective of reducing transboundary flows from the United States to Canada to 2 million metric tons or less.

Acknowledgments

This chapter was originally written in April 1988. A short postscript has been added at the end of the chapter to comment on developments between then and November 1989.

The views expressed herein are those of the author and not necessarily those of the Government of Canada.

Notes

1. Clean Air Amendments of 1970, 42 U.S.C. § 1857 (1982) (amending 42 U.S.C. § 1857 (1967)).
2. Clean Air Act, ch. 47 (Can. 1971).
3. Calculations based on data from Environment Canada and the U.S. Environmental Protection Agency.
4. *See Report on the Transport of Air Pollutants*, 80 U.S. DEP'T ST. BULL. 4 (Jan. 1980). *See also* ACID RAIN AND FRIENDLY NEIGHBORS: THE POLICY DISPUTE BETWEEN CANADA AND THE UNITED STATES 76 (J. Schmandt & H. Roderick eds. 1985) [hereinafter ACID RAIN AND FRIENDLY NEIGHBORS].
5. Foreign Relations Authorizations Act, Fiscal Year 1979, § 612, Pub. L. No. 95–426, Oct. 7, 1978, 92 Stat. 990, 42 U.S.C. § 7415 Historical Note (1983).
6. A. Altshuller & G. McBean, *The Long-Range Transport of Air Pollutants Problem in North America: A Preliminary Overview*, United States-Canada Bilateral Consultation Group (Oct. 1979).
7. *Id.*; *Second Report of the United States-Canada Bilateral Research Consultation Group on the Long-Range Transport of Air Pollutants* (Oct. 1980).
8. *See* ACID RAIN AND FRIENDLY NEIGHBORS, *supra* note 4, at 62; Memorandum of Intent Between the Government of Canada and the Government of the United States Concerning Transboundary Air Pollution, Aug. 5, 1980, Canada-United States, 80 U.S. DEP'T ST. BULL. 21 (Oct. 1980).
9. For a discussion of the Work Groups' final reports, see ACID RAIN AND FRIENDLY NEIGHBORS, *supra* note 4, at 80–82.
10. Report of the Acid Rain Peer Review Panel (Chaired by W.A. Nierenberg) (July 1984); Office of Science and Technology Policy, Executive Office of the President, news release, June 28, 1983. A summary of the panel's findings can be found in Nat'l Acad. Sci., 33 NEWS REPORT 6 (July–Aug. 1983).

11. NATIONAL RESEARCH COUNCIL, NAT'L ACAD. SCI., ACID DEPOSITION: ATMOSPHERIC PROCESSES IN EASTERN NORTH AMERICA, Washington, D.C. (Nat'l Acad. Press 1983).

12. ROYAL SOCIETY OF CANADA, REPORT OF THE PEER REVIEW GROUP (1983).

13. President Reagan's State of the Union Address, Jan. 25, 1984, WEEKLY COMP. PRES. DOCS., Vol. 20, No. 4, at 91 (Jan. 30, 1984).

14. D. LEWIS & W. DAVIS, JOINT REPORT OF THE SPECIAL ENVOYS ON ACID RAIN 5, U.S. Dep't of St., Washington, D.C. (Jan. 1986) [hereinafter JOINT REPORT OF THE SPECIAL ENVOYS].

15. *Id.*

16. Statement of the Principal Deputy Press Secretary to the President, March 19, 1986, WEEKLY COMP. PRES. DOCS., Vol. 22, No. 12, at 389–90 (Mar. 24, 1986).

17. JOINT REPORT OF THE SPECIAL ENVOYS, *supra* note 14, at 32.

18. *Id.* at 31–35.

19. *Id.* at 31.

20. *Id.* at 29–30.

21. Statement by President Reagan, Mar. 18, 1987, WEEKLY COMP. PRES. DOCS., Vol. 23, No. 11, at 269–70 (Mar. 23, 1987).

22. President Ronald Reagan, *Address to the Canadian Parliament*, Apr. 6, 1987.

23. Joint Report to Bilateral Advisory and Consultative Group (BACG), *Status of Canadian/U.S. Research in Acidic Deposition* (Feb. 25, 1987).

24. Confidential document not released publicly.

25. Discussions between Canadian and U.S. officials, Bilateral Advisory and Consultative Group (BACG), Jan. 25, 1986.

26. Confidential document not released publicly.

27. Clean Air Act Amendment, Bill C–51 (Can. 1980).

28. *Canada's Acid Rain Control Program*, prepared by Canadian Embassy, Washington, D.C., at 1 (1989).

29. Statement by Canadian Federal and Provincial Environment Ministers, Mar. 6, 1984.

30. Statement by Canadian Federal and Provincial Environment Ministers, *Federal and Provincial Environment Ministers' Agreement on Apportionment by Province of Sulphur Dioxide Emission Reductions*, Montreal, Quebec, Feb. 5, 1985.

31. Environment Canada Press Release # PR HQ 085–16, *Federal Acid Rain Control Program Unveiled—Landmark Decision in Environmental Protection*, Hull, Quebec, Mar. 6, 1985.

32. *Id.*

33. *Canada's Acid Rain Control Program*, prepared by Canadian Embassy, Washington, D.C., at 2 (1989).

34. *Progress Report: The Canadian Acid Rain Control Program*, prepared by Canadian Embassy, Washington, D.C., at 1 (1989).

35. *Canada-United States—Acid Rain*, prepared by Canadian Embassy, Washington, D.C., at 1 (1989).

36. *Id.*

37. *Id.* at 4.

38. Treaty Relating to the Boundary Waters and Questions Arising Along the Boundary Between the United States and Canada, Jan. 11, 1909, United States-Canada, 36 Stat. 2448, T.S. No. 548.

39. Trail Smelter (U.S. v. Can.), 3 R. Int'l Arb. Awards 1905 (1938 & 1941).

40. *Id.* at 1965.

41. REPORT OF THE UNITED NATIONS CONFERENCE ON THE HUMAN ENVIRON-MENT, June 16, 1972, U.N. Doc. A/CONF.48/14 and Corr., *reprinted in* 11 I.L.M. 1416, 1420 (1972).

42. Agreement of Cooperation Regarding Transboundary Air Pollution Caused by Copper Smelters Along Their Common Border, Jan. 29, 1987, United States-Mexico, *reprinted in* 26 I.L.M. 33 (1987).

43. Convention on Long-Range Transboundary Air Pollution, Nov. 13, 1979, T.I.A.S. No. 10541, *reprinted in* 18 I.L.M. 1442 (1979).

44. Protocol to the Convention on Long-Range Transboundary Air Pollution of Nov. 13, 1979, Concerning Monitoring and Evaluation of Long-Range Transmission of Air Pollutants in Europe (EMEP), Sept. 28, 1984, *reprinted in* 24 I.L.M. 484 (1985).

45. NATIONAL ACID PRECIPITATION ASSESSMENT PROGRAM, INTERIM ASSESS-MENT ON THE CAUSES AND EFFECTS OF ACID RAIN, Executive Summary (U.S. Government Printing Office 1987).

46. Federal/Provincial Research and Monitoring Coordinating Committee, *A Critique of the U.S. National Acid Precipitation Assessment Program's Interim Assessment Report*, at 1, 2 (Dec. 1987), *reprinted in* 1 INT'L ENVTL. AFF. 57 (1989).

47. *Id.* at 2.

48. *Id.*

49. *Id.* at 3.

50. *Id.* at 25.

51. *Canada's Acid Rain Control Program*, prepared by Canadian Embassy, Washington, D.C., at 2 (1989).

52. Discussions between Canadian and U.S. officials, Bilateral Advisory and Consultative Group (BACG), Jan. 25, 1989.

53. *Id.*

54. JOINT REPORT OF THE SPECIAL ENVOYS, *supra* note 14, at 30.

55. H.R. 3030, 101st Cong., 1st Sess. (introduced July 27, 1989); S. 1490, 101st Cong., 1st Sess. (introduced Aug. 3, 1989).

Chapter 14
International Law and the Canada–United States Acid Rain Dispute

Edward G. Lee

The United States has a responsibility, in international law, to reduce the transboundary flow of sulphur dioxide emissions to the point where they are not causing significant damage in Canada. Canada's legal position, which has been specifically expressed to the United States during discussions on this subject, is based on a principle of responsibility in international environmental law that was first enunciated during a previous Canada–United States dispute over damage due to sulphur emissions.[1] In the 1941 *Trail Smelter* case, however, the situation was reversed. In addition to admitting liability and paying some $390,000 to the United States in damages, Canada accepted the Arbitral Tribunal's finding that

No state has the right to use or permit the use of its territory in such a manner as to cause injury by fumes in or to the territory of another . . . when the case is of serious consequence and the injury is established by clear and convincing evidence.[2]

This specific principle of responsibility for injury by fumes was broadened in two other international decisions dealing with state responsibility: the 1949 *Corfu Channel*[3] and the 1975 *Lac Lanoux*[4] cases. The modern statement of the principle, now generalized to cover all environmental damage, has been incorporated into the corpus of customary international law,[5] and is found in Principle 21 of the Stockholm Declaration, adopted at the 1972 United Nations Conference on the Human Environment.[6] Principle 21, which is accepted by the United States,[7] provides, in part, that States have "the responsibility to ensure that activities within their jurisdiction or control do not cause damage to the environment of other States or of areas beyond the limits of national jurisdiction."[8]

In this chapter, I will examine several specific legal issues that flow from Principle 21. In doing so, I hope to dispel certain myths that have been used to forestall action on acid rain.

First, it is a well-established principle that the international liability a State may incur for acts of private persons—in this case, primarily U.S. coal-fired electric power plants—is a function of that State's control over the activities concerned.[9] There is a convincing argument to be made that, as regards acid rain, the U.S. Government is the one actor that has both the knowledge of the problem and the ability to regulate it in an effective way.

Second, Canada can establish both that significant damage to our environment has occurred and that the fault is due, in part, to the United States. With regard to the damage, some 14,000 Canadian lakes are already dead, 150,000 others are today being acidified, and 150,000 more are vulnerable.[10] Nine salmon-bearing rivers are dead in one province alone.[11] Almost 85% of the best agricultural land in eastern Canada receives unacceptably high levels of acid rain.[12] More than 50% of forests in eastern Canada grow in areas where rainfall is acidic, and even Canada's maple sugar industry is in jeopardy.[13] More than 80% of all Canadians live in areas where acidic deposits are high.[14]

On the question of fault, the United States knows its emissions are crossing the border. Indeed, in endorsing the Joint Report of the Special Envoys on Acid Rain,[15] released January 1986, the United States went further and admitted that acid rain remains a serious transboundary environmental problem.[16]

What then is left in dispute? Two things, I suggest. First, the United States questions the cause and effect linkage between U.S.-origin sulphur dioxide emissions and the damage in Canada. This appears to be the basis for U.S. arguments that more research is required before action can be taken. Second, the United States is unwilling to subscribe to any particular control program until it is satisfied, again on the basis of clear scientific evidence, that the remedy would be effective, from both a technical and an economic point of view.

On the first issue, we believe that a significant body of expert scientific evidence already exists to the effect that acid rain pollution is causing damage to natural resources and public health in Canada and that much of the damage can be traced to sources in the United States. Among the reports that support the Canadian position are the 1981 Report of the U.S. National Commission on Air Quality;[17] the 1982

Report of Work Group No. II prepared pursuant to the 1980 Canada–United States Memorandum of Intent;[18] the U.S. Environmental Protection Agency's own 1982 Air Quality Criteria Document;[19] the 1986 Joint Report of the Special Envoys on Acid Rain;[20] and the 1988 Assessment of Air Pollution Effects on Human Health in Ontario.[21]

Indeed, scientists at Environment Canada verify the following: acid deposition in much of eastern Canada is at levels causing significant damage to the environment; the damage is getting worse at current levels of emissions and depositions; it is possible to identify the levels of emissions and deposition at which significant damage will not occur; and it is possible, both in specific and in general cases, to identify by atmospheric modeling the extent to which Canadian and U.S. sources are contributing to the levels of deposition.[22]

What scientific evidence is the United States relying on then, when it rejects, as it did in January 1988, Canadian demands for targeted reductions of sulphur dioxide emissions over a specific time period? In September 1987 the U.S. National Acid Precipitation Assessment Program (NAPAP) issued a report.[23] It consists of four volumes of some 1,200 pages. The science in it is good solid work, as far as it goes. The qualification "as far as it goes" is necessary, first, because the report is an interim report, and, second, because it does not include Canadian information that the authors chose to ignore.[24]

Moreover, the Executive Summary, the only portion of the report that most people will have time to read, is so flawed it raises questions about the use of scientific information in this debate. For example, why choose a pH of 5 and not 6 when environmental damage is already starting to occur at the higher level?[25] Why exclude lakes under ten acres?[26] Why exclude waterways?[27] Why the selectivity of the data? Why forecast U.S. emission reductions based on an assumption of a 300% increase in nuclear power generation?[28] Why was the Executive Summary, which was 67 pages long, itself not peer-reviewed?

Regardless of the answers to those questions, the political fallout is clear. Nontechnical agencies and officials find it difficult to contradict scientific work, and the negative effect of the Executive Summary has been put to predictable use in Congress and the Administration by those with nontechnical reasons for opposing action on acid rain. Furthermore, in our view, U.S. decision-makers must recognize that scientific information can only assist in public policymaking. Science cannot and should not be the sole determinant of public policy. To do so is to put scientific investigation in a role for which it is neither designed nor equipped. As Canada's Environment Minister Tom McMillan stated: "To our mind, science should contribute to public policy; public policy should not dictate science."[29]

The international protocol on stratospheric ozone depletion, signed in Montreal in September 1987, is an excellent example of the role of science in public policymaking.[30] Science gave us an indication that we had a serious problem with the ozone layer and what was causing the problem, that is, the release of chlorofluorocarbons (CFCs) into the atmosphere.[31] To say we know far more about the science of acid rain than we do about the science of stratospheric ozone depletion is an understatement. Yet the international community, including the United States—indeed, led by the United States[32]—was able to band together to slash worldwide releases of CFCs. If U.S. decision-makers can support actions to protect the ozone layer, there is no scientific rationale standing in the way of a bilateral accord on acid rain. In summary, even assuming that the correct standard of proof is "clear and convincing," that standard has been met: the transboundary flux of sulphur dioxide from the United States to Canada is causing serious damage in Canada.

On the second question still in dispute between Canada and the United States, that is, whether the United States has the right to refrain from taking action until it is satisfied as to the effectiveness of the control measures, we take the position that the answer is clearly "no." The Canadian position can perhaps best be explained by putting the question another way. Should Canada continue to be exposed to significant environmental damage and its associated costs from U.S. sulphur emissions because the United States is unwilling to accept the risk of investment decisions regarding cleanup programs that might turn out to be less than 100% effective?

In summary, the United States is obligated by principles of international law to reduce the transboundary flow of sulphur dioxide from the United States into eastern Canada. The United States also has a neighborly duty to do so.[33] In order to fulfill these duties, as is explained in Chapter 12 the United States should reduce the transboundary flux from the 1980 level of 4 million metric tons to approximately 2 million metric tons per year (one metric ton—or "tonne"— equals 1.102 "short" tons, as the latter term is used in the United States). Canada and the United States ought to conclude a bilateral agreement that would include definite targets and schedules for that reduction.[34]

Postscript

Several developments have occurred since the time this chapter was originally written in August 1988. The most significant occurrence is that President George Bush proposed new legislation in June 1989 that would reduce annual U.S. domestic sulphur dioxide emissions by 10 million short tons.[35] The Canadian Government, whose position on the acid rain issue has remained essentially unchanged, has determined that such a 10 million short ton reduction would reduce the transboundary flow of sulphur dioxide from the United States to Canada to 2 million metric tons or less. The conclusion of a bilateral Air Quality Accord would be the logical result of the efforts expended by both countries to date.

Acknowledgments

This chapter is adapted from a presentation on August 7, 1988, at a panel discussion on acid deposition at the Annual Meeting of the American Bar Association in Toronto, Canada. A short postscript to this chapter brings the chapter up-to-date on developments between August 1988 and November 1989. Chapter 15, *infra*, by Scott Hajost, then-Deputy Associate Administrator of the U.S. Environmental Protection Agency, is also adapted from a presentation at the Toronto 1988 panel.

The views expressed in this chapter are those of the author and not necessarily those of the Government of Canada.

Notes

1. Trail Smelter (U.S. v. Can.), 3 R. Int'l Arb. Awards 1905 (1938 & 1941).
2. *Id.* at 1965.
3. Corfu Channel (U.K. v. Alb.), 1949 I.C.J. 4 (Judgment of Apr. 9).
4. Lac Lanoux (Fr. v. Spain), 24 I.L.R. 101 (1957) (English), 12 R. Int'l Arb. Awards 281 (1957) (French).
5. *See, e.g.*, Protection of the Atmosphere: International Meeting of Legal and Policy Experts, *Meeting Statement*, note to art. A.5 ("[Principle 21] contains a relevant principle of international law").
6. Declaration of the United Nations Conference on the Human Environment, prin. 21, Stockholm, U.N. Doc. A/CONF.48/14 & Corr. 1, *reprinted in* 11 I.L.M. 1416 (1972) [hereinafter 1972 Stockholm Declaration].
7. *See, e.g.*, Agreement of Cooperation Between the United States of America and the United Mexican States Regarding Transboundary Air Pollution Caused by Copper Smelters Along Their Common Border, Jan. 29, 1987, Mexico-United States, Preamble, *reprinted in* 26 I.L.M. 33 (1987) ("*Reaffirming* Principle 21 . . ."); Chapter 15, *infra.*
8. 1972 Stockholm Declaration, *supra* note 6, prin. 21.
9. *See, e.g.*, Trail Smelter (U.S. v. Can.), 3 R. Int'l Arb. Awards 1905 (1938 & 1941); Corfu Channel (U.K. v. Alb.), 1949 I.C.J. 4; *cf.* U.S. Diplomatic and Consular Staff in Tehran (U.S. v. Iran), 1979 I.C.J. 7.
10. DEPARTMENT OF FISHERIES AND OCEANS, ACIDIFICATION OF SURFACE WA-

TERS IN EASTERN CANADA AND ITS RELATIONSHIP TO AQUATIC BIOTA (Scientific Information and Publications Branch, DFO, 1986).

11. International Joint Commission, *Work Group I Impact Assessment* (Feb. 1983).

12. Environment Canada, *The Effects of Acid Rain on Canada's Prime Resource Lands* (Canadian Land Inventory Series, Lands Directorate 1978).

13. D. LEWIS & W DAVIS, JOINT REPORT OF THE SPECIAL ENVOYS ON ACID RAIN 23, U.S. Dep't of State, Washington, D C. (Jan. 1986).

14. *Id.*

15. *Id.*

16. Statement by the Principal Deputy Press Secretary to the President, Mar. 19, 1986, WEEKLY COMP. OF PRES. DOCS., Vol. 22, No. 12, at 389–90 (Mar. 24, 1986).

17. REPORT OF THE NATIONAL COMMISSION ON AIR QUALITY, TO BREATHE CLEAN AIR (U.S. Gov't Printing Office 1981).

18. Memorandum of Intent Between the Government of Canada and the Government of the United States Concerning Transboundary Air Pollution, Aug. 5, 1979, Canada-United States, 80 U.S. DEP'T ST. BULL. 21 (Oct. 1980). For a discussion of the Work Groups' final reports, see ACID RAIN AND FRIENDLY NEIGHBORS: THE POLICY DISPUTE BETWEEN CANADA AND THE UNITED STATES (J. Schmandt & H. Roderick eds. 1985).

19. U.S. Environmental Protection Agency, *Air Quality Criteria for Particulate Matter and Sulphur Oxides* (Environmental Criteria and Assessment Office 1982).

20. *Supra* note 13.

21. Ontario Hydro, *An Assessment of Air Pollution Effects on Human Health in Ontario* (Economics and Forecasts Division Mar. 1988).

22. *See* International Joint Commission, *Work Group 2—Atmospheric Sciences and Analysis* (Nov. 1982); M.P. Olson, E.C. Voldner & K.K. Oikawa, *Transfer Matrices from the AES-LRT Model* (Air Quality and Inter-Environmental Research Branch, Atmospheric Environment Service May 1983).

23. NATIONAL ACID PRECIPITATION ASSESSMENT PROGRAM (NAPAP), INTERIM ASSESSMENT ON THE CAUSES AND EFFECTS OF ACID RAIN (U.S. Gov't Printing Office 1987) [hereinafter NAPAP REPORT].

24. *See, e.g.*, Federal/Provincial Research and Monitoring Coordinating Committee, *A Critique of the U.S. National Acid Precipitation Assessment Program's Interim Assessment Report*, esp. at 4, 6, 11 (Dec. 1987), *reprinted in* 1 INT'L ENVTL. AFF. 57 (1989).

25. NAPAP REPORT, *supra* note 23, vol. 1, at 2–3.

26. *Id.*, vol. 1, at 30–31.

27. *Id.*

28. *Id.*

29. Speech by Honorable Tom McMillan, Canadian Minister of the Environment, to the National Conservation and Parks Ass'n, Washington, D.C., Sept. 28, 1987.

30. Montreal Protocol on Substances that Deplete the Ozone Layer, Sept. 16, 1987, *reprinted in* 26 I.L.M. 1541 (1987).

31. *See, e.g.*, *Atmospheric Ozone 1985: Assessment of Our Understanding of the Processes Controlling Its Present Distribution and Change*, World Meteorological Organization Global Ozone Research and Monitoring Project, Report No. 16 (1985).

32. Durkee, *EPA Administrator Lee Thomas Emphasizes Need for Ozone Agreement, Explores Complexity of Acid Rain Issues, International Priorities for Agency*, [10 Current Report] Int'l Env't Rep. (BNA) 461 (Sept. 9, 1987).

33. *See generally* Michel Virally, *Preface*, in VOISINAGE ET BON VOISINAGE EN DROIT INTERNATIONAL (Editions A. Pedone Paris 1980).

34. For discussion of the Canadian and U.S. positions regarding such a bilateral agreement, see *supra* Chapter 13 and *infra* Chapter 15.

35. H.R. 3030, 101st Cong., 1st Sess. (introduced July 27, 1989); S. 1490, 101st Cong., 1st Sess. (introduced Aug. 3, 1989).

Chapter 15
Acid Rain: A United States Policy Perspective

William A. Nitze

The U.S. Administration fully appreciates that acid rain is an important environmental concern for both Americans and Canadians. It is a basic Administration policy to continue the cooperative relationship with Canada on acid rain that has existed almost since scientists first identified the potentially serious environmental problems connected with long-range transport of byproducts of fossil fuel emissions.

Long-Standing Cooperation with Canada

United States–Canada bilateral efforts regarding acid rain actually date back over forty years to the *Trail Smelter* case in which an arbitration panel held that "no state has the right to use or permit the use of its territory in such a manner as to cause injury by fumes in or to the territory of another."[1] The first United States–Canada joint response to deal specifically with acid deposition was a bilateral research consultation group established in 1978 to report the extent and significance of long-range air pollution.[2] Additionally, in 1978, the U.S. Congress called upon President Jimmy Carter to make every effort to negotiate a cooperative agreement with the Government of Canada aimed at preserving the mutual airshed of the United States and Canada.[3]

These negotiations, in turn, led to a joint statement on Transboundary Air Quality of July 26, 1979,[4] and a Memorandum of Intent of August 5, 1980,[5] in which the two governments recognized explicitly the potential seriousness of acid rain and accepted a mutual commitment to work toward a bilateral agreement as soon as possible. Although a bilateral air quality agreement was not reached under the

Memorandum of Intent because of fundamental scientific differences between the two sides on the nature and effects of acid rain, much useful work was done and bilateral cooperation focused on coordinating scientific research continued in the years thereafter.

Then on March 17 and 18, 1985, President Ronald Reagan and Canadian Prime Minister Brian Mulroney met in Quebec City to discuss a wide range of bilateral issues, including the environment. Both leaders acknowledged publicly that acid rain was a serious concern affecting our bilateral relations. The two leaders noted the 75-year history of cooperation in dealing with the environment and expressed determination to continue in that historic spirit in dealing with acid rain. They each appointed a Special Envoy (Drew Lewis of the United States and William Davis of Canada) to review jointly the acid rain issue and to make recommendations for their next meeting in the spring of 1986.

The Special Envoys completed their work and issued a joint report, endorsed by the President and the Prime Minister, in March 1986. The United States, the Special Envoys found, had made good progress in reducing emissions of sulphur dioxide under the Clean Air Act of 1970. National ambient air quality standards for SO_2 and NOx had been attained as controls on new emission sources had been put in place. As a result, total U.S. emissions of SO_2 had declined by 27% from 1973 to 1985.[6]

Unfortunately, Canada believes that environmental degradation continues and is due to present levels of SO_2 and NOx emissions in both Canada and the United States. As a result, the envoys agreed that acid rain remains a serious transboundary environmental problem. They also concluded that only a limited number of potential avenues exist to achieve major reductions in acidic air emissions, all of them carrying high socioeconomic costs. The envoys recognized that the acid rain issue is politically divisive in the United States and that if an expanded emissions reduction program were to be pursued immediately, it would have to choose from a limited list of control options—coal washing, coal switching, or flue-gas scrubbing—none of which provides a simple or easily affordable solution and all of which may soon be obsolete as new technologies are developed and deployed.

In response, the Special Envoys made three basic recommendations. First, they proposed that the U.S. Government "implement a five-year, five-billion dollar control technology commercial demonstration program,"[7] with the federal government providing half the funding, $2.5 billion, for projects proposed by industry and for which industry is prepared to contribute the other half of the funding. The primary purpose of the program is to encourage development of cheaper and more efficient technologies that might underlie a future emissions control program. They recommended that this program be carried out in a way that produces near-term reductions in emissions affecting Canadian ecosystems. They also recommended that a panel, headed by a cabinet-level official and including Canadian participation, be appointed to oversee the program and select demonstration projects.

Second, the Special Envoys suggested a series of administrative measures to enhance bilateral cooperation and consultation. And third, the envoys called for a cooperative program of research in areas of special value to decision-makers in guiding the development of environmental policies, including (1) deposition monitoring, (2) forest effects, (3) aquatic environment impacts, (4) materials damage, and (5) the role of heavy metals.

The Administration regards the joint report of the Special Envoys on acid rain as the primary framework for continued bilateral cooperation on acid rain. Accordingly, it has moved expeditiously to implement the report's recommendations.

With respect to the envoys' first recommendation, the Administration has urged Congress to provide the full $2.5 billion in federal funding recommended by the envoys for innovative control technologies.[8] It supports a recent solicitation for private interests to propose demonstration projects on innovative clean coal technologies.[9] To qualify, the proposal must be projected to meet or exceed all current Clean Air Act regulations and to do this at lower costs per ton of SO_2 and NOx emissions reduced than is achieved by the current control options. Some of the technologies are new burning processes that are expected to be twice as stringent for both SO_2 and NOx removal than are now required for any newly constructed power plant.

This is in addition to the ongoing Clean Coal Technology Program[10] enacted prior to the envoys' report and related federal, state, and private clean coal research, development, and demonstration efforts on which more than $6 billion will be expended through 1992.[11] Several states are also participating in independent programs to bring new, cleaner technologies into the marketplace through demonstration cost-sharing and by other financial incentives.[12] These include states that historically have had high emissions—such as Pennsylvania, Ohio, and Illinois.

Moreover, the Department of Energy has established an advisory panel with Canadian participation—the Innovative Control Technology Advisory Panel—to advise on the Department's funding and selection of innovative control technology demonstration projects. Several meetings of that advisory panel have already taken place, and the panel provided detailed project selection criteria that are being used in a current solicitation for demonstration projects. Advisory committees to the panel are conducting two studies, one reviewing and evaluating the existing clean coal technology program and the other examining commercialization incentives at the federal and state levels.[13]

Finally, the United States has carried out the envoys' other recommendations regarding reviewing the existing U.S. air pollution programs, reviewing the mechanisms by which the United States informs Canada of proposed changes in U.S. laws or regulations that may have transboundary effects, and participating in the joint Bilateral Advisory and Consultative Group. Those developments are described in Chapter 16.

Uncertainty About Causes Remains a Real Problem

To put the issue in perspective, I must point out that clear differences between the United States and Canada still remain about how to protect our respective interests. Acid deposition has been proposed as the cause of a variety of effects, including acidification of lakes and streams (with consequent damage to fish and other aquatic populations), deforestation or retardation of forest growth, damage to buildings and structures, reductions in visibility, and threats to human health from inhalation of sulfate particles and from the dissolution of heavy metals in water supplies. Nevertheless, scientific uncertainty remains about the link between the acid precursor pollutants and possible damage. Much of the concern about acid rain reflects the fact that its effects in specific localities are not yet known with sufficient precision.

The relative contribution of the various chemical emissions to acid deposition remains an important unknown. As we have seen, acidification results from a complex interaction of emitted compounds, which include sulphur dioxide, oxides of nitrogen, and volatile organic compounds (VOCs). Sulphur dioxide by itself is certainly not the sole determinant of acid deposition. Nitrogen oxides are precursors of nitric acid; both sulphur dioxide and the nitrogen precursors require oxidants to form the corresponding acids in the atmosphere. Such oxidants are derived from a complex sequence of photochemical reactions involving the oxides of nitrogen and VOCs. The oxidants themselves can cause damage to plants and animals at sufficient concentrations, in addition to producing acidic substances.

At the same time, sulphur dioxide emissions have not shown any pronounced long-term trend over the past sixty years. Annual emissions in the United States for 1985 were only about 10% higher than in 1925.[14] There have been fluctuations of as much as 20 to 30% from the average level over this period. Increased electrical utility use of coal has been offset by more stringent pollution controls, the demise of the coal-fired locomotive and the virtual disappearance of coal-fueled home heating systems, causing this roughly constant pattern in emissions. National annual sulphur dioxide emissions also have, as noted, declined considerably (by about 40%) since their historic peak in 1972, even though our use of coal has grown by two thirds.[15] The rate of decline in rain acidity has been slower than the decline in sulphur dioxide emissions due to the nonlinear character of the atmospheric processes. Also, emissions of nitrogen oxides grew as fossil fuel use (including the increases attributable to automobiles) increased until the mid-1970s. Then nitrogen oxide controls, especially on automobiles, caused a leveling, followed by a slight decline in these emissions. VOCs are associated to a great extent with automobiles and grew steadily until about 1970, when they too began to decline by about 25% from the historic peak. Interestingly, the acidity of rain generally decreases during winter because of the lower concentration of oxidants, even though that is the season of greatest sulphur dioxide emissions.[16] These facts suggest that efforts to control acid deposition had best not focus exclusively on controlling sulphur dioxide emissions.

Another major uncertainty in the acid deposition process has to do with the mechanisms of atmospheric transport. The areas of North America that have most clearly demonstrated the effects of acid deposition are the lakes and streams in the glaciated terrain in Canada and the Adirondack Mountains. These areas are generally downwind of the U.S. eastern and midwestern power plants and Canadian smelters which are the main sources of the sulphur dioxide emissions. We cannot trace specific fractions of the acid deposition in the Adirondacks, however, to a cause originating in New York, Pennsylvania, Quebec, Ohio, Ontario, or more distant states or provinces.

Effects Are Not Clearly Understood

Acid deposition may be in dry or liquid form. Yet neither the United States nor Canada has put in place comprehensive monitoring networks for dry deposition. Thus, a major quantitative dimension of the overall pattern of acid deposition is not yet clearly understood. Visible damage to forests appears to be largely confined to trees above cloud base (3,500–5,000 feet) in the Appalachian Mountains; these mountain-peak areas account for less than one-tenth of 1% of U.S. forests.[17]

There are several competing hypotheses regarding harm to these forests from pollution, including theories identifying ozone and hydrogen peroxide (that is, oxidants) as the main causes of damage.[18]

Sensitivity of lakes and streams to acidification varies greatly, depending on the presence or absence of naturally occurring neutralizing chemicals (mainly carbonate minerals) in the watersheds. Extensive sampling under our National Acid Precipitation Assessment Program (NAPAP)[19] has shown that only a small percentage of the lake area in the Adirondacks is acidic to a degree that makes it difficult or impossible for most fish to survive.[20] The health danger of heavy metals in water supplies is potentially serious, but there is no definitive evidence yet as to the degree to which toxic metals may be contributing to pollution problems. Furthermore, most water supplies are treated in municipal plants or, for seasonal homes, are flushed to remove the metallic taste from water pipes that have not been in use.

Costs of New Controls Could Be Prohibitive

Unfortunately, our ability to analyze costs and benefits adequately is quite limited. While the benefits obtained by controlling emissions of acid precursors are not easily quantifiable with any degree of certainty, some of the measures that have been proposed to reduce emissions would clearly be very costly. Because the bulk of the sulphur dioxide emitted today in the United States comes from coal-fired electrical power plants, most recent sulphur dioxide emission control strategies involve switching to coal with lower sulphur content, removing some of the sulphur before combustion ("coal washing"), or removing the sulphur during or after combustion by "gas cleaning" devices.

The actual cost of achieving any particular reduction in emissions will depend on how the reduction is achieved—whether through scrubbing of flue gases, fuel switching, substitution of new capacity and technologies for old plants, or some combination of methods. Cost estimates also depend on projections of future electricity demand. Thus, cost estimates are uncertain, but have been estimated (for sulphur dioxide reductions amounting to approximately 10 million tons per year below current levels) to be in the range of several billion dollars per year in present value over the period 1990–2010.[21]

Because sulphur dioxide by itself is not the sole determinant of acid deposition, any control strategy focused on sulphur dioxide emissions alone may not produce a proportional reduction in acid deposition. Costs of a control program aimed at nitrogen oxides and VOCs in addition to sulphur dioxide would add to the cost of proposed sulphur dioxide control programs.[22]

The Administration's Policy Response

As already noted, the Administration's policy response to the problem of acid deposition begins with its commitment to the steps outlined in the envoys' recommendations. The five-year, $5 billion research effort to develop a commercial control technology demonstration program provides a framework for aggressive pursuit of cleaner coal-burning technologies. And progress in this area is already being made. For example, integrated gasification combined cycle technologies are potentially cheaper than scrubbing, and gasification can remove as much as 99% of the sulphur dioxide and 90% of the nitrogen oxides. The Administration is committed to further work to demonstrate the commercial feasibility of new coal-burning technologies in the belief that several of the technologies, once adequately demonstrated, will be the economic choice of utilities needing to expand to meet demand.

At the same time, the scientific uncertainties surrounding the causes and effects of acid deposition will be reduced through further research. In the United States, this effort is coordinated through the National Acid Precipitation Assessment Program (NAPAP) mechanism.[23] NAPAP—which is described in greater detail in Chapter 16—is an interagency program jointly financed by the Environmental Protection Agency, the National Oceanic and Atmospheric Administration, and the Departments of Agriculture, Energy, and Interior. NAPAP's research agenda includes sources of acid precipitation, atmospheric processes, deposition monitoring, aquatic and terrestrial effects, effects on materials and cultural resources, and control technologies. Progress in resolving remaining areas of uncertainty will have direct relevance to policy. For example, a better understanding of the mechanisms of atmospheric transport could tell us whether any U.S. effort to reduce acid deposition in Canada should emphasize emissions reductions from the states bordering Canada.

We should also keep in mind that the price of haste could be unacceptably high. Because of the long lead times for power utility plant investments, an emissions control program based on the wrong technology could impose irreversible—and severe—economic inefficiencies. We must take the time needed to ensure sound decisions—based on appropriate cost-benefit analysis—before embarking on major new investments. Otherwise we risk getting locked into costly obsolete technologies. Certainly, it would seem that the way *not* to proceed is to require expensive scrubbers now, when the same investment in new technologies will almost certainly produce greater reductions, more efficiently, in the not too distant future. Alternative, low-cost, short-term mitigation strategies, such as liming of certain sensitive lakes, must also be examined; such practices to maintain fish populations have been carried out in some areas for decades.

At the same time, we need time to review environmental and regulatory policies to determine whether they may be contributing to the problem of acid deposition. Coal-fired power plants constructed before 1972, when performance standards were imposed on new stationary sources, are not being rebuilt or replaced as quickly as expected, in part, due to lower than projected growth in electricity demand. The downward trend we have seen in SO_2 emissions may level off or even turn up slightly in the near term as a result of using older power plants at higher capacity. However, as these old plants are eventually replaced or rebuilt, stationary source emissions can only decrease. Clearly, any "anti-new source bias," which prolongs the life of older facilities and makes it more difficult to build newer, cleaner plants, should be reexamined. For example, some argue that reluctance by local regulators to allow utilities to include costs of equipment under construction in their rate base impedes construction of new plants or retrofitting of control technology. Where this is true, efforts could be made to eliminate regulatory impediments to the adoption of newer technologies. Again, control strategies ought to be avoided that would tend to lock the utilities into obsolete techniques.

Relevant Principles of International Law

There is an important, but still developing, body of international environmental law addressing the nature and scope of a State's obligation in the context of transboundary pollution. Various aspects of that body of law are discussed in Chapters 3, 4, 7, 14, and 16; the last two focus specifically on the United States–Canada situation. A few general comments follow.

Principle 21 of the Stockholm Declaration on the Human Environment, the *Trail Smelter* arbitration, the *Corfu Channel* case, and the Long-Range Transboundary Air Pollution Convention form a significant part of the relevant legal framework. The United States–Canada *Trail Smelter* arbitration of the 1930s and the *Corfu Channel* case of 1947 represent two of the earliest pronouncements on the issue of state responsibility in regard to transboundary pollution. In the *Trail Smelter* case, Canada stipulated its liability for environmental and property damage in the United States caused by fumes from a smelter located in British Columbia. In deciding that the smelter should be required to refrain from causing damage in the United States in the future, the tribunal stated that "no State has the right to use or permit the use of its territory in such a manner as to cause injury by fumes in or to the territory of another or the properties of persons therein, when the case is of serious consequence and the injury is established by clear and convincing evidence."[24] The *Corfu Channel* case, in which Albania was found liable for damage incurred by a British vessel in passage through a channel laid with Albanian mines, sets forth a generalized State obligation "not to allow knowingly its territory to be used for acts contrary to the rights of other States."[25]

These decisions were followed by the adoption of Principle 21 in June 1972 by the U.N. Conference on the Human Environment. Principle 21, which is viewed as reflecting customary principles of international law on this subject, provides that

States have, in accordance with the Charter of the United Nations and the principles of international law, the sovereign right to exploit their own resources pursuant to their own environmental policies, and the responsibility to ensure that activities within their jurisdiction or control do not cause damage to the environment of other States or of areas beyond the limits of national jurisdiction.[26]

Seven years after the adoption of Principle 21, negotiations on a multilateral agreement addressing the problem of transboundary air pollution were concluded. This agreement—the Convention on the Long-Range Transboundary Air Pollution—requires its parties to "endeavor to limit and, as far as possible, gradually reduce and prevent air pollution including long-range transboundary air pollution."[27] It further provides that the parties shall develop policies and strategies to combat the discharge of air pollutants "taking into account efforts already made at national and international levels."[28] At present, there are 32 contracting parties to the Convention, including the United States and Canada.[29]

Recommendations on the control of transfrontier pollution have also evolved. The member countries of the Organization for Economic Cooperation and Development adopted in 1974 a Recommendation on Principles Concerning Transfrontier Pollution which exhorts countries to take, individually and jointly, "all appropriate measures to prevent and control transboundary pollution and harmonize as far as possible their relevant policies."[30] The recommendation also states that "[c]ountries should endeavor to conclude, where necessary, bilateral or multilateral agreements for the abatement of transfrontier pollution."[31]

The United States and Canada have a history of bilateral commitment and cooperative practice in the field of transboundary air pollution. This history includes (as described earlier) a Joint Statement on Transboundary Air Quality issued on July 26, 1979;[32] a Memorandum of Intent on Transboundary Air Pollution signed by the two Governments on April 5, 1980;[33] the appointment in 1985 of Special Envoys to examine the acid rain problem; and in 1986 the endorsement by the United States and Canada of the joint envoys' report and recommendations,[34] as well as continuing discussions on acid rain by the President and the Prime Minister at summit meetings.

Of course, international law does not impose an absolute prohibition on transboundary pollution. For instance, the proscription enunciated in the *Trail Smelter* case is applicable where the case is of *serious consequence* and the injury is established by both *clear and convincing evidence*,[35] suggesting that where the pollution is insignificant or the causes and effects uncertain, the prohibition does not pertain. Moreover, Principle 21 maintains a careful balance between the sovereign right of a State to exploit its resources and its responsibility to avoid serious transboundary pollution. The principle does not purport to resolve (or even address) the issue of the extent to which the State's right is circumscribed or expunged by its responsibility. Logic suggests that a rule of reason be applied in striking this balance.

One prominent legal scholar, Pierre-Marie Dupuy, describes a State's responsibility to avoid transboundary environmental damage as an obligation of "due diligence."[36] In this regard, nearly eighteen years ago, the United States enacted major legislation to protect air quality.[37] Efforts to protect health and the environment through the control of air pollution pursuant to U.S. legislation have resulted in substantial reduction in sulphur dioxide and other air pollutants.[38]

U.S. Domestic Legislation

The Clean Air Act[39] is the principal U.S. legal authority for controlling air pollution. The Act contains two complementary air pollution control strategies: (1) an ambient air quality approach for all emissions sources; and (2) a technology-based standard approach directed primarily at minimizing emissions from newly constructed facilities.

The ambient air quality approach is designed to assure that the surrounding air is of sufficient quality to protect health and the environment. A national ambient air quality standard (NAAQS) is established by the U.S. Environmental Protection Agency under this approach for widely emitted pollutants—such as sulphur dioxide or nitrogen oxides. A national primary NAAQS is set based on public health considerations, such as the vulnerability of such sensitive populations as asthmatics. A secondary NAAQS is established to prevent adverse welfare or environmental effects, such as accelerated damage to crops or building materials. After the establishment of the NAAQS for a given pollutant, each state must prepare a state implementation plan (SIP) to assure achievement of those ambient air standards in *all* regions within its territory. The Clean Air Act also contains a program to prevent significant deterioration of air quality in areas where air pollutant levels are presently cleaner than those required by national air quality standards.

The Clean Air Act's requirement of technology-based emission standards for new stationary sources supplements the Act's ambient air quality requirements. The purpose of the technology-based emission standards—known as new source performance standards (NSPS)—is to assure that new stationary sources do not emit unacceptable levels of pollutants. Existing power plant boilers constructed prior to 1972 are subject to NSPS if they undergo a major construction or operating change.

Section 115 of the Clean Air Act is the statutory provision which deals with international air pollution. It provides the Environmental Protection Agency with the legal authority to require revisions to SIPs to prevent or eliminate air pollution originating in the United States which may reasonably be anticipated to endanger public health or welfare in a foreign country. An important prerequisite to reliance on section 115 is a finding of "endangerment"—a determination that there is reason to believe that "any air pollutant or pollutants emitted in the United States cause or contribute to air pollution which may reasonably be anticipated to endanger public health or welfare in a foreign country."[40] The implementation of section 115 is described in Chapter 16.

To support an effective and equitable program addressing transboundary air pollution explicitly, there must be sufficient understanding of the link between emissions and their effects. To put this in the acid rain context, the development of a more substantial understanding of transboundary flow measurement and the chemical, physical, and biological processes associated with acid deposition is critical from a legal standpoint to make and defend all of the complex scientific judgments linking the acid deposition effects of concern with the actions required by a new regulatory program. As an aside, it is worth noting that none of the petitions filed pursuant to the domestic analogue of section 115—section 126 of the Clean Air Act—has been granted so far, in part because of insufficient data and scientific uncertainty about the long-range transport of air pollutants and the lack of an adequate long-range transport model.[41]

An Action Program

Acid rain continued to be high on the agenda when President George Bush and Prime Minister Brian Mulroney met for their first annual Summit Meeting in Ottawa on February 10, 1989. At that meeting, President Bush confirmed what he had said a day earlier in his budget address to the U.S. Congress[42]—that he attached high priority to working with Congress on comprehensive legislation that would include acid deposition precursor emission reduction targets and time-tables. The President indicated that subsequently discussions on a bilateral accord with Canada could begin. Prime Minister Mulroney welcomed the initiative, urging that the United States match Canada's decision to reduce polluting emissions by at least 50%.

The acid rain element of the President's proposed package of Clean Air Act amendments submitted to the Congress on June 12, 1989, calls for a 10 million ton reduction in SO_2 emissions by 2000.[43] Initial reductions in sulphur dioxide emissions would be required after December 31, 1995, and a second phase of reductions would be required after December 31, 2000. The Administration's proposal recognizes the benefits to the environment from improvements in coal-burning technology and provides incentives, not only for demonstrating these new technologies, but for deploying them as solutions to the acid rain problem. This proposal would allow sources which choose certain repowering technologies as viable control options to receive a three-year extension of the December 31, 2000, deadline. In addition, those boilers amenable to cost-effective retrofit with low-NOx burners would be required to install such devices by the end of the year 2000. Such a program will reduce NOx emissions in 2000 by 2 million tons.

Consistent with the Administration's commitment to use market forces wherever possible, the proposal would allow maximum flexibility in obtaining reductions. The plan permits utilities to trade required reductions of sulphur oxides and nitrogen oxides so that they will be achieved in the least costly fashion. In the first phase, allowances can be transferred among affected sources within a state and within an interstate utility company. In phase two, broad interstate trading within an eastern region and a western region would be allowed.

While Canadian officials have been eager to begin negotiations toward a bilateral agreement that would incorporate targets and time-tables for emissions reductions, they recognize that formal talks cannot precede congressional action. Preliminary discussions with Canada that focus on reaching consensus on the main elements of a possible accord have taken place, however, to clear the way for formal negotiations once the outcome in Congress is clear.

In addition to targets and timetables, elements of an accord should include, in the Administration's view, collection and analysis of scientific and economic information and exchanges of information concerning the operation and effectiveness of programs being undertaken by each country to improve its air quality. Appropriate reporting to both the Canadian and U.S. Governments of the results of each country's air management programs should also be an element of any accord. Moreover, an accord should formalize regular review, consultation, and information exchange on air quality in both countries.

Such an accord would, in the Administration's opinion, be a constructive agreement for continued bilateral action. It would provide a sound basis for efforts in both countries to deal effectively with what we all agree is a serious environmental and economic problem.

Acknowledgments

This chapter was updated as of September 1989.

The views expressed herein are those of the author and not necessarily those of the United States Government.

Notes

1. Trail Smelter (U.S. v. Can.), 3 R. Int'l Arb. Awards 1905, 1965 (1938 & 1941).

2. *See Report on the Transport of Air Pollutants*, 80 U.S. DEP'T ST. BULL. 4 (Jan. 1980). *See also* ACID RAIN AND FRIENDLY NEIGHBORS: THE POLICY DISPUTE BETWEEN CANADA AND THE UNITED STATES 76 (J. Schmandt & H. Roderick eds. 1985) [hereinafter ACID RAIN AND FRIENDLY NEIGHBORS].

3. Foreign Relations Re-authorization Act of 1978, § 612, Pub. L. No. 95–426, 92 Stat. 963 (1978).

4. *See* ACID RAIN AND FRIENDLY NEIGHBORS, *supra* note 2, at 62.

5. Memorandum of Intent Between the Government of Canada and the Government of the United States Concerning Transboundary Air Pollution, Aug. 5, 1980, Canada–United States, 80 U.S. DEP'T ST. BULL. 21 (Oct. 1980).

6. D. LEWIS & W. DAVIS, JOINT REPORT OF THE SPECIAL ENVOYS ON ACID RAIN, U.S. Dep't of St., Washington, D.C. (Jan. 1986).

7. *Id.* at 3.

8. *E.g.*, President Ronald Reagan requested this in March 1987.

9. *Innovative Clean Coal Technology Program Opportunity Notice OE–PS101–88FE61530*, Feb. 22, 1988.

10. Statement by President Reagan, Office of the Press Secretary, Mar. 18, 1987.

11. *Id.*

12. *See, e.g., Ohio Coal Development Agenda*, Jan. 1988.

13. *Report to the Secretary of Energy Concerning Factors to be Considered in the First Innovative Clean Coal Technologies Program Solicitation*, Dec. 1987.

14. NATIONAL ACID PRECIPITATION ASSESSMENT PROGRAM, ANNUAL REPORT TO THE PRESIDENT, 1986 at 3 (U.S. Gov't Printing Office 1986).

15. NATIONAL ACID PRECIPITATION ASSESSMENT PROGRAM, INTERIM ASSESSMENT ON THE CAUSES AND EFFECTS OF ACID RAIN, Executive Summary (U.S. Gov't Printing Office, 1987) [hereinafter NAPAP].

16. *Id.* Vol. II, at 1–36; Vol. III, at 5–64.

17. *Id.* Vol. IV, at 7–6.

18. *Id.* Vol. IV, at 7–22 to 7–24.

19. *See infra* text accompanying note 23; Chapter 16, *infra.*

20. NAPAP, *supra* note 15, at Vol. IV, 8–72.

21. Statement of Lee M. Thomas, Administrator of the U.S. Envt'l Protection Agency, Before the Sen. Comm. on Env't and Public Works, Apr. 22, 1987, at 9–10.

22. National Ass'n of Manufacturers, *Acid Rain Legislation and the Economy*, Washington, D.C. (Sept. 1987).

23. NAPAP was established by the Acid Precipitation Act of 1980, Pub. L. No. 96–294, Title VII.

24. Trail Smelter, 3 R. Int'l Arb. Awards at 1965.

25. Corfu Channel (U.K. v. Alb.), 1949 I.C.J. 4, 22 (Judgment of Apr. 9).

26. REPORT OF THE STOCKHOLM CONFERENCE, U.N. Doc. A/CONF.48/14 & Corr. 1, at 7 (1972), *reprinted in* 11 I.L.M. 1416 (1972).

27. Convention on Long-Range Transboundary Air Pollution, Nov. 13, 1979, art. 2, T.I.A.S. No. 10541, *reprinted in* 18 I.L.M. 1442 (1979). For a discussion of the Convention, see *supra* Chapter 12.

28. *Id.* art. 3.

29. U.S. Dep't of State, TREATIES IN FORCE 343 (1988).

30. OECD, Recommendation of the Council on Principles Concerning Transfrontier Pollution, O.E.C.D. Doc. C(174)224 (1974), *reprinted in* 14 I.L.M. 242, 244 (1975) [hereinafter O.E.C.D. Rec.]. For a discussion of OECD activities concerning the environment, see *supra* Chapter 12.

31. O.E.C.D. Rec., *supra* note 30.

32. *Supra* note 4.

33. *Supra* note 5.

34. *Supra* text accompanying note 6.

35. *See supra* text accompanying note 24.

36. *See* Dupuy, *International Liability of States for Damage Caused by Transfrontier Pollution, reprinted in* O.E.C.D., LEGAL ASPECTS OF TRANSFRONTIER POLLUTION 345, 353 (1977); *see also supra* Chapter 3.

37. Clean Air Act of 1970, Pub. L. No. 91–604, 84 Stat. 1676.

38. U.S. Envt'l Protection Agency, *National Air Quality and Emissions Trends Report, 1985*, 3–15.

39. Clean Air Act (as amended), 42 U.S.C. §§ 7401–7642 (1982).

40. 42 U.S.C. § 7415(a) (1982).

41. Section 126 of the Clean Air Act, 42 U.S.C. § 7426 (1982), provides a mechanism for abatement of interstate air pollution that can be shown to be preventing a state from attaining NAAQS or interfering with its ability to comply with certain other requirements established pursuant to the Clean Air Act. Under section 126, a state or political subdivision may petition the Administrator of the Environmental Protection Agency for a finding that an out-of-state source is in violation of the Act's interstate air pollution provisions. If the Administrator finds that a violation exists, he may prohibit the construction or

Chapter 16
International Legal Implications of United States Policy on Acid Deposition

Scott A. Hajost

Introduction

This chapter addresses from a U.S. perspective the legal aspects of acid rain, more properly known as acid deposition, as they relate to the United States and Canada. More specifically, this chapter responds to the frequent assertion that the United States is not really doing something about acid deposition and that, either explicitly or implicitly, it is not living up to its international obligations by clarifying what the United States is doing to meet its obligations.

At the outset, one can safely say that the United States and Canada agree on a number of points, namely, that acid deposition is a serious environmental and transboundary problem; that the two countries subscribe to a similar body of international law and principles; and that the two countries have a common history of cooperation on environmental problems, including a common commitment to find a cooperative solution to transboundary acid deposition. It is to be hoped that both countries would also agree that progress has been made. The United States, for its part, is currently considering sweeping changes in the Clean Air Act to control emissions of acid deposition precursors further, while continuing research to resolve scientific uncertainties related to acid deposition. As is described in the preceding chapter, the United States has also committed significant efforts up to now in cooperation with Canada to reduce scientific uncertainty while pursuing alternative technologies to ensure that control programs are cost effective. The U.S. assessment is that its efforts to date, both alone and in cooperation with Canada, fully meet the United States' international obligations, whether conventional or customary.

continued operation of new or existing sources found to be in violation or require that they comply with a schedule to meet more stringent emission limits.

42. President George Bush, Address to the U.S. Congress, Feb. 9, 1989.

43. President Bush's proposal was included in legislation introduced in Congress later that summer. *See* H.R. 3030, 101st Cong., 1st Sess.; S. 1490, 101st Cong., 1st Sess.

The International Legal Framework

As noted above, the United States and Canada subscribe to a common body of international law and principles relevant to transboundary pollution. I will not embark on a comprehensive dissertation on this body of law, but will simply note that it incorporates basic principles of compliance with treaty obligations,[1] the duty to cooperate and negotiate on the basis of good neighborliness,[2] and the obligation to exercise due diligence in order to avoid transboundary pollution consistent with a balancing of equities.[3]

With respect to conventional law, there are two relevant agreements, one bilateral and the other multilateral: the 1980 United States–Canada Memorandum of Intent on Transboundary Air Pollution (MOI)[4] and the 1979 Convention on Long-Range Transboundary Air Pollution (LRTAP Convention),[5] respectively. The key provisions of the MOI called for development of a bilateral agreement on transboundary air pollution, for action to combat transboundary air pollution, and for a number of scientific and technical work group projects.[6] The work group projects have been concluded,[7] and the United States remains committed to the development of a bilateral accord on transboundary air pollution while continuing to take appropriate and long-standing domestic air pollution control action, as is described below.[8] Both Canada and the United States are party to the LRTAP Convention.[9] It requires parties to "endeavor to limit and, as far as possible, gradually reduce and prevent air pollution including long-range transboundary air pollution"[10] and that parties shall develop policies and strategies to combat the discharge of air pollutants "taking into account efforts already made at national and international levels."[11] (In July 1989, the United States also became party to the NO_x Protocol to the Convention.)[12] The U.S. obligations under both the MOI and the LRTAP Convention are fully met by U.S. programs under the Clean Air Act, which is described below under "The U.S. Regulatory Control Program."

Part of the international legal framework, of course, includes the seminal United States–Canada *Trail Smelter* arbitration[13] of the 1930s and Principle 21 of the 1972 Stockholm Declaration on the Human Environment,[14] which is in part based on the *Trail Smelter* case. In the *Trail Smelter* case, Canada stipulated its liability for environmental and property damage in the United States caused by fumes from a smelter in British Columbia, with the arbitral tribunal to assess damage. In deciding that the smelter should be required to refrain from causing damage in the United States in the future and compensate Washington State farmers for any such damage to their crops, the tribunal stated that "no State has the right to use or permit the use of its territory in such a manner as to cause injury by fumes in or to the territory of another."[15] The panel limited this proscription, however, to cases in which the injury is of "serious consequence" and is established by both "clear and convincing evidence,"[16] thereby suggesting that where the causes and effects are uncertain the proscription does not pertain.

This declaration was embodied in Principle 21 of the Declaration by the 1972 United Nations Conference on the Human Environment, which is now viewed as reflective of principles of customary international law.[17] It provides that "States have . . . the sovereign right to exploit their own resources pursuant to their own environmental policies, and the responsibility to ensure that activities within their jurisdiction or control do not cause damage to the environment of other States or of areas beyond the limits of national jurisdiction."[18] Other cases that reflect the same fundamental principle, albeit in nonpollution disputes,[19] include *Corfu Channel* (a State has the obligation "not to allow knowingly its territory to be used for acts contrary to the acts of other States"),[20] *Lac Lanoux* (potential upstream source States are required to "take into consideration in a reasonable manner the interests of the downstream State"),[21] and *United States Diplomatic and Consular Staff in Iran* (Iran was held accountable for not "taking appropriate steps to ensure the protection" of the U.S. Embassy and staff).[22] Each of these cases requires States to take the interests of other States into account, and two of them (*Corfu Channel* and *Diplomatic and Consular Staff*) recognize the responsibility of States to regulate nongovernmental activity within their jurisdiction. Also relevant is the general principle *sic utere tuo ut alienum non laedas*, that is, that one has the duty to exercise one's rights in ways that do not harm the interest of other subjects of law, which may be a "general principle" of law within the meaning of article 38(1)(c) of the Statute of the International Court of Justice.[23]

International environmental law, as enunciated in the *Trail Smelter* case and confirmed in Principle 21, does not impose, however, an absolute prohibition on transboundary pollution. First of all, the causes in relation to the effects must be clear. For example, the broad issue of U.S.-Canadian acid deposition is not comparable to the harm caused by a discrete smelter which was the subject of the *Trail Smelter* arbitration. Acid deposition is the product of many different, geographically dispersed sources whose individual contributions and effects cannot be pinpointed as with the Trail smelter.

Moreover, Principle 21 of the Stockholm Declaration maintains a careful balance between the sovereign right of a State to exploit its resources and its responsibility to avoid serious transboundary pollution. The Principle does not purport to resolve (or even to address)[24] the issue of the extent to which the State's rights are circumscribed by its responsibility. As such, there must be a balancing between a State's right to act and another State's right not to be affected, on which there is no clear-cut answer. This balance is consistent with a State's responsibility to exercise due diligence to avoid deleterious transboundary impacts on another.[25] This principle thus requires the State to take all necessary steps, through the introduction of domestic legislation and controls, to prevent substantial pollution to the environment of another State. Further support for a balancing test is provided by the *Lac Lanoux* case, which calls for an examination of whether the potential source State took account of the downstream State's interests in a "reasonable" manner.[26] A contrary reading would seem to require a State to bar *all* pollution from crossing into any other State—an impossibility in the case of air pollutants.

Analysis of U.S. Efforts to Control Acid Deposition

The United States has made an extensive effort to cooperate with Canada in addressing acid deposition. Cooperation between the two countries on environmental issues dates back to the Boundary Waters Treaty of 1909[27] and includes the Great Lakes Water Quality Agreement,[28] most recently amended in 1987,[29] the 1980 MOI,[30] the Special Envoys Report on Acid Rain of 1986,[31] summit meetings between the two heads of government, and a myriad of other forms. In fact, U.S.-Canadian relations on environmental protection are replete with cooperative efforts and include significant efforts on the United States' part to consult as well as Canadian access to U.S. courts, Federal agencies, Congress, and press. More specifically, as is explained in detail below, the United States is aggressively implementing its domestic regulatory control program under the Clean Air Act, conducting research under the National Acid Precipitation Assessment Program, carrying out the recommendations of the Special Envoys on Acid Rain, and is pursuing discussions with Canada on a comprehensive agreement to protect air quality in both nations. In light of this situation, the United States is meeting its international legal obligations outlined above ("The International Legal Framework") with respect to acid deposition.

The U.S. Regulatory Control Program

The U.S. Clean Air Act[32] sets out the most comprehensive air pollution control program in the world.[33] The Clean Air Act, however, is not perfect. In fact, by focusing on the preservation of local air quality, some of its provisions—section 123 on tall stacks, for example[34]—may have exacerbated other, longer-range air pollution problems such as acid deposition. Nor are its programs specifically directed at acid deposition. Yet, despite these limitations, the Clean Air Act has resulted in impressive gains in controlling the two pollutants most closely associated with the acid deposition phenomenon: sulphur dioxide and nitrogen oxides. After marked reductions in the early and mid-1970s, U.S. sulphur dioxide emissions have dropped another 21% since 1977;[35] and, despite considerable growth in the electric utility and industrial sectors and increased mobile source activity, nitrogen oxide emissions have decreased from 21.0 million metric tons in 1977 to 19.3 million metric tons in 1986.[36]

Moreover, in June 1989 President George Bush proposed major amendments to the Clean Air Act that, among other provisions, would reduce annual SO_2 and NO_x emissions by 10 million tons and 2 million tons, respectively.[37]

President Bush's proposal and the general approach and mechanics of the Clean Air Act have been described earlier in Chapter 15. In this chapter, I will focus on section 115 of the Act. As the subject of litigation between EPA and several environmental groups and New England states, section 115 has special implications for acid deposition control which might be undertaken in the United States. According to section 115,[38]

Whenever the [Environmental Protection Agency] Administrator upon receipt of reports, surveys or studies from any duly constituted international agency has reason to believe that any air pollutant or pollutants emitted in the United States cause or contribute to air pollution which may reasonably be anticipated to endanger public health or welfare in a foreign country . . . the Administrator shall give formal notification thereof to the Governor of the State in which such emissions originate.

Such notification is contingent, however, on the Administrator's finding of "endangerment." Formal notification, in turn, would require a state to revise its implementation plan to prevent or eliminate the endangerment. Section 115 also specifies that it will apply only to a foreign country which the Administrator determines has given the United States essentially the same rights with respect to the prevention or control of air pollution occurring in that country.[39]

In 1985, the U.S. District Court for the District of Columbia held in *Thomas v. New York* that letters from former Environmental Protection Agency (EPA) Administrator Doug Costle to then-Secretary of State Edmund Muskie and Senator George Mitchell, and a press release, imposed on the current Administrator a duty to identify States responsible for emissions contributing to acid deposition in Canada and to order those States to revise their implementation plans.[40] In 1986, this decision was overturned by the U.S. Court of Appeals.[41] The court ruled that, because Administrator Costle's statements regarding "endangerment" and "reciprocity" had been issued without following rule-making procedures, they did not bind the Agency. The court held that the timing and methods of regulatory actions under section 115 are "within the agency's discretion and not subject to judicial compulsion."[42]

Several environmental groups and New England states have petitioned the EPA Administrator to make the finding of "endangerment."[43] Even though these petitions are still pending before EPA, the petitioners have brought litigation in the U.S. Court of Appeals for the D.C. Circuit, contending that EPA has either denied the petitions or unreasonably delayed acting on them.[44] The cases have been briefed and are scheduled for oral argument in February 1990.

Although some might argue that section 115 may provide the legal basis necessary to design, implement, and defend an acid deposition control program as soon as we have achieved—through the assessment programs described in the next part of this chapter—a sufficient understanding of the causes and effects of acid deposition and the President's Clean Air Act proposal would provide a superior framework for comprehensive control.

The National Acid Precipitation Assessment Program (NAPAP)

The United States is also conducting a massive research program to reduce scientific uncertainties regarding the sources and effects of acid deposition and to assess the results in terms of control strategy. The Acid Precipitation Act of 1980[45] set up the National Acid Precipitation Assessment Program (NAPAP), a comprehensive ten-year research program developed and guided by an Interagency Task Force of twelve federal agencies the directors of four National Laboratories and four presidential appointees. The program is directed, among other purposes, at (1) identifying the sources of atmospheric emissions contributing to acid precipitation; (2) establishing and operating a nationwide long-term monitoring network to detect and measure levels of acid precipitation; (3) conducting research on atmospheric physics and chemistry to facilitate understanding of the processes by which atmospheric emissions are transformed into acid precipitation; (4) developing atmospheric transport models to enable predicting of long-range transport of air pollutants; and (5) defining geographic areas of impact through deposition monitoring, identification of sensitive areas, and identification of areas at risk.[46]

The first NAPAP Research Plan was developed in 1980–81. Research began in earnest in 1982, and results began to be published in significant numbers in 1985. The scientific research supported by NAPAP has resulted in over a thousand peer-reviewed papers and articles in the scientific literature, which have been supplemented by many additional studies carried out in both the United States and other countries. Scientific results to date have greatly improved our understandings of (1) the sources, quantities, and reactivities of acid deposition precursors; (2) the current status and future potential of control technologies; (3) the chemical and physical processes by which acids and oxidants are formed and then transported in the atmosphere; and (4) their effects on agricultural crops, forests, and aquatic systems. This increased understanding will ensure that control strategies are designed for a variety of pollutants that cause the acid rain. This includes the issues of timing and financing, and new technologies such as clean coal technology.

To date, the United States has spent close to $500 million on the NAPAP program. A major NAPAP international conference will be held in February 1990; NAPAP is scheduled to publish its Final Integrated Assessment in September 1990.

Implementation of the Special Envoys' Report

The appointment of the Special Envoys on Acid Rain and their recommendations have been described in Chapter 15. So also are the facts that the United States is working to implement the envoys' major recommendation of a five-year, $5 billion "technology commercial demonstrator program" in the United States to encourage the development of cheaper and more efficient control technologies, and, in keeping with another of the envoys' recommendations, the Secretary of Energy has established an advisory panel (the Innovative Control Technology Advisory Panel), with Canadian participation, to advise him on the Department's funding and selection of innovative control technology demonstration projects.

The United States is also carrying out the envoys' other recommendations. In May 1987, for example, the United States completed a review of its existing air pollution programs and legislation to identify opportunities, consistent with existing law, for addressing environmental concerns related to transboundary air pollution. This review concluded that, while the current Clean Air Act was designed primarily to address domestic problems, programs instituted under the Clean

Air Act have achieved a significant improvement in air quality, including reduction in transboundary flows. Moreover, it was found that section 115 of the Clean Air Act might provide a legal mechanism to address transboundary air pollution, but after we have achieved a better understanding of the chemical, physical, and biological processes associated with the acid deposition phenomenon.[47]

In keeping with other recommendations of the Special Envoys, U.S. agencies have reviewed the mechanisms by which the United States informs Canada of proposed changes in U.S. law and regulations which could have transboundary effects and concluded that these procedures are working well. The acid deposition issue has remained a priority item at high-level meetings, being raised most recently by the two heads of state at their bilateral summit in April 1988, at the Toronto Economic Summit in June, and again at the bilateral summit in February 1989. President Bush has indicated his support for development of a bilateral accord following passage of the Clean Air Act amendments. Research on deposition monitoring, rates of aquatic change, aquatic biology, forests effects and materials damage is being carried out under NAPAP, as described in the preceding section on NAPAP.

Finally, the United States was an active participant on the Bilateral Advisory and Consultative Group (BACG), a joint body of diplomatic and environmental officials from both nations, which the Special Envoys recommended to assess the international environmental problems associated with transboundary air pollution. The BACG has met on numerous occasions since its first meeting in June 1986, alternating between Ottawa and Washington, D.C. (It may be noted that the focus of attention between officials of the two governments has been on an accord and that some functional equivalent of the BACG may well be subsumed under a new accord.)

Negotiations on an Air Quality Accord with Canada

The final element of the U.S. strategy, in accordance with President Ronald Reagan's April 1988 and subsequently President Bush's February 1989 commitment to Prime Minister Brian Mulroney, is to consider a bilateral accord with Canada on acid deposition. The purpose of such an accord would be to establish targets and timetables for reducing the emissions of acid deposition precursors, to promote a better understanding of the causes and effects of acid deposition, and to encourage identification and deployment of innovative emissions reduction methods. Preliminary U.S.-Canadian discussions toward an accord are under way, with conclusion of an agreement linked to congressional action on completion of new Clean Air legislation. (Further details on an accord are addressed in Chapter 15.)

Conclusion

Over the years, the United States has undertaken an aggressive program to address air pollution, from both regulatory and scientific perspectives, and under the Bush Administration intends to go even further to deal with acid deposition. Taking into account the complexity of the issue, the United States' actions to date have met both its treaty and customary law obligations and have represented a reasonable balance as reflected in Principle 21 of the Stockholm Declaration.

Acknowledgments

This chapter is based on remarks made while the author was Deputy Associate Administrator for International Activities, U.S. Environmental Protection Agency, at a panel discussion on the Canada–United States Acid Rain Dispute on August 7, 1988, in Toronto, Canada, at the Annual Meeting of the American Bar Association; Chapter 14 is also based on remarks made on that panel. The present chapter was updated as of December 1989. The author thanks Jamison Koehler and Thomas Marshall for their assistance in preparing this chapter.

The views expressed herein are those of the author and not necessarily those of the United States Government or of any other organization.

Notes

1. *See, e.g.*, RESTATEMENT (THIRD) OF FOREIGN RELATIONS LAW OF THE UNITED STATES §§ 102, 111 (1987).
2. *See* United Nations Environment Programme, *Report of the Executive Director on Cooperation in the Field of Environment.*
3. *See* Dupuy, *International Liability of States for Damage Caused by Transfrontier Pollution, reprinted in* O.E.C.D., LEGAL ASPECTS OF TRANSFRONTIER POLLUTION 345, 353 (1977); *see also supra* Chapter 3.
4. Memorandum of Intent Between the Government of Canada and the Government of the United States Concerning Transboundary Air Pollution, Aug. 5, 1980, Canada-United States, 80 U.S. DEP'T ST. BULL. 21 (Oct. 1980) [hereinafter MOI].
5. Convention on Long-Range Transboundary Air Pollution, Nov. 13, 1979, T.I.A.S. No. 10541, *reprinted in* 18 I.L.M. 1441 (1979) [hereinafter LRTAP Convention].
6. MOI, *supra* note 4, arts. 1 and 2.
7. *See, e.g., Executive Summaries: Work Group Reports* [United States/Canada

Coordinating Committee, established in the Annex to the MOI, *supra* note 4] (Feb. 1983).

8. *See infra* parts of third section on an air quality accord with Canada and the U.S. regulatory control program.

9. *Supra* note 5; *see* U.S. Dep't of State, Treaties in Force 343 (1988).

10. LRTAP Convention, *supra* note 5, art. 2.

11. *Id*. art. 3.

12. Protocol to the 1979 Convention on Long-Range Transboundary Air Pollution Concerning the Control of Emissions of Nitrogen Oxides or Their Transboundary Fluxes, Nov. 1988, *reprinted in* 28 I.L.M. 214 (1989). For a description of the NO_x Protocol, see *infra* Chapter 12, at text accompanying notes 50–59.

13. Trail Smelter (U.S. v. Can.), 3 R. Int'l Arb. Awards 1905 (1938 & 1941).

14. Declaration of the United Nations Conference on the Human Environment, prin. 21, Report of the Stockholm Conference, U.N. Doc. A/CONF.48/14 & Corr. 1, at 7 (1972), *reprinted in* 11 I.L.M. 1416 (1972) [hereinafter 1972 Stockholm Declaration].

15. Trail Smelter (U.S. v. Can.), 3 R. Int'l Arb. Awards 1905, 1965 (1938 & 1941).

16. *Id*.

17. *See, e.g.*, Statement of the Meeting of Legal and Policy Experts, Ottawa, Canada, art. 5 Note (Feb. 22, 1989) (Principle 21 "contains a . . . principle of international law").

18. 1972 Stockholm Declaration, *supra* note 14, prin. 21.

19. An *environmental* case in the International Court of Justice implicitly reaffirmed *Trail Smelter*, but there was no express statement of the rule. Nuclear Tests (Austl. v. Fr.), 1973 I.C.J. 99 (Interim Protection Order of June 22).

20. Corfu Channel (U.K. v. Alb.), 1949 I.C.J. 4, 22 (Judgment of Apr. 9).

21. Lac Lanoux (Fr. v. Spain), 24 I.L.R. 101, 140 (1957) (English), 12 R. Int'l Arb. Awards 281 (1957) (French).

22. United States Diplomatic and Consular Staff in Tehran (U.S. v. Iran), 1979 I.C.J. 7.

23. 59 Stat. 1055, T.S. 993, 3 Bevins 1179.

24. *See supra* text accompanying note 18.

25. *Supra* note 3.

26. Lac Lanoux, *supra* note 21. For a brief discussion of "reasonableness," see *supra* Chapter 2.

27. Boundary Waters Treaty, Jan. 11, 1909, United States-Great Britain, 36 Stat. 2448, T.S. No. 548.

28. Agreement Between the United States of America and Canada on Great Lakes Water Quality, Apr. 15, 1972, 13 U.S.T. 301, T.I.A.S. No. 7312.

29. Protocol Amending the 1978 Agreement Between the United States of America and Canada on Great Lakes Water Quality, as amended on Oct. 16, 1983, Nov. 18, 1987.

30. *Supra* note 4.

31. D. Lewis & W. Davis, Joint Report of the Special Envoys on Acid Rain, U.S. Dep't of St., Washington, D.C. (Jan. 1986).

32. Clean Air Act (as amended), 42 U.S.C. §§ 7401–7642 (1982).

33. The United States has spent over $200 billion since 1970 on programs and control measures instituted under the Clean Air Act.

34. 42 U.S.C. § 7423 (1982).

35. Total sulphur dioxide emissions in the United States fell from 26.9 million metric tons (mmt) per year in 1977 to 21.2 mmt per year in 1986. EPA, *National Air Quality and Emission Trends Report, 1986* (Feb. 1988).

36. *Id.*

37. President Bush's proposal was included in legislation introduced in Congress later that summer. *See* H.R. 3030, 101st Cong., 1st Sess., 135 CONG. REC. H4458–59 (daily ed. July 27, 1989); *Fact Sheet: President Bush's Clean Air Plan*, Office of the Press Secretary, the White House, June 12, 1989.

38. 42 U.S.C. § 7415(a) (1982).

39. *Id.*

40. New York v. Thomas, 613 F. Supp. 1472 (D.D.C. 1985), *rev'd*, Thomas v. New York, 802 F.2d 1443 (1986), *cert. den.*, 482 U.S. 919 (1987).

41. Thomas v. New York, 802 F.2d 1443, 1447 (D.C. Cir. 1986), *cert. denied*, 482 U.S. 919 (1987).

42. *Id.* at 1448.

43. New York v. Thomas, *supra* note 40. The most recent litigation is Ontario v. EPA, No. 88–1778 (D.C. Cir. filed Nov. 1, 1988).

44. *See* Ontario v. EPA, *supra* note 43.

45. Pub. L. No. 96–294, Title VII, 94 Stat. 770 (1980) (codified at 42 U.S.C. §§ 8901–8912 (1982)).

46. *Id.*

47. U.S. Environmental Protection Agency, *Review of Existing U.S. Air Pollution Authority Pursuant to the Special Envoy's Report on Acid Rain* 4 (May 1987).

Contributors

ANDRONICO O. ADEDE was Director of the Legal Division (the Legal Advisor) of the International Atomic Energy Agency, 1983–1987. He is currently Deputy Director for Research and Studies, Codification Division, Office of Legal Affairs, United Nations.

IAN BROWNLIE is Chichele Professor of Public International Law, Oxford University; Fellow of All Souls College; member of the English Bar; Bencher of Grays's Inn; and Queen's Counsel.

PIERRE-MARIE DUPUY is Professor of Law, University of Law, Economics and Social Sciences of Paris; Director, Institut des Hautes Etudes Internationales de Paris; and Editor-in-Chief, Revue Générale de Droit International Public.

JAMES N. GALLOWAY is Professor, Department of Environmental Sciences, University of Virginia.

ROSS GLASGOW is First Secretary and Head, Environment Section, Canadian Embassy, Washington, D.C.

L.F.E. GOLDIE is Professor and Director, International Legal Studies Program (Emeritus), Syracuse University College of Law.

SCOTT A. HAJOST was Associate General Counsel for International Activities, U.S. Environmental Protection Agency, when this chapter was finalized, and currently is Senior Attorney, Environmental Defense Fund.

GÜNTHER HANDL is Professor of Law, Wayne State University.

JOHAN G. LAMMERS is Professor of International Law, University of Amsterdam, Netherlands, and Deputy Legal Advisor, Ministry of Foreign Affairs, Netherlands. He participated, among other endeavors, in negotiating the 1988 NO_x Protocol to the 1979 Convention on Long-Range Transboundary Air Pollution.

EDWARD G. LEE is Legal Advisor and Assistant Deputy Minister for Legal, Consular and Immigration Affairs, Department of External Affairs and International Trade, Canada. As Undersecretary for U.S.A. Affairs in the Department of External Affairs and International Trade, Canada, during the early 1980s, he headed the Canadian delegation in the first set of negotiations with the United States for an acid deposition accord.

DANIEL BARSTOW MAGRAW is Associate Professor of Law, University of Colorado, and Visiting Scientist, Environmental and Societal Impacts Group, National Center for Atmospheric Research (1989–1990).

STEPHEN C. McCAFFREY is Professor of Law, University of the Pacific, McGeorge School of Law, and Member, United Nations International Law Commission.

WILLIAM A. NITZE was Deputy Assistant Secretary of State for Environment, Health and Natural Resources, U.S. Department of State, when this chapter was written, and currently is a Visiting Scholar at the Environmental Law Institute.

PAUL SZASZ was Deputy to the Legal Counsel, and Director, General Legal Division, Office of Legal Affairs, United Nations.

Index

This book was set in Baskerville and Eras typefaces. Baskerville was designed by John Baskerville at his private press in Birmingham, England, in the eighteenth century. The first typeface to depart from oldstyle typeface design, Baskerville has more variation between thick and thin strokes. In an effort to insure that the thick and thin strokes of his typeface reproduced well on paper, John Baskerville developed the first wove paper, the surface of which was much smoother than the laid paper of the time. The development of wove paper was partly responsible for the introduction of typefaces classified as modern, which have even more contrast between thick and thin strokes.

Eras was designed in 1969 by Studio Hollenstein in Paris for the Wagner Typefoundry. A contemporary script-like version of a sans-serif typeface, the letters of Eras have a monotone stroke and are slightly inclined.

Printed on acid-free paper.